Mousetraps and the Moon

Mousetraps and the Moon

The Strange Ride of Sigmund Freud and the Early Years of Psychoanalysis

Robert Wilcocks

LEXINGTON BOOKS
Lanham • Boulder • New York • Oxford

LEXINGTON BOOKS

Published in the United States of America
by Lexington Books
4720 Boston Way, Lanham, Maryland 20706

12 Hid's Copse Road
Cumnor Hill, Oxford OX2 9JJ, England

British Library Cataloguing in Publication Information Available

Library of Congress Cataloging-in-Publication Data

Wilcocks, Robert.
    Mousetraps and the moon : the strange ride of Sigmund Freud and the early years of psychoanalysis / Robert Wilcocks.
        p. cm.
    Includes bibliographical references and index.
    ISBN 0-7391-0158-7 (hardcover : alk. paper)
        1. Psychoanalysis—History—19th century. 2. Psychoanalysis—History—20th century. 3. Freud, Sigmund, 1856-1939. I. title.

BF173 .W5473 2000
150.19'52092—dc21   00-030153
Printed in the United States of America

♾™ The paper used in this publication meets the minimum requirements of American National Standard for Information Sciences—Permanence of Paper for Printed Library Materials, ANSI/NISO Z39.48–1992.

For Felix, Robert, and Mariane

"They were learning to draw . . . and they drew all manner of things—everything that begins with an M— . . . such as mouse-traps, and the moon, and memory, and muchness."

LEWIS CARROLL,
Alice's Adventures in Wonderland

"There is, as the conjurers say, no deception about this tale."

RUDYARD KIPLING,
The Strange Ride of Morrowbie Jukes

Contents

Reference Abbreviations

Masson 1985   *The Complete Letters of Sigmund Freud to Wilhelm Fliess, 1887-1904*. Tr. and ed. Jeffrey Moussaieff Masson. Cambridge, Mass.: The Belknap Press of Harvard University Press, 1985.

P.F.L.   *The Pelican Freud Library*. 15 vols. General ed. Albert Dickson. Harmondsworth, U.K.: Penguin, 1973-1985.

S.E.   *The Standard Edition of the Complete Psychological Works of Sigmund Freud*. 24 vols. Edited by James Strachey; translated in collaboration with Anna Freud, assisted by Alix Strachey and Alan Tyson. London: Hogarth Press and the Institute of Psycho-Analysis, 1953-1974.

G.W.   *Sigmund Freud, Gesammelte Werke*. 18 vols. Edited by Anna Freud, with the collaboration of Marie Bonaparte, E. Bibring, W. Hoffer, E. Kris, and O. Isakower. London: Imago Publishing Company, 1940-1952.

Studies   *Studies on Hysteria*. Josef Breuer and Sigmund Freud. New York: Basic Books, 1957.

Acknowledgments

In a work such as this, which covers so many disparate disciplines—the history of medicine, psychiatry, psychoanalysis, as well as certain literary areas—many people are almost inevitably involved in aspects of the research and writing (the ultimate responsibility for which is solely the author's). The many encouragements given have been as diverse as the disciplines of those helpful colleagues on both sides of the Atlantic. It is a genuine pleasure to thank them in public for their years of attentive solidarity in the pursuit of a common purpose—the search for *what really happened* in those early years of psychoanalysis.

On this side of the Atlantic the first acknowledgment must go to Frederick Crews, who has provided years of moral support and specialist advice and who, furthermore, has shown immense personal patience with the whims of, as he recognized some years ago, a "fellow maverick." Mavericks are awkward beasts, and I am not as irenic in disposition as Professor Crews. It is therefore a double delight to thank him in public for his perseverance and for the many hours he spent on earlier drafts of the first five chapters. Professors Adolf Grünbaum of Pittsburgh and Harold Merskey of London (Ontario) have continued to show encouraging and thoughtful critical interest. Professor Merskey read through several chapters where psychiatric material is foremost, and he unfailingly gave prompt telephoned responses and suggestions. It is a pleasure to acknowledge his participation in the long-term enterprise.

In England, I have had much specialist advice and information from the consultant psychiatrist at Leeds University, Dr. Karel de Pauw. His frequent postings of photocopied articles have indeed made of our correspondence almost an Open University in matters psychiatric. He deserves my deepest thanks for his continuing efforts to educate me beyond my primary discipline. Dr. de Pauw was also the initiator of a most helpful correspondence with the French psychiatrist Dr. J.-P. Luauté of Romans-sur-Isère (France). By the same token, Allen Esterson, the author of *Seductive Mirage: An Exploration of the Works of Sigmund*

xiii

Freud, gave unsparingly of his time to read carefully the first drafts of most of the chapters. I am immensely grateful to him for the care and intelligence so willingly offered. And it is an additional pleasure to record my thanks for the many hours of trans-Atlantic phone conversations dealing with the finer points of Freudiana.

Raymond Tallis, professor of geriatric medicine at the University of Manchester, has been a stalwart champion over the years, ever since he took delight in my first Freud escapade, *Maelzel's Chess Player: Sigmund Freud and the Rhetoric of Deceit*. I am most appreciative of his continuing efforts on my behalf. I record his kind support and specialist assistance with the warmest thanks. Richard Webster, the author of *Why Freud Was Wrong*, was very generous in his published appreciation of my earlier work and was responsive in our subsequent correspondence.

I would like to thank my son (who lives in London) for his speedy expedition of books by return of post. He has been as helpful and efficiently supportive for this volume as he was for my first Freud book.

The reference staff members at the Rutherford Library of the University of Alberta have been efficient beyond expectation. I thank them for their prompt and courteous assistance. I also thank the helpful staff at the John W. Scott Health Sciences Library at the University of Alberta.

It is a pleasure to record my appreciation of Terry Butler for his careful production of the computer-generated typesetting of this book. The technical support he has offered was, for me, enhanced by the friendly enthusiasm he has shown for the project over the months of our collaboration. By the same token, I would like to thank Nancy Nassef for her very careful typesetting and for her very great patience.

Introduction

A Canadian psychiatrist (now professor emeritus), after having read the first three chapters of this book in typescript with apparent pleasure, suggested that they needed an introduction to place, as it were, the position from which this work emerges. He had not, at that time, read my earlier *Maelzel's Chess Player: Sigmund Freud and the Rhetoric of Deceit*, and was, in consequence, in a kind of intellectual quandary as to where I was coming from. Given what is to follow, his expression of amused unease was quite understandable. A practicing French neuro-psychiatrist, who *had* read my first book on Freud, asked me if the present work (then *en chantier*) was intended as a follow-up to the earlier work. He hoped it would be; it is.

Perhaps the quickest way to make my position known from the outset is to quote the words that Frank J. Sulloway uses at the very end of his exhaustive 1979 study of the founder of psychoanalysis, *Freud, Biologist of the Mind: Beyond the Psychoanalytic Legend*.[1] In his last chapter, and after some five hundred pages of extensive research, Sulloway writes: "Perhaps only Aristotle and Darwin have equaled Freud's marriage of theory and observation in the broad realm of the life sciences" (Sulloway 1979 [1992], 500).

Sulloway's last paragraph reads:

> In many respects, then, Freud will always remain a crypto-biologist, his self-analysis will always be seen as heroic and unprecedented, and his years of discovery will always partake of a "splendid isolation" and an inscrutable genius. After all, Freud really was a hero. The myths are merely his historical due, and they shall continue to live on, protecting his brilliant legacy to mankind, as long as this legacy remains a powerful part of human consciousness. (Sulloway 1979 [1992], 503)

To traduce Eliot (among others), "in *his* end is *my* beginning." Either Sulloway hadn't understood Aristotle, or Darwin, or—and more likely—he had been seduced by the aura of purpose, prescience, and power that has surrounded the activities of Sigmund Freud—a consequence of the latter's literary and organizational skills. In modern North America such a position is not unusual; it is, nonetheless, completely unfounded. Freud was never a great observer, if by "observer" we mean one who observes without *a priori* premises coloring the observation. (But then was Aristotle a "great observer"?—Bertrand Russell somewhere remarks in a sly mood that Aristotle could have *empirically* checked the number of teeth that women have by asking Mrs. Aristotle to open her mouth for a moment so he could *count* them!) One more sinister implication of Sulloway's comparison of Freud with Aristotle may be gleaned from this observation—about the philosopher's negative qualities and/or effects—also by Russell, who of course has immense praise for the genius from Stagira: "His present-day influence is so inimical to clear thinking that it is hard to remember how great an advance he made upon all his predecessors (including Plato), or how admirable his logical work would still seem if it had been a stage in a continual progress, instead of being (as in fact it was) a dead end, followed by over two thousand years of stagnation."[2] I think it may be safe to assume that Freud's incursions into medicine will not be followed by two thousand years of stagnation in that discipline. His century of massive influence is now coming to an end.

Freud's reputation among the intelligentsia, including the various species of psychologists who appear in the attempted scientific justification for the good standing of psychoanalysis in Fisher and Greenberg,[3] is little different from the one presented in the closing pages of Sulloway's study. Since Sulloway's volume first appeared, much new material has come to light about the reality behind the sedulously invented myth of the early years of psychoanalysis. The careful and intensive scholarship of researchers as diverse as Mikkel Borch-Jacobsen, Frederick Crews, the late Henri Ellenberger, Allen Esterson, Han Israëls, Jeffrey M. Masson, Paul Roazen, Max Scharnberg, and Peter Swales has led to a situation where one can no longer begin with Sulloway as a guide to Freud's years of inventing psychoanalysis. If anything, then, this book is intended as an exposition of the self-serving muddles that made the invention of psychoanalysis possible.

In other words, without being "anti-Sulloway" (he did, after all, carry out splendid and original research, much of which is still valuable about aspects of the nineteenth-century German scientific *Zeitgeist*, even if it is not—or no longer—relevant to an examination of Freud's first twenty years of "therapeutic" practice and theorizing), this is nevertheless a book which could never honestly come to the conclusions reached by Sulloway and quoted above. To place Freud on a level with Aristotle or Darwin is to commit the kind of blunder that Freud himself would have appreciated and did occasionally indulge in. The psychologist Hans J. Eysenck placed Freud in his *Decline and Fall of the Freudian Empire*[4] close to Hans Christian Andersen or the brothers Grimm—"tellers of fairy tales"—and it is certainly in that category that I would place this self-confessed *conquistador* of late-nineteenth-century Vienna. Conquistadors created long-lasting havoc—one recalls Herzog's film *Aguirre der Zorn Gottes* (*Aguirre, The Wrath of God*). In his incursions into the extensive unexplored (or poorly explored) realms of psychology, psychiatry, and mental health care, Sigmund Freud was, in every sense of the word, a *conquistador*. For once his use of metaphor was precise, accurate, and horribly prescient.

Freud has had an immense influence on the thinking of modern western peoples; this should never be denied. Whether that influence has been a force for good or evil is another matter. Much real harm has come from Freud's overrating (and misunderstanding) of the significance of sexuality in human affairs. The mendacious reporting of his "cases" and the rhetoric of fiction employed throughout the many publications of his private hunches—the so-called theoretical essays—have been largely responsible for a widespread diffusion of false and dangerous ideas about memory and the mind. Freud was the "biologist of the mind" for Sulloway, and, for my psychiatrist friend, Freud's originality lay in his reputed attempt to uncover the workings of the human mind and to elaborate "for the first time" an overall theory of the mind. Neither of these positions takes cognizance of *how* the Freud of the early years of psychoanalysis actually carried out his medical duties and his research interests. When these matters are considered close-up, as they now can be to some extent thanks to the efforts of Jeffrey Moussaieff Masson and Peter Swales in unearthing and publishing the epistolary material that was contemporary with the invention of what was to become "psychoanalysis," then the picture that emerges is less than flattering to Freud. It is even less acceptable than the image offered by Richard Webster in his recent *Why Freud Was Wrong: Sin, Science, and Psychoanalysis*. Webster has been quite unreasonably harassed by pro-Freudian commentators for his decision to expose the elements of error in Freud's early foray into an overall theory of the mind. But the truth of

Freud's years of inventing psychoanalysis is far more unpleasant than even Webster reveals. Time and again Webster attempts, sometimes with an elegant and inventive sophistry, to get Freud off the hook of his own dishonesty or incompetence. Having studied this man and the medicine of his time (for some twenty years now), I have come to the firm conclusion that Freud was frequently dishonest and mostly incompetent. In the cruel but accurate assessment of Raymond Tallis, professor of geriatric medicine at the University of Manchester, Freud was the Lysenko of psychiatry and of literary studies.[5] He was a great writer—a "teller of tales," as Eysenck ironically says—he *really* was! His gifts lay in literature and not in medicine. He did not have the great insight into human beings that the great novelists have; but he did have a mastery of language and a polyglot culture that permitted him to produce case histories and theoretical essays that have the rhetorical power of great narrative.

Notes

1. Frank J. Sulloway (1979 [1992]). *Freud, Biologist of the Mind: Beyond the Psychoanalytic Legend*. New York: Basic Books. This book was reissued with its text unchanged by Harvard University Press in 1992; the pagination of the earlier edition has been retained. This printing contains a new "Preface to the 1992 Edition" on pages xi-xv. In this preface Sulloway writes that he has benefited in the intervening decade by the important publications of scholars such as J. Allan Hobson (*The Dreaming Brain*), Adolf Grünbaum (*The Foundations of Psychoanalysis*), and Frederick Crews (*Skeptical Engagements*), and by works of investigative journalism such as *The Wolf-Man Sixty Years Later* by Karin Obholzer.
2. Bertrand Russell ([1946] 1979). *History of Western Philosophy*. London: Unwin Paperbacks, 206.
3. Seymour Fisher and Roger P. Greenberg, eds. (1978). *The Scientific Evaluation of Freud's Theories and Therapy: A Book of Readings*. New York: Basic Books. See also their latest joint overview (1996), which includes commentary on Adolf Grünbaum, *Freud Scientifically Reappraised: Testing the Theories and Therapy*. New York: John Wiley and Sons.
4. H. J. Eysenck (1985). *Decline and Fall of the Freudian Empire*. New York: Viking/Penguin.
5. See "Deconstruction in Performance," *Times Literary Supplement*, March 12, 1999, 17. This letter is Tallis's swingeing response to an article by Michel Chaouli (*TLS*, February 26) which suggests the use of Freudian

psychoanalytic constructs in university courses on literature. Tallis's immediate reaction to this is worth quoting for its pungent common sense:

> Never mind that Freud made up the data that supported his massive theories about mankind, never mind that he lied endlessly about the effectiveness of his treatments, never mind that he and his followers have caused immeasurable damage to vulnerable people—we can still use his theories to reveal the nature of literature to students. . . . May we therefore look to theorists for a Lysenkoist interpretation of the Rougon-Macquart cycle, for Flat Earth perspectives on Jules Verne, Hoddle-based reflections on *Richard III*, and an L. Ron Hubbardian approach to Donne's cosmology? (*TLS*, March 12, 1999, 17)

1

The Medawar Sentence

Sir Peter Medawar, the greatest scientific essayist of all, once described
science as "the art of the possible." On the evidence of Piltdown and his
successors, "plausible" would be a better choice. STEVE JONES[1]

Two men, an Australian and an American, have each devoted over a
quarter of a century to a meticulous examination of, respectively, the
validity of psychoanalysis and its widespread appeal in America. In the
recent MIT paperback edition of his *Freud Evaluated: The Completed
Arc*, the Australian professor of psychology, Malcolm Macmillan, has
praise for the "cogent data . . . recovered by Hale (1971, 1995) in his
study of the response to and spread of psychoanalysis in the United
States."[2] The American, Nathan G. Hale Jr., began a work (orginally a
doctoral thesis) entitled *Freud in America* in the late sixties. The first
volume, *Freud and the Americans*, takes the story of Freud's transatlantic
adventures up to 1917. It was published by Oxford University Press in
1971. The second volume, *The Rise and Crisis of Psychoanalysis in the
United States: Freud and the Americans, 1917-1985*, came out in 1995.[3]
A reading of both of these works (Macmillan's and Hale's) is essential for
anyone contemplating a serious study of any aspect of Freudian theory
and of its influence in America. Their scholarship is wide-ranging,
cautious, and thorough; their bibliographies give a virtual "CD-ROM"
glimpse of psychoanalytic writings.

Any person in the humanities who is using Freudian (or Lacanian)
notions for the purposes of explication of texts, or movements, or
individual artistic crises, *and who has not consulted* these two works is
running the risk of being charged with charlatanry, or at the very least

with an amateurism which is ignorant of the ill-founded status of psychoanalytic doctrines. The literature on Freud is vast, as Macmillan notes in the thirty-eight-page afterword prepared for the MIT edition:

> In this Afterword I wanted to reconsider the arguments and conclusions of *Freud Evaluated* in the light of the post-1989 literature, but a search of the *PsycLit* data base quickly showed that goal was unattainable. Between 1990 and 1995 some 3,500 journal articles or book chapters and 250 books appeared with "Freud" or "psychoanalysis" or both (or derivatives) in their titles, numbers that increase approximately three times if the search is based on those words in the content descriptions. (Macmillan 1997, 629)

Faced with such dimensions of scholarship, propaganda, and polemical literature, the neophyte may well wonder where to begin. Apart from the short, intensive course offered so cogently in the first five chapters of Frederick Crews's magnificent *Skeptical Engagements*,[4] my suggestion would be to start with these two works; with Hale, if the primary interest is the multidisciplinary nature of Freud's American transplantation; with Macmillan, if the primary interest is an evaluation of Freud's clinical data and subsequent metapsychological theorizings.[5] Material not directly covered by Hale or Macmillan is frequently mentioned in the titles of works in their excellent bibliographies.

The first two paragraphs of Hale's 1971 volume are worth quoting in full because they state so succinctly the legendary nature of the status of psychoanalysis as (once) seen by its proponents and as (once) seen by its adversaries.

> Any study of Freud's influence in the United States must begin with two myths, the first created by the founders of American psychoanalysis, the second, by their enemies. The first legend holds that Freud transformed neurology, psychiatry, the social sciences, education, and child raising; that before Freud there had been mostly darkness, inhumanity, a narrow constraint which ignored sexuality and childhood. This was the myth created by Freud's first militant followers, especially those who were in their mid-twenties or early thirties in 1909 when he visited America, and who became the first historians of psychoanalysis.[6] The enemies of psychoanalysis constructed their counter-legends. These began, perhaps, with the neurologist Francis X. Dercum, the humanist Paul Elmer More, and reached their apogee in Oscar Cargill, the literary historian, and the sociologist Richard La Pierre. "Freudian doctrine," they held, prescribed

primitivism, sexual liberation, pessimistic determinism, permissiveness, and decadence. (Hale 1971, xi)

In the twenty-five-odd years that Hale spent on his magnum opus many changes have taken place in the United States with respect to the good standing of psychoanalysis. It is now not favored as a treatment of choice for someone suffering from depression or marital difficulties. And although it may still have a certain cachet in Hollywood and Manhattan (witness Woody Allen's lifelong flirtation with its central notions), it is no longer seen as a set of psychological theories of almost universal significance and applicability. Indeed in 1989 the editor in chief of *Neuropsychiatry, Neuropsychology, and Behavioral Neurology* declared bluntly at the opening of an otherwise modest editorial: "Other than psychoanalysis, which is now in Chapter 11, I know of no conceptual framework which offers a detailed explanation of why people do what they do."[7] Nonetheless, it is still an active force in the humanities (specifically the studies of literature, sociology, and anthropology), and it has been responsible for a widespread secondary intellectual industry where it has been applied—often with disastrous results—to many fields of social concern. Some of these—mainly those dealing with the familial, societal, educational, criminological and anthropological effects of psychoanalytic enthusiasms—have been documented by clinical and research psychiatrist E. Fuller Torrey in a book whose title indicates the indictment to be found between the covers, *Freudian Fraud: The Malignant Effect of Freud's Theory on American Thought and Culture.*[8]

Torrey's book is a robust, no-nonsense slash at the various high-falutin'—and sometimes low-falutin'—lunacies visited upon Americans by those who believed they were Freud's disciples. In Torrey's index, however, there is no place for Nathan G. Hale Jr., nor for his careful record of the many consequences of Freud's visitation. Neither is there any reference to such eminent philosophers of science as Adolf Grünbaum[9] or to such tireless sleuths as Peter Swales or Jeffrey M. Masson (who, as projects director of the Freud Archives, first broke the taboo surrounding Freud's correspondence with his Berlin otorhino-laryngologist friend Wilhelm Fliess).[10] Torrey, in short, is interested in the evident disasters, as he sees them, in a practical way. The niceties of theory do not interest him. Nor do the serious investigations of people such as Grünbaum, who have immeasurably raised our sense of awareness of the "Freudian Fraud" that has indeed affected so much of Western civilization.[11]

Hale's second volume, which appeared in 1995, has taken cognizance of the changes in fashion and, more importantly, of the changes in scholarship since he began his mammoth task. Neither Frederick Crews nor Peter Medawar was present in the earlier volume. Now they have, almost, pride of place: they are both forcefully present in his prologue. In his conclusion, Hale himself refers to the practical consequences of psychoanalytic practice in America:

> Part of the current difficulty of psychoanalysis has been its practitioners' insistence that it is a science within the context of medicine. But what kind of a "science" is it? Far more than medicine, psychoanalysis is an art and a skill, based on a structure of systematic theory for the therapist's guidance in the labyrinth of the patient's life and words. Its theories resemble those of some of the social sciences far more closely than they do the experimental sciences, except that the social sciences are not challenged to "treat" patients. Many of these issues of scientific "status" were exacerbated by the medical rhetoric and model psychoanalysts traditionally chose. Moreover, replicable results have been made acutely desirable by soaring medical expenses and third party payers' insistence on 'cost effectiveness.' (Hale 1995, 384-85)

The Australian, Macmillan, writes toward the end of his seven-hundred-page study, "In the face of its limited value as a therapy, its acknowledged weaknesses as a theory, and its reliance on a suspect method of enquiry, the continuing appeal of psychoanalysis requires explanation" (Macmillan 1997, 663). So, one might add, does scientology. Macmillan, however, has seen this difficulty coming and in an early chapter has castigated belief in previous existences and astral notions of spiritual existence.[12] Macmillan places Freud's attempt at "recovered memories" somewhere between Bridey Murphy and the scientologists (Macmillan 1997, 214-15).

Macmillan does not directly accuse Freud of charlatanry, nor does Hale—nor, indeed, does the recent volume by the English researcher Richard Webster, *Why Freud Was Wrong: Sin, Science, and Psychoanalysis*.[13] One of the most interesting phenomena in recent Freudian studies has been the reluctance of many of the critical commentators to investigate the material provided by Jeffrey Masson when he managed to get Harvard University Press to publish the complete correspondence of Freud with Wilhelm Fliess.[14] That correspondence provides—in spades—evidence of Freud's ability to "invent" the truth according to the needs of the moment; it also demonstrates what I have called "the truth of Freud's bizarre beliefs about human motivations and . . . his self-proclaimed ability to discern their workings."[15]

"Was Freud a liar?"[16]—the question first publicly raised in 1974 by the American philosophy teacher resident in England, Frank Cioffi—has been decorously ignored even by those who refuse Freud's claim to cogent and valid medical theory (e.g., Grünbaum, Hale, Macmillan, Webster). Five years later, in November 1979, in a double review of Frank Sulloway's *Freud, Biologist of the Mind* and Sherry Turkle's *Psychoanalytic Politics: Freud's French Revolution*, Cioffi, still without the evidence of the unexpurgated letters to Fliess but with sufficient information to rephrase the question as a clear statement of fact, rounded on Sulloway not for the inadequacy of his scientific research but for Sulloway's refusal to confront the consequences of his own careful findings:

> When is a lie not a lie? When it is a myth. Sulloway has made some interesting discoveries about Freud's relation to Albert Moll, a sexologist hostile to psychoanalysis. He has been able to consult Freud's own copy of Moll's 1897 work, *Libido Sexualis*, with passages underscored by Freud. These show that although on the occasion of the publication in 1907 of Moll's book, *The Sexual Life of Children*, Freud accused him of plagiarising the idea of infantile sexuality from his own *Three Essays on Sexuality*, published in 1905, he knew that in fact it was rather Moll who had anticipated him. Sulloway's comment on this episode illustrates how difficult it is, even for an aspiring iconoclast, to stand upright in the presence of the Freud legend: "Freud's claim of priority had symbolic status . . . Freud's accusation of plagiarism against Albert Moll must be seen in this light." . . . Carry on lying.[17]

With the evidence now available we know that Cioffi's hunch was correct. For example, in a letter to Fliess on November 14, 1897, Freud mentions Moll's work and notes: "I have often had a suspicion that something organic plays a part in repression; I was able once before to tell you that it was a question of the abandonment of former sexual zones, and I was able to add that I had been pleased at coming across a similar idea in Moll." But Freud immediately adds, in parentheses: "(Privately I concede priority in the idea to no one)" (Masson 1985, 279). Nor would he, ever. Prior to the publication of the complete Freud–Fliess correspondence it was difficult to assess the elements of "economy with the truth" in Freud's writings. Since then, it has become evident that the mythological version of Freud (initiated by himself in fact)[18] needs serious investigation *before* any scientific credit is given to psychoanalysis. The Nobel laureate for medicine, Sir Peter Medawar, was sufficiently infuriated—and, interestingly enough, with neither access to, nor knowledge of, the unexpurgated Freud–Fliess correspondence—by the pretensions of North American psychoanalysts to draft what has probably become the most repeated and most reprinted phrase of him or, indeed, of any Nobel laureate ever.

The British scholar, currently in charge of renaissance studies at the ETH Zurich (Swiss Federal Institute of Technology), Brian Vickers, used Medawar's sentence in his Yale University Press diatribe against various foolish trends in much recent Shakespeare criticism, *Appropriating Shakespeare: Contemporary Critical Quarrels.*[19] Richard Webster in *Why Freud Was Wrong* quotes it. The late Ernest Gellner quotes it in his *The Psychoanalytic Movement, or the Coming of Unreason.*[20] Frederick Crews quotes it in the 1980 essay "Analysis Terminable" reprinted in *Skeptical Engagements* (1986) and refers to it again in *The Memory Wars: Freud's Legacy in Dispute.*[21] I myself use it in my earlier book *Maelzel's Chess Player: Sigmund Freud and the Rhetoric of Deceit,*[22] and it has been recycled to effect in innumerable articles and newspaper columns.

Medawar's phrase comes from a book review published in the *New York Review of Books* in early 1975. He was praising the courage and medical lucidity of the neurosurgeon Irving S. Cooper, who had written of his intervention for patients suffering from DMD (*dystonia musculorum deformans*), a rare and dreadful neuromuscular disease, in an account called *The Victim Is Always the Same.*[23] Several of Cooper's young patients had been clients or, more accurately, victims of psychoanalysis before being sent to him for brain exploration and neurosurgery using innovatory techniques of precisely controlled and focused liquid nitrogen (at -196°C) to inactivate "through freezing . . . a group of cells deep in the thalamus, the part of the brain through which sensory impulses pass on their way to the cerebral cortex and which has important motor connections with the cortex" (Medawar 1975, 17). Their psychoanalytic treatment did nothing for their neurophysiological condition and, if anything, made their day-to-day existential misery worse. The moral culpabilization of the patients, their siblings, and/or parents was the sole and disastrous result of psychoanalytic intervention.

We are now in a position to know (i.e., those of us who are neither Nobel laureates for medicine nor even medical doctors) that the outcome of psychoanalytic treatment for these patients could not have been other than it was. What is interesting about Medawar's assessment of psychoanalysis is that it was the consequence of two things: (a) an awareness of the hideous deficiencies in medical knowledge associated with psychoanalysis;[24] (b) a medical grasp of the innovatory surgical techniques of Irving Cooper and an understanding of *why* they were right and of *how* nothing else could relieve these patients. A further interesting aspect of Medawar's (quite correct) assessment of the medical situation of Cooper's patients is that when he drafted this review for the *New York Review of Books* he was unaware of the duplicities and ignorances at the very heart of psychoanalysis from its inception. Any alert reader nowadays has access (thanks to Masson's decision to publish the complete correspondence of Freud and Fliess during the very years which saw the creation of the discipline called psychoanalysis) to material that in Freud's own words shows clearly the disastrous combination of ignorance, ambition, and cocaine intoxication that produced a latter-day version of the Inquisition (minus the rack and the stake) as far as the close interrogation of suspects from baseless premises was concerned.[25]

Here is the essence of what Medawar wrote in the extract quoted, for example, by Ernest Gellner:

> Psychoanalysts will continue to perpetrate the most ghastly blunders just so long as they persevere in their impudent and intellectually disabling belief that they enjoy a "privileged access to the truth" (M. H. Stern, *International Journal of Psycho-Analysis*, 53, 13, 1972). The opinion is gaining ground that doctrinaire psychoanalytic theory is the most stupendous intellectual confidence trick of the twentieth century.[26]

Richard Webster in his recent *Why Freud Was Wrong* tries to subvert the value of Medawar's caustic demolition. He does not quote the first half of this famous statement concerning the probable perpetuation of "the most ghastly blunders" that would result from psychoanalysts persevering "in their impudent and intellectually disabling belief that they enjoy a 'privileged access to the truth.'" Medawar was writing less *ex cathedra* as a Nobel laureate than as a highly qualified researcher in internal medicine. (The Nobel Prize he won was for work which led to the correct bio-chemical treatment of transplant patients, and many now standard organ-transplant operations would not be possible without the knowledge provided by Medawar's research.) Webster leaves his challenge to Medawar to his last section, part 3, entitled "Psychoanalysis, Science and the Future." This is by far the weakest section of his book where, after a careful examination of some of Freud's mistakes, he launches into a speculative search for an overarching foundation theory for human psychology without which, he implies, we may not properly criticize Freud.[27] It is, perhaps, significant that this extravaganza begins with an ill-considered assault on one of the greatest medical researchers of the twentieth century.

His objections to Medawar begin: "In the first place psychoanalysis cannot fairly be described as a 'confidence trick.' For this description quite clearly implies a conscious and deliberate attempt to deceive" (Webster 1995, 437). Webster goes on to haul out hoary instances of pseudo-science, like astrology, as having, *nonetheless*, been useful in the long run. If this sounds to the reader like a desperate scraping of the barrel, be assured, it is. Webster confidently quotes Galileo's refusal to credit Copernicus on lunar tidal effect as an instance of overweening scientific hubris. Copernicus, however, did not set out to establish a worldwide organization that would perpetuate Copernican theory. Freud *did* set out "consciously and deliberately" to found a universal organization that would perpetuate his notions. And as we now know, he personally contrived, via a tendentious differential diagnosis of "repressed homosexuality" and suggestions on divorce to be followed by remarriage to an heiress, the ruin of four lives in order to enroll Dr. Horace Frink as president of the psychoanalytic community in New York and in order to ensure the financial prosperity of his "cause"—psychoanalysis.[28]

The Frink affair, which has been succinctly and acerbically discussed by Esterson,[29] is a telling instance of the deliberate attempt by Freud to obtain at the same time continuing personal authority status in the U.S. psychoanalytic community (by the recommendation of his own "hand-picked" analysand-candidate—Frink—for the presidency of the New York Psychoanalytic Society) and the prospect of immense funding for his new organization from wealthy heiress Angelika Bijur (a former patient of Frink's) upon her Freud-recommended divorce from her millionaire husband Abraham Bijur (so that she could marry the newly divorced

Horace Frink). The whole tale of twisted emotional disaster is sickening to read; one feels immense empathy for Doris Frink and her two children; her letters to her husband accepting the Freud divorce proposal are heart-rending. (Freud, one should realize, had never met either Doris Frink or the other targeted victim, Abraham Bijur.)

The one person who stands out in this miserable affair for his humane lucidity and his professional caring is the Swiss-American psychiatrist, one of the founders of modern American psychiatry, Adolf Meyer.[30] He was both a teacher of the young Horace Frink and, in the crucial 1920s, his psychiatric physician. Apart from the professional issue of deontology, Meyer felt that Freud had made a "colossal clinical misjudgment" in not recognizing the seriousness of Frink's manic-depressive (or bipolar) disorder. As Lavinia Edmunds notes, Adolf Meyer "would label the case 'nauseating,'" adding, "The attitude of Freud was evidently one of encouragement and suggestion rather strongly in contrast to his usual pretension that these factors are left out of consideration" (Meyer, quoted in Edmunds 1988, 42). Perhaps the most nauseating single documentary evidence in this affair is the letter from Freud to the still undecided (and not yet divorced) Frink in November 1921:

> May I suggest to you that your idea Mrs B. had lost part of her beauty may be turned into her having lost part of her money. . . . Your complaint that you cannot grasp your homosexuality implies that you are not yet aware of your phantasy of making me a rich man. If matters turn out all right let us change this imaginary gift into a real contribution to the Psychoanalytic Funds. (Edmunds 1988, 45)

A better example of a self-serving intellectual confidence trick would be hard to imagine. To those who would argue that Medawar's charge was against a total system of thought (psychoanalysis) rather than against a specific instance of what one might call "mere abuse," the answer, alas, is that the distinction between the totality of Freud's enterprise and this particular episode involving the Frink family circumstances is not even one of degree. It is par for the course. A more elaborate and long-running confidence trick has been the quite conscious deception of scholars (and hence of the public) undertaken by the internal Hays Office of the psychoanalytic movement under the direction of Anna Freud on behalf of her father's reputation to so censor archival material that only now is some of the ghastly truth about the true origins of psychoanalysis coming, piecemeal, to light.

Nonetheless, even a reading of the censored correspondence of Freud with Karl Abraham from 1907 to the latter's early death in 1926 reveals most painfully the consequences of a loyal and intelligent disciple being ensnared in a web of treatment methods and diagnostic procedures that appeared to have been entirely dependent upon Freud's theories of pyscho-sexual development. That hay fever can be "treated successfully by psychoanalysis," according to one enthusiastic letter from Abraham, may not necessarily imply "a conscious and deliberate attempt to deceive" (Webster 1995) on the part of the pupil; but the absence of rebuttal from Freud on reading of his pupil's "first looking for the psycho-sexual roots of the hay fever" is evidence of medical incompetence or of the confidence of the trickster–seer—irrespective of medical incompetence—on the part of Freud.[31] Perhaps Freud was relying on the innocence of a man whose doctoral thesis had been on "The Developmental History of the Budgerigar."[32]

Freud's deceptions are so enormous and so frequent that one is amazed at Webster's challenge to Medawar. Curiously, the immediate consequence of reading part 3 on *this* reader of *Why Freud Was Wrong* was to go back to the beginning and to reread the first two parts retailing Freud's various adventures. And what one finds upon a second reading of Webster is a stylistic feat of legerdemain whereby many of Freud's deliberate confabulations are ignored or excused in such a way that one wonders who was the subject of this book. It certainly wasn't the Freud that I have discovered from my own researches into his methods and uses of persuasive rhetoric. Nor was it the Freud of whom Frederick Crews wrote in the conclusion of *The Memory Wars* and including himself as an honorable "Freud-basher":

> What passes today for Freud bashing is simply the long-postponed exposure of Freudian ideas to the same standards of non-contradiction, clarity, testability, cogency, and parsimonious explanatory power that prevail in empirical discourse at large. Step by step, we are learning that Freud has been the most overrated figure in the entire history of science and medicine—one who wrought immense harm through the propagation of false etiologies, mistaken diagnoses, and fruitless lines of enquiry. (Crews et al. 1995, 298)

The reason—or one of the reasons—that Webster's challenge to Peter Medawar backfires is that when one returns to Webster's accounts of

Freud's emerging practice, one discovers that, although Freud's errors are discussed in substantial detail, there is silence or invented (sometimes jesuitical) excuse for the multiple duplicities; hence Webster's title—*Why Freud Was Wrong*—uses the adjective in its empirical and not in its moral sense.

To the question provocatively proposed by Frank Cioffi a quarter of a century ago—"Was Freud a liar?"—we can now answer "Yes!" This affirmative gives the present author neither pleasure nor embarrassment. It will be recorded, demonstrated, and analyzed in as neutral a tone as I can manage; but that tone will not exclude moments of irony. The "yes" is—nowadays—to far many more issues than Cioffi at that time (1974) could have realized. Freud lied to—and about—his patients (see the next chapter), lied to his colleagues, lied to the world at large in *The Interpretation of Dreams*, where we can now show that the so-called "specimen dream" of Irma's Injection, supposed to underwrite the value of dream-interpretation for the whole book, is a tissue of lies and innuendoes that could not have occurred when and how it is claimed with the analysis attributed to it. And, incidentally, Wilhelm Fliess, the *Zauberer* (magician) from Berlin, seems to have been the first to have realized the lies within the published version of the dream.

It goes without saying (but needs nonetheless to be said) that the philosopher Frank Cioffi and the literary scholar Frederick Crews are absent from what was published—as recently as 1991—as *The Cambridge Companion to Freud*.[33] This collection of essays, which concludes with an attempted rebuttal by David Sachs of Grünbaum's *The Foundations of Psychoanalysis*, is at once a sign of the ability of psychoanalysis to live, and thrive, in a world aware of the stringent and accurate revelations of the last quarter century and a testament to the willful blindness of the many contributors listed as "advanced candidates" at several psychoanalytic institutes in the United States. To be an "advanced candidate" means, apparently, among other things, to be immune to the process of careful investigation of the honesty and accuracy of the founder of one's chosen sect. It is sad to read, for example, that Gerald Izenberg, once the author of an excellent existentialist critique of Freud, is now listed as "an advanced candidate and instructor at the St. Louis Psychoanalytic Institute." The whiff of what George Steiner once called "the Jewish mode of Christian Science"[34] is evidently intoxicating.

Whether Freud was infected with the malady of Messiah-isis is another question. Webster argues that Freud *was* so afflicted and that because he saw himself as a latter-day Moses he allowed his vision to get the better of his actual understanding of science and psychology. He allowed this vision to override his empirical findings. Stated that bluntly, Webster's solution—or, as I would say, Webster's cop-out[35]—could be a perfect starting point for an intellectual biography (but *not* an exposé) of L. Ron Hubbard. A biography of Hubbard or of the Church of Scientology would not require the detailed investigation into late-nineteenth-century French medicine at the Salpêtrière under Jean-Martin Charcot (which was in many respects a kind of human zoo for the training for performance of indigent invalids)[36] or the extensive examination of hypnosis and hysteria as a medical condition that Webster's text provides. This is one intensely documented and informative aspect of Webster's book, the fruit of years of careful personal research into medical history with the aid (generously acknowledged) of several British neurologists and medical historians. If Webster has not always understood the intricacies of his subject—and several psychiatrists have found flaws in his grasp of hysteria and in his understanding of brain lesions and their sequelae—one feels like congratulating him on his industry while reserving judgment about its ultimate utility when dealing with the writings and organizational aptitudes of Freud.

To be fair, Webster can be devastatingly, and accurately, blunt in his assessment of Freud's scientific, medical, or simply intellectual standing. Witness this passage toward the beginning of part 3:

> Freud made no substantial intellectual discoveries. He was the creator of a complex pseudo-science which should be recognized as one of the great follies of Western civilisation. In creating his particular pseudo-science, Freud developed an autocratic, anti-empirical intellectual style which has contributed immeasurably to the intellectual ills of our own era. His original theoretical system, his habits of thought and his entire attitude to scientific research are so far removed from any responsible method of inquiry that no intellectual approach basing itself upon these is likely to endure. (Webster 1995, 438)[37]

If Webster's verdict is correct—as I believe it is—then certain questions occur concerning certain silences, and not only those of Webster in the first two parts of his book. For these silences are those of the academic community, including scholars in medicine, psychology, philosophy, and especially in literature or literary studies including "theory," who have written at length on Freud's writings and activities without once raising the issue of dishonesty. Freud seems to have the Teflon quality of a Reagan.

Here, in brief, are some of the crucial silences of the academic community (and of Webster) concerning the origins of psychoanalysis: the dishonesty of presentation of the *Studies on Hysteria*; the irresponsible mismanagement of the Emma Eckstein fiasco and its sequels; the true origins of the Oedipus scenario; the true circumstances and dates of the "Dream of Irma's Injection"; the rhetoric of deceit; the presentation of self as scrupulous.

Had Medawar had access to these features of psychoanalysis, one can imagine the charge that would have been added to the review of Irving Cooper's book. To accuse Freud of lying, and of lying in his presentation of his own case histories, in a first chapter is to run the risk, paradoxically at the end of the twentieth century, of being accused of some kind of nefarious lèse-psychoanalysis which will irritate not merely "the believers" (as Grünbaum refers to the disciples of Freud) but also those who nonetheless were convinced of a fundamental, if misguided, honesty in the origins of psychoanalysis. As a recent instance of this touchiness about the Master's supposed foibles, let me quote from the review in the London *Times* of the British edition of Crews's *The Memory Wars* by the English psychotherapist Anthony Storr. Having noted his agreement with Crews about the excellence of Mark Pendergrast's *Victims of Memory*, Storr unleashes this broadside:

> However, agreement with Crews in this respect does not commit anyone to go along with the rest of his attack upon Freud, which is so intemperate that even psychiatrists like myself who are highly critical of Freud feel appalled by Crews's portrayal of Freud as a dishonest crook, and his lack of appreciation of the positive aspects of Freud's legacy.[38]

The reason why Medawar would be livid could he know of the present state of affairs is twofold: (1) how *could* a medical doctor so falsify his case histories? and (2) how *could* psychoanalysis be usefully examined for its probative qualities and potential heuristic value if its very origins and the reporting thereof were a tissue of inventions? Even toward the end of the essay critical of psychoanalytic methodology, "Further Comments on Psychoanalysis" (first published in 1972, reprinted in *Pluto's Republic*),

Medawar seems to throw up his hands and limit his comments on Freud's duplicity to the rhetoric of the presentation of the discipline: "A critique of psychoanalysis is, in the outcome, never much more than a skirmish, because (as I tried to explain) its doctrines are so cunningly insulated from the salutary rigours of disbelief" (*Pluto's Republic*, 71).

There are those who know this, alas, and who happily manage to embroider suggestive interpretations around the very evidence before their eyes, so that, once again, Freud comes out as the juggernaut of psychology. One particularly well-documented work is the entertaining volume, sexily—and accurately—entitled *Freud's Women* (1992), jointly written by Lisa Appignanesi and John Forrester.[39] This book, which is magnificently informed about all the gossip of the heroic early days of psychoanalysis—one learns, for example, the real identity of the famous predator of the "Dora" case history, "Herr K.," and of his ambiguous, adulterous wife "Frau K." (Herr and Frau Zellenka)—had the benefit of the publication of Harvard University Press's edition of the unexpurgated Freud–Fliess letters. This reference source is quoted, frequently, and to effect. For those who have also studied these letters, however, the effect is quite congruent with what Freud would have wanted from his disciples: silence on certain matters and "careful" reading on others. As we will see in the next chapter, the power of documentary evidence to disabuse the "believers" is limited. And the continuing legacy of deception is as great as it ever had been in the hands of the father and daughter of psycho-analysis.

Appignanesi and Forrester, following in the footsteps of the hagiographical Peter Gay, do not deal, in *Freud's Women*, with anything so vulgar as Freud's scientific qualifications and achievements. Their book is solely directed to an appreciation of the brilliant and courageous ingenuity of Freud's handling of his patients, his circle, and his "metapsychological" extravaganzas. Malcolm Macmillan's book, which should have been known to them, is absent from their bibliography and references, though they do cite an article by him on Freud's possible debt to Delboeuf and Janet in his treatment of Emmy von N.[40]

Forrester and Appignanesi are clearly happy denizens of that dark "intellectual underworld" whose various modes of disenlightenment (not all, by any means, related to psychoanalysis) Medawar has explored in the collection of essays and papers entitled *Pluto's Republic*. In his introduction to the collection Medawar writes of a cultural and a medical problem (anti-Semitism and ulcerative colitis, respectively) in a way that suggests his distance from the Freudian and/or Lacanian inhabitants of the Night's Plutonian shore:

> I cite a whole number of psychoanalytic aetiologies and do not believe that any honest-minded man can read them—especially that which relates to a matter so grave and socially so important as anti-Semitism . . . —without thinking that, so far from being unjust, my reference to their 'Olympian glibness' was if anything rather temperate. I single out for special censure . . . the passage that deals with the psychotherapy of ulcerative colitis, a disease now widely regarded as 'auto-immune' in character—as a miscarriage of the immunological defence system in which the immunological defences of the body have turned against one of its own constituents.[41]

In *Freud Evaluated* Macmillan writes of Freud's "scientific" work in neurohistology and clinical neurology (none of which, incidentally, required the involvement of another living human):

> Freud was no more competent later in conducting experiments or entirely reliable in reporting their results. The methodological deficiencies of his (1885/1974) experiment on the effects of cocaine on muscular strength and reaction time are marked . . . and he lied over the addictiveness of the cocaine with which he "experimentally" attempted to wean Fleischl from his morphine addiction during 1884-1885. . . . His reports on this latter episode seem to presage his hiding his change of mind over the reality of the seduction memories.
>
> There are parallels with his work on the causes of neurosis. It required a method best described as quasi-experimental, but his use of it violated the canons on which it was purportedly based, and Freud was less than truthful about what he actually found. He also claimed incorrectly that he had not been led to the sexual etiology of psychoneuroses by those quasi-experimental methods. (Macmillan 1997, 658-59)[42]

The situation may be even worse in France.[43] Adolf Grünbaum, who wrote to me in 1997 to send me the recent publication of the French version of *The Foundations of Psychoanalysis* (*Les Fondements de la psychanalyse*, Paris: Presses Universitaires de France, 1996), mentioned the series of university seminars being given in Paris by the Freudian–Lacanian (which is beginning to sound like "Marxist–Leninist") Elisabeth Roudinesco under the general title "La haine de Freud." These seminars purport to examine historically the various historical "resistances" to Freudiansism, that is, "a Jewish science," "a petit-bourgeois science," and so on, according to whether the society was a capitalist economy, a soviet socialist economy, a dictatorship, or even under the thrall of wicked empiricists or thinkers such as Karl Popper. One thing that Roudinesco does not do, apparently, is to investigate, or to ask her students to investigate, how the movement began and on what premises. Or with what honesty.[44]

When the Cambridge University journal *Behavioral and Brain Sciences* ran a special issue (vol. 9, no. 2, June 1986) giving an "Open Peer Commentary" on Adolf Grünbaum's *The Foundations of Psychoanalysis,* not one of the responses of any of the many internationally recognized commentators confronted the issue of Freud's devious troping with the term *Naturwissenschaft* (or Hard Science) as a metaphor with its inbuilt implication that his *method* was equally rigorous. Secondly, and more importantly, nobody mentioned that, even within the license offered by this freeplay with language, Freud frequently had recourse to invented or distorted accounts of "patients." I put the word patients in quotation marks because sometimes the apparent "patient" is Freud himself disguised for the recounting of a theoretical teasing—as in the celebrated fraud on "Screen Memories," which has been known for the last fifty years to be a highly contrived presentation of a theoretical position made believable by its observational aspects being attributed to the presence of a "patient"—none other than Freud himself in fact.[45] Even the daring Frank Cioffi concludes his criticism of Grünbaum's *Foundations* thus:

> The right procedure would have been to examine the specimens of consilience put forward by Freud and to have shown that not only do they fail to surpass that of rival accounts but they generally fail to meet the standards of plausible story telling (vague as these are) current in good historical, biographical, or forensic practice.[46]

The "right" procedure (*pace* Cioffi and Grünbaum) would have been to question the veracity of the material presented in the guise of "medical case histories" as prone to error as any others *but at least as accurately presented*. None of the commentators raises the issue of Freud's duplicity. Curiously enough, the one contributor who *does* raise the issue of Freud's rhetorical "pure salesmanship" is Grünbaum himself.

As recently as 1997, Malcolm Macmillan (1997, 665) in the afterword to his revised *Freud Evaluated* can cite and agree with my own findings about the fiction of the "Dream of Irma's Injection" as it is presented in *The Interpretation of Dreams*[47] without, however, seeing fit to follow up the implications of this discovery. Those implications are, in a very important sense, far more damning of the whole enterprise called psychoanalysis than any of the many attempts to validate its scientificity. Those knowing mendacities, which are but part of the whole enterprise (and which have no place in Richard Webster's "messianic" version of Freud's adventures), were, unfortunately, par for the course in the cocaine-inspired years which saw the creation of psychoanalysis. Adolf Grünbaum, for example, has written of Mikkel Borch-Jacobsen's recent exposure *Remembering Anna O.* that it is "[t]he most unsparing point-by-point critical comparison yet of the 1882 and 1895 case histories of Josef Breuer's celebrated patient Anna O., documenting the mendacity of the claim of successful treatment outcome."[48] In my view, the distinguished neurophysiologist Breuer was less the willing perpetrator of a medical deception than the seduced victim of his younger colleague's enormous persuasive powers. And the consequence of this seduction was *Studies on Hysteria* brought out in 1895, the year of the Emma Eckstein disaster (about which every commentator in the *Behavioral and Brain Sciences* review was silent, as indeed was Grünbaum in *The Foundations of Psychoanalysis*).

In addition to what Macmillan calls "its limited value as a therapy, its acknowledged weaknesses as a theory, and its reliance on a suspect method of enquiry" (Macmillan 1997, 663), psychoanalysis is, or has been, virtually preordained by its founder to be revealed as a brilliant exercise in persuasion with some felicitous (but scarcely original) insights into human psychology. These insights are accompanied by—and sometimes confused with—errors about human developmental psychology so momentous that the "medical" validity of psychoanalytic treatment was doomed from the very start.

Such was the power of the rhetoric and such has been the skill of the international organization that a century has not been sufficient to remove the dangers to individual patients or to the collectivity of arts undergraduates (in psychology departments as well as in literature departments). And, incidentally, if "contamination by suggestion" was the bugbear of the analytic hour, consider the extension of this effect in university classrooms all over the continent, where the authority invested in the professor was enhanced in its deleterious efficacity by the (understandable) ignorance of the undergraduates about the origins of the texts presented as authoritative.

What has to be challenged is the cornucopia of conceits whereby the world has fallen victim to the artful Freud's invitation, "Share my obsession!" Beyond the contrivances of rhetorical persuasion, there was a genuine obsessional fascination and revulsion with genitalia and their male infant manifestations that Freud wished the world to share. The combination of authentic obsession and literary genius is responsible for the fictionalizations of human experience that make up Freud's case histories (beginning with *Studies on Hysteria*) and his theoretical essays (including *The Interpretation of Dreams*).

The "fictionalizations of human experience" do not merely refer to the improper reporting of case histories; they also refer to the presentation of the master-narrator of those histories, Freud himself. What is fictionalized in Freud's presentation of himself is (at least) double in intent and effect. In the first place, without the evidence of Freud's relatively uncensored ruminations in the letters to Wilhelm Fliess, we would not be in a position to ascertain the extent of Freud's contemporaneously held weird pseudo-medical beliefs that informed the patient confrontations so lovingly reworked in the "clinical" presentations. These are not the biographical indiscretions of youth, which it would be unchivalrous (and quite inaccurate) to present as the considerations of the mature man; these letters do not begin until Freud is more than thirty-one (November 24, 1887, is the date of the first), some six and a half years after he had received his medical degree, and some three and a half years after he had begun the regular absorption of cocaine. They cease with the letter of July 27, 1904, when Freud was in his forty-eighth year. In other words this important correspondence coincides exactly with Freud's maturity and, more significantly, with the elaboration of what was to become psychoanalysis.

That said, the careful reader (even without access to the Freud–Fliess correspondence) can have already discovered strange admissions in—to cite a famous example—the Dora case history. One learns there that it is "well known that gastric pains occur especially often in those who masturbate."[49] Freud obviously moved in the wrong circles, where sexual enlightenment was tardy, for even in late-nineteenth-century Europe there were sophisticates (and no doubt innocent shop-girls) who were aware of the egregious and chauvinist lunacy of such notions. Even Virginia Woolf was moved to write to her friend Molly MacCarthy at the time when the

Hogarth Press was "setting up" the proofs of the English translation of Freud: "I glance at the proof and read how Mr. A. B. threw a bottle of red ink on to the sheets of his marriage bed to excuse his impotence to the housemaid, but threw it in the wrong place, which unhinged his wife's mind—and to this day she pours claret on the dinner table. We could all go on like that for hours; and yet these Germans think it proves something—besides their own gull-like imbecility."[50] One can hear in these lines the workings of that stern and lucid intelligence that was Virginia Woolf's forte; she would have been among the first to despise those Freudian-based elucubrations on her own life—including the feminist ones—and, one feels, with very good reason.

In the second place, there is a presentation of knowing ironic gravitas in the narrator (similar to the presentation of self that Freud offers Karl Abraham in their correspondence) that is likely to provoke, in the innocent reader, a sense that indeed, odd as it may seem, what is recounted *must* have happened as it was recorded and, furthermore, *must* have the significance intended by the recorder. As discussed in chapters six and seven, Rudyard Kipling—one of Freud's favorite models among the English writers (and perhaps ultimately more significant than Conan Doyle as a literary influence)—had not merely anticipated the style of the case histories in his Indian tales but indeed imaginatively invented the future history of what psychoanalysis would become (with all its internecine quarrels) in a tale written at the end of the nineteenth century. Freud's fascination with Kipling's tales is clearly demonstrated in the correspondence with Fliess. For all the suitably literary references— Goethe, Shakespeare, Heine, and so on, that elegantly embroider the Freudian oeuvre—the narrative master who was most formative in the development of the style adopted by Freud both in the case histories and later in the narratives of the "theoretical" essays was Kipling.

There remains a disturbing question that requires some kind of accommodation concerning the extent to which Freud was, indeed, at the time of the elaboration of psychoanalysis, self-deceived and not the knowing trickster that Medawar and, later, Cioffi and Crews have presented. This is a difficult issue. On the one hand, some of Freud's beliefs are *so* bizarre (whether as a consequence of cocaine abuse or as an instance of his personality) that one is reluctant to conclude that the man was a charlatan ever aware of his misdemeanors—he was simply, and grossly, mistaken and all the time was totally convinced of the rightness of his beliefs. On the other hand, the more evidence one has of his early maneuvers in case management and case reporting, the more one is inclined to credit the arguments of Cioffi and Medawar (and, more recently, Crews).

Reading the late letters (of the 1920s and 1930s)[51] to such eminences as Romain Rolland (Nobel Prize, 1915), Albert Einstein, and Arnold and Stefan Zweig, one is almost seduced by what an academic friend once called "Freud's wisdom." The "wisdom" of these late letters (and of those to Lou Andreas-Salomé) is certainly a powerful presence. Was it the result of a valid, and unpopular, insight into mankind? Or was it part of the "trickery" of presentation that was paramount in Freud's writings? Or did Freud, in fact, come to a genuine change of personality, as much as of analytical credo, such that these late letters reveal a man who, through all the tribulations of a vexed professional career, had entered upon a new territory—as Moses was not allowed to—where the wisdom of old age replaces the vanished moments of youthful or mature impetuosity?

A thorough reading of these late letters reveals that, although the style had matured and the presentation is indeed that of the "sage," the early notions about human sexual development and its ongoing influence are still the forces at work behind the new persona that Freud has brilliantly— and perhaps unwittingly?—crafted for himself. There was no change in the paradigms of human behavior. It may well be that the Freud who could write to Rolland and others in the 1920s and 1930s with such calm majesty had come to credit the beliefs engendered during the dangerously cocaine-brushed years of the last quarter of the nineteenth century. (But one cannot ignore the fact that it was this same "wise Freud" who also wrote to Horace Frink.)

So when did the self-deception begin? In a review article in the *Times Literary Supplement* for May 16, 1997, Richard Webster raised this issue in his assessment of the English publication of Frederick Crews's *The Memory Wars*. He writes:

> One of the questions which Crews does not address is whether Freud consistently and deliberately misrepresented his methods of working or whether, perhaps because of the very power of his messianic self-belief, he fell victim to self-deception on a colossal scale. Crews's tendency to take the former view, and his use of terms such as "fraudulence" and "fakery," renders his essay more offensive to the Freudian faithful than it need have been.[52]

That last phrase is puzzling. Why does the demonstration (and Crews certainly demonstrates his case) have to consider possible "offense" to the "Freudian faithful"? The "offense" to free debate and to free informed discussion about tendentious notions has been for nearly a century that committed by what Webster (rightly) calls the "Freudian faithful." To this day many Freud archives remain sealed for years to come. And those who attempt to prize the truth from the documents are chastised for their scurrilous courage. Crews's terms such as "fraudulence" and "fakery" are, as this book will show, perfectly correct assessments of how Freud chartered the course for what he called "the cause," that is, his new-found "science" of psychoanalysis. Crews's tough language is specifically limited to those years when Freudian psychoanalysis was being invented, and in those years (roughly 1895-1915) Freud was, indeed, both a fraud and a fake (however much the fakery was the consequence of almost willed self-deception). I doubt if Crews would deny the obsessive sincerity with which Freud elaborated his theories. Where the strong language ("fraud," "fakery") comes into play is (1) in what we can glean of his handling of patients; (2) in what we can now prove of his "economy with the truth" in his public and published presentations of "clinical" findings; (3) in his role as *magister ludi* presiding over the discussions of his pupils.

Webster's saving notion of "messianic self-belief" requires a re-reading (what Derrida would happily call a "deconstruction") of what actually occurred in those formative years. Webster's "messianic" version of Freud—given that he has seriously studied the period—is ultimately irrelevant to the merits of Freud's theories or how they were really developed. Freud was a brilliant writer but obtuse about human behavior. Although my own researches have shown that there were certainly moments of deep stupidity in Freudian solutions to human predicaments, I have not discovered serious grounds for elevating this late-nineteenth-century "monomaniac" (as Freud referred to his local reputation in 1894)[53] to the status of Messiah or even of Deceived Messiah, or even, to borrow from Ken Russell on Gaudier-Brzeska, "Savage Messiah." The Freud writing to Fliess from 1887 to 1904 was a confused, cocaine-intoxicated man, enslaved to Fliess's notions about periodicity and the power of the nose and intent on charting his own version of mental hygiene and, later, on thrusting it upon the world. His slowly emerging gift was for convincing narrative. In that he was eminently successful.

Notes

1. Steve Jones (1997). "Crooked Bones." *New York Review of Books* (February 6): 23. Jones, the professor of genetics at University College, London, was reviewing an exposé of the Piltdown fraud, *Unraveling Piltdown: The Science Fraud of the Century and Its Solution*, by John Evangelist Walsh. Medawar was known for his vigorous expressions, as proponents of psychoanalysis have learned to their cost. It may be worth recording here his thunder about "The Piltdown Skull" (see P. B. and J. S. Medawar 1983. *Aristotle to Zoos: A Philosophical Dictionary of Biology*, 215): "[T]he term 'hoax,' widely used to describe the episode, is unduly euphemistic: this was a carefully executed crime carried out with the intention of deceiving."

2. Malcolm Macmillan (1997). *Freud Evaluated: The Completed Arc*. Cambridge, Mass.: The MIT Press, 663.

3. Nathan G. Hale Jr. (1971, 1995). *Freud and the Americans: The Beginnings of Psychoanalysis in the United States, 1876-1917*. New York: Oxford University Press, 1971; and *The Rise and Crisis of Psychoanalysis in the United States: Freud and the Americans, 1917-1985*. New York, Oxford University Press, 1995.

4. Frederick Crews (1986). *Skeptical Engagements*. New York: Oxford University Press. In my view, the five essays reprinted in this paperback edition are by far the most trenchant, the most succinct, and (given the limits of space) the most informed of the currently available writings on Freud. Anyone who has read and understood these invigorating essays and who is attending a course in literary studies where Freudian (or Lacanian) dogma is being offered as a tool in literary criticism may be expected to raise awkward questions in class discussions. One instance of the lasting significance of these essays (beyond their own intrinsic value) is the argument they offer to university students caught in the web of sexy "intellectualism" of Freudian conceits. Armed with an understanding of the thought at work in Crews's book, students will prove difficult clients; and the quality of the integrity and scholarship of graduate courses may accordingly be improved.

5. I say "*subsequent* metapsychological theorizings" thinking of famous essays such as *Beyond the Pleasure Principle* (1920); but in fact Freud's "metapsychological theorizings" predated most of the "clinical" data. Already, in a letter dated March 10, 1898, we find Freud writing to his mentor Fliess: "(I am going to ask you seriously, by the way, whether I may use the name metapsychology for my psychology that leads behind consciousness)" (Masson 1985, 301-302).

6. Hale's accurate historical assessment of early American enthusiasms and of the myths accordingly created by Freud's "militant followers" passes silently

over the crucial issue of Freud's *prior* mythification of his activities and their reception in Vienna. It may be that his commitment to Freudianism has allowed this otherwise scrupulous historian to omit material relating to the *reality* of Freud's Viennese activities.

7. Michael Alan Taylor (1989). "Editorial." *Neuropsychiatry, Neuropsychology, and Behavioral Neurology* 2, no. 4, 237-38. My thanks to Dr. Karel de Pauw, consultant psychiatrist at St. James's University Hospital, Leeds (U.K.), for bringing this article, and several others, to my attention. For the benefit of readers not familiar with American law, "Chapter 11" refers to a form of bankruptcy.

8. E. Fuller Torrey (1992). *Freudian Fraud: The Malignant Effect of Freud's Theory on American Thought and Culture.* New York: HarperCollins.

9. Adolf Grünbaum (1984). *The Foundations of Psychoanalysis.* Berkeley: University of California Press. His second volume on psychoanalysis, Grünbaum (1993), is *Validation in the Clinical Theory of Psychoanalysis.* Madison, Conn.: International Universities Press.

10. Jeffrey M. Masson (1985). *The Complete Letters of Sigmund Freud to Wilhelm Fliess, 1887-1904.* Cambridge: Harvard University Press (The Belknap Press).

The reason for the absence of these scholars from Torrey's index may have less to do with censorship than with carelessness. His book has all the evidence of having been stitched together from diverse material gathered by several graduate research assistants and not properly integrated by the overseer (whether the HarperCollins in-house editor or Torrey himself). The poorly presented unnumbered chapter endnotes do in fact refer to an article by Peter Swales and to Nathan G. Hale's first volume and to Jeffrey M. Masson's *The Assault on Truth* and to his edition of the unexpurgated Freud–Fliess correspondence; all of this material is sufficiently important to merit an index entry.

11. Although Grünbaum has chosen to present a "best-case scenario" of Freud's invention and is discreet, to the point of silence, about the latter's abuse of cocaine and its consequences, his section (in *The Foundations of Psychoanalysis*) dealing with the Specimen Dream—of Irma's Injection—accuses Freud in one paragraph of falsehood, incompetence, and pretension (see Grünbaum 1984, 222).

12. Macmillan gives careful (one may wonder, tongue in cheek?) reference to the hyponotist M. Bernstein's 1956 publication *The Search for Bridey Murphy.* New York: Doubleday.

13. Richard Webster (1996). *Why Freud Was Wrong: Sin, Science and Psychoanalysis.* New York: Basic Books.

14. An exception may be made for retired British lecturer in mathematics and physics Allen Esterson. In 1993 he published with Open Court in Chicago *Seductive Mirage: An Exploration of the Work of Sigmund Freud*. His article, "Jeffrey Masson and Freud's Seduction Theory: A New Fable Based on Old Myths," *History of the Human Sciences* 11, no. 1 (February 1998): 1-21, is a detailed and perceptive reading of the seduction theory episode. Like me, Esterson sees deception, self-deception, and the pursuit of an obsession (probably) inspired by—certainly aggravated by—the long-term abuse of cocaine as some of the real cornerstones of psychoanalysis. He does not think, however, as E. M. Thornton did, that cocaine is an important element in relation to Freud's post-1897 theorizing. I should like to thank Allen Esterson for an early typescript draft of this paper.

15. Robert Wilcocks (1996). "Freud and his Defenders." *Times Literary Supplement* (October 11): 19.

16. Frank Cioffi (1974). "Was Freud a Liar?" *Listener* 91: 172-74. Readers should realize that this question was raised over twenty years ago in a prestigious BBC publication. Frank Cioffi has been haranguing the world for a good quarter of a century about the philosophical and scientific inadequacies of psychoanalysis. This *vox in deserto* should have been heard, or listened to, a long time ago (the more so in that his scathing assessments of the philosophical and scientific status of psychoanalysis were published well before our present knowledge of Freud's dishonesty). Among Cioffi's many publications on the status of psychoanalysis are: (1970) "Freud and the Idea of a Pseudo-science," in R. Borger and Frank Cioffi, eds., *Explanation in the Behavioural Sciences* (471-99), Cambridge: Cambridge University Press; (1972) "Wollheim on Freud," *Inquiry* 15: 171-86; (1973) introduction to F. Cioffi, ed., *Freud: Modern Judgements* (1-24), London: Macmillan; (1985) "Psycho-analysis, Pseudo-science, and Testability," in G. Currie and A. Musgrave, eds., *Popper and the Human Sciences* (13-44), Dordrecht: Nijhoff. Most of Frank Cioffi's Freud essays were published by Open Court (Chicago) in 1998 under the title: *Freud and the Question of Pseudoscience*.

17. Frank Cioffi (1979). "Freud—New Myths to Replace the Old." *New Society* (November 29): 503-504. This quotation comes from page 504.

18. See, for example, Freud's "history" of his movement in "An Autobiographical Study," in *S.E.* 20: 7-74. But the earliest public presentations of self as magister go back to his chairing (from 1902, when he was forty-six years old) of the Psychological Wednesday Evenings in his own home. These later became the Vienna Psychoanalytic Society meetings, and the current translation of these activities is the excellent *Minutes of the Vienna Psychoanalytic Society* (vols.1-4), edited by Herman Nunberg and Ernst Federn and translated by M. Nunberg, New York: International Universities Press,

1962-1975.

19. Brian Vickers (1993). *Appropriating Shakespeare: Contemporary Critical Quarrels*. New Haven: Yale University Press. The chapter which includes the Medawar quote (on p. 280), "Psychocriticism: Finding the Fault," is prefaced by this telling passage from Alasdair MacIntyre's (1971) *Against the Self-Images of the Age* (London: Duckworth, 7-8):

> In the cultural desert created by the prejudices of the liberal intelligentsia of New York or of the Californian cities, the questioning of the scientific pretensions of psychoanalysis is restricted almost entirely to those concerned with the philosophy of science. The therapeutic needs of such aids perhaps makes intelligible the extraordinary situation whereby a theory that is certainly no better informed—and perhaps not as well confirmed—as witchcraft or astrology should have gained the credence it has.

20. Ernest Gellner (1985). *The Psychoanalytic Movement, or the Coming of Unreason*. London: Paladin. The subtitle "The *Cunning* of Unreason" is the one intended by Gellner; but my London paperback edition (Paladin Books, Granada, 1985) clearly and only gives "The Coming of Unreason" which is perhaps even more pertinent.

21. Frederick Crews et al. (1995). *The Memory Wars: Freud's Legacy in Dispute*. New York: New York Review Books. Crews's comment this time on the crucial phrase in Medawar that doctrinaire psychoanalytic theory is "the most stupendous intellectual confidence trick of the twentieth century" is, simply: "He could have added that like many another such instrument of deception, its first and most enduring dupes are its own practitioners" (135).

22. Robert Wilcocks (1994). *Maelzel's Chess Player: Sigmund Freud and the Rhetoric of Deceit*. Lanham, Md.: Rowman & Littlefield.

23. Irving S. Cooper (1974). *The Victim Is Always the Same*. New York: Harper and Row. In the first paragraph of his review, Medawar explains Cooper's choice of a phrase from a French Nobel Prize winner (literature, 1957) for his title:

> In a passage in "Bread and Freedom" Camus expresses his revulsion at the way in which, in political arguments, one atrocity may be bartered for another: if one protests at some enormity of the communists, three American negroes are "thrown in one's face." In any such disgusting attempt at outbidding, Camus says, one thing does not change—the victim, freedom. It is this reflection that gives Irving Cooper's book its title: the victim is the patient, and the aptness of the Camus quotation becomes very clear as the book goes on. (Medawar 1975, 17)

24. It is important to understand that in the United States, where most

psychoanalysts are M.D.s, medical knowledge, especially of neurology, gained in training appears to be ignored in psychoanalytic case assessments. As a consequence, for these analysts the beliefs they have come to embrace have overpowered the knowledge they had once acquired (or begun to acquire).

25. The Inquisitorial image is not gratuitous. Freud writes to Fliess on January 24, 1897, that he has just placed an order for the *Malleus Maleficarum* (*The Hammer of Witches*), and adds later in the same letter: "I dream, therefore, of a primeval devil religion with rites that are carried on secretly, and understand the harsh therapy of the witches' judges" (Masson 1985, 227).

One of the most useful modern American editions of this all-purpose guide to witchery and how to recognize it and deal with it (almost a fifteenth-century version of an M. F. K. Fisher cookbook—*"First, catch your witch"*) is *The Malleus Maleficarum of Heinrich Kramer and James Sprenger*. Translated with introductions, bibliography, and notes by Rev. Montague Summers. New York: Dover, 1971.

26. Gellner (1985), 222. The original review under the title "Victims of Psychiatry" was published in the *New York Review of Books* for January 23, 1975, 17.

27. This bizarre contention of Webster has, recently, been trounced by Frederick Crews in a letter response to *The Times Literary Supplement* where Crews writes, "The idea that a body of unfounded speculation as megalomaniacal in its pretensions as Freud's needs to be 'replaced' before it can be refuted makes no more sense than saying the same thing about palmistry or UFOlogy. If Webster fails to grasp this elementary point, it is because he himself shares Freud's desire to play Prometheus" ("Freud and the Judaeo–Christian Tradition," *TLS*, June 20, 1997, 17).

28. See the revelations of Mrs. Kraft (daughter of Dr. Frink) reported in the excellent article by Lavinia Edmunds, "His Master's Choice," *Johns Hopkins Magazine* 40, no. 2 (April 1988): 40-49. This article is, curiously, absent from the bibliography of Richard Webster's *Why Freud Was Wrong*, as is any mention of the whole Frink business.

Lavinia Edmunds's article is mandatory reading for anyone who still feels able to credit one of the other Freudian (and Freud-originated) myths, namely his diagnostic acumen and his intransigent honesty. It is also worth reading for what it reveals of current psychoanalytic excuses in the face of the evidence. For example, Edmunds quotes Albert Dreyfus as an assistant professor of psychiatry who had been a practicing psychoanalyst for more than thirty years: "He [Freud] was in an incredibly difficult position in connection with bringing out the primary sexual issue at a time when Victorian mores made the concept itself taboo" (Edmunds 1988, 49). That a long-established analyst could come out with such rubbish shows an immense ignorance of Freud's Vienna—not known for its "Victorian mores"—unless it is yet another disturbing example of the analytic tendency to deceive to save the practice and its reputation.

29. See Allen Esterson (1993), 121-23.

30. Meyer himself said of his own position in his presidential address (see *The American Journal of Psychiatry*, 1928: 8, 1-31):

> My own preoccupation becomes the individual patient examined and discussed in staff meeting and considered as an experiment of nature, with special attention to the modifiable factors, and followed to an adjustment or, in case of death, to autopsy and beyond autopsy, with a study of reaction sets and the factors at work.

This is reported in B. S. Fogel, R. B. Schiffer, S. M. Rao, eds. (1996), *Neuropsychiatry*. Baltimore: Williams and Wilkins, 7. In their first chapter, "Evolution of Neuropsychiatric Ideas in the United States and United Kingdom—1800-2000," Randolph B. Schiffer and Barry S. Fogel write:

> In the United States, psychoanalytic ideas gained an even more rapid and unqualified acceptance. An important figure in the facilitation of this process was Adolf Meyer, who was unquestionably the dominant intellectual figure in American psychiatry during the early years of the 20th century. Meyer had come from Switzerland and had participated in neuropathological and neurological research. He emigrated to the U.S. and in the early 1890s was appointed pathologist at the Illinois Eastern Asylum in Kankekee.

31. Hilda C. Abraham and Ernst L. Freud, eds. (1965). *A Psycho-Analytic Dialogue: The Letters of Sigmund Freud and Karl Abraham, 1907-1926*. Tr. Bernard Marsh and Hilda C. Abraham. London: Hogarth Press and the Institute of Psycho-Analysis. See Abraham's letter of August 9, 1912, 121-22.

These letters, incidentally, are not *complete* but were selected and censored on the "advice" of Miss Anna Freud according to the editors' preface (following the same principles which some ten years earlier had led to the highly misleading publication of the expurgated Freud–Fliess correspondence). Dr. Edward Glover contributes an introduction which includes the recommendation that the volume "should be read by psychiatrists who have not already sold the pass to neuro-physiology and by any general psychologist who is prepared to learn by what steps the principles and practices of (unconscious) psychology came to be applied to everyday life and character." The present author finds himself in total agreement with Glover about the value of this work for understanding the history of psychoanalysis.

32. Abraham/Freud letters, 131, note 3: "Abraham wrote his doctoral thesis on an embryological subject: '*Entwicklungsgeschichte des Wellensittigs*' [The

Developmental History of the Budgerigar]."

33. Jerome Neu, ed. (1991). *The Cambridge Companion to Freud.*
Cambridge: Cambridge University Press. The volume, introduced by Jerome
Neu, begins with the famous "In Memory of Sigmund Freud" by Auden—"if
often he was wrong and, at times, absurd,//to us he is no more a person//now
but a whole climate of opinion//under whom we conduct our different lives"—
and continues with Neu's extravagant claim: "He gave us a new and powerful
way to think about and investigate human thought, action, and interaction. He
made sense of ranges of experience generally neglected or misunderstood"
(Neu, 1991, 1). Wellington's "Sir, if you believe that, you'll believe anything!"
comes to mind; but Neu's introductory patter is, in fact, quite an accurate
indication of what one will find in the volume; no recent criticism, with the
exception of Grünbaum, is seriously discussed, and the *magister ludi* is allowed
right of way.

34. George Steiner (1988). "The Great Liberator." *The Sunday Times*
(London). May 22, G2. This is a review of Peter Gay's *Freud: A Life for Our
Time.*

35. Webster's book is a massively researched and, in many ways, a very
valuable piece of work. If I use the pejorative "cop-out" it is simply because the
Freudian material Webster had to hand as his book was being completed was
no different from the material I had at my disposition when I wrote *Maelzel's
Chess Player.* Either his nerve failed him and he invented 'understandable'
excuses for Freud's wierd conduct, or his readings of the Freud–Fliess
correspondence were superficial; or perhaps both. In any case it is a great pity
that a large book as well-produced and well-marketed as *Why Freud Was
Wrong* should miss what I consider to be the essential moral indictment of
psychoanalysis—that it was founded upon the shifting sands of calculated
deceit (no doubt compounded by massive, if intermittent, self-deception).

36. A close reading of the many "medical" research papers from the mid-
1880s on dealing principally with the trio of hysteria, hypnosis, and
magnetism (in the literal sense of the application to the left or right
hemispheres of the cranium of ordinary magnets), to be found in the volumes of
La Revue philosophique de la France et de l'étranger (usually simply referred
to as *La Revue philosophique*), edited by Théodule Ribot, gives the impression
of much frenetic activity, much professional rationalization, and much
unnecessary and sometimes downright irresponsible tormenting of incarcerated
patients.

The fad for amateur hypnotism was such that even the philosopher Henri
Bergson (then a teacher at Clermont-Ferrand) found time to experiment and
write up his findings on schoolboy subjects for *La Revue philosophique*, "De la
simulation inconsciente dans l'état d'hypnotisme" (Tome 22, 1886, 525-31).

Nonetheless several genuine neurological discoveries were made at the Salpêtrière, notably by Joseph Babinski, Pierre Marie, and Gilles de la Tourette. But their findings were not the consequence of hypnotism or magnetism.

37. This echoes the resounding final sentence in Allen Esterson's (1993) *Seductive Mirage: An Exploration of the Work of Sigmund Freud*:

> It may well be that the rise of psychoanalysis to a position of prominence in the twentieth century will come to be regarded as one of the most extraordinary aberrations in the history of Western thought. (Esterson 1993, 254)

38. Anthony Storr (1997). "Battle for the No Man's Land of the Mind." *The Times* (London), June 12. Storr's very next sentence is a statement of belief, or credo, which partly explains his anger with Crews: "Freud was *a great clinical observer* and a great writer [my emphasis]." There is no empirical evidence whatever to support the first half of that sentence. There is, on the contrary, much material coming, piecemeal, to light that clearly demonstrates the numerous instances of Freud's clinical blindness. For a more representative view of current British psychiatric devaluation of the analytic mythology around Freud's career, see Raymond Tallis's review of Webster in *The Lancet* (1996: 347, 669-71). Tallis uses the Nobel laureate Richard Feynman's description of Freud as a "cargo cult scientist" and adds that he "was closer to L. Ron Hubbard than to Einstein."

39. Lisa Appignanesi and John Forrester (1992). *Freud's Women*. London: Weidenfeld and Nicolson.

40. Malcolm Macmillan (1984). "Delboeuf and Janet as Influences in Freud's Treatment of Emmy von N." *Journal of the History of Behavioral Sciences* 20: 340-58.

41. Sir Peter Medawar (1984). *Pluto's Republic*. New York: Oxford University Press, 4.

42. The date 1974 in the first paragraph refers to Robert Byck's American reprint of Freud on cocaine (see Byck 1975 in my bibliography). Macmillan's reference regarding the deficiencies of Freud's cocaine experimental studies is to S. Bernfeld (1953), "Freud's Studies on Cocaine," *Journal of the American Psychoanalytical Association* 1: 581-613.

43. In fairness, one has to distinguish between psychiatric hospital practice and "intellectual" and popular press presentations of psychoanalysis in France. The latter are as avid as ever about Freud's invention. For instance, a cover-story dossier in the monthly *Science et Vie* for June 1995 on the French appearance of Antonio Damasio's *Descartes' Error* is headlined *"Freud avait raison. Des expériences le prouvent,"* and Damasio (whose whole book contains only one brief reference to Freud's *Civilization and Its Discontents*) is

presented as a neurological witness for Freud's scientific accuracy.

The former—French hospital psychiatrists—(from the evidence of my own research) are, for the most part, increasingly heartily disabused. It used to be standard practice for young psychiatrists to undergo a pedagogical analysis prior to completing their medical requirements. This has been abandoned for some years now as a suggested initiatory procedure and French psychiatrists do not recommend psychoanalysis as a treatment of choice for those suffering from depression or from many of the neurotic symptoms of modern patients. Those suffering from psychosis were rarely recommended for psychoanalysis, even in the past.

44. This was written before the delicious scandal provoked in France by the publication of *Impostures intellectuelles* (1997, Paris: Odile Jacob) by the physicists (American and Belgian) Alan Sokal and Jean Bricmont. Lacan's pseudo-scientific musings are given short shrift, and the vacuity of much French intellectual "problematizing" around matters Freudian and Lacanian is mercilessly revealed.

45. See Siegfried Bernfeld's honest examination in "An Unknown Autobiographical Fragment by Freud," *American Imago* 4 (1946), 3-19. Bernfeld's discovery is discussed by Henri Ellenberger (1970), 494-95.

46. Frank Cioffi (1986). "Did Freud Rely on the Tally Argument to Meet the Argument from Suggestibility?" *Behavioral and Brain Sciences* 9, no. 2 (June): 231.

47. See the arguments developed in Wilcocks (1994), 227-80.

48. Adolf Grünbaum, prepublication commentary printed on the back page of Mikkel Borch-Jacobsen, *Remembering Anna O.: A Century of Mystification*, New York: Routledge, 1996. Mikkel Borch-Jacobsen is professor of French and comparative literature at the University of Washington. His recent extensive and probing interview with Dr. Herbert Spiegel on the origins (in America) of the syndrome known as Multiple Personality Disorder is a splendid example of dispassionate lucidity. See Mikkel Borch-Jacobsen (1997), "Sybil—The Making of a Disease: An Interview with Dr. Herbert Spiegel," *The New York Review of Books* (April 24): 60-64.

49. Sigmund Freud, *Case Histories I: 'Dora' and 'Little Hans.'* Tr. Alix and James Strachey; ed. James Strachey, assisted by Angela Richards and Alan Tyson. Present volume edited by Angela Richards. Harmondsworth, U.K.: Penguin (*P.F.L.*, vol. 8, 1977, 115).

It is significant—and highly damaging to the public myth of Freud the psychological seer, or even "liberator"—that this strange notion and others conceived while Freud was under the joint influence of Fliess and cocaine (for instance, the belief that "gastralgias of this character . . . can be interrupted by an application of cocaine to the 'gastric spot' discovered by him [Fliess] in the nose") were retained in all subsequent editions, including the revised edition of 1924 and the last edition (1932), to appear in Freud's lifetime.

50. Virginia Woolf–Molly MacCarthy, October 2, 1924. Nigel Nicolson, ed., *A Change of Perspective: The Letters of Virginia Woolf*, vol. 3 (1923-1928), 134. Quoted in Clark (1980), 417. The reference is to Freud's *Introductory Lecture, 17*, "The Meaning of Symptoms." A "Gestalt" interpretation of this was given in 1955 by Fritz Schmidl, "The Problem of Scientific Validation in Psycho-Analytic Interpretation," *International Journal of Psychoanalysis*, March-April 1955. It is discussed by Frank Cioffi (1998) in *Freud and the Question of Pseudoscience*. Chicago: Open Court, 70-71. Virginia Woolf's response remains the best in its recognition and dismissal of the sly tendentious rhetoric of Freud's lecture; though Cioffi does write that "doubts may be raised as to the authenticity of the data" (71).

51. See the "selected and edited" edition of Ernst L. Freud (1960), *Letters of Sigmund Freud,* tr. Tania, and James Stern. New York: Basic Books.

52. Richard Webster (1997). "The Bewildered Visionary." *The Times Literary Supplement* (May 16): 10-11. This quotation is from page 11. Crews responded at some length ("Freud and the Judaeo–Christian Tradition") in *The Times Literary Supplement* (June 20, 1997): 17.

53. In the early summer of 1894, while he was working on drafts of *Studies on Hysteria* and on an elaboration of the sexual basis of the neuroses, he writes to Fliess (letter of May 21, 1894): "I am pretty much alone here in the elucidation of the neuroses. They look upon me as pretty much of a monomaniac, while I have the distinct feeling that I have touched upon one of the great secrets of nature" (Masson 1985, 74).

2

From the Baltic to the Correspondence

[N]o one can still claim to be unaware that the official history of psychoanalysis is a vast anthology of tall tales. MIKKEL BORCH-JACOBSEN[1]

If the "official history of psychoanalysis" is, as Mikkel Borch-Jacobsen claims (and has frequently demonstrated with evidence in hand), a concatenation of tall tales, what of the *un*official history? Are those tales even taller? Does Sigmund Freud become less an Isaac Newton and more an ersatz Marco Polo of psychology? In *Remembering Anna O.*, Borch-Jacobsen has carefully examined the evidence for the validity of the case presentation of "Anna O." as the first episode in *Studies on Hysteria*. He has shown convincingly that, although there is a shred of truth in the presentation of the "case" of Bertha Pappenheim as it is used to introduce *Studies on Hysteria*, it is hedged around with so much "mystification" (Borch-Jacobsen's courteous euphemism for rhetorical deception) that it is worse than useless as a medical document. No physician or psychotherapist could use this material as an aid to understanding aspects of his or her own profession.[2] So what may have been intended as a book, jointly authored with an established physiologist, to enhance Freud's emergence on the medical stage may be seen in hindsight as a first powerful presentation of the rhetoric of deceit that was to remain a continuing feature of his career.

After the appearance of the book, Breuer gave a lecture on November 4, 1895, to the Vienna College of Physicians [*Medizinisches Doktor-collegium*] and—or so Freud wrote to his Berlin friend Wilhelm Fliess—"introduced himself as a *converted* adherent to the sexual etiology" (Masson 1985, 151). However, what Breuer actually said—reported in the

Wiener medizinische Blätter (no. 18 [1895]: 716-17)—was less fulsome.

> One point on which the speaker [Breuer] does not agree with Freud is the overvaluation of sexuality; Freud probably did not want to say that every hysterical symptom has a sexual background, but rather that the original root of hysteria is sexual. . . . The objection might also have been raised that a lack of coherence makes itself felt in Freud's disquisitions; now, there is something to that, but one should not forget that we have provisional conclusions before us, that every theory is a temporary structure.[3]

This reticent approach (so typical of Breuer) enraged the fiery Freud. He immediately confided to Fliess, in the sentence after the one just quoted from his letter of November 8, 1895: "When I thanked him for this in private, he spoiled my pleasure by saying, 'But all the same, I don't believe it.' Do you understand this? I don't." Freud's apparently genuine puzzlement at Breuer's response indicates the extent to which, at least at this early stage of his psychological researches—what one may call the paleo-psychoanalytic period—he was a sincere believer in his "discoveries" even while we know that he was "cooking the books" (of his case reports) so that they would appear to fit the developing theories on which they were based. The Freud of this period was an extremely labile individual, and his theories about human motivation and the dire consequences of early sexual experience (of almost *any* sort, though not yet during the first eighteen months of life as they were later to be) were as unstable as their author. What the Freud–Fliess correspondence shows is that these rapidly shifting schemata of human behavior were in fact constant in only one respect, and that was the bemused and alarmed fascination with sexuality. If Freud was hoist by his own petard, it was scarcely a petard at the outset; it was more an obsessive intellection which, among other things, years of cocaine absorption had intensified.

In fact the publication of the famous *Studies on Hysteria* (1895) marked both the high point and the nadir of Freud's relations with Josef Breuer. The joint work had been in active preparation for some three years. The first mention made to Fliess occurs in a letter of June 28, 1892, and two weeks later, on July 12, 1892, Freud can write:

> My hysteria has, in Breuer's hands, become transformed, broadened, restricted, and in the process has partially evaporated. We are writing the thing jointly, each on his own working on several sections which he will

sign, but still in complete agreement. No one can yet say how it will turn out. In the meantime, I am using a cerebrally dull period to read psychology. (Masson 1985, 32)

In a letter to Fliess of February 7, 1894, Freud noted, "The book on hysteria I am doing with Breuer is half-finished; just a few of the total number of case histories and two general chapters are still outstanding" (Masson 1985, 66). Freud was, perhaps, a trifle optimistic about the little left unfinished. He was still reporting active, frenzied bouts of writing in the spring of 1895,[4] while Emma Eckstein was recuperating (at least *physically*) from the practical consequences of the theoretically based ministrations of Freud and Fliess.

Breuer, having been bitten once—and one feels that Breuer felt he *had* been bitten—was reluctant to repeat the experience. (He never again collaborated with Freud on a volume of clinical psychology.) Indeed he was so incensed by Freud's obsessive interests in sexual matters and his claims that they were of paramount determining significance in the etiology of virtually any nervous complaint in an adult that he wrote privately to Wilhelm Fliess (whom he had introduced to Freud in the first place) to distance himself from the findings of *Studies on Hysteria*. Freud responded to this when Fliess passed on Breuer's letter:

I was less angry about Breuer's letter than I had expected to be. I could console myself that the colorblind turns so quickly into a judge of colors, and I at least could understand why he held a low opinion of the etiology of the n[euroses]: because of my statement that trivial noxae may produce neurosis in persons who, it is true, never masturbated, but who nevertheless exhibit from the beginning a type of sexuality that has the same appearance as if they had acquired it through masturbation. (Masson 1985, 175)

Later, in the same paragraph, Freud confides the disaster that has overtaken his personal day-to-day relations with Breuer:

Our personal relationship, mended on the surface, casts a deep shadow over my existence here. I can do nothing right for him and have given up trying. According to him, I should have to ask myself every day whether I am suffering from *moral insanity* or paranoia scientifica. Yet I regard myself as the psychically more normal one. I believe he will never forgive that in the Studies [on Hysteria] I dragged him along and involved him in something where he unfailingly knows three candidates for the position of one truth and abhors all generalizations, regarding them as presumptuous. (Masson 1985, 175; my emphasis)[5]

Breuer's reaction to the outcome of the *Studies on Hysteria* proposal, as recounted by Freud to Fliess, rings true to my own estimation. I believe that a serious physiologist, who had been momentarily entranced by the "cathartic" treatment of young Bertha Pappenheim (some thirteen years previously), had agreed, albeit unwillingly, to contribute to Freud's suggested jointly authored volume on hysteria. The fact that all of the cases to be presented would be Freud's with the exception of the first one—"Anna O."—should have warned Breuer as to the likely consequences of publication.[6] Breuer's postpublication recommendation that Freud should consider seriously the charge of "moral insanity" was evidently not appreciated. With the wisdom of hindsight and a hundred years of psychoanalysis behind us, we can perhaps regret that Breuer's caution was not followed.

What the reader should bear in mind, *at all times*, is the curious contemporary "system" of beliefs in Freud's mind as he was, retrospectively, reviewing the appearance of *Studies on Hysteria*. This volume appeared, one recalls, after the operation on Emma Eckstein's middle turbinate bone—the middle left nasal concha—by Fliess (in February 1895), and after the continued fiasco of Freud's persuasive, and successful, attempt to convince Eckstein that she alone was responsible for her post-operative hemorrhages. These ghastly events (mentioned in more detail in chapter 3) were merely the physical preliminaries to a career of grotesque blunders—neurological, psychological, psychiatric— that were to mark Freud's ventures onto the stage of human history. As Raymond Tallis has recently remarked in his *Enemies of Hope*:

The alibi of wisdom can be used to cover up a good deal of ordinary incompetence and to support the asymmetrical power relation between patient and doctor. Both of these are vividly illustrated by the case of Freud, the emblematic figure of medical wisdom, the doctor who saw 'deeper' into the suffering soul of humanity, the paradigmatic healer. The truth that has slowly leaked out about Freud is that he was a monster—a monster of genius, but a monster none the less. He was a strikingly incompetent diagnostician, incapable of learning from his own mistakes because he could not acknowledge them, preferring to rationalise them away; and he was a bully who forced his patients to provide him with confirmatory evidence of the groundless notions he had thought up at a time when he was addicted to cocaine. (1997, 171-72)

This same letter to Wilhelm Fliess of March 1, 1896, concludes with a paragraph of quite stunning mathematical—and even common or garden—stupidity (or, to be charitable, of wide-eyed gullibility, the kind that Virginia Woolf excoriated; her phrase, one recalls, was "gull-like imbecility"), which was to be cited verbatim, and approvingly, by Fliess in his master volume *Die Beziehungen zwischen Nase und weiblichen Geschlechtsorganen* (*The Relationships Between the Nose and Female Sexual Organs*).[7] Freud, a firm believer in Fliess's 23 and 28 day periodicity theory (numerology for the cognoscenti),[8] gave the following account of his wife's, Martha's, pregnancy with his last-born, Anna Freud:

> Perhaps it will interest you, as an aside, that Martha felt the first movements, with Annerl, on July 10. The birth occurred on December 3. The menstrual period occurred again on February 29. Since puberty Martha has always been regular. The interval between menstrual periods is a little over 29 days, let's say $29\frac{1}{2}$. Now, from December 3 to February 29, there are 88 [days] = 3 x $29\frac{1}{3}$:
>
> $$\begin{array}{r} 28 \\ 31 \\ 29 \\ 88 \div 3 = 29\frac{1}{3} \text{ days} \\ \hline -\ 28 \end{array}$$
>
> From July 10 to December 3, there are 5 x $29\frac{1}{5}$:
>
> $$\begin{array}{r} 21 \\ 31 \\ 30 \\ 31 \\ 30 \\ 3 \\ 146 \div 5 = 29\frac{1}{5} \\ \hline -\ 46 \\ -\ \ 1 \end{array}$$

Thus, for a period of a little over 29 days, the birth occurred at precisely the right time, and the first movements occurred at the time of the fifth menstrual period. (Masson 1985, 175-76)

The thoughts (as it were) offered in Freud's concluding paragraph to Fliess were contemporaneous with the ongoing "treatment" of Emma Eckstein and with his own postpublication reactions to *Studies on Hysteria*; they were, hence, quite posterior to any of the "case histories" reported by him in the collaborative work with Breuer. They testify to a confusion of mind such that one would not readily trust one's future (or an interpretation of one's past) to such a person. Gypsy Petrulengo would be preferable.

Two years earlier, and so contemporary to the elaboration of the cases to be published in *Studies on Hysteria*, though well after the treatment of Frau Emmy von N., notions such as those listed in Freud's postscript to his letter to Fliess of May 30, 1893, show the closing-down of Freud's diagnostic searches for the origins of nervous complaints: the field was to be limited to sexuality (and in particular to masturbation) with an adjacent interest in the properties of the nose. Here Freud fastens onto Fliess's hypotheses about the supposed *causative* feature of the nose as a third possibility for what he has called "juvenile neurasthenia":

> Undoubtedly there exist cases of juvenile neurasthenia *without* masturbation, but *not* without the usual preliminaries of over-abundant pollutions—that is, precisely as though there had been masturbation. I have only the following unproven surmises for the understanding of these cases:
> (1) Innate weakness of the genital and nervous systems
> (2) Abuse in the prepubertal period
> (3) Could it not be that organic changes of the nose produce the pollutions and thereby the neurasthenia, so that here the latter develops as a product of the nasal reflex noxa?
> What do you think, and do you know something about it?
> (Masson 1985, 50; emphasis in the original)

Freud's patients were not to know, of course, of the private correspondence with Wilhelm Fliess (nor, judging by Anna Freud's censorship, was posterity to be allowed access to these eccentricities of belief of her father—eccentricities which seemed, moreover, to be central to the emerging invention of psychoanalysis). One consequence (still with us in North America) of the general ignorance about Freud's beliefs at the time of the creation of psychoanalysis has been the widespread acceptance that his efforts in psychology were no less than the honestly reported case histories—and cogent theorizing therefrom—of a (relatively) objective medical scientist. The quaint, and totally mistaken, belief that "organic changes of the nose produce the pollutions and thereby the neurasthenia" was an early example of Freud's credence in Fliess's back-to-front understanding of the parasympathetic nervous system linking the nose and the genitals and an instance of Freud's crediting Fliess's "discovery" (which few in Vienna credited) of the infamous "nasal reflex neurosis." Several years later, and well after the publication of the "breakthrough" *Die Traumdeutung* (*The Interpretation of Dreams*), Freud was still accepting these strange notions of his friend Fliess. In a letter dated July 4, 1901, Freud was to write suggesting that Fliess take over a case of his (this was not unusual; Freud and Fliess seemed to have had a developing network of family relations and patients whom they introduced to each other for treatment):

> Mr L. was easy to diagnose: *no* actual sexual cause, not a psychological case, but neurasthenia; *so earlier realities must have been retained by way of alterations of the nose.* (Masson 1985, 444; my emphasis)

We now know that the "objective medical scientist" was an imaginative construction fostered originally by Freud himself (and no doubt partly and deeply believed in by him); we also know that what were taken to be "honestly reported histories" were a series of confabulations that no person with access to the truth would ever have credited with medical value. Many people, especially those in the various Western universities (in England, John Forrester at Cambridge is merely one recidivist; Malcolm Bowie at Oxford is another)[9] and those who claim to be dedicated to relieving the suffering of the abused, either refuse to recognize the uncomfortable truth before their eyes or have chosen to remain ignorant of the real origins of the doctrines of psychoanalysis.

What do we mean when we say of scholars that they have "chosen to remain ignorant"? We mean, it seems to me, at least two things: in the first place we implicitly acknowledge their qualities for research and discovery (otherwise there would be no "choice" involved in the "ignorance"); in the second place we infer from their publications of their research that, given their demonstrated intelligence and archival acuity, they have opted to pretend that the uncomfortable evidence unearthed in their researches either (a) does not exist (although at some level of their consciousness they must know it does), or (b) may be interpreted in such a way so as to protect the mythological status acquired by their subject.

Now it is not the business of scholars to protect mythology. A scholar—a historian, for instance—who writes "to protect a mythology" becomes at once propagandist for a particular dogma: thus we have witnessed "Nazi" historians, "Soviet" historians, "Maoist" historians and so on. A scholar's business is to investigate *in a scholarly way* and to present in publication the nearest approximation he or she can get to the accuracy of the significance of the material investigated. And if that investigation uncovers lapses in honesty or inventions of incident that confound the presuppositions of the historian, then the historian is honor-bound to present this information.[10]

In the introduction to his brief but well-documented book on Anna O., Borch-Jacobsen comments acidly on the power of the myth and (not incidentally) on the value of the myth in the various rewritings of the beginnings of psychoanalysis. He writes (of the *Studies on Hysteria*):

> The case histories are not so much faithful accounts of treatment (impossible to verify in any case, since theoretically they would be protected under medical confidentiality) as models to be imitated, and no less by psychoanalysts than by their patients. In other words, the case histories have no scientific or historical function; their function is one of identification and emulation, with every new version retroactively confirming and justifying the model. Any possibility of validation or experimental control is excluded on principle, so it goes without saying that the model can be validated only by its own replication. This is true of all of Freud's great paradigmatic cases, but especially of the *ur*-paradigm that is the case of Anna O. (Borch-Jacobsen 1996, 11)

In the bitter aftermath of the break with Breuer, Freud was to invent (his word was "reconstruct") the story of a pseudocyesis (hysterical false pregnancy) of Anna O.—in real life, Bertha Pappenheim, the future Austrian socialist and woman's movement pioneer. Freud must have brooded over this story for many years; as late as 1932 he wrote to Stefan Zweig to correct "an error" in the Italian translation of Zweig's *Mental Healers* about the case of Anna O. and to recount the tale of Breuer's unprofessional flight from his patient. Freud adds, "I was so convinced of this reconstruction of mine that I published it somewhere."[11] Whether this last sentence is a deliberate fiction or the forgetfulness of old age (Freud was now seventy-six) will probably never be known; suffice it to say that no such publication has ever come to light.

Lisa Appignanesi and John Forrester in *Freud's Women*, in what Borch-Jacobsen terms "a laudable effort to exonerate Freud," suggest that the "Dr. B." of Freud's letter refers not to Breuer but to Dr. Breslauer, director of the Inzensdorf sanatorium (where Bertha Pappenheim had been placed). Borch-Jacobsen then adds maliciously:

> But Appignanesi and Forrester are out of luck, since this hypothesis is tenable only for the published English translation of the letter to Stefan Zweig, where the phrase "Dr. B." is indeed distinguished from "Breuer," which, being spelled out, would seem to indicate that two different people are involved. In the original German version, however, there can be no doubt that we are dealing with Breuer, whose name Freud repeatedly abbreviates as "Br.," as he also does in the incriminating passage: *"Jetzt kommt das Kind, das ich von Dr. Br. habe."*[12]

But Borch-Jacobsen is only dealing here with an endnote possibility raised by Appignanesi and Forrester (on their pages 488-89). With even more whimsicality and the inevitable dash of psychoanalytic naughty sexuality in the main body of the text dealing with Anna O., Appignanesi and Forrester craft an ingenious invention of their own on the triple basis of (1) the truth of the pseudocyesis story, (2) the accuracy of Breuer's account of Anna O.'s curious ability (or need) to recount decisive emotional moments of her life with a lapse of one calendar year, (3) the assumed date and time of the conception of Breuer's daughter Dora. Their paragraph of pro-Freudian supposition is well worth quoting:

> We can venture a speculative explanation of how this phrase concerning Dr. B.'s baby became linked to Dora Breuer's birth—and in this way show why it so unnerved Breuer. Breuer recounted how Bertha's 're-living of the previous year continued right up until the illness came to a definitive conclusion in June 1882.' If on 7 June 1882 she was reliving the events of 7 June 1881, she might well have been reliving Breuer's (and his wife's) experiences of that day: 7 June 1881 is almost exactly nine months before Dora Breuer's birthday. With her cry 'Now Dr. B.'s child is coming!', 'she recognised (and wanted her doctor to know that she recognised) that events in his personal life as well as in her own had taken place at the time, 7 June 1881'. The 'now' of the baby that is coming was the 'now' of 1881, not 1882.[13]

It is a measure of the disgrace into which Freudian tenets have fallen that such a passage can be offered by "historians" of psychoanalysis—even if it is only offered as "a speculative explanation." This is not an explanation; it is not "speculative" except in the etymological sense of a looking-glass world where Alice encounters irrationality for real. The question that remains, of course, after one's initial reaction to the high jinks, is: What in heaven's name did the two "historians" think they were playing at? And why did they see fit to invent such a preposterous scenario (which proposes, at the very least, that Dr. Breuer while treating his patient regaled her with intimate—indeed climactic—moments of his conjugal bliss)?

The answer, or *one* answer, lies in the Freudian texts themselves. We have to do with the "identification" and "emulation" of the Freudian case histories whose peculiar mode of presentation Borch-Jacobsen has mentioned. An early indication of Freud's acute awareness of the importance of literary presentation is to be found in some of his editorial suggestions (postmarked February 8, 1893) for a paper on the "nasal reflex neurosis" that Fliess had sent him for commentary:

> Now to the sexual question. I believe that in this respect one can act more like a literary businessman. The way you present sexual etiology, you are attributing to the audience a knowledge which it, after all, possesses only in latent form. It knows, and yet behaves as though it knew nothing. . . . I think that you cannot avoid mentioning the sexual etiology of neurosis without tearing the most beautiful leaf out of the wreath. So do it immediately in a manner suitable to the circumstances. Announce the forthcoming investigations; describe the anticipated result as that which it really is, something new; show people the key that unlocks everything, the etiological formula; and if in the process you give me a place in this by incorporating a reference such as "a colleague and friend," I shall be very pleased rather than angry. I have inserted such a passage on sexuality for you, merely as a suggestion. (Masson 1985, 45-46)

Much of post-Freudian psychoanalytic history has been drafted in the "house-style" invented by the master, and it is a credit to Freud (as an imaginative writer) that the epigones have not succeeded in matching his rhetorical skills. They have tried, many of them, for many years and in many languages; but the "emulation" has not prevented the discovery of trite attempts to save the wreckage from the flames. Myths have been built upon myths—and sometimes with internecine quarrels, as with Anna Freud's hostility to the child analyses published by Melanie Klein, or, in France, with Lacan's private Hegelianization of Freud for personal purposes—and myths have been built upon these myths built upon myths. The book by Appignanesi and Forrester is an excellent example of the truly transcendental power of rhetoric and myth over serious historical investigation and sober assessment. To the extent that their work flourishes, so will psychoanalysis as an aspect of human experience, irrespective of the holes that one can find in it. It is also likely that L. Ron Hubbard's invention will be with us for the next century. (Hubbard, it will be remembered, was a very strange man who wrote science fiction and who had a gift for the international organizing of a cult based on his understanding of human psychological needs.)

Anna O. was never one of Freud's patients. Her story interested him because it created a network of associated "medical" endeavor between himself and Josef Breuer and because it began the notion of "the talking cure"—that strange Cheshire Cat of a method that was to transfix Freud because of its rhetorical possibilities. Much has been made of the reputed three-stage progress of Freud's clinical attempts with (or "on"?) his patients: the "cathartic" (following from Breuer's manipulations of Anna O., or of hers of him); the "hypnotic," whereby the pressure of the hand upon the forehead of the patient, whose eyes were closed, induced recall of reputedly hidden experiences; the "associationism," which produced material from the "basic rule" of psychoanalysis to say whatever came into one's mind and to leave the interpretation and commingling of significance to the psychoanalyst. As far as one can gather from Freud's intimate correspondence (with Fliess, with Abraham, with Jung, with Jones) there was never a complete break with any one of these phases, and Freud seems, in fact, to have alternated between various combinations for the rest of his therapeutic career, although outright attempts at hypnotism—and certainly the technique of hand pressure on the patient's forehead—seem to have been absent from the case of Dora on.[14]

A footnote by the editors to the case of "Miss Lucy R.," following Freud's description in the text of his having witnessed and been impressed by Hippolyte Bernheim's use of the "hand-pressure on the forehead" technique, states:[15]

We have fairly exact information upon the period of Freud's use of hypnotism proper. In a letter to Fliess of December 28, 1887 (Freud, 1950*a*, Letter 2) he wrote: 'During the last few weeks I have taken up hypnosis.' [see Masson 1985, 16–18]. And in a lecture given before the Vienna 'Medizinisches Doktorencollegium' on December 12, 1904 (Freud, 1905*a*, *Standard Ed.*, 7, 260) he declared: 'I have not used hypnosis for therapeutic purposes for some eight years (except for a few special experiments).' His use of hypnotism therefore fell approximately between the years 1887 and 1896. (*Studies*, 110-11)[16]

With Frau Emmy von N., Freud's own first illustration of his "Studies on Hysteria," we are most certainly in the realm of the Anton Mesmer side of Freud. His "literary businessman" has been hard at work. We are deep in the realm of deception where the artful narrator of the case history allows his inventive fictional disguise of the several encounters with Frau Emmy free rein. If you thought you could feel the fresh breezes from Scandinavia wafting across the rock-pools, or smell the maritime air from the reeds and dunes of the Baltic shores, you were mistaken. Even the authorized, and no doubt dutifully respectful, editors of the *Standard Edition* are in doubt as to when her treatment started, why it started, and where it took place.[17] Not even the most recent edition of Freud's collected works—the *Pelican Freud Library*—indicates that the shores of the Baltic Sea are a Freudian fictional invention for a castle on a Swiss lake!

Fanny Moser, the widowed second wife of a rich industrialist, was born in 1848 of the German Swiss family of Sulzer-Wart. She had married the sixty-five-year-old widower Heinrich Moser at the age of twenty-three in 1871. Within a year the first child, also named Fanny, was born. In 1874 a second daughter (Mentona) was born, and within days of her birth Herr Moser—now aged 68—collapsed and died of an apparent heart attack. Rumours circulated at the instigation of the children of the first marriage of Herr Moser that the twenty-six-year-old Fanny had poisoned her husband to profit from the immense wealth of his estate. The corpse was exhumed, but no trace of poison was found in the post-mortem autopsy. As Appignanesi and Forrester (1992) state:

> As in the classic detective stories, the basis of the rumour was obvious: Fanny and her daughters inherited the most valuable part of her husband's enormous fortune. She was now one of the richest women in Europe, but her name was, at least in many circles, so surrounded by scandal that, when she visited health resorts and spas, she sometimes forbade her children to tell people their name. When Fanny attempted to gain access to a court, the rumours and scandal forced her away. Instead, she became a salon hostess. (*Freud's Women*, 92)

And as such she established her own court at the Schloss on a Swiss lake which she purchased in 1887 and where Freud visited her. It was there that she became, eventually, the patient to be pseudonymed as "Frau Emmy von N."[18] As Elisabeth Roudinesco writes in her preface to *Freud avant Freud*:

Thanks to two historians [Ola Andersson and Henri Ellenberger] we now know that Fanny Moser did not invent the famous scene of modern psychoanalysis—even if the phrase is authentic—and that she was never cured of her neurosis either by Freud or by the doctors who followed him. Fanny Moser was moreover more melancholic than hysteric and her life was a mix of the detective story and a tale by Balzac.[19]

The wealthy, elegant, and tormented forty-one-year-old widow seemed destined, almost, to have her convoluted existence written into literature by the young mesmerist to whom she was introduced by Breuer. The thirty-three-year-old Freud seized the opportunity and spent much time with his recalcitrant patient, and on more than one extended occasion: there seem to have been three treatment periods beginning with the weeks in May-June 1888 (for which Freud provides the daily case notes); a second course of some eight weeks beginning in May 1889; a third course at her home in Switzerland (i.e., on "her Baltic estate") in May 1890. He tried faradic excitation of the foot muscles, lukewarm baths, cool baths, bran baths, massages, and, on each occasion, hypnosis.

From the first paragraph of his text Freud establishes his recognition of two (related) aspects of Frau Emmy's personality. The second sentence of the tale reads:

She was a hysteric and could be put into a state of somnambulism with the greatest ease; and when I became aware of this I decided that I would make use of Breuer's technique of investigation under hypnosis, which I had come to know from the account he had given me of the successful treatment of his first patient. (*Studies*, 48)[20]

Frau Emmy was, apparently, what Dr. Herbert Spiegel has rated as a "grade five"—someone eminently suitable for hypnotic suggestion.[21] Whether she was *therefore* a "hysteric," as Freud was to insist even in later years, is another question. Richard Webster, who, as one knows, denies the very existence of "hysteria" as a disease entity, writes of this case:

By incorporating Frau Emmy's helpful rationalisation into his own theories, and by taking advantage of a slight amelioration of her symptoms which was probably spontaneous, Freud is thus able to represent a negative outcome as a partial therapeutic success. A further rationalisation of failure is introduced in his summary of the case when he points out that he has applied two different kinds of therapy to the same illness, making use both

of direct suggestion under hypnosis and of the cathartic method—
'psychical analysis.' For this reason, he suggests, the case of Frau Emmy
'cannot strictly be used as evidence for the therapeutic efficacy of the
cathartic procedure.' In view of the case's negative outcome, Freud's claim
might well be seen as part of an essential defensive strategy. (Webster, *Why
Freud Was Wrong*, 148)[22]

What is peculiar about this early case and—given the subsequent
authority of psychoanalysis for "recovered memories" in the stage of
treatment called *anamnesis*[23]—peculiar about Freud's curative intentions
is that Freud claimed to be able to *obliterate* memories by the use of
hypnosis.

It is a strange turn of events that the hypnotic-suggestive treatment
used by Freud in the late 1880s and early 1890s often had as its goal the
elimination of, or the conscious suppression of, memories of past events
whose recollection apparently caused contemporaneous states of anxiety
or dismay. This was, of course, a continuation—in a way—of what Freud
had gleaned from Breuer's treatment of Anna O. If, under the power of
hypnosis and hypnotic suggestion, memories with supposed traumatic
consequence could be removed, then the patient would recover (recover,
that is, from the unwanted intrusion of these memories into her present-
day life). Freud, at this time, wrote as if he credited the positive
assessment of cure in the case of Anna O. as a consequence of Breuer's
hypnotic therapy.

Two points to bear in mind here are: (1) Freud believed then—and in
fact never lost this belief—that early memories of supposedly disturbing
experiences were psychological antecedents of present anxiety
(represented by somatic symptoms);[24] and (2) that *removal* of these
memories by hypnosis was both possible and necessary for the somatic
symptoms of unease to be made to disappear permanently. By the turn of
the century, Freud had discarded the second of these hypotheses and had
come to think of the effects of hypnosis as merely "cosmetic" and not
long-lasting. But when he was investigating the cases in *Studies on
Hysteria*, and throughout the formative years of what was to become
psychoanalysis, he relied on the apparent efficacy of hypnotic suggestion
with—increasingly—an emphasis on early sexual encounters as an area
for deep examination. Frau Emmy (unlike the later 'Dora') was spared the
inquiries concerning her infantile and childhood masturbatory habits. One
almost has the impression that one of the things *not* seriously discussed by
patient and doctor was sex. It was on Freud's mind, as the footnotes

reveal. Against this, however, one must place Freud's disingenuous comment in the concluding part of the book, "IV. Psychotherapy of Hysteria (Freud)":

> When I began to analyse the second patient, Frau Emmy von N., the expectation of a sexual neurosis being the basis of hysteria was fairly remote from my mind. I had come fresh from the school of Charcot, and I regarded the linking of hysteria with the topic of sexuality as a sort of insult—just as the women patients themselves do. (*Studies*, 259-60)

"Sexuality" was not a topic for conversation between the wealthy client and the fledgling mesmerist. The one would propose her *"règles du jeu"* and the other would, advisedly, follow them.

In his description of various stages of the treatment, Freud is quite categorical about the reputed *obliteration* of noxious memories when his patient is (apparently) under the spell of his hypnotic strategies. "My therapy consists in wiping away these pictures, so that she is no longer able to see them before her. To give support to my suggestion I stroked her several times over the eyes" (*Studies*, 53). On the following day (May 10, according to Freud's notes), he removed under hypnosis the "spastic" speech impediment associated with a carriage ride with her children during a thunderstorm (this is a reference to her "clacking" phenomenon). Freud writes of this hypnotic attempt to relieve an adult-originated symptom of fear: "I extinguished her plastic memory of these scenes, but asked her to imagine them once more. She appeared to try to do this and remained quiet as she did so; and from now on she spoke in hypnosis without any spastic impediment" (*Studies*, 58). Later that same day Freud hears of her (adult) memories of a lunatic who "had walked into her room several times at night by mistake" (this was when Frau Emmy was in a sanatorium at Freud's behest) and, Freud insists, in his final paragraph of that day's notes: "I wiped out all these memories, woke her up and assured her she would sleep well tonight, having omitted to give her this suggestion in her hypnosis" (*Studies*, 59).

One morning, during Freud's last visit to Switzerland (hence, May 1890?), he entertained his host as they were "walking . . . along an avenue that led from the house to an inlet in the sea" (i.e., "the Baltic," i.e., the Swiss lake) with an example of post-hypnotic suggestion that he promised, Anton Mesmer-like, would be fulfilled at lunchtime. It is a measure of Freud's confidence and of the general atmosphere of "psychiatric Vienna" that he could (a) have perpetrated this party trick and (b) published it with some confidence that the story would be credited and that its credit would redound on Freud himself. Fanny Moser, having expressed "a fear that in future she was likely to be less obedient under hypnosis than before," Freud accepts the challenge to his authority thus:

> I wrote a few words on a piece of paper, handed it to her and said: 'At lunch to-day you will pour me out a glass of red wine, just as you did yesterday. As I raise the glass to my lips you will say: "Oh, please pour me out a glass, too," and when I reach for the bottle, you will say: "No thank you, I don't think I will after all." You will then put your hand in your bag, draw out the piece of paper and find those same words written on it.' This was in the morning. A few hours later the little episode took place exactly as I had pre-arranged it, and so naturally that none of the many people present noticed anything. When she asked me for the wine she showed visible signs of an internal struggle—for she never drank wine—and after she had refused the drink with obvious relief, she put her hand into her bag and drew out the piece of paper on which appeared the last words she had spoken. She shook her head and stared at me in astonishment. (*Studies*, 84-85)

This is certainly a splendid rhetorical number on which to finish a case history. And this is how Freud chooses to end the narrative part of "The Case of Frau Emmy"—the subsequent last section, appropriately for a medical history, is entitled "Discussion." A reading over of that last powerful narrative reveals (1) that Frau Emmy was under hypnosis at the time of the stroll near the lake; (2) that Freud *knew* that Frau Emmy did not drink wine; (3) that she would therefore refuse the offer of a glass; (4) that Freud's words, as written on the piece of paper, were also spoken to Frau Emmy as the piece of paper was being handed over. The whole show, in other words, is indeed an amusing party trick; it is not, however, an indication of either psychological insight or of the value (scientific or otherwise) of the newly developing psychoanalysis. It is when reading paragraphs like this that Medawar's sentence comes to the fore. One is almost inclined to replace "the most stupendous intellectual confidence trick of the twentieth century" with "the most stupendous intellectual *party trick* of the twentieth century."

The "Frau Emmy" case is embroidered, as Freud had said it would be, by a series of extensive discursive footnotes referring to earlier and later cases treated by him. Some of these take over two pages of presentation, and the reader is left with the sense of being faced with the literary version of a Romanian counterpane, where exquisite designs are subsumed into the whole. The last two of this series of footnotes are worth assessing here. In the penultimate note (*Studies*, 100-101), Freud recounts his investigation of a young woman (in the presence of her father, an elderly physician). According to Freud two "leading authorities in Vienna" had examined this young woman: one had thought she was suffering from multiple sclerosis; another thought she was a hysteric and recommended her to Freud for treatment. Freud, who (unawares?) gives an excellent illustration of multiple sclerosis in his description of the poor girl, chooses to believe that this diagnosis is wrong. Accordingly, having shown and refused the diagnosis of multiple sclerosis, Freud begins a treatment program which has nothing to do with neurological problems and everything to do with supposed *psychological* origins.

He records the father's recollection of a recent bout of good humor in the girl[25] and of her singing "Ein freies Leben führen wir."[26] As a consequence of this choral enthusiasm, the girl broke her umbrella by banging it too hard on the sidewalk. Freud refers to this incident as a way of "explaining" his own foolish suggestion:

> Of course she herself had no notion that she had wittily transformed a nonsensical suggestion [this is Freud playing the *faux-naïf* who claims to have "given a suggestion to an inanimate object," the umbrella] into a brilliantly successful one. Since her condition was not improved by assurances, commands and treatment under hypnosis, I turned to psychical analysis and requested her to tell me what emotion had preceded the onset of her illness. (*Studies*, 100)

(One should note, in parenthesis, Freud's investigative techniques: in the first place, between a disputed multiple sclerosis finding and a possible hysteria finding, he opts for the latter; having been unsuccessful with hypnotic suggestions, he opts for "psychical analysis" to determine the *psychological* origins of the girl's physical impairment, rather than revert to the potentially accurate alternative diagnosis of the neurological impairment, multiple sclerosis.) Freud had "suggested" that the umbrella might break and that the girl would be liberated of her illness as a result. This is one instance of Freud playing Jesus and, apparently, failing, and— by the inclusion of this footnote—admitting his failure. Freud's moment of self-recollected anger is described in the sentence immediately preceding the Robbers' Chorus:

> One day, after she once more came tottering into the room, one arm supported on her father's, the other on an umbrella whose tip was already

much worn down, I lost patience and shouted at her in the hypnosis: 'This has gone on too long. Tomorrow morning that umbrella of yours will break in your hands and you'll have to walk without it, and from that time on you will never need an umbrella again.' (*Studies*, 100)

It is difficult to assess whether this intriguing footnote (a case history by itself) is an instance of Freud's honesty, Freud's dissembling, or of Freud's growing awareness of his rhetorical power to persuade. If it is to be seen as an instance of Freud's "honesty," it certainly cannot be seen as an instance of his diagnostic ability. Freud's mistake was clearly diagnostic and yet his keeping of this footnote demonstrates that his confidence in his sexual etiologies was stronger than his understanding of either the origins of multiple sclerosis or of the long-term physical effects of some suspected childhood sexual abuse. The parallel with Jesus is from Mark 2, verses 8-11, where Christ rebukes the scribes' disbelief in his powers:

Why reason ye these things in your hearts?

Whether it is easier to say to the sick of the palsy, Thy sins be forgiven thee; or to say, Arise, and take up thy bed, and walk?

But that ye may know that the Son of man hath power on earth to forgive sins, (he saith to the sick of the palsy,)

I say unto thee, Arise, and take up thy bed, and go thy way into thine house.

The young woman did not take up her bed (or umbrella) and walk. And, alas, multiple sclerosis (from which she almost certainly suffered, in spite of Freud's disclaimer) cannot be cured by such injunctions. Freud continued his (psychological) interrogation of the young patient. He concluded that the death of a young relative of hers to whom she had considered herself "for many years" engaged was not the initiating factor (Freud's method of investigation of neurological illness is demonstrated here for all to see). There must have been some event prior to that. Freud drafted, in the following fashion, the last two sentences of his footnote (which he was to retain in subsequent editions):

At this she gave way to the extent of letting fall a single significant phrase; but she had hardly said a word before she stopped, and her old father, who was sitting behind her, began to sob bitterly. Naturally I pressed my investigation no further; but I never saw the patient again. (*Studies*, 101)

This is an interesting example of Freud's knowledge of the power of his language in Vienna. He makes no statement that a court of law could question. He notes that he never saw his patient again (but does not tell us why). He allows us, indeed he incites us, to consider an inference that, while it has nothing to do with multiple sclerosis, has everything to do with the sexual abuse by a father of a daughter. We know from his correspondence with Fliess that Freud himself was to dream of a sexual encounter with his firstborn, Mathilde; we know from this correspondence of his increasing dependence upon cocaine; we know that abuse of cocaine creates sexual scenarii that are difficult to surmount. We should, therefore, question the inference that Freud has implicitly offered us. Here was a young woman who had gone through menarche, who had established a loving relationship with a male relative to whom "she considered herself engaged," and who had been struck down with a neurological disorder that had made her unable to walk or organize her physical movements properly. Having, on Freud's own account, successfully traversed the developmental aspects of her sexuality, could this young woman be seen as the victim of some earlier father–daughter incest? Could she be seen as one whose incest trauma was such that she could no longer walk unaided? And was her inability to walk a hysterical consequence of her implied earlier abuse?

One is drawn ineluctably to Medawar's anger at the psychoanalytic treatment of the young victims of DMD (*dystonia musculorum deformanas*) before they encountered the intelligent and neurologically appropriate treatment of Dr. I. S. Cooper. (All their psychoanalytic "therapies" had been based on such Freud-based mock-hysterical traumas.) Freud's successors have certainly not changed his ability to run roughshod over reality—and at the patients' expense. Freud's words have not only contributed to the strange and *un*medical beliefs of his disciples, they have also infected those who have realized the fraudulence (or some of it) of the entire enterprise. Jeffrey M. Masson, in his diatribe against psychoanalysis, *The Assault on Truth*, cites this very footnote and writes: "It now seems possible that Freud is here depicting a scene where a young girl accuses her father of having raped her, upon which the man begins to sob, acknowledging his guilt."[27]

Such an interpretation could only "seem possible" to a person who had no understanding of neurological disorders such as multiple sclerosis and who still, for reasons unknown, was prepared to give credence to Freud's "medical" findings. One would like to ask Masson just how many cases he has ever encountered of a young woman suffering from the physical impairments so carefully described by Freud where these impairments can be seriously imputed to some form of prior incestuous abuse. That *these* presenting symptoms are truly representative of Freud's hypothetical (and a priori) guess of paternal abuse makes that guess quite beyond belief. The rhetoric of courteous prudence that Freud employs— "Naturally I pressed my investigation no further"—followed as it is by the last concessive phrase of the footnote—"but I never saw the patient again"—has seduced Masson, and others like him, into forgetting the motor neurone difficulties of the young woman (with the detailed description of which Freud began this case footnote) and into attributing to the deliberately provocative, ambiguous, and yet curiously *empty*—"a single significant phrase"—a heady mixture of parental mayhem, doubtless responsible for the girl's sessions with Freud in the first place. Freud has, in other words, rhetorically hooked his readers (some of them) onto the baited snare of his own misjudgments.

If—and it is a very big "if"—Freud's account of the abrupt ending of this tale is veridical, then one may well ask whether the physician-father's bitter sobs were not rather a sorrowful reaction to the irrelevance of the line of Freud's questioning. Could they not, and much more reasonably, represent the bitter realization that the Viennese medical rumors currently circulating about Freud's obsessions were indeed justified and that *this was the wrong person, the last person, to help his daughter*? Was her illness, then, incurable?

Freud's rhetorical sophistication here is that he has allowed for the reading of a possible "misjudgment" on his part in the first half of the story and yet, by the end, we are sorely tempted to "read" into his last phrases the sexual meanings implicit in them for him—and, by extension, for us. And if we do so, we become his complicit allies; herein lies Freud's rhetorical strength. It has outlived him; it may even outlive the collapse of his movement.

The last footnote of "Frau Emmy von N.," and on which the whole chapter concerned with her case closes, was added to the text in 1924, the year of Fanny Moser's death and some thirty-five years after the initial encounter of the young hypnotist and the wealthy patron. For Richard Webster, this page of small print represents "a tragic and seemingly cruel valediction, the woman whose intelligence and energy Freud had chauvinistically rated as 'no less than a man's' and whose 'benevolent care for the welfare of all her dependents' he had praised, is described by her daughter as a 'ruthless tyrant' and Freud, noting the daughter's doctor's degree and married status, appears to accept the judgement" (Webster 1995, 154).

In fact, this note is far more than a kind of backhanded valediction to a recently deceased and uncured patient. It is also an ingenious, but totally mistaken, *mea culpa* which opens with the Old Freud revealing, with the experience of years on his shoulders, the simplicities and errors of his first attempt at Breuer's cathartic treatment. Unfortunately, by the end of the first paragraph, we recognize that those "years of experience" had not radically altered the serious diagnostic deficiencies of the case. Freud begins this 1924 note thus:

> I am aware that no analyst can read this case history today without a smile of pity. But it should be borne in mind that this was the first case in which I employed the cathartic procedure to a large extent. For this reason I shall leave the report in its original form. I shall not bring forward any of the criticisms which can so easily be made on it today, nor shall I attempt to fill in any of the numerous gaps in it. I will only add two things: *what I afterwards discovered about the immediate aetiology of the illness* and what I learned of its subsequent course. (*Studies*, 105; my emphasis)

What Freud "afterwards discovered" about the "immediate etiology of the illness" is revealed in the next paragraph, which refers to an incident where a younger man had offered to marry Frau Emmy. Freud here, however, is no different from the Freud of earlier years who had seen continued sexual abstinence—her late husband had been dead for some fifteen years when Freud first encountered her—as a prime mover of his patient's hysteria. Thanks to the careful researches of Ola Andersson, we now know that Fanny Moser led a kind of latter-day Madame de Staël existence in her Swiss Schloss with a multiplicity of male lovers drawn from her intellectual and medical acquaintances. Absence of sexual gratification was the very least of her problems.

She may have had the savvy to refuse marriage, given her sense of maternal responsibility toward her daughters and to her late husband's munificent estate; but she also had the savvy to enjoy sexual relations without any of the hang-ups that Freud was prepared to place on her. Freud himself had hinted in his case history that Frau Emmy had probably given him a bowdlerized version of her love life. He writes (*Studies*, 103), "What I was allowed to hear was no doubt an *editio ad usum delphini* of her life-story. The patient behaved with the greatest and to all appearances with the most unforced sense of propriety, without a trace of prudishness."[28]

Now, either Freud could not, or *would not,* abandon his hypothesis that absence of regular sexual congress leads to the kinds of problems—chiefly of speech impairment (the "clacking"), awkward gestures, persistent phobias, and some sort of generalized depression (why don't the Popes suffer from these disabilities?)—that Frau Emmy suffered from, or he was *genuinely* as unaware of the reality of her day-to-day life as he evidently was, clinically, of the real source of her discomfort; and he assumed that her physiological symptoms were an example of the evidence he needed for his a priori theory. Two instances from the text of the case itself:

> (1) A footnote on page 65 which reads: "At the time I wrote this I was inclined to look for a *psychical* origin for all symptoms in cases of hysteria. I should now explain this sexually abstinent woman's tendency to anxiety as being due to *neurosis* (i.e. anxiety neurosis)."

> (2) On page 88 (in the Discussion section): "It is necessary, I think, to adduce a *neurotic* factor to account for this persistence [of these phobias]—the fact that the patient had been living for years in a state of sexual abstinence. Such circumstances are among the most frequent causes of a tendency to anxiety."

The Freud note that terminates the case in 1924, thirty-five years after the initial treatment and—much more significantly for what it reveals about the absence of later sophistication in Freud (or *any* sophistication in those who credit the value of these texts—and this includes Forrester, Appignanesi, and their ilk)—*after* the publication of most of the doctrinal volumes of psychoanalysis, is *no more perceptive* in its understanding of Fanny Moser's ailment than the pages of the case history recording his visits to her from more than thirty years before. One should not forget that, after Breuer's "III. Theoretical," Freud, in his "IV. The Psychotherapy of Hysteria," had written of the Frau Emmy case:

When I go through my notes on this case today there seems to me to be no doubt at all that it must be looked on as a case of severe anxiety neurosis accompanied by anxious expectation and phobias—*an anxiety neurosis which originated from sexual abstinence and had become combined with hysteria.* (*Studies*, 260; my emphasis)

Freud's reference in the 1924 footnote to a letter (of 1918) received from the elder daughter of Fanny Moser has tempted Lisa Appignanesi and John Forrester once again onto the paths of historical invention. Their quotation of the (English) version of Freud's reply to the daughter concludes: "By nature your mother was a highly estimable, serious, and morally austere woman who was guided by the strictest sense of duty—it is [quite?] possible that this noble character was ruined by *the unsolved conflicts of her life*" (*Freud's Women*, 101; my emphasis). They add this expansive commentary (a different conclusion to that of Webster, but still completely wrong):

> There was no question of Freud, thirty years on, siding with the daughters against the mother; his responsibility still lay with his ex-patient. The elder daughter, the addressee of this letter, was, he implied, still one of those unsolved conflicts. And she was still one of those conflicts, not only because she was a daughter, but also because she was a doctor. As Freud intimated in his case history, and as we can infer from our additional information about her style of life, Fanny's relations with the medical profession were always fraught and passionate. (*Freud's Women*, 101)

Leaving aside the fond notion that Freud ever assumed he had a "responsibility" toward "his ex-patient," one should treat with caution the "inferences" that Appignanesi and Forrester claim to draw from documentary sources, especially when they are conveniently given in some English translation. As Borch-Jacobsen had caught the wily pair out over Freud's letter to Stefan Zweig, so this is an example where one must challenge the "inferences" created from the "conflicts" of Fanny Moser's life. It would appear from the Appignanesi and Forrester version that Freud was referring to a series of difficulties encountered by Moser with her daughters, with the medical profession, and so on. But this is *not* what Freud wrote in his original German. He simply and (I suspect) sincerely—however mistakenly—referred to a basic unresolved conflict that Fanny Moser had not overcome. He was wrong to do so because (a) he had not understood the probably neurological basis of her illness; (b) he had a limited—and quite inaccurate—grasp of her then-present sexual situation; (c) his slowly emerging fascination with sexual explicanda based on supposed infantile experiences was mistaken. The crucial sentence in Freud's letter to the elder daughter reads:

> Ursprünglich ist ihre Mutter eine hochachtbare, ernsthafte, sittenstrenge
> von dem strengsten Pflichtgefühl geleitete Frau gewesen leicht (?) möglich,
> *dass dieser edle Character in dem ungelösten Konflikt ihres Lebens zu
> Grunde gegangen ist.*[29]

The italicized phrase reads in English: "that this noble character has been brought down by the unresolved conflict of her life." Freud uses the *singular* for "conflict" with the definite article, and by no stretch of the imagination can that phrase be read to refer to Fanny Moser's ongoing problems as a parent with her daughters, or as an heiress with her wealth, or as a patient with her doctors.

If Freud's first presented case, "Frau Emmy von N."—and the most detailed in narrative—was based on false medical assumptions, false existential assumptions (of the reality of her day-to-day experiences), and false treatment assumptions (of her supposed, if temporary, improvement under Freud's care), what is one to say of the other cases offered to the reader for contemplation? Richard Webster, who has been much maligned for his overinsistence on neurological lesions of no psychological etiology whatever in his examinations of the cases of Charcot and Freud, is most helpful in his very careful assessment of these cases and in his judicious refusal of Freud's fantasies of etiology—and hence of successful treatment outcome.

His commentary on the Elisabeth von R. case—which Appignanesi and Forrester refer to gushingly as "The First Full-Length Analysis"—is an exemplum of common sense. What Webster refuses to ignore is Freud's growing insistence on, and delight in, his discovery of pun-like relationships between somatic disorders and hypothesized emotional states in the patients. (Both the puns and the hypothesized emotional states were Freud's inventions.) This was to be a continuing feature of his assessments of those who came into his orbit. Dora, one recalls, would be accused of having "made a false step" because of an observed dragging leg. Likewise, in *Studies*, Elisabeth von R. has pains in her legs not from rheumatism or some other muscular or motor-neurone problem but because of the "repressed" wish that her dead sister's husband might become her own husband. Webster's comments on these etiological futilities are pertinent:

> Disregarding her repeated objections, however, Freud clings to his view that Elisabeth von R.'s rheumatic pains are the product of unrequited love, and in the final stages of the case seeks to 'get rid of the excitation which

had been piling up for so long by "abreacting" it'[reference omitted]. At this point in the analysis Elisabeth von R.'s supposed hysterical symptoms should, according to the theory promulgated by Breuer and Freud, have disappeared 'permanently and immediately.' Freud, however, is obliged to admit that, although he brought his patient's treatment to an end on the assumption that she was cured, her symptoms subsequently recurred. . . . Perhaps the most interesting and most characteristic feature of Freud's arguments is the manner in which he assumes that since *he* is able to perceive or construct a link between two discrete phenomena, then this link has some kind of operative reality: Freud's own internal and idiosyncratic logic is treated as though it were a real, external chain of causality. The most charitable observation we can make about this kind of reasoning is that it is neither odd nor abnormal. For it is exactly the kind of reasoning habitually encountered in necromancy, astrology, phrenology and many other forms of investigation with which psychoanalysis is not normally associated. (Webster 1995, 163-66; his emphasis)

My examination of *The Studies on Hysteria* suggests that Webster has hit the nail on the head and that Freud's self-perceived causal links are not merely misconstruals of the situation but also an unadmitted evidence of diagnostic failure. (I have the suspicion that Breuer was of this opinion as well.) Against this assessment of Webster, however, one must in fairness place the following position: that when an examining doctor makes links between "two discrete phenomena," he does not *thereby create* a self-imposed "real, external chain of causality"—he may well be *observing* it (and it may well be real), noting it, and, with appropriate attention, treating it—if the condition is treatable. The one fundamental difference between a patient and a doctor is that the latter has (or is reputed to have) a knowledge of a discipline unknown to the sufferer; plus, of course, the third-party status which allows for objectivity of judgment.

In these early cases Freud may well not have demurred from this objection to Webster and may well have been justified, on occasion, in such a rebuttal. We know now, from an accumulation of background information—of two sorts: (a) more sophisticated awareness of neurological disabilities, (b) more archival material relating to Freud's patients and to Freud himself—that he was frequently and grossly mistaken in his assumptions (the case footnote in the "Frau Emmy" story dealing with the probable multiple sclerosis girl provides an excellent, if unwitting, illustration). Freud's patients suffered from this ignorance (or, sometimes, "imposed" ignorance).

Does that, by itself, make him a charlatan or a sorcerer's apprentice? Not necessarily; and quite irrespective of the subsequent temporary triumph of his invented discipline—psychoanalysis. It may, on the other hand, make him one of medicine's Great Incompetents; and here one would wish to temper Webster's flattering phrase about Freud's handling of the "Frau Emmy von N." case: "Given his medical training, his undoubted skill as a diagnostician and his own familiarity with the organic aetiologies of many neurological diseases, it is entirely conceivable that he was still afflicted by doubt as to the correctness of his diagnosis" (Webster 1995, 153).

But it is when one puts in parallel context the musings, presented with a certain rhetorical flair, of those early case histories up to 'Dora' (terminated abruptly by Dora herself on December 31, 1900; published in 1905) with the "thinking-aloud" of the private letters to Fliess that some kind of discredit inevitably emerges. Webster's phrase, "his undoubted skill as a diagnostician," would be laughable were it not for the human suffering perpetuated precisely by Freud's repeated failures as a diagnostician. Webster, who had the advantage of the publication of the complete correspondence with Fliess, does not use it as rigorously as he should have. To his credit, he does not use it as willfully and as inventively as Appignanesi and Forrester. Nonetheless, had he considered it dispassionately for what it reveals of the mentation of Freud at the moments of the invention of psychoanalysis, he might well have come to a far less favorable assessment of his hero. His excuses on behalf of Freud's demonstrated mendacity would have been less prominent. He does, however, in his chapter 10, "Freud, Fliess and Infantile Sexuality," discuss Freud's increasing intellectual dependence on Fliess and examines the Fliess errors concerning the "nasal reflex neurosis" and the influence of Ernst Haeckel's "biogenetic law" on both correspondents (and on Adolf Hitler!).[30]

It is a question of great importance whether the Freud who was writing to Fliess from 1887 to 1904 was as clearheaded and as perceptive of the criteria for diagnostic accuracy as Webster appears to claim. He argues that Fliess and, by contagion, discipleship, or some influential effect of the contemporary 'scientific' *zeitgeist*, Freud himself, was in thrall to the biogenetic law propounded by Ernst Haeckel. A close reading of the correspondence of Fliess and Freud does not convince me that Freud was in any discernible way writing as an aficionado of Haeckel. This seems to me to be a case of making high-falutin' excuses for the evidence—in letter after letter—of the ravages on careful thinking that are the consequence of the long-term abuse of cocaine.[31] It should be recalled that both correspondents were regular and enthusiastic users and promoters of the Bolivian marching powder;[32] that Fliess had claimed to find a "cocaine spot" in the nose and regularly recommended cocaine to his patients; that Freud was, at one stage, notorious in Vienna for his greathearted ministrations of the substance to all and sundry, and for his complicity in the cocaine narcosis death (in 1891) of Ernst Fleischl von Marxow.

Freud's lies about Fleischl von Marxow's subcutaneous injections of cocaine and his lies about having ever recommended such a procedure, despite the fact that in his 1885 paper he recommended precisely this—"I should unhesitatingly advise cocaine being administered in subcutaneous injection." ("On the General Effect of Cocaine," paper read before the Psychiatric Society, March 1885, 117)—are dexterously gift-wrapped for the public by Webster in the following excuse:

> Lies may be among the most common of moral sins but they are not the most simple and often spring from complex motives. The scientific lie which Freud told about Fleischl-Marxow is no exception. For there seems every reason to suppose that Freud had persuaded himself that in this case his particular lie hid a general truth—a truth so important that its enunciation should not be muffled by too many moral scruples. (Webster 1995, 50)

There is, on the contrary, no reason to suppose that Freud had these general notions clearly before him, or that, with the integrity and courage that his future Association (the International Psychoanalytic Association, or I.P.A.) so often imagines for him, he had recognized a "general truth" from which the "Fleischl von Marxow case" was merely an unfortunate abnormality. There is, however, every reason to believe that Freud was either unable to judge of the dangers of cocaine absorption (this must be the charitable interpretation of his recommendation to Martha Bernays that his fiancée begin taking the substance), or that he was indifferent to their consequences for a friend who had succumbed to his suggestions. Freud was prepared to eliminate from his curriculum vitae any awkward publications that appeared to put him in an unfavorable light with the authorities. There are no written Freud acknowledgments for his measure of responsibility concerning the death of Fleischl von Marxow; just as there is no written Freud recognition of his other *known* medical disasters—for example, Emma Eckstein (beyond the private "so we had done her an injustice" to Fliess), the suicide of Victor Tausk, or the 1921 mess resulting from his greedy and crass interventions in the life of Dr. Horace Frink.

When Webster quotes from Freud's letter to Fliess of June 22, 1897, where Freud anticipates the pleasures of meeting his Berlin friend at Aussee: "At Aussee I know a wonderful wood full of ferns and mushrooms,[sic] where you shall reveal to me the secrets of the world of lower animals and the world of children[,]," he misses the delicate Shakespearean reference—"I know a bank whereon the wild thyme blows//Where ox-lips and the nodding violet grows"—but also, and more significantly as far as Freud's medical progress is concerned, the intended revelation. Webster writes: "when Freud spoke of 'the secrets of the world of lower animals and the world of children,' he was referring to Fliess's application of contemporary Darwinian biology to child-psychology—to Fliess's theory of infantile sexuality" (Webster 1995, 228).

Was he? A straight reading of the letter not only does *not* indicate this, it shows that the subject is none other than Freud's infatuation with Fliess's chimerical periodicity system (as it had been in the already-quoted letter of a year before, March 1, 1896, elaborating Anna Freud's birth statistics). Whatever lunacies were prevalent in Haeckel's "biogenetic law" notions, they were quite irrelevant to Fliess's homespun numerology. And it was to news of Fliess's mathematical punning on the combinatory felicities of 23 and 28 that Freud was looking forward in the summer of 1897. To make this point crystal-clear to the reader, here is the complete paragraph (of which only one phrase was quoted by Webster) of Freud's mock-Oberon delight:

> In Aussee I know a wonderful wood full of ferns and mushrooms where you must reveal to me the secrets of the world of lower animals and the world of children, I have never before felt so stupidly expectant in the face of your disclosures, but hope the world will not hear of them before I do and that instead of a short article you will within a year present to us a small book which solves the organic secrets in series of 28 and 23. (Masson 1985, 254)

Neither Haeckel, nor Darwin, nor yet "Darwinian biology" is present on the horizon. Haeckel, incidentally, is never once referred to in the whole of Freud's correspondence with Fliess. Freud's continuing credence in Fliess's ability to manipulate numbers into epistemological marvels (complete with their own divinatory qualities) was to outlast their friendship and their correspondence. He was unable to pursue this Fliessian line of inquiry into the riddles of reality because of a self-acknowledged deficiency in mathematics. (Had he been as sharp as Martin Gardner he would have seen through Fliess's nonsense in no time!) Nonetheless, Freud never retracted his belief in Fliess's genial comprehension of the world. He was loyal, at least, to what he felt was one aspect of the intellectual substance of their relationship. If this loyalty was an instance of Freud's grasp of what had been intellectually significant in his years of correspondence with Fliess, then one must confess to a certain disappointment in his intellectual acuity.

And yet, by all accounts, Freud was a brilliant man of rare intellectual endeavor and of rare linguistic gifts—a polyglottal punster as avid and, almost, as knowing as his linguistic counterpart, James Joyce (Freud, himself, once suggested that the French equivalent of his own name would be *M. Le Joyeux*). It is, however, possible that these very gifts were to prove a curse. Combined with the heightened but muddled grasp of reality offered by cocaine and the demands of scientific medicine to which he was both strangely recalcitrant and ambitiously attracted, Freud, during the years of correspondence with Fliess, became, I believe, less able to distinguish between genuine human suffering and the limited means we have to counter it. He became ever more enmeshed in a highly idiosyncratic belief in theories of human psychological development which had more to do with his own ongoing crises—not all the consequence of cocaine—and with his Fliess-based beliefs in the periodicity to which human nature was subject.

For the reader of the Freud–Fliess correspondence, three things stand out that make the reading of these letters a strange and estranging experience. In the first place, the repetition by Freud of his own nasal disasters (the direct and inevitable consequence of repeated painting of the mucous membrane of the nostrils with cocaine)[33] makes this correspondence not one to be read at the breakfast table. The frequent accounts of the purulent secretions from the nostrils, and Freud's loving descriptions of the distinctions between old pus and new pus, make the reading of these letters an exercice in stoicism that would have been appreciated by Ignatius Loyola. Here, for example, is Freud writing to Fliess at the time of his completion of the draft for the *Studies on Hysteria* in the letter of May 25, 1895:

I discharged exceedingly ample amounts of pus and all the while felt splendid; now the secretion has nearly dried up and I am still feeling very well. I propose the following to you: it is neither the congestion nor the flow of pus that determines the distant symptoms. The flow of pus does nothing; pus congestion, infectious swelling, and so forth make for local symptoms allochirally transposed, probably according to specific logical rules (and according to the law of eccentric projection). (Masson 1985, 130)

This passage continues with a page-length disquisition on the significance of the varieties of nostril pus which I will spare the reader. (It reminds this reader of Alfred Jarry's snotty opening to *Ubu Roi*: *"De par ma chandelle verte, Mère Ubu!"*).[34] Unsurprisingly, passages like this are absent from the saucy selection chosen by Appignanesi and Forrester. Of the three things mentioned above, this is the first estranging experience on reading the Freud–Fliess correspondence.

The second is the sheer intensity of Freud's gullible belief in Fliess's notions of the 23-day (male) and 28-day (female) periodicity cycles (with their concomitant birthdates and predicted death-dates) and his frenetic attempts to keep abreast of Fliessian mathematics. That this reaction is in no way one of twentieth-century smug anachronism is made quite clear when one 'listens' to the tenor of Fliess's words as he addressed, on December 11, 1896, the gathering of Berlin gynecologists on his numerological theories and attempted to counter the sudden outbursts of unprofessional but doubtless spontaneous hilarity provoked by his talk (which was pure Teutonic Monty Python *avant la lettre*):

For each one of these series of dates, I could also include the birthdates of the siblings on the mother's side, the uncles and aunts. I see, gentlemen, that this proposal stimulates your laughing muscles in a dubious manner. But I can reveal to you that we are dealing here with a great law of nature, and I promise you, the time will come when you will be struck dumb by the greatness of this law! (Reported in Masson 1985, 233-34)[35]

Freud (letter of March 29, 1897) was deeply appreciative of the paper's "unbelievable power of condensing thoughts" and sympathetic to Fliess's need to make "the remark about the audience's changing expression" (Masson 1985, 233).

The third estranging experience is the sudden confrontation, which must be quite unnerving for a first-time reader whose acquaintance with Freud is limited to, say, *The Psychopathology of Everyday Life* or *The*

Introductory Lectures on Psychoanalysis, with the Freud of the correspondence and with his zany and sudden spurts of hypothetical psychological discovery (one meets, for real, the Mr. Hyde behind the Dr. Jekyll of public performance). An instance—but, for the duration of the seventeen years of the correspondence, the pattern was to continue—is the excited letter of Monday, January 11, 1897:

> Dear Wilhelm,
>
> I am sending you, red-hot, two ideas which occurred to me today and which appear to me to be viable; they are based, of course, on the results of the analyses.
>
> (1) The determination of a psychosis (that is, amentia or a confusional psychosis—a psychosis of being overwhelmed, as I called it earlier) as opposed to a neurosis seems to be that sexual abuse occurs before the end of the first intellectual stage, that is, before the psychic apparatus has been completed in its first form (before the age of 1¼ to 1½ years). It is possible that the abuse dates back so far that these experiences lie concealed behind the later ones and that they can be revived from time to time. Epilepsy, I believe, belongs to the same period. . . .
>
> (2) Perversions regularly lead to zoophilia and have an animal character. They are explained not by the functioning of erogenous zones that later have been abandoned, but by the effect of erogenous *sensations* that later lose their force. In this connection one recalls that the principal sense of animals (for sexuality as well) is that of smell, which has been reduced in human beings. As long as smell (or taste) is dominant, urine, feces, and the whole surface of the body, also blood, have a sexually exciting effect. The heightened sense of smell in hysteria presumably is connected with this. (Masson 1985, 221-23)[36]

Freud's "red-hot ideas," based, one notes, "on the analyses," were followed the very next day by a letter with this extraordinary request:

> Dear Wilhelm,
>
> Would you please try to search for a case of childhood convulsions that you can trace back (in the future or in your memory) to sexual abuse, specifically to *lictus* [licking] (or finger) in the anus. There must, after all, be some indications or reasons to suspect this where it has occurred. This would then cover the [well-]known functional category in the literature: worm irritation, dyspepsia, and the like. For my newest finding is that I am able to trace back with certainty a patient's attack that merely resembled epilepsy to such treatment by the tongue on the part of his nurse. Age 2

years.—Substitute early infancy and you get the semblance of epileptic psychosis in the reproduction [of the scene]. I have firm confidence in this novelty as well as in yesterday's about the precondition of age in psychosis. (Masson 1985, 223-24)

These were the thoughts of a forty-one-year-old "nerve specialist" with some ten years of 'medical' experience behind him writing to his trusted colleague. And these letters, one remembers, were subsequent by two years to what Breuer had called the "lack of coherence . . . in Freud's disquisitions" in the *Studies on Hysteria*. They were contemporaneous in fact with the early drafts of what was to become *The Interpretation of Dreams*. Freud, throughout this correspondence, is revealed as credulous—of his own fantastic notions of human psychology (usually presented with "certainty" or "great confidence") as much as of Fliess's mathematical calculations—and, alas, as one who has rejected empirical research for the conceits of his own strange grasp of alleged early, that is infantile, experiences. I say "alleged" because Freud's letters to Fliess indicate that his "findings" of early infantile sexual abuse (in this case of Nanny licking the baby's bottom) have been drawn from the responses of his adult patients, as have the "memories" of childhood convulsions. The causative link between the two—both implausible and impossible—has been inferred by Freud himself, of course. In what circumstances were these reputed infantile memories elicited? Or invented? We have here an instance, one of many, of Freud busily at work in his consulting office seeking infantile moments which, he thinks, account for his adult patients' present unhappiness.

We are a long way from the Baltic and the leisurely strolls by the water's edge with a hypnotized patient who would prove one's genius by responding at lunchtime to one's post-hypnotic suggestions. We are now—in 1897—deeply into the subject that Freud wanted to call (but he was to request Fliess's formal approval) "metapsychology." In the letter of March 10, 1898, Freud asks in parenthesis: "(I am going to ask you seriously, by the way, whether I may use the name metapsychology for my psychology that leads behind consciousness)" (Masson 1985, 301-302). This labyrinth, together with Freud's self-obsessed rooting around within it, were to provide the true Freudian origins of "psychoanalysis"—we have lived with its fictions for a century. Two years before these strange letters, Freud began his deceitful treatment of Emma Eckstein—the woman whom analysts would prefer to have never existed.

Notes

1. Mikkel Borch-Jacobsen (1996). *Remembering Anna O.: A Century of Mystification* (tr. Kirby Olson in collaboration with Xavier Callahan and the author). New York: Routledge, 34. Borch-Jacobsen's phrase relates to the rumor of Anna O.'s pseudocyesis (false pregnancy) and Breuer's hasty departure from her therapy. Borch-Jacobsen points out that, although psychoanalysts tend to see Ernest Jones's "mistakes" as a convenient and likely origin for inaccurate mythology, "here as elsewhere, Freud himself is to blame" (34).

2. Of the many attempts that have been made to make psychiatric sense of the case of "Anna O." the most persuasive, and the most sober, in my view, is that of the emeritus professor of psychiatry at the University of Western Ontario, Dr. Harold Merskey. His careful documentary research was not limited to the misleading account published in *Studies on Hysteria*. His study, which opts for the suggestion of a severe depressive illness followed by a long-term cognitively maintained recovery, is not mentioned in Borch-Jacobsen's book and is dismissed by Macmillan (Macmillan 1997, 632) with the cavalier phrase: "new diagnoses are always functions of whatever is currently fashionable." No, they're not; not always. I am at a loss to understand this tetchy reaction from Macmillan; has he *read* this paper? Harold Merskey is not a trendy jet-setting charismatic. I recommend his thoughtful paper to those interested in pursuing the dilemmas of Bertha Pappenheim's illness. See Merskey (1992), "Anna O. Had a Severe Depressive Illness," *British Journal of Psychiatry* 161: 185-94. I am grateful to Dr. Karel de Pauw for bringing this paper to my attention.

Merskey is rightly critical of the American psychiatrist Alison Orr-Andrawes's assumption of "temporal lobe epilepsy" favorably reported by Richard Webster. Webster also, I should mention, speaks of "multiple sclerosis" as a hypothetical diagnostic category; but this is quite impossible if one takes into consideration—as one should—the many years of productive, active social life that followed her departure for Germany. Her founding of the *Jüdischer Frauenbund* in 1904 (i.e., some twenty two years after the 1882 Breuer case notes) and her active work in the Weimar period make nonsense of multiple sclerosis as a disease entity in her case, given the progressive, ultimately unremitting, nature of this degenerative disease.

3. Translation by Lotti Newman in Masson 1985, 151, n. 1.

4. See, for example, the letter to Fliess of Wednesday, March 13, 1895: "The only thing I remember of last week is that I have written fifty-two printed pages on the psychotherapy of hysteria; I shall give you the galley proofs to read" (Masson 1985, 119).

5. The italicized phrase, "moral insanity," is in English in the original,

according to Masson's note 4 (176).

6. Although "Anna O." is the only case described in chapter detail by Breuer, one should note that in the long part 3 "Theoretical" by Breuer there is (211-12 in the Basic Books edition of *Studies on Hysteria*) an excellent brief example of treatment by Breuer of a twelve-year-old boy subjected to a pedophilic assault in a public urinal. The rapid benefit of Breuer's non-hypnotic treatment (which seems to have consisted in the establishment of the lad's confidence and in the "talking out" in the presence of his "clever and energetic mother" of the sexual approach) is quite contrary to Freud's grasp of the repressed infantile origins of neurosis. See Wilcocks (1994, 208-209) for discussion.

7. Wilhelm Fliess. *Die Beziehungen zwischen Nase und weiblichen Geschlechtsorganen: In ihrer biologischen Bedeutung dargestellt.* Leipzig and Vienna: Franz Deuticke, 1897. As I noted in *Maelzel's Chess Player* (see chapter 3, endnote 27, 105), Fliess had no understanding of the parasympathetic nervous system and thus came to erroneous conclusions about the supposed "relationship" between the nose and female genitalia. It is true that some females will experience a stuffy nose and engorgement of the mucous membrane surrounding the nasal concha during excitation of the vagina; but this is a secondary "parasympathetic" effect; the nose neither causes nor is "responsible" for these effects. Had Fliess understood this, Emma Eckstein would have been spared much misery. Frank Sulloway (1979 [1992]) mentions this citation of Freud by Fliess (181).

8. See Martin Gardner's (1966) devastating critique of the Fliessian numerical mumbo jumbo in "Freud's Friend Wilhelm Fliess and His Theory of Male and Female Life Cycles," *Scientific American* 215 (July): 108-12. That Freud was to credit this nonsense until his dying days is something that psychoanalysts and their fellow believers seem to overlook in their encomia of the sage.

9. Malcolm Bowie has, it is true, been quite scathing about the limitations of the tunnel-vision of Freudian psychoanalysis (see his *Freud, Proust and Lacan: Theory as Fiction*, Cambridge, U.K.: Cambridge University Press, 1987). His book is an elegant essay on Freud's cultural significance and includes an interesting study of Freud's continuing employment of the "archaeology" analogue. He has, nonetheless, opted for a kind of Lacanian revisionism which allows him to write of John Forrester's recent collection of essays *Dispatches from the Freud Wars*, "[H]e is an outstanding Freud scholar who brings a scrupulous sense of history to everything he does." As I demonstrate with citations later on, this is the last thing Forrester does.

10. This paragraph was written before I had read Wayne Koestenbaum's *Double Talk: The Erotics of Male Literary Collaboration* (New York: Routledge, 1989). The first chapter of this book is entitled "Privileging the

Anus: Anna O. and the Collaborative Origin of Psychoanalysis." As Koestenbaum remarks at one stage, having confused Frau Emmy von N.'s daughter with the patient herself (32) and committed other elementary blunders of fact, interpretation, and presentation, "I recover this drama not to unseat Freud, but to reupholster him for the purposes of gay criticism." If I were to "decode" Koestenbaum's sentence in the way he chooses to treat his selected texts, there would be much nudge-nudge, wink-wink, salacious grade 12 commentary on what is *implied* by "*unseat* Freud" followed, as it is, by "*reupholster* him." This is neither gay, nor is it criticism.

That Koestenbaum's first acknowledgment thanks are to Elaine Showalter is not surprising. The thoughtful homosexual writer and critic, Edmund White, wrote this in his review of Showalter's *Sexual Anarchy*: "But her Freudianism, used to sniff out patriarchal conspiracies, even in complex works of art, joined by her willingness to play footsy with vague and frightening concepts such as decadence, the apocalypse and AIDS-as-metaphor, reveal her to be coarsened by feminism and a confused, even reactionary social thinker" (*The Times Literary Supplement*, April 12, 1991, 6).

11. Ernst L. Freud (1960), 413. The letter, numbered 265 in Ernst Freud's collection, is dated June 2, 1932.

12. The text that Borch-Jacobsen has consulted is from Stefan Zweig, *Briefwechsel mit Hermann Bahr, Sigmund Freud, Rainer Maria Rilke und Arthur Schnitzler*, herausgegeben von Jeffrey B. Berlin, Hans-Ulrich Lindken und Donald A. Prater (Frankfurt am Main: S. Fischer Verlag, 1987), 200. Borch-Jacobsen's quote is from footnote 12 on page 35 of his book.

13. L. Appignanesi and J. Forrester (1992). *Freud's Women.* London: Weidenfeld and Nicolson, 83-84.

14. One should perhaps point out that there seems to have been no distinct treatment mode ever recommended by Freud for the diverse categories— hysteric, obsessional neurotic, neurotic, and so on—which his differential diagnoses claimed to recognize. This may have been because these diagnostic distinctions were a lure to catch the unwary, or simply because Freud was more interested in investigating (as he would say) the *origins* of his patients' discomforts.

15. This was during his brief visit to Hippolyte Bernheim's clinic/laboratory in Nancy (France) in the summer of 1889. In 1888 Freud's translation into German (as *Die Suggestion und ihre Heilwirkung)* of Bernheim's *De la suggestion et de ses applications à la thérapeutique* had appeared. In August 1890 Bernheim published *Hypnotisme, suggestion, psycho-thérapie: Etudes nouvelles*, which was translated by Freud as *Neue Studien über Hypnotismus, Suggestion und Psychotherapie*. Mikkel Borch-Jacobsen has written a fine comparative study of Bernheim's and Charcot's approaches to hypnotism, in the French (Nanterre) review *Corpus* under the title "L'effet Bernheim

(fragments d'une théorie de l'artefact généralisé)." See Borch-Jacobsen. 1997. "Delboeuf et Bernheim. Entre hypnose et suggestion," *Corpus*, no. 32: 147-73.

16. One thing that is not explained by this editors' note is what Freud was doing with patients in hypnosis in the early years of the correspondence with Wilhelm Fliess. The fourth letter—dated May 28, 1888, hence prior to his move to the famous Berggasse, 19—seems to imply some kind of restorative hypnotic repose not requiring the doctor's attention: "I have at this moment a lady in hypnosis lying in front of me and therefore can go on writing in peace . . ." and two paragraphs later a rapid end to the letter: "The time for the hypnosis is up. I greet you cordially. In all haste, your Dr. Freud" (Masson 1985, 21-22). I have no idea what the woman was doing in Freud's office in "hypnotic sleep," and the editors of the *Standard Edition* have either not known or not seen fit to tell us what was happening.

17. My Basic Books edition (1957) is a reprint of volume 2 of the *Standard Edition*. The sentence, "She lives at present in a country seat on the Baltic near a large town" (50), provokes the following coy footnote: "This is referred to later on as 'D—.' There is reason to believe that, in order to disguise his patient's identity, Freud had transferred her home from quite another part of Europe" (50, note 1). This edition concludes with an Appendix A on the vexed chronology of the Frau Emmy case (307-309). The probity of this editorial discussion, however, detailing the internal inconsistencies of Freud's own dating—did the treatment begin in 1888 or 1889?—is marred by the series of statements of "fact" about Freud's visits to the Baltic. The editorial footnote cited above already indicates that the Baltic was far from the geographical location of Freud's visits. Why, then, do the editors insist on replicating Freud's fiction in their Appendix?

18. The material relating to the truth about "Frau Emmy" was collected variously by the late Swedish scholar Ola Andersson and revealed to the public by the indefatigable Henri Ellenberger. See the recent "Présentation" by Elisabeth Roudinesco and Per Magnus Johansson in Ola Andersson, *Freud avant Freud: La préhistoire de la psychanalyse (1886-1896)*. (traduit de l'anglais par Sylvette Gleize). Le Plessis-Robinson: Synthélabo Groupe, Collection Les Empêcheurs de penser en rond, 1997. The original title of Ola Andersson's essays was "Studies in the Prehistory of Psychoanalysis: The Etiology of Psychoneuroses and Some Related Themes in Sigmund Freud's Scientific Writings and Letters, 1886-1896." It was published (in English) by Scandinavian University Books at Stockholm in 1962.

19. E. Roudinesco, "Présentation" in *Freud avant Freud*, 18 (my translation). The "famous scene" refers to the reputed invention of the out-of-sight position of the analyst seated on a chair behind the couch.

20. The "confabulation" mentioned earlier begins with this opening paragraph. Frau Emmy was *not* hysteric; Breuer's treatment of Anna O. was

not successful; she was *not* his first patient. That Freud was aware of this is the reason for my use of the word "confabulation," which implies, inter alia, a conscious attempt to deceive—and not merely the lay public, but the medical audience for whom this text was originally conceived.

21. See Herbert Spiegel, "The Grade Five Syndrome: The Highly Hypnotizable Person," *The International Journal of Clinical and Experimental Hypnosis* 22 (1974): 303-19. See also Mikkel Borch-Jacobsen, "Sybil—The Making of a Disease: An Interview with Dr. Herbert Spiegel," *The New York Review of Books* (April 24, 1997): 60-64.

22. Webster suggests that Frau Emmy may have been a "Touretter" and mentions in an endnote the following article: Else Pappenheim, "Freud and Gilles de la Tourette: Diagnostic Speculations on 'Frau Emmy von N.,'" *International Review of Psychoanalysis* (1980) 7: 265-77. Tourette syndrome is a neurological disorder (which may indeed give rise to the various "clacking" sounds reportedly produced by Frau Emmy) and has nothing whatever to do with antecedent psychological experiences. *If* Fanny Moser *was* suffering from this neurological complaint, then none of Freud's procedures would have made the slightest difference to her treatment outcome. Freud throughout treats the "clacking" as a combination of *tic* and "the putting into effect of antithetic ideas," as a kind of "hysterical conversion" of *ideational* origin. Her "clacking," needless to say, was not cured by Freud.

Perhaps the best documented paper on this complaint is the excellent recent article by Howard I. Kushner, "From Gilles de la Tourette's Disease to Tourette Syndrome: A History," *C N S Spectrums (The International Journal of Neuropsychiatric Medicine)* 4, no. 2 (February 1999): 24-35. It is an objective, succinct history of the problem and includes an extensive, virtually exhaustive bibliography on the subject. One aspect of the dangers for medical research in the United States in the 1960s and 1970s of the then dominant position in psychiatry of psychoanalysis is revealed in this sentence:

> The widespread acceptance of psychoanalytic assumptions, combined with the power that the psychoanalytic community wielded over medical journal editorial boards, made it extremely difficult for those few practitioners who were convinced that TS [Tourette syndrome] had an organic etiology to gain a professional platform in the 1970s. (Kushner 1999, 32)

Kushner then uses the case of successful TS treatment with dosages of haloperidol by the husband and wife team (Arthur and Elaine Shapiro) as an instance of the nonperson treatment meted out by the psychoanalytic-dominated editorial boards: "The Shapiros' article was rejected for publication by every major American psychiatric journal, only finding a home in 1968 in the *British Journal of Psychiatry*" (Kushner 1999, 32). Howard Kushner has recently published what *Nature* describes as "a 'must' for anyone interested in the history of medicine, neurology and psychiatry as well as Tourette syndrome": *A Cursing Brain? The Histories of Tourette Syndrome*, Cambridge, Mass.: Harvard University Press, 1999.

23. "Anamnesis" is a contrived term developed from "amnesia" and implies the "lifting" of "amnesia" by the methods of analysis. The *anamnesis* is that part of a psychoanalytic treatment which "recovers" supposedly repressed and supposedly inaccessible memories. The "recovered memory" movement in the United States is merely one modern strand of the psychoanalytic procedure. The neurological impossibility of the enterprise as far as infantile so-called repressed memories is concerned has been amply demonstrated by the French surgeon Gérard Zwang in his (truly) monumental—1,000 pages!—*La Statue de Freud*, Paris: Robert Laffont, 1985.

24. I add "supposedly" because it is evident from a reading of Freud's works that he never recorded or examined "serious" traumatic experiences. When he mentioned them—for example, the "shell-shock" problems of soldiers returning from the Great War or the anxieties of survivors of train crashes—in later years in *Beyond the Pleasure Principle* (1920), he was too far gone in his Fliess-and-cocaine-based sexual etiologies to offer more than the following: "the mechanical violence of the trauma would liberate a quantity of sexual excitation which, owing to the lack of preparation for anxiety, would have a traumatic effect" (*P.F.L.*, 11, 305).

25. This is perfectly consistent with the multiple sclerosis diagnosis. The disease includes, inter alia, an occasional unusual buoyancy of feeling even given the disastrous inadequacy of the motor neurones.

26. "We live a free life," from the popularly-sung Robbers' Chorus in Schiller's play *Die Räuber* according to the editorial addition to *Studies*, 100.

27. Jeffrey M. Masson, *The Assault on Truth: Freud's Suppression of the Seduction Theory*. New York: Viking-Penguin, 1985, 85.

28. The *editio ad usum delphini* [edition for the use of the Dauphin] refers to the carefully pruned and hence politically and morally correct version of the Latin classics prepared for the Dauphin (heir to the Bourbon throne in France) during the reign of Louis XIV.

29. My emphasis. Quoted from Ola Andersson, *Freud avant Freud*, 273. The French translation in the Roudinesco edition cited also gives a convenient plural for Freud's singular. Why? one wonders.

30. For this unanticipated connection with the Führer, Webster cites (and recommends) the book by Daniel Gasman, *The Scientific Origins of National Socialism: Social Darwinism in Ernst Haeckel and the German Monist League*, New York: Macdonald, 1971. See Webster 1995, 589, note 33.

31. See in this connection the German pharmacologist Louis Lewin, *Phantastica. Die Betäubenden und Erregenden Genussmittel für Ärzte und*

Nichtärzte, Berlin: Verlag von Georg Stilke, 1924. The chapter "Der Kokainismus" is translated in Robert Byck, ed., *Cocaine Papers: Sigmund Freud*. New York: Meridian Books, 1975. The English medical historian Elizabeth Thornton makes this point in her pioneering book *Freud and Cocaine: The Freudian Fallacy*. London: Blond and Briggs, 1983; this was republished by Paladin in 1986 under the title *The Freudian Fallacy: Freud and Cocaine*. Richard Webster and Allen Esterson, who have both corresponded with Thornton, have reservations about the certainty of some of her findings. I share these hesitations; but I think she has done an immense service to scholarship in her careful analysis of some of the reasons for Freud's beliefs.

32. As the European supplier of refined cocaine, E. Merck of Darmstadt wrote in "Cocaine and its Salts": "Cocaine is a stimulant which is peculiarly adapted to elevate the working ability of the body, without any dangerous result. Its action is stronger than that of alcohol. Its use for this purpose in marching or mountain climbing is self-evident" (in Byck 1975, 79).

The chemist Merck (founder of what was to become Merck, Sharpe and Dohme) published "Kokain und seine Salze" in *Klinische Monatsblätter für Augenheilkunde*, Zeherder: vol. 22, November 1884; the translation appeared in the American *Chicago Medical Journal and Examiner* 50 (February 1885): 157-63. The complete translation is included in Byck (1975), 77-81. Webster quotes from Merck's paper, attributing it, mistakenly, to Freud (Webster 1995, 565, note 19).

33. Freud regularly "brushed" the inside of his nostrils with a solution of liquid cocaine. This abuse of the tissues of the nose led to immense pain, tissue necrosis, and a cancerous degeneration of the inner nasal cavities and the adjacent hard palate—the roof of the mouth—so that surgical removal was necessary to limit the spread of the cancer. Freud underwent this last surgical intervention in his sixties and lived with a prosthesis separating his mouth from his nose for the last twenty years of his life.

An example of Freud's mistaken use of cocaine (to relieve pain or swelling caused by the use of cocaine in the first place) is offered in his letter to Fliess of January 24, 1895:

> Last time I wrote to you, after a good period which immediately succeeded the reaction, that a few viciously bad days had followed during which a cocainization of the left nostril had helped me to an amazing extent. I now continue my report. The next day I kept the nose under cocaine, which one should not really do; that is, I repeatedly painted it to prevent the renewed occurrence of swelling; during this time I discharged copious amounts of thick pus; and since then I have felt wonderful, as though there never had been anything wrong at all. Arrhythmia is still present, but rarely and not badly. (Masson 1985, 106)

The irregular (and frightening) heartbeats (arrhythmia) were a continuing nightmare for Freud from his late thirties on; that they were a direct consequence of his frequent massive doses of cocaine was neither recognized by him nor revealed by his personal physician (Max Schur) in his biography of Freud.

34. A "chandelle verte" (literally "green candle") is a slangy reference to hanging, dripping nasal mucus.

35. This is reminiscent of Freud's phrase to Fliess two and a half years earlier (quoted at the end of the previous chapter), when he had written of his reception in Vienna: "They look upon me pretty much as a monomaniac, while I have the distinct feeling that I have touched upon one of the great secrets of nature" (Masson 1985, 74).

36. The Keynote Address given by Dr. Alan A. Stone to the American Academy of Psychoanalysis on December 9, 1995, "Where Will Psychoanalysis Survive?" is an honest, if muddled, recantation by a leading analyst. What Stone says of Freud's adventures of 1895-1896 is an instance of what anyone could divine from the frantic last years of the nineteenth century: "What one discovers is that Freud had a new hypothesis every day. It is astonishing to see how little evidence he needed; a single patient hour was enough to launch a whole new theory of mental illness" (Stone 1997, *Harvard Magazine* 99, no. 3 [January-February 1997]: 34-39; this passage is on page 37).

3

From the Correspondence to the Sanatorium Loew

> I am now making this diagnosis very often and agree with you that the nasal reflex is one of the most frequent disturbances. Unfortunately, I am never sure what to do then. The tie to sexuality too is becoming ever tighter; it is a pity we cannot work on the same cases. FREUD TO FLIESS, May 30, 1893[1]

This letter of May 30, 1893, confirms that as Freud was elaborating his share of the book-in-progress, *Studies on Hysteria*, he was not simply under the sway of Fliess's influence within the private confines of their correspondence; he was actively producing diagnoses of his own patients which agreed with Fliess's hypothesis of a nasal reflex neurosis. This neurosis implied previous *abusus sexualis* (which Latin term meant, for Fliess, masturbation rather than "seduction" by another), according to Fliess's paper read at the Twelfth Congress of Internal Medicine at Wiesbaden held from April 12-15, 1893. Freud, we recall, had advised on Fliess's presentation in his "literary businessman" letter (postmarked February 8, 1893; see chapter 2, page 42 above). To a certain extent, then, Freud himself was a "partner" as much as a follower in Fliess's notions about the nature of noses. It is, however, possible—and most likely—that his efforts to help Fliess in his presentation were of more literary, or propagandistic, than medical significance.

This might explain the sense of helplessness, having made the nasal reflex neurosis diagnosis, of Freud's sentence: "Unfortunately, I am never sure what to do then." When Freud ends the paragraph with the phrase "it is a pity we cannot work on the same cases," one recognizes a plea for cooperative clinical endeavor. In less than two years Freud's wish would be amply fulfilled, and a guinea pig for Dr. Wilhelm Fliess's surgical interventions on the nose would be found among Freud's patients.

Before we consider in detail the particular case that led to the Sanatorium Loew, we might ask some questions about the implications for Freud's methods of medical inquiry that this letter suggests. One might ask, for example, what Freud meant when he wrote to Fliess about the nasal reflex neurosis that "I am now making this diagnosis very often and agree with you that the nasal reflex is one of the most frequent disturbances." As for the second half of those two statements: Does Freud mean most frequent in *his* practice? Or most frequent in Vienna among nerve doctors (*Nervenärzte*)? Or, most frequent among *nonorganic* presenters? If, as I suspect is the case, Freud is *merely* referring to his own case load, then that second half of his two statements teeters straight back on to the first half: "I am now making this diagnosis very often"; and the thought naturally occurs—on what grounds had this diagnosis suddenly found favor?

Had Freud's patient population radically changed in its presenting symptoms? If so, why do we have no record of such an apparent sudden and radical shift of patient symptomatology? If not, had Freud himself changed his grasp of those presenting symptoms and discovered a new significance for them? If so, the question inevitably emerges: What was the validity of the various previous diagnoses? And, a subsidiary question: On what were *they* based? Were they all mistaken? Or had Freud now understood a complex of symptoms revealing a "crossed" or combinatory form of disease entity where before he had only perceived a single ailment? This is what Freud writes in the paragraph immediately following the quotation at the head of this chapter:

> Recently I too encountered something like crossed reflexes. Furthermore, a short time ago I interrupted (for one hour) a severe migraine of my own with cocaine; the effect set in only after I had cocainized the opposite side as well; but then it did so promptly. I see a good possibility of filling yet another gap in the sexual etiology of the neuroses. I believe I understand the anxiety neuroses of young persons who must be presumed to be virgins and who have not been subjected to abuse. I have analyzed two cases of this kind; it was a *presentient dread* of sexuality, and behind it things they had seen or heard and half-understood—thus, the etiology is purely emotional but nevertheless of a sexual nature. (Masson 1985, 49; Freud's emphasis)

How Freud "analyzed" the two mentioned cases we do not know. Why they had been sent to him we do not know. Whether he initiated the inquiries about attitudes to sexuality we do not know. Nor do we know whether this is the fruit of the kind of interrogation whereby Freud elicited "memories" of sexual encounters (between domestics, for example) "overheard" when the now-adult patient was in swaddling clothes. The classic instance of this did not come until some four years later (letter of January 24, 1897), when Freud claimed that he could hear the conversation "recorded" by the patient at the age of eleven months. It requires direct quotation, or the reader may—quite understandably— imagine that I am inventing:

> Thus I was able to trace back, with certainty, a hysteria that developed in the context of a periodic mild depression to a seduction, which occurred for the first time at 11 months and [I could] hear again the words that were exchanged between two adults at that time! It is as though it comes from a phonograph. (Masson 1985, 226)

The neurological impossibility of such a scenario having any validity has not prevented many "repressed memory" advocates from invoking the authority of Freud for their cause.[2] One thing that they have not understood is that in this area Freud is not to be, and never should have been, considered an authority. For this to have happened, the mythology of the movement must have replaced serious scholarship of the history of medicine.

Freud's confused sequence of thoughts in his 1893 paragraph leads one to believe that "crossed reflexes" have somehow, in Freud's mind, become linked (a memory of his Paris experience of eight years earlier?) with the left/right dichotomy of cranial magnetism that he had observed at the Salpêtrière and that he has now employed (or, re-employed) to his satisfaction on his own remission from migraine by cocainizing both nostrils.[3] The absence of careful (as opposed to compulsive) introspection is evident. What is less evident is Freud's ability to pursue the establishment and investigation of a serious patient history.[4] It is when one recalls the last hypothesis of this letter (quoted in chapter 2) that one becomes aware of Freud's fundamental inability to consider a patient other than as an instance of his own emerging fantasies. That hypothesis was: "Could it not be that organic changes of the nose produce the pollutions and thereby the neurasthenia, so that here the latter develops as a product of the nasal reflex noxa?" The Freud who wrote these thoughts was also the Freud who was "examining" his patients on a daily basis.

It is an almost perfect example of poetic justice that the country which now, of all Western countries (including the United States), remains most surely and most intellectually and (even) most popularly within the sphere of Freudian belief is France (a French psychiatrist informs me that Brazil and Argentina are now hotbeds of Lacanian–Freudianism). France was Freud's discovery of a world of psychological investigation where the statements of the patient were interpreted according to the tenets of the doctor. (With Lacan this has been elevated into High Theory, irrespective of the known blunders of the Master's treatment—e.g., his long-term analysis of the Marxist theoretician and wife-murderer Louis Althusser.)[5] "Charcot's Mistake" is the title of one of Richard Webster's early chapters. Webster is not wrong (he is talking of the mistakes of the *later* Charcot already celebrated for his genuine histological discoveries). Of the many lunacies perpetrated in the name of science at the Salpêtrière in the nineteenth century, Charcot's "invention" of "Les Grandes Hystériques" was merely one. That Charcot *could* continue in this way with his *folie de grandeur* says much about the intellectual, and moral, climate of the time. That Fulgence Raymond, who succeeded Charcot, was uninterested in such characteristics of abnormal human behavior and that he decided to use his administrative powers in other directions (he nonetheless allowed Pierre Janet to keep a psychological unit of inquiry) demonstrates the ephemeral nature of the "findings" of medical science under Charcot's imperium. The more one examines the tail end of Charcot's career, the more the relevance of the Peter Principle is felt. Here was an excellent example of a first-class researcher being promoted beyond the competence of his earlier achievements. And yet it was precisely the incompetent, if magisterial and Napoleonic, Charcot who fascinated Freud.

Freud found in the writings of *La Revue philosophique* and in the general atmosphere at the Salpêtrière from October 1885 to late February 1886 a brand-new world which would color his vision of "scientific" inquiry for ever after. The Fechner or Haeckel influences which Webster adduces are total irrelevancies when compared to the seductions that France offered Freud. An excellent chapter on this strange fascination with hysteria is given in Martha Noel Evans's splendidly researched *Fits and Starts: A Genealogy of Hysteria in Modern France*.[6] I am firmly convinced that Freud's French experiences, however brief (some five months in Paris—October 1885 to February 1886—plus a brief later visit to Bernheim in Nancy), were instrumental in shaping the course of his treatment of his patients and in his willing acceptance of Wilhelm Fliess's strange notions about the divinatory power of the nose. Fliess represented for Freud the nearest German equivalent of the kind of "medical" science to which he had been exposed in Paris. Fliess was, for Freud, almost a youthful Charcot, and the intellectual allegiance that Freud unquestioningly gave him for so many years (even after their break in 1904) is a testimony to this. One inevitable consequence, of course, was Freud's tendency to treat patients as aspects of his continuing "investigations" (just as the later Charcot had) rather than as human individuals with their own discrete dilemmas. If anything, the Paris experience confirmed Freud in his belief that "patients" were objects of study for theoretical elaboration rather than fellow humans with medical problems who needed his medical aid for recovery. If this is the case, then Charcot's influence on the young Freud has had a pernicious effect, one which is still working its way through the consulting rooms of many continents.

When he was confronted with a young woman suffering from irregular periods, stomach cramps, and a generalized depression, the scene was set for a fiasco that should have been the end of a "medical" career. The scene was also set for a long-term combination of deceit and duplicity first practiced on the patient, later exercised upon the medical world, and, finally, on the public at large, by Freud's Stalinist erasure of Emma Eckstein from the history of psychoanalysis. This was continued after Freud's death by the equally Stalinist removal of references to Eckstein by daughter Anna Freud in her highly censored version of the Freud–Fliess correspondence. This tale of chicanery has recently been given a new lease of life by the pro-Freudian phantasmagoria erected by Appignanesi and Forrester in their enthrallingly deceitful version of this affair in *Freud's Women*.

The test case for Freud, it seems to me, is not that of Anna O., as Borch-Jacobsen asserts; it is, and much more importantly, because it concerns a case that Freud actually handled (or *mis*handled) himself, that of the wretched Emma Eckstein.[7] This case concerns not merely maltreatment of a patient (that according to Freud's own personal physician, Max Schur, could have landed Wilhelm Fliess in court—even in the nineteenth century—on charges of medical malpractice) in the physical sense; it concerns the sustained and continued psychological maltreatment of Eckstein by her premier physician, Sigmund Freud.

We do not know what prompted Emma Eckstein to come to Freud for treatment. We do know, however, what the presenting symptoms of this young woman of twenty-nine were. She suffered from menstrual cramps and had, hence, abdominal pains, her periods were difficult and irregular, she was generally depressed. Few doctors now or then—that is, at the end of the benighted nineteenth century—would have suggested that she should therefore have the structure of her nose surgically altered as a therapeutic measure. Freud, however, had a close and trustworthy friend, Wilhelm Fliess, who recommended just such a tactic for this young woman. Gastric pains? She must be a masturbator! Masturbator? And female? The removal of the middle left nasal concha (turbinate bone) will remedy this! No problem!

This cartoon fast-forward to the events of February 1895 is not as unrealistic as cartoon sequences usually are. The reality was, of course, both more complex and, most certainly, no laughing matter. Freud himself, who appears to have initiated the involvement of Fliess,[8] was relying on the authority of Fliess's hypotheses relating to the supposed relationship between the nose and female sexual organs and on the subsidiary hypothesis that female masturbation caused gastric pains (gastralgias) which could be resolved by the removal of the middle left turbinate bone. Whether Fliess meant that such surgical intervention would stop the gastric pains or prevent further attempts at self-gratification—or both—is not clear. (Though one can well imagine that the desire for masturbation on the part of a patient recovering from a Fliess operation must have been extremely limited.) It seems evident, from his own writings on the subject, that the primary motive behind Fliess's ill-conceived operation was to arrest female masturbation. This puts him on par with those contemporaries of his in New York who recommended (and indeed practiced) clitoridectomy for the suppression of animal instincts in "decent" women. This parallel by itself should give pause for thought to those "feminist" Freudians who imagine that Sigmund Freud was in any sense a "liberator" of women or of the open expression of sexuality untrammeled by current social hypocrisies.

Why Fliess should have been called in for Eckstein is not clear either. The stomach cramps associated with difficult or irregular periods are in no conceivable manner to be associated with the (erroneously) imagined effects of female masturbation. Hence, the first questions to be asked of Freud (and of those Freudians who still credit the value of this intervention) are: (1) Did he believe that female masturbation caused gastric pains?—Answer, Yes; (2) Did he believe that the removal of the middle left nasal concha would end these pains (and the associated masturbation)?—Answer, Yes; (3) Did he think that Eckstein was a suitable candidate for Fliess's surgery?—Answer, Yes.

Now comes the most important question: the one that relates, inevitably, to Freud's "clinical work" on his patients. Given Eckstein's presenting symptoms, *how* did the subject of masturbation ever occur as an item for detailed discussion in Freud's consulting room? It cannot have occurred with Eckstein's producing some Viennese equivalent of "Doctor, I've been jerking off, and now I've got these pains, right here, just below my tummy." It must have occurred with Freud taking cognizance of the patient's presenting symptoms and introducing to her the central theme of his own medical curiosity—masturbation. On the assumption of naive (and foolish, as it turned out) honesty on the part of Emma Eckstein, one can assume that she replied positively to his interrogations. Yes, she had masturbated; yes, she did masturbate. This allowed Freud to invoke the (so far) unproven powers of the Berlin magician, the nasal reflex neurosis specialist, and to suggest to his patient something like: "My colleague, the renowned Berlin otorhinolaryngologist Wilhelm Fliess, will be in Vienna in the month of February. I will arrange for him to provide you with suitable surgical treatment while he is here. You will be cured!"

Of *what* would she be cured? From *what* was she suffering when she first encountered Freud's responses? How could Freud be so certain that (a) his diagnosis (no doubt of the nasal reflex neurosis) was right and (b) his proposed solution was appropriate and viable?

Freud himself, when we return to the correspondence with Fliess, shows great uncertainty about the prospective operation. The letter dated January 24, 1895, which begins with the now-familiar descriptions of the state of his own nose: "The next day I kept the nose under cocaine, which one should not really do; that is, I repeatedly painted it to prevent the renewed occurrence of swelling; during this time I discharged what in my experience is a copious amount of thick pus" concludes with Freud's thoughts about Fliess's forthcoming visit to Vienna. His first suggestion is that Fliess should work with one of the leading plastic surgeons in Vienna, Gersuny:[9] "How would it be if you *first* experimented on the preparation jointly with Gersuny? According to Breuer and Rie, he worked intensively on the matter after he had overcome his initial hesitation." This first suggestion of Freud's, for the participation of a reputed local surgeon in the *preparations* for the operation, indicates a certain hesitancy about allowing Fliess surgical free-play in the patient's treatment. (It also implies, incidentally, that Fliess had never before actually practiced the turbinate bone removal operation.) Freud's hesitancy was, we now know, quite justified; however, a doubt remains. Was Freud hesitant about Fliess's accomplishments as a surgeon? Or about the efficacy of the operation itself? If the latter, then three further questions may (and *should*) have been present in Freud's mind: (1) Was the diagnosis of nasal reflex neurosis well-founded?—that is, in *this* particular case? (Freud having already for some two years believed that there *was* such a disease entity); (2) if so, Was Fliess's operation the correct procedure? and (3) Was it a *safe* procedure?

Freud then writes a paragraph of what I have elsewhere called "white-knuckled panic"[10] when he considers the fast-approaching reality of what he and Fliess have, so far, merely hypothesized. It says much for Freud's residual reality-testing abilities that he should express such terror:

> Now only one more week separates us from the operation, or at least from the preparations for it. The time has passed quickly, and I gladly avoid putting myself through a self-examination to ascertain what right I have to expect so much from it. My lack of medical knowledge once again weighs heavily on me. But I keep repeating to myself: so far as I have some insight into the matter, the cure must be achievable by this route. I would not have dared to invent this plan of treatment on my own, but I confidently join you in it. (Masson 1985, 106-107)

"The cure must be achievable by this route" is an interesting phrase. Which cure? For which malady? Already Eckstein's fate has been sealed, even before Fliess has set off on the train for Vienna. She now suffers from a disease for which Fliess has invented a cure—the nasal reflex neurosis. This correspondence between Freud and Fliess raises so many issues at different moments. And the Eckstein moment is particularly full of such unanswered (and, perhaps, unanswerable?) questions. For example, in that paragraph just cited: *why* did Freud write "I would not have dared to invent this plan of treatment on my own"? What are the implications of this lack of daring? Are they a secret, hidden (yet known) fear that the whole thing is "bachelors' baloney" about the pains that women sometimes suffer at times of menstrual stress—and which have nothing to do either with noses or with the masculine imagined moments of female erotic fantasy?

What was Fliess doing in Vienna in February 1895? Was he merely visiting an old friend and sorting out a diagnostic dilemma? Was his visit to Vienna solely the consequence of Freud's desperate letters? The February 1895 visit of Wilhelm Fliess to Vienna was indeed part of his professional progress through the medical ranks. It is most likely that, quite irrespective of Freud's invitation, Fliess would have been in Vienna in February 1895.

He had already arranged a series of demonstrations with a Viennese maternity clinic to show that the administration of cocaine to the nostrils of women with labor pains would efficiently remove these difficulties. Fliess used his cocaine experimentations in the clinic of Professor Chrobak (one of the leading Viennese gynecologists). His work was reported in the local press. The *Wiener allgemeine Zeitung* for February 26, 1895, had a half-column report entitled *"Eine neue medizinische Entdeckung"* ("A New Medical Discovery") which included an interview with Fliess: "As Dr. Fliess himself tells us, he has not yet been able to form a conclusive opinion about the significance of the discovery he has made."[11] The "conclusive opinion" rapidly made by the Viennese medical community was that Fliess's "discovery" was an unmitigated failure and that no relief was obtained by the expectant mothers in their laying-in.

Freud, aware of Fliess's touchiness about public reputation, wrote immediately (letter of March 4, 1895) to calm his friend's fears about the consequences of the mistaken "labor-pain therapy" and its reporting in the Viennese press:

> Breuer thinks there is nothing to be done about it because you are quoted only as asserting that the matter has not been brought to a conclusion, and that you cannot dispute. I believe one should let it go; it is not worth the effort; as long as you have assured Chrobak that you are blameless, all possible harm has been prevented. For the rest, the whole thing does not matter. Naturally, they are now talking a lot about your experiments and spreading the word that they did not succeed. (Masson 1985, 113)

The medical gossip in Vienna about the incompetences and ill-founded theorizing of Fliess was rife, and Freud was to take it into consideration when accepting his friend's suggestions to "isolate" himself from his medical colleagues.[12] The 1895 Fliessian visit to Vienna provided two calamities in fact: the first, related to Fliess's unsuccessful cocaine medication for mothers-to-be in labor; the second, which concerns us here, was the ghastly mismanagement of the operation on Emma Eckstein. Although the Eckstein failure was fairly rapidly hushed up (and neither

Freud nor Fliess had the temerity, or strategic foolishness, to base a publication on the incident), the failure of the cocaine-for-mothers-to-be experiment was to redound on Fliess once again within three years. The publication of Fliess's *The Relationship between the Nose and the Female Sexual Organs* by Deuticke in 1897 produced a swingeing attack on Fliess in 1898 in the *Wiener klinische Rundschau* by Dr. Benjamin Ry.[13]

Ry pours scorn on someone who can invent a relationship between the tonsils and the eyes and quotes Fliess:

> I saw a 2½-year-old cross-eyed child become straight-eyed after an intervention of this sort [namely, scraping of the tonsils with a fingernail]; since I know [sic!] that the eye muscles of the infant become functional at critical periods, so that the initial strabism characteristic of infants disappears in spurts, I should like to interpret the above observation in the sense that in this case the diseased tonsils inhibited this periodical maturation of the eye muscles. (Masson 1985, 310, note 4; square brackets with exclamation point are Ry's own)

Dr. Benjamin Ry concludes: "That is indeed disgusting gobbledygook! No wonder that in not a few places the reader of this book has the impression that the author is making fun of him."

Prior to this decisive demolition of Fliess's major work, *The Relationship between the Nose and the Female Sexual Organs*, Benjamin Ry has pointedly mentioned the failure of the notion "that it is possible to remove labor pains by the cocainization of certain parts of the nasal mucosa." He adds, thoughtfully:

> The reviewer, having made inquiries at obstetrical clinics [i.e., in Vienna], learned that experiments in respect thereof—which at the time were also widely discussed in the daily press [i.e., in February 1895]—did not lead to positive results; therewith any need to deal further with this point of Fliess's work is obviated. The rest of what the book contains has nothing to do with medicine or natural science. For if one nowadays seeks to render such mystical nonsense that aspires to be intellectual wealth capable of discussion, the attempt founders on the realization that it is not the business of science to embark on a critique of the fantasy creations of every author, for such idle disquisitions can be neither refuted nor confirmed.[14]

This savage, but accurate, assessment of Fliess's contributions to medicine is a kind of pre-Popperian assault on the irrational which shows that Virginia Woolf was too general in her condemnation of the "gull-like imbecility" of the Germans (or Austrians)—it all depends on whom you read! Incidentally, Webster, who quotes parts of this trenchant review of Fliess, makes the mistake of assuming that "Freud immediately sent a copy of the review to Fliess" (Webster 1995, 223). This is not the case. One wonders, in fact, that *had* Freud sent a copy of this review to Fliess, what would have been the motives behind such cruelty? Freud first mentions Ry's devastating review in his letter of April 14, 1898, where he calls it "an example of that type of impertinence which is characteristic of absolute ignorance" (Masson 1985, 309). In fact, he did *not* send the review to Fliess, as is made perfectly clear in the very next letter of April 27, 1898, where Freud announces his resignation (as a protest against Ry) from the editorial board of the *Wiener klinische Rundschau*, adding: "I intentionally did not send you the review in question" (Masson 1985, 311).

I sympathize with Webster's mistake here; the Freud–Fliess correspondence has to be read very carefully and *repeatedly* and, even then, one can get tripped up by an unnoticed reference.[15] It is a biographical minefield. I recall how, after my research for my earlier Freud book, Allen Esterson had observed things that I had ignored and I had unearthed things that Esterson had not perceived; and we had both realized things that were apparently hidden from Masson, who was responsible for putting the whole correspondence together in the first place! Webster has sometimes come a cropper quite innocently; and Appignanesi and Forrester have had a field day "interpreting" the letters to the greater glory of Freud. This is a grave disservice to the history of medicine as much as to the general public who become victims of the misinformation so artfully offered by the pair.

Apart from the "Eckstein" letters themselves in the correspondence, two texts deserve to be read almost in conjunction with one another as a demonstration of how scholarship, propaganda, the pursuit of a hobby-horse, can lead to mutually contradictory commentaries on the very same texts. The two passages are Jeffrey M. Masson, *The Assault on Truth* ("The Theory of Periodicity" and "The Witch must Die," 94-106, of the Viking-Penguin edition) and "Emma Eckstein and the Wish Theory of the Psyche" on pages 133-141 of *Freud's Women* by Appignanesi and Forrester. For the latter, irrespective of their knowledge of Freud's beliefs at the time (which led to his accepting Fliess's clumsy and unnecessary surgical intervention), the whole wretched business is yet another instance of Freud's burgeoning brilliance as a psychoanalyst: "What is remarkable is the sureness of touch he displays in wending his way towards using the traumatic bleeding scene for the purposes of advancing Emma's *analysis*. And it is here, again, in the context of a transference interpretation, that we find him employing the term 'wish'" (Appignanesi and Forrester 1992, 137).

In the case of Emma Eckstein, Appignanesi and Forrester have nothing whatever to add to the archival efforts of Jeffrey Masson. Masson's pages mentioned above (from *The Assault on Truth*)—with the addition of "Appendix A: Freud and Emma Eckstein," 241-58—provide the substantial material from which he has drawn a totally divergent conclusion. Masson, here, sees no "sureness of touch" and, unlike Appignanesi and Forrester, details the dreadful events to which Eckstein was submitted. And these events include not merely the cackhandedness of Fliess, who left half a meter of gauze in the ruptured cavity, with the inevitable consequence that it could not heal properly or healthily, given the suppuration beneath the lint; but equally the months of indoctrination by Freud to convince his patient that her bleeding—the many hemorrhages suffered in the months subsequent to the operation (and the postoperative operations to deal with the mess left behind by Fliess)—was the physiological consequence of her repressed erotic desire to see him at her bedside in attendance. For Appginanesi and Forrester, this was an early discovery by Freud of the erotic "transference." For this monstrous abuse alone of medical historiography, this pair should be drummed out of the academic court.

Although they don't whitewash Fliess, they certainly whitewash Freud's reprehensible treatment of this first victim of Freudian psychoanalysis, imagining it as *deep* investigation of the damaged psyche of Emma, rather than as the self-serving confabulations of a worried *Nervenarzt*:

> But a year after Emma had nearly bled to death because of Fliess's error, Freud was finding a history of bleeding in her case, turning the dramatic events of her 'bleeding scene' to psychoanalytic use. In other words, he took Emma's response to that scene as evidence of her transference, and reconstructed her prehistoric wishes from the new material." (*Freud's Women*, 136)

What seems to have been conveniently forgotten by Appignanesi and Forrester is *why* Emma Eckstein was ever in Freud's consulting room in the first place. In the process, by the way, they have even forgotten what "prehistoric wishes" meant for the Freud who compounded amateur paleoanthropology with individual life experiences. For Freud "prehistoric" referred to extreme infancy, prior to the acquisition of language in the child. In the passage from the letter of May 17, 1896, used by Appignanesi and Forrester to illustrate their defense of the master, Freud's references are all to recollections of the pubescent Emma and to her difficulties with menstruation, for example:

> [S]he joyously welcomed her severe menstrual bleeding as proof that her illness was genuine, a proof that was also recognized as such by others. She described a scene from the age of fifteen, in which she suddenly began to bleed from the nose when she had the wish to be treated by a certain young doctor who was present (and who also appeared in the dream). When she saw how affected I was by her first hemorrhage while she was still in the hands of Rosanes, she experienced this as the realization of an old wish to be loved in her illness, and in spite of the danger during the succeeding hours she felt happy as never before. (Masson 1985, 186)

Freud has evidently chosen a theme—ideationally provoked bleeding—and attempted to provide Fliess with "analytical" material which will get them both (Freud and Fliess) off the hook. But, so far, this material has not been "prehistoric," and it was only later to become so in Freud's impossible credulity about hearing a conversation "overheard" by an eleven-month-old baby (in actuality, an adult patient "regressing," possibly Emma) as clear as if it were on a phonograph. By using these letters of Freud as clear indications of the already valuable and valid method of what was to become "psychoanalysis," Appignanesi and Forrester are treading on dangerous ground. If proof were needed of the dishonest ingenuity at the heart of the enterprise, they have provided it, in full.

Masson has been frequently criticized for his provocative treason toward psychoanalysis and for his too-ready acceptance of the arguments of that branch of the radical feminist movement which has seen incestuous fathers at work all over the place (as, indeed, in his moments of fantasy, did Freud). Many of these criticisms seem pertinent to me; I have the feeling that Masson has been following a hobbyhorse that has become a virtual obsession so that clear and cogent thinking has been replaced by splenetic outrage at supposed parental transgressions. His lack of perspective and careful scholarship has led him into untenable positions which have, indirectly, had dreadful consequences for many innocent people.

Having said this, I must quote his powerful and accurate paragraph on the Eckstein episode, which seems to me unassailable as to the facts and unassailable (with one exception to be mentioned below) as to their interpretation. Without any hoo-ha about the putative analytical abilities of Freud, and with scant reverence for the numerology of Fliess, Masson, I believe, tells the truth about the disaster that occurred to one human guinea pig in Vienna in February 1895:

> Fliess's immediate response to the hemorrhage was to seek an explanation in terms of 28 and 23 rather than in terms of what he had done to the patient. While Freud could not go along with this in Emma's case without abandoning his scientific view, he, like Fliess (and no doubt for the benefit of Fliess), turned his investigation away from the operation, that is, away from an external source, and sought the cause of the bleeding in Emma Eckstein herself. To Emma Eckstein it would have been little comfort that Freud's was the more sophisticated procedure. The truth is that the source of her bleeding was to be found neither in series of 23-day and 28-day cycles nor in hysterical longing, but in an unnecessary operation which was performed because of a *folie à deux* on the part of two misguided doctors. (Masson, *The Assault on Truth*, 99)

Masson's last sentence is an eloquent and accurate assessment of the situation of Emma Eckstein as she was taken, with the surgeon Ignaz Rosanes (who had discovered the half-meter of gauze left in the nose by Fliess and removed it, thereby unleashing an almost fatal massive hemorrhaging),[16] from her private apartment to the Sanatorium Loew on Wednesday, March 6, 1895. It was there that Rosanes and Gersuny, and later Gussenbauer and Gersuny, carried out the next series of post-operative procedures to remedy the mistakes of Fliess, the surgeon, and of Freud, the physician, who had accepted the need for this bizarre intervention.

In spite of the many justified criticisms that have been leveled at *The Assault on Truth*—and it certainly stirred up a hornet's nest in the psychoanalytic community[17]—it contains, at moments, a profound ring of truth about Freud's cowardice when confronted with the choice between opting for an attempted exoneration of comrade Fliess (which was the path Freud chose) or an honest recognition of Fliess's misadventure and his own foolishness in accepting the validity of Fliess's nonsense about periodicity, about the relationship between the nose and female sexual organs, and about the nasal reflex neurosis.

In *The Assault on Truth*, Masson gives some direct (translated) citations from Fliess's infamous *Die Beziehungen zwischen Nase und weiblichen Geschlechtsorganen* (*The Relationship between the Nose and Female Sexual Organs*). One case instance mentioned by Fliess includes the periodicity theorem and the removal of the middle nasal concha of a fifty-three-year-old patient, Frau N. The reported operation was carried out a year after the Eckstein Vienna catastrophe of February 1895—in Berlin on March 12, 1896. Masson has done a great service to the public at large by indicating, by quotation and by commentary, the sheer imbecilities credited by Fliess himself (since he put them in his book) which gave rise to Benjamin Ry's amazed disgust that such a volume could appear under the imprint of a reputable medical publisher, Deuticke.

This little paragraph should be treasured by those who still imagine that Sigmund Freud had the slightest grasp of human behavioral or physiological responses in 1895.[18] This is a snippet of what Masson offers:

> On March 12, 1896, Fliess probed what was left of her left middle concha, which had been removed earlier (most likely by Fliess himself). As he was carrying out this examination, she developed massive bleeding, which could only be stopped by a very tight packing. At the same time, tears mixed with blood came pouring out of her right eye. On the night of the 13th she had a bloody discharge from her vagina. Fliess "explained" to her right away that the bleeding was vicarious (*Die Blutung wurde sofort als vicariirende angesprochen*). Proof: between March 1, 1892, and March 12, 1896, 1,472 days had elapsed, that is 64 times 23, her male period. (*The Assault on Truth*, 98-99)

But the truth—as far as Freud is concerned—is far worse than even Masson allows.

Masson writes that Freud could not go along with Fliess's periodicity theses "in Emma's case *without abandoning his scientific view.*" We know that over a year after Emma Eckstein's operation Freud was computing the supposed accuracy of Fliess's numerology with respect to the birth of his last child, Anna, (see chapter 2, page 37 above). At the end of the following month (letter of April 26, 1896)—hence a year after the postoperative interventions on Eckstein—Freud, whose sessions with Eckstein teaching her how the hemorrhages had been neurotically self-induced were always faithfully reported to Fliess, writes to the Berlin magician:

> First of all, Eckstein. I shall be able to prove to you that you were right, that her episodes of bleeding were hysterical, were occasioned by *longing*, and probably occurred at the sexually relevant times (the woman, out of resistance, has not yet supplied me with the dates). (Masson 1985, 183)

In other words, in this case—as in so many others—Freud had *no* "scientific view," for his "scientific views" were little else than a personal grasp of the various notions bruited about by Fliess. This is equally true, incidentally, for Freud's understanding of his own frequent heart arrhythmia. He had been troubled by this for some years and had even consulted Breuer about it, fearing a dilation of the heart (letter to Fliess of April 25, 1894). But his letter of June 12, 1895, confirms his acceptance of Fliess's diagnosis that the nose was the causative organ of the heart's irregularity.[19]

Hence the importance of the letter of 1893 which opens this chapter. "Nasal reflex neurosis"—without any apparent change in patients' presenting symptoms—had suddenly, and rapidly, become Freud's chief diagnosis of those innocents who came to see him. And he appeared to be completely dependent upon Fliess for any postoperative recommendations. In the letter of March 4, 1895, referring to the disappointment of the cocaine technique for women in labor, Freud's fourth paragraph concerns Emma Eckstein:

> Eckstein's condition is still unsatisfactory: persistent swelling, going up and down "like an avalanche"; pain, so that morphine cannot be dispensed with; bad nights. The purulent secretion has been decreasing since yesterday; the day before yesterday (Saturday) she had a massive hemorrhage, probably as a result of expelling a bone chip the size of a heller [a small coin]; there were two bowls full of pus. Today we encountered resistance on irrigation; and since the pain and the visible edema had increased, I let myself be persuaded to call in Gersuny. . . . He explained that the access was considerably narrowed and insufficient for drainage, inserted a drainage tube, and threatened to break it [the bone?] open if that did not stay in. To judge by the smell, all this is most likely correct. Please send me your authoritative advice. I am not looking forward to new surgery on this girl. (Masson 1985, 113-14)

This same letter of March 4, 1895, mentions Freud's discussions with Breuer about this case and about their joint volume, *Studies on Hysteria*. Freud notes: "I visited him on Sunday evening and once again won him over—probably only for a short time—by telling him about the analysis of Eckstein, with which you are not really familiar either" (Masson 1985, 114). The first thought that occurs to *this* reader on considering these phrases of Freud is *why* had Fliess not been made familiar with "the analysis of Eckstein"? It is not now, in the twenty-first century, nor was it then, in the late nineteenth century, customary for a physician to recruit a surgeon for a case without having previously informed him of the standing of the case and of the need for his intervention.

That Freud should have accepted Fliess's intervention *without* the latter knowing the details of the reasons for the intervention argues gross malpractice on Freud's part as the physician looking after Emma Eckstein. Even if Freud felt confident about the mumbo jumbo of Fliess's "nasal reflex neurosis," he should have fully informed the intervening surgeon of the grounds for the intervention. Against this standard deontological objection, of course, one can respond (though the response is scarcely to Freud's credit) that knowing, as he did, the significance for Fliess of the nasal neurosis complex and knowing, as he did, the reasons for the turbinate bone operation proposed by Fliess and its intended objectives, Freud had no need to consult his friend further on the diagnosis arrived at on his patient. He evidently believed that his patient suffered from the "nasal neurosis complex" and that her state would be remedied by the surgical magic of Fliess.

There is an indication that, at one stage in the several crises of the postoperative traumas, Freud began to doubt the original diagnosis he had made and, in consequence, the necessity of Fliess's weird operation. In the letter of Friday, March 8, 1895, which recounts Rosanes's pulling at the piece of iodoform gauze left behind by Fliess and unleashing a massive hemorrhage (this is the incident in the Eckstein apartment which prompted the urgent removal of the patient to the Sanatorium Loew), Freud disclaims that it was the sight of so much blood that overwhelmed him; it was rather his strong emotional reactions to the sickening realization that he and Fliess had made a dreadful mistake. He writes:

> So we had done her an injustice; she was not at all abnormal,[20] rather, a piece of iodoform gauze had gotten torn off as you were removing it and stayed in for fourteen days, preventing healing; at the end it tore off and provoked the bleeding. (Masson 1985, 117)

The mixture of panic, sheer terror, and the scrambled beginnings of a "schoolboy" exculpation of Fliess—which the rest of the letter expands upon—is a moving testimony to Freud's sudden awareness of the disaster he had wrought.

One helpful consequence of this "sincerity" of a Freudian confessional letter, never intended for publication, has been the overlooking by historians and critics of psychoanalysis of the real significance and implications of what Freud wrote. There are two points to bear in mind, neither to Freud's credit, but both definitely indicated in his comments. The first is the obvious non sequitur of the reality of Eckstein's mental state and the mess created by Fliess's surgical error in leaving the length of gauze behind. It does not follow *because* Fliess had left some gauze behind, that *therefore* Eckstein was *gar nicht abnorm*. The corollary of this would be that had Fliess not been remiss in the operation and *not* left any gauze behind, then Eckstein would have been abnormal.

The second, and much more disturbing, point is this: nowhere in his panicky, and hence deeply sincere, confession does Freud deny either the appropriateness of Fliess's operation on the turbinate bone or its ultimate utility to the patient. A mistake in diagnosis is recognized (for quite the wrong reasons, by the way); but this is implicitly followed by the notion that *had* the diagnosis been correct, then the operation would have been justified. In other words, Freud had learned *nothing*, scientifically or medically, from Fliess's mistake. He still gave credit to the validity of the operation *for the right person*. This is precisely what one would expect from an examination, from a medical or even largely empirical point of view, of Freud's writings. The comments on his footnoted case of the (probable) multiple sclerosis girl in *Studies on Hysteria*, as well as the understanding of the case of Frau Emmy von N., even thirty-five years later, are no different. Ignorance, arrogance, and what the French call *suffisance* are the hallmarks of Freud's case histories. It is almost as if he refuses to recognize his errors, *deliberately*.

Freud's subsequent letters to Fliess during the lengthy aftermath of the Eckstein débâcle show that his momentary glimpse of the reality of the situation (which was, in effect, also a misunderstood glimpse) was quickly cast aside with the ongoing "therapy" of Emma Eckstein. She had moments of night hysterias in the Sanatorium Loew. On March 15, 1895, Freud wrote to Fliess (much too optimistically, as it turned out):

Surgically, Eckstein will soon be well, [but] now the nervous effects of the incident are starting: hysterical attacks at night and similar symptoms which I must start to work on. It is now about time you forgave yourself the minimal oversight, as Breuer called it. (Masson 1985, 120)

Freud has now, apparently, but using the diplomatic cover of a phrase by Breuer, recognized that Fliess had indeed erred and was the one responsible for the young woman's hemorrhages. Nonetheless, this "self-evident" error of Fliess's was not to be the subject of Freud's continuing sessions with Eckstein. Freud was frequently called upon to continue his impressive suggestions to her that "she had always been a bleeder" and that her continuing discomfort was the result of ideation by her, based upon erotic longing. The error in diagnosis—"So we had done her an injustice, she was not at all abnormal"—was soon forgotten in the ensuing indoctrination of the convalescent Eckstein.

A serious issue that needs to be addressed here is whether having recognized—and so written to Fliess—the obvious surgical error of the latter, Freud therefore realized that the hemorrhages were indeed the inevitable and quite normal physiological response to this kind of surgical mishap. The above-quoted letter of March 15 leaves little room for doubt about this, even given the double rhetorical use of Breuer's authority—it allowed Freud to mention the fact that Fliess had made a mistake in practice, and at the same time it allowed Freud to minimize the extent of the error. This raises great problems for those who cherish the myth of Freud's integrity as well as for those (like Appignanesi and Forrester) who claim to see, in the "psychological" management of Emma Eckstein's mental stability as she was weaned off the intensive morphine medication necessitated by the severe pain subsequent to the Fliess operation, the "sureness of touch" of the creator of psychoanalysis. The bright and cheerful way in which Appignanesi and Forrester reinvent the precocious early maturity of psychoanalysis is quite endearing—as long as one remains in ignorance about what really happened and why, and the immense, and continuing, pain involved for the victim. Once one has knowledge of the reality, then the Appignanesi and Forrester approach becomes hideously and doubly chilling—because of its denial of an individual human suffering (that of Emma) and because of its support for an understanding of medical intervention based on such disasters.

Either Freud, in spite of the letter of March 15, had not grasped the effects of such wrongly performed invasive techniques (a clear sign of elementary medical incompetence); or he had indeed understood the necessary physical consequences of Fliess's error, and he was prepared, nonetheless, to ensure that the patient be convinced that her physiological distress was the consequence of a preexisting personality pattern.

The either/or scenario presented here offers two possibilities: Freud was a credulous incompetent; Freud was a conniving liar. There remains, it is true, a third possibility (which I tend to favor): Freud was *both* a credulous incompetent (this has to be the case given his continuing credence in the value of Fliess's operation)[21] *and* a conniving liar (this has to be true for the way he conducted the post-operative suggestive therapy of Emma). By the time he had finished with her "analysis" a couple of years or so later, Eckstein had become convinced of the dangers of childhood masturbation (she even wrote a pamphlet on the subject),[22] of her own ideational responsibility for the events of February 1895, and became, with teenage female patients of her very own, the first practicing female psychoanalyst certified by Freud himself. That the first victim becomes the first analyst and the first propagandist for the faith is a telling indication of the powers of persuasion of Sigmund Freud.

Who, in February 1895, including Freud himself, anticipating—albeit with tight-lipped anguish—the successful outcome of Fliess's operation, would have imagined that from this fiasco would come an innovatory approach to human ailments and from the patient herself, the first person, apart from Freud, to apply his principles to others? The injunction "take up thy bed and walk" may not have worked on the young woman probably suffering from multiple sclerosis reported in the footnote to the Frau Emmy von N. case in *Studies on Hysteria*; but it worked with spectacular success on poor Emma Eckstein (with the exception, it must be said, of precisely the ability to walk without pain; see below).

Jeffrey Moussaieff Masson has an interesting coda to the Eckstein affair. In his Appendix A at the end of *The Assault on Truth*, Masson finds what he believes to be a reference to Emma Eckstein in Freud's very late work "Analysis Terminable and Interminable"—I think Masson's educated hunch is perfectly correct. He quotes Freud (*S.E.*, 23, 222) and mentions the problems with walking that a certain patient of his had. Although Freud's report of this unnamed patient is self-congratulatory in a deceptive way ("The successful analytic treatment took place so long ago that we cannot expect too much from it"), Masson argues—and I think with sound judgment—that it is indeed a reference to Emma Eckstein and her treatment in 1895. We know from the letters to Fliess that Eckstein did suffer from difficulty in walking and that Freud thought he was being successful in improving her walking. For example, the last paragraph of the letter of May 25, 1895, states: "Emma E. is finally doing very well and I have succeeded in once more alleviating her weakness in walking, which also set in again" (Masson 1985, 130).

Freud has no explanation that I have discovered, either in the correspondence with Fliess or elsewhere in any published papers, for the walking difficulties of Emma Eckstein (nor, of course, are they anywhere discussed, or even mentioned, by Appignanesi and Forrester). This is an important gap in our understanding of Freud's early psychoanalytic work; Emma Eckstein came to him with problems relating to irregular and painful periods; but she may also have presented herself as one who had difficulty walking. Could Freud resolve or at least alleviate that problem? If such was the case (of her presenting symptoms), it makes the intervention of Fliess and his nasal solutions even more problematic. (And it raises the matter of whether Freud ever broached the issue of the walking impairment of Eckstein to Fliess before the operation.) Freud claims in his letter to Fliess to have alleviated "her weakness in walking." That alleviation was temporary and, according to her nephew, Albert Hirst, was followed by frequent relapses. It should be noted, for what it reveals of the limitations of the obsessive sexual themes chosen by Freud for the "management" of Eckstein's recovery from the Fliess operation, that in none of the reports sent to Fliess does Freud once suggest that the difficulty in walking has been a thematic subject of the "analysis." For the last ten years of her life she was virtually confined to a couch.

From the Jones Archives in London, Masson unearthed an intriguing interview by K. R. Eissler (then in charge of the New York Freud Archives) with the nephew of Emma Eckstein, Albert Hirst, who had himself undergone an analysis with Freud. Hirst, *pace* Borch-Jacobsen, refers to his aunt as Freud's "first patient"—that is, first *psychoanalytic* patient. The commentary and quotation of Masson are worth citing here. They demonstrate so clearly the way in which Freud manipulated people and events, and the memory of those events, so that the reality of the original situation was forever lost in a fog of specious rhetoric:

> Freud writes that the analysis of this patient was a success. Hirst also wrote an autobiography, *Analysed and Reeducated by Freud Himself*, which was never published. (Albert Hirst's niece, Dr. Hanna E. Kapit, in New York, kindly sent me a copy of this autobiography.) He begins the chapter entitled "Aunt Emma" with these words:

One of Freud's earliest successes as an analyst, perhaps his earliest, was the cure of the neurosis of my aunt Emma.

In the interview with Eissler he said:

I think it was of importance to him [Freud] in his practice that he had this great success, this well-known girl, this girl of a well-known family. Now she was a very beautiful woman and after he had this great success, she for several years led a perfectly normal life. . . .

As for the symptoms of not being able to walk, Hirst (autobiography) writes that "she spent all her days on her couch, never left her room, not even for meals, could not walk." (This is also mentioned in a letter to Fliess.) Freud writes that "she proved inaccessible to a further attempt at analysis," and Hirst (interview) says: "There was a time when . . . Freud would come to her and try to continue the analysis. There was a conflict between him and her." Freud ends by saying that "she remained abnormal to the end of her life." Hirst (autobiography) writes: "Emma . . . soon returned to her couch on which she had lived so long. She survived, as a hopeless invalid, for another ten years." (Masson, *The Assault on Truth*, 255-56)

Those interested in pursuing this further can consult Appendix A of *The Assault on Truth*, which is a mine of intricate information collected by Masson. What emerges quite clearly from his researches, and from my own reading of the Freud–Fliess correspondence, is that Emma Eckstein did not suffer from a "nasal reflex neurosis," that she did not benefit from Freud's postoperative suggestions, that her walking impairment was not improved by Freud's methods of therapy. In short, her experiences with Sigmund Freud were totally negative. That Freud should later conveniently remember this as a "success" (even an anonymous one) is understandable.

During the early months of Eckstein's indoctrination, roughly coincidental with the spring of 1895, Freud was still dealing with the remnants of the other disaster of Fliess's Viennese visit—the failure of his clinical experiment on the use of cocaine in the nostrils to alleviate the pains of women in labor. In the already quoted enclosure (dated March 15) to the letter of March 13, 1895, prior to discussing Eckstein's progress, Freud begins with some comments on the "unreliability" of the gynecologist Chrobak—at whose clinic Fliess had conducted his cocaine experiments—and notes the rumors already circulating about Fliess's experimental efforts:

But listen, the two letters from Chrobak are precisely what we know here as an addition to Chrobakian *bonhomie*: pettiness and unreliability. This confirms the reports that are making the rounds. Gersuny says Chrobak always adopts the opinions of those around him. I am indeed convinced that your reply is dignified and that this matter will be settled in a few weeks. What kind of hair-splitting entitles him to say the labor pains have *not* been eliminated by your experiment? (Masson 1985, 119)

Nearly two weeks later (letter of Thursday, March 28, 1895) Freud returns to the vexed topic of the Viennese failure of Fliess's explorations and suggests that he confound Chrobak by using his Berlin experiments, which would allow him to outweigh numerically the failures in Vienna:

I think you will soon have worked your way out of it and then tackle the labor pains first. By chance, I recently had a conversation with Chrobak about them. My impression was unfavorable. I would like to see you dispense with all his cases, which, moreover, you do not need. The public will misunderstand [your article on] "labor pains" as "painless birth," which would be claiming too much. These should have been distinguished and so forth. Make sure you get well, publish forty cases, and make him [i.e., Chrobak] a present of his four. I do not know whether I should infect you: I am so very annoyed. (Masson 1985, 122)

Freud's use of "forty cases" is biblical hyperbole and no doubt an attempt to encourage Fliess. Two months later (letter of May 25, 1895) Freud suggests, more seriously, the need for Fliess to publish a paper on the Vienna painless-birth experiments: "There seems to me to be an urgent need for communicating the labor pain story. Do you already have twenty-five cases? Let Chrobak be a little angry—or a lot, if he prefers" (Masson 1985, 129). Thereafter, for the remainder of the correspondence there is no word either of Chrobak or of Fliess's Viennese attempts to render labor painless by the administration of cocaine to certain parts of the nostrils of the women in waiting.

As for Fliess's other Viennese endeavor—on Eckstein—her name rumbles on through the correspondence for over two years, with Freud detailing various outbreaks of pain and hemorrhaging through to the summer of 1895. His "analysis" (which went on until 1897 at least) of her predisposition to bleeding has traced this to a sense of childhood deprivation of affection, so that Emma, Freud suggests, "used" her apparent tendency to bleed easily to gain affection. We have no empirical knowledge of these Freudian-based "recollections" of Emma's childhood.

They were, it is true, highly convenient for Freud at that time.

These instances of an early pattern of "compensation-through-illness" have no empirical relevance whatever to the consequences of the Fliess procedure. Neither have they necessarily any empirical relevance to the childhood experienced by Emma and later subject to "rememoration" oriented by the theme chosen by Freud. His choice of theme inevitably limits the accuracy of significance of the assumed recall. But, even supposing that Emma's childhood recollections were not contaminated by Freud's selective approach, and were, largely, accurate—*of what were they an accurate recall*? Of a childhood deprived of natural affection and love and caring? Perhaps. Or of a childhood remembered as having been so deprived by an overdemanding child whom no amount of affection would satisfy? Also perhaps.

It is here in this nonempirical dilemma of any attempt at therapy by recourse to patient-rememoration that medical or moral or philosophical psychotherapy ceases to be a scientific investigation and inevitably becomes (as many sensitive and valuable therapists—like Peter Lomas in Britain—recognize) an art where, for successful treatment outcome, an intuitive response to, and understanding of, the patient's present personality is essential for any improvement in the patient's contemporary sense of self-worth. Whether Freud was (as he sometimes declared himself to be) the originator of such an art is another matter altogether. Certainly his handling of the Emma Eckstein case is no evidence for his recognition of the importance of an open-minded, non-a-priori listening to the patient; but that was clearly not his goal in her case.

There are some comments by C. G. Jung from his lecture "Analytical Psychology and Education" which are pertinent to Freud's analytic examination of the convalescing Eckstein (and indeed to most of Freud's subsequent known case histories):

> Naïveté is out of place in psychotherapy. The doctor, like the educator, must always keep his eyes open to the possibility of being consciously or unconsciously deceived, not merely by his patient, but above all by himself. The tendency to live in illusion and to believe in a fiction of oneself—in the good sense or in the bad—is almost insuperably great. . . .
>
> Since there is no nag that cannot be ridden to death, all theories of neurosis and methods of treatment are a dubious affair. . . . A doctrinal system like that of Freud or Adler consists on the one hand of technical rules, and on the other of the pet emotive ideas of its author.[23]

Writing as someone who is not a "Jungian," I confess to a great appreciation of the elementary sanity of these lines. It is almost as if Jung had had access to the case notes on Eckstein and were writing a critical response to them. Jung, as we know, had access neither to any case notes on Eckstein, nor to the intimacies of the Freud–Fliess correspondence. It remains to his credit, I believe, that he could have had such intelligent and moral insight on the dangers of certain kinds of psychotherapy as early as 1924 (the year of Freud's last revision of the case of Frau Emmy von N.), when this lecture was first given, in English, in London.

In January 1897, Freud was delving into fantasy sequences reported by Eckstein—or so he claims to Fliess—where, by a curious but understandable combination, his own contemporary interest in the treatment by the Inquisition of suspected witches was linked to "scenes" phantasmagorically recalled by her in analysis. We never discover, incidentally, whether these sequences of medieval diabolism were suggested to Eckstein by Freud, or whether, by a sheer fluke, as it were, she was privately and independently studying those topics which happened to coincide with Freud's current preoccupation. This late "deep" investigation of Eckstein's mental state is still fraught (if the correspondence with Fliess is to be credited) with an overwhelming concern to exculpate the Berlin magician from any responsibility for Emma's physical damage. An instance of this is the letter of January 17, 1897. Freud writes: "Eckstein has a scene [that is, remembers][24] where the diabolus sticks needles into her fingers and then places a candy on each drop of blood. As far as the blood is concerned, you are absolutely without blame!" (Masson 1985, 224-25). Freud's exculpatory phrase is not called for by anything previous in this letter (or even in the preceding one); it indicates more Freud's continuing alarm than Fliess's badgering of some two years earlier for a "testimonial letter" from Gersuny that the operation on Emma Eckstein had been carried out correctly.[25]

One minor point about this quotation that requires comment is Masson's use of editorial square brackets to explicate the phrase "has a scene": "[that is, remembers]." This implies an interpretation of the facts that is not wholly justified. One must recognize that, when he was compiling the unexpurgated correspondence for Harvard University Press, Masson—although highly critical of what he saw as Freud's reneging on the "seduction hypothesis"—was nonetheless still an uncritical adherent of the early work of Freud.[26] He has elsewhere commented on Freud's various uses of the German "Szene" and suggested that Freud's use of this term changed from one of "recollected event" to one of "imagined event." His editorial intervention—"that is, remembers"—is more a remnant of his earlier Freudian indoctrination than an objective and informative editorial remark. We have no reason to believe that Emma Eckstein "remembered" such a fantasy where the devil and candy and blood are inextricably interwoven into themes of medieval Freudian significance. On the assumption that Freud did not invent this story for the edification of friend Fliess, one is left with two possibilities not allowed for by Masson's editorial intervention. Either Emma was producing inventive fantasies to please her analyst (this is what Appignanesi and Forrester generously call "her eager collaboration in her analysis"; see *Freud's Women*, 137), or she was embroidering possible, partial recollections of moments of past fantasizing with images that suited the present charged atmosphere of the hours spent with Freud. Masson's "that is, remembers" is totally misleading and needs to be changed in any new edition of the Harvard volume. There is no way that Masson can substantiate his claim that Eckstein's reported fantasy responses to Freud were "memories"—even of past fantasies.

A week later on January 24, 1897, Freud, in the letter which begins with his tale of the phonographic recall of a patient (unnamed, but perhaps Eckstein?) of a conversation overheard at age eleven months, makes a series of statements (some of them uncritically reported by Appignanesi and Forrester) that bring to mind Breuer's earlier remark that Freud should consider "moral insanity" as one of his characteristics.

The letter begins with Freud responding to an observation by Fliess about the origin of convulsions.[27] The mentality responsible for the opening paragraph is not that of the sober, aware physician; it is that of the cocaine-encumbered mind discovering impossible etiologies within phantasmagoria of its own creation. Freud writes, and one really needs to read this paragraph to understand the grotesqueries being performed in Vienna in the closing years of the nineteenth century,

> Most of my hunches *in neuroticis* [in regard to neuroses] subsequently turned out to be true. Incidentally, the whole thing is based on a case in which epileptiform convulsions could with certainty be traced back to similar excitations in later months. I do not yet have new material. The early period before the age of 1½ years is becoming ever more significant.
> I am inclined to distinguish several periods even within it. Thus I was able to trace back, with certainty, a hysteria that developed in the context of a periodic mild depression to a seduction, which occurred for the first time at

11 months and [I could] hear again the words that were exchanged between two adults at that time! It is as though it comes from a phonograph. The temporal determination of epilepsy (hysterical) and hysterical psychosis therefore lies further back. But there is also a psychotic feature in the periodicity of the mild depression. (Masson 1985, 226)

This is the paragraph Appignanesi and Forrester should have exploited; it deals solely and explicitly with what they call the "prehistoric" period. One has to bear in mind that Freud is, in each case mentioned here (there seem to be two patients involved), talking about the reputed infantile recall of the adults he is dealing with. Apart from the obvious idiocy of the phonographic recall from a baby aged eleven months (and conjured, if the patient was indeed Emma Eckstein, from a young woman now in her late twenties), the rest of this paragraph deserves close scrutiny. Some phrases make no sense at all; some phrases—for example, the last one, "But there is also a psychotic feature in the periodicity of the mild depression"—only make sense if one incorporates into them the "periodicity" theorems of Fliess. The sentence before this—"The temporal determination of epilepsy (hysterical) and hysterical psychosis therefore lies further back"—offers a splendid example of Freud's inability, or refusal, to recognize that he does not understand what epilepsy is (it is *not* ideational; it is the product of a neurological lesion that has nothing to do with the psychology of the patient) and also that what he calls "hysterical psychosis" must have originated in a psychological impairment created by a "seduction" before the age of eleven months! His "therefore" links this comment to the previous one concerning the impossible (and thus contrived—but by *whom*? by the patient? by Freud himself? by the patient with Freud's help?) "phonographic" replay of an overheard conversation. If, on the other hand, this is an early instance of "constructions in analysis"—and it is—then it is sheer confabulation even within the intimacy of a communication to (*Teurer*) 'Dear' Wilhelm.

There are five grave errors in this paragraph which need to be mentioned, given that they were to become essential aspects of what was to evolve as doctrinaire Freudianism and that many of them were to remain on the books of those who saw themselves as "post-Freudian revisionist" analysts. They concern, respectively:

(1) the search for "origins" of an ideational (that is, psychological) nature;

(2) the notion that the discovery of these origins is necessary for the "cure" of the patient;

(3) the belief that accurate recall of the earliest months of life is accessible to people;

(4) the related belief that absence of such recall is evidence of "repression" (itself conceived of as an ideational activity) or of some other damaging psychological character trait;

(5) the refusal (or at least minimization) of neurological deficiencies unresponsive to psychological approaches.

Later on in the same letter, Freud invokes the strange rites of imagined cults in the Semitic East. Appignanesi and Forrester prune their quotation cleverly and present it, without challenging any of its implications, as a follow-up report to Fliess on what Freud has obtained from his interrogations of Emma. Here is Freud's paragraph (unpruned):

> I am beginning to grasp an idea: it is as though in the perversions, or which hysteria is the negative, we have before us a remnant of a primeval sexual cult, which once was—perhaps still is—a religion in the Semitic East (Moloch, Astarte). Imagine, I obtained a scene about the circumcision of a girl. The cutting off of a piece of the labium minor (which is even shorter today), sucking up the blood, after which the child was given a piece of skin to eat. This child, at age 13, once claimed that she could swallow a part of an earth-worm and proceeded to do it. An operation you once performed was affected by a hemophilia that originated in this way. (Masson 1985, 227)

Appignanesi and Forrester have this to say about the part of the above paragraph that they have chosen to quote (they begin at "Imagine"):

> Emma's longing, her eager collaboration in her analysis, gave Freud much precious material; she had the ability to provoke him emotionally—'So this is the strong sex!'—and to contribute substantial changes and fundamental new elements to his theories: the wish theory of psychosis and dreams;[28] the transferential reconstruction of her early pleasures in menstruation and its prehistory in her battles with her family; fantastic scenes from her inner life, in the no-man's land between fantasy and memory, resonating with the sadistic acts and fantasies of a former historical epoch. And she showed Freud how his ideas and techniques would finally make their way in the world. Not through publications, books and lectures, but along the prolonged and painful path by which his unhappy and neurotic patients would themselves become analysts. (*Freud's Women*, 137)

There certainly is a fine frenzy rolling through their phrases. This passage reads—if read silently—like the back-cover blurb for some Harlequin romance. It sounds—if read aloud—like the dark chocolate baritone voiceover urging one to see the movie being previewed, soon coming to a cinema near you. Try it in the privacy of your own bathroom! It answers, however, none of the many issues raised by Freud's extravagant words. The reason (and incidentally the *only* reason) that Appignanesi and Forrester assume this passage to be entirely about Eckstein is the footnote given by Masson to the last sentence: "An operation you once performed was affected by a hemophilia that originated in this way." Masson (Masson 1985, 228) notes of this sentence: "A reference to the operation on Eckstein."

Masson doesn't *know* this; he has merely hypothesized that, given what we can deduce of the Freud–Fliess relationship, the sentence *must* refer to Emma Eckstein's unfortunate brush with fate. He may not be wrong; indeed he is probably correct. If he is right, then he should also have questioned, and in the very same footnote, Freud's understanding of how "hemophilia" originates. It does not originate from surgical malpractice; and, in any case, Eckstein was not a hemophiliac—if she had been, she would have been dead before Freud could have begun his sagacious transformations of reality on her.

Another difficulty avoided both by Masson and by Appignanesi and Forrester is that of the length of the *labium minor* —or of one of them (they are situated either side of the vulva)—"which is even shorter today." This weird passage begins, we recall, with "I obtained a scene about the circumcision of a girl." We are not told how Freud "obtained" this "scene," which is a pity. It is inaccurate with respect to real "female circumcision" (or "genital mutilation" as it is rightly referred to today), whereby in some customs—but not all—the removal from both sides of the vulva of the *labia minora* is called for as well as the clitoridectomy, which is a universal feature of the practice. What is unusual about Freud's tale to Fliess is that he steps out of the role of raconteur of patients' memories/fantasies and remarks in parentheses, and *in the present tense*, "which is even shorter today." This puts us, as readers of the Freud–Fliess correspondence, into an awkward position. Are we to take on trust what he himself has (apparently) taken on trust? Or are we to imagine a moment at Berggasse 19 or at the Sanatorium Loew where Emma, thrusting modesty aside for the sake of science, reveals her pubic disequilibrium? Freud's present tense—"which is even shorter today"—allows no hesitation. And what was Fliess supposed to make of this communication?

This extract from Freud's letter to Fliess about his continuing (and suggestive) postoperative treatment of Emma Eckstein—whether the fantasy was induced by Freud or produced "spontaneously" and submissively by Eckstein—is perhaps among the first recorded nineteenth-century psychoanalytic instances of what has become a current plague in "therapeutic" North America, the kind of present-day recovered memory of abuse so comprehensively examined by Mark Pendergrast in his excellent and wide-ranging *Victims of Memory*.[29] As the clinical psychologist Janet D. Feigenbaum succinctly notes in her review of Pendergrast's study:

> In order to highlight the unbelievability and unscientific nature of the debate, Pendergrast examines some of the claims of proponents of recovered memories. He cites cases of women who are still virgins claiming to have had intercourse; claiming to have eaten the remains of their own twin for whom there are no records of the birth; and to have been videotaped during bizarre and horrific events for which no copy of any video has ever surfaced.[30]

How on earth, in other words, did Freud know that one half of the vaginal lips of Emma was shorter than the other half? Appignanesi and Forrester, with the wisdom of the converted, do not address silly issues such as this. They are safe and happy within the mythological realm they have opted to inhabit. And as long as they stay within their Hobbit precincts, no harm will come to them. Outside the Frodo fantasy of Appignanesi and Forrester, more serious issues are involved.

Such issues include: serious and accurate medical diagnosis; serious and accurate reporting of a case history; serious and accurate historiography; serious and accurate recognition of deception when it is encountered; in short, serious and accurate history. Obviously pretty boring stuff. No! decided Appignanesi and Forrester, let's go for the sexy legend. And our success will prove Freud's everlasting value—at least to authors who, as true believers, seem intent on retailing passionate propaganda of misinformation as if it were serious and accurate (and honest) medical history. No doubt there were some readers of *Freud's Women* who believed that they were being given the inside story. The value of the present little volume will be to show without rhetorical flourish that the *real* inside story has yet to be written. When it is, the future public will have probably forgotten the importance that Freud once had for their parents' and grandparents' generations. He will be remembered as an Anton Mesmer of the history books who once wreaked havoc on at least two generations of American (and French) psychiatric scholarship.

It is clearly time for an interlude so that we can relax and observe Freud's treatment of a young woman who was also a singer. Or should I have said, a young singer who was also a woman?

Notes

1. See Masson 1985, 49.

2. Of the many objections to the likelihood of such an "overheard" conversation being recollected by a patient, two are preeminent (one of which Freud should have realized): (a) at the age of eleven months the linguistic proficiencies of the child are insufficient to have "recorded" the speech patterns of the "overheard" adults (Freud here has forgotten his Latin and the reason why "infants" are so called—from the Latin *infans*, present participle of the verb *infari*, to be incapable of speech); (b) the myeline sheathing necessary for long-term memory circuits has scarcely begun to be developed at this age—see the comments of the French surgeon and sexologist Gérard Zwang in *La Statue de Freud* (Paris: Robert Laffont, 1985).

3. This may be an appropriate place to mention that the critical psychoanalytic terms "transference," "resistance," and "suggestion" were *all* borrowed by Freud from current language at the Salpêtrière dealing with hypnotism, hysteria, and magnetism. "Le transfert" (in German *Übertragung*) originally referred, at the Salpêtrière, to two kinds of supposed response (muscular and ideational) to the placement of ordinary magnets (not electromagnets) on the left or right side of the cranium, or to the left or right side extremities.

Perhaps the most comprehensive discussion on "transference" (*"le transfert"*—still the current psychoanalytic term in France for the emotional reaction of the patient to the analyst, which assumes a reinvestment of forgotten infantile memories whereby the analyst becomes a parent analogue—as is "transference" in English), and which Freud almost certainly consulted, appeared in the *Revue philosophique* a couple of months before Freud's descent upon Paris. This was the extensive article by A. Binet and Charles Féré, entitled "L'hypnotisme chez les hystériques: Le transfert," *La Revue philosophique*, Tome 19 (janvier-juin 1885): 1-25. It includes references to Charcot and Bernheim and to various types of induced partial paralyses.

In fact, a study of this article makes many of Freud's early literary productions—whether case histories or theoretical essays—comprehensible (though no more reliable). For those who read French, here is one article which embraces the threesome: hysteria, hypnotism, magnetism. I will translate one paragraph (from *La Revue philosophique* 20) to give the flavor:

> The transference action of the magnet deserves to be considered in a special manner in the *localised paralyses*. One can transfer a host of these paralyses. Let us choose the one which consists in the forgetting of a name. We suggest to one of our female patients the forgetting of the name of M. Féré whom she has known for more or less ten years. When she is awakened from hypnosis, it is impossible for her not only to articulate this name, but to recognize it when it is pronounced; and although she can spell all the letters which compose it, she is unable to read it, and even more, to write it (incidentally, her writing skills are very poor). She is, therefore, subject, relative to this name, to a complex aphasia. Everything is there: motor aphasia, agraphia, verbal blindness. We apply a magnet near her right arm: after seven minutes, there is a slight trembling of her right hand, the patient complains of a right-sided headache, a little forward and a little below that produced in the case of experimenting on her arm. Then, the pain passes to the left and offers several oscillations determining an indefinable sensation. The patient says: "It's as if there were swing doors between the two sides of my brain." A moment later she says without hesitating: "M. Féré" and she recognizes the name in all its forms. The magnet is withdrawn, and the subject is asked to repeat the name without interruption. She repeats it correctly a dozen times, Féré, Féré, Féré . . . etc., then she says Féry, Férou . . . finally she stops and says "I can't take any more" ["*Je ne puis plus*"].

4. There is no published evidence of Freud ever having done what all medical students are now required to do—that is, to take a serious, objective history of the patient prior to any recommendation concerning possible treatment plans.

The nearest Freud comes to this is in the opening section "I. The Clinical Picture" in the Dora case. But this prelude is so craftily woven into the narrative of the whole, including the presentation of material whose significance would be revealed only later in the tale, that the very pleasure one takes in reading it (or indeed in rereading it as a kind of vintage Kipling yarn with the quiet, sobersides voice of the narrator guiding our steps into his world) is precisely that of a kind of "willing suspension of disbelief" as one submits to the seduction of a master narrator. Medical students are, fortunately, *not* trained to write "histories" in this fashion.

5. But see also, for further neurological and medical incompetencies, the scathing review of Elisabeth Roudinesco's biography of Lacan in *The Times Higher Education Supplement* (October 31, 1997, 20), appropriately entitled

"The Shrink from Hell," by English neurologist and gerontologist Raymond Tallis.

6. Martha Noel Evans. *Fits and Starts: A Genealogy of Hysteria in Modern France*. Ithaca: Cornell University Press, 1991. See, in particular, the first chapter, "Charcot and the Heyday of Hysteria," 9-50, for a well-documented account of the atmosphere at the Salpêtrière during Charcot's time.

7. Borch-Jacobsen has said that he does not consider the Eckstein case to be the necessary founding case of psychoanalysis. I agree with him. It is an instance, one among very many, of Freud's diagnostic mistakes. It is, by virtue of the Freud–Fliess correspondence, the best-documented case to date of Freud's endeavors to produce a "therapy" that would be more than merely physical. The medical catastrophes that had appeared to begin with Freud's infatuation for the Anna O. scenario were doubtless widespread; but we do not have the evidence to convict. As I see it, the Emma Eckstein case is merely one instance of what was an ongoing pattern in Freud's Viennese practice.

8. Whether Freud approached Fliess with a direct request for surgical intervention, or succumbed to Fliess's enthusiasm for the nose operation, or was, against his better judgment, persuaded—seduced—into allowing it to take place is not known. What is evident, however, is that it was Freud who first mentioned the patient Eckstein to Fliess and, presumably, as an instance of the nasal reflex neurosis which he had been diagnosing "very often" as "one of the most frequent disturbances" for nearly two years. Freud's letter of March 8, 1895, clearly states: ". . . how wrong I was to urge you to operate in a foreign city where you could not follow through on the case . . ." And, again, his letter of March 13, 1895, recounting the miserable post-operative problems of Emma Eckstein, implies that it was indeed Freud who initiated the intervention of Fliess: "In my thoughts I have given up hope for the poor girl and am inconsolable that I involved you and created such a distressing affair for you." (Masson 1985, 121)

9. Robert Gersuny (1844-1924) was the first director of the hospital called the Rudolfinerhaus and was a well-known plastic surgeon; he later became involved in the attempt to repair Fliess's damage to Eckstein. See below.

10. See Wilcocks, *Maelzel's Chess Player*, chapter 3, 92.

11. See Masson 1985, note 1, 112-13, for information relating to this event.

12. It is important to realize that the "isolation" recalled by Freud in his own self-serving memoir of the beginnings of psychoanalysis was *not* imposed by his Viennese colleagues as he implies; it was self-originated, following his willing acceptance of Fliess's requests to keep his distance from his Viennese medical peers. Fliess's motives seem to have been that Freud was the potential "weak link" in the chain of his (Fliess's) medical reputation.

13. This is an unusual surname, even in the Europe of the Austro-

Hungarian Empire. Frank J. Sulloway in *Freud, Biologist of the Mind* suggests, without explanation, that it is an abbreviation (using the first and last letters of the surname) for Dr. Benjamin Rischawy. But Sulloway appends a question mark ["?"] to show his uncertainty. Whether it was written by "Ry" or by "Rischawy," the commentary deserves serious reading. The name "Ry" will be used in the following text.

14. See Masson 1985, 310, note 4. Ry's last point is as relevant today as when he first wrote it. Webster, who quotes this passage (223), seems not to accept its validity or current relevance to the contemporary "Freud Debate," to judge from his response to Frederick Crews in their quarrel over *The Memory Wars*. See Webster, "Freud and the Judaeo–Christian Tradition," *The Times Literary Supplement* (July 4, 1997): 17. And yet, what Benjamin Ry wrote about Fliess would have been just as pointedly accurate had it been directed at Freud's writings then or later. Was Ry, or Rischawy, a medically informed precursor of Sir Karl Popper? Or a one-man Sokal and Bricmont?

15. One of the amusing Miss Marple aspects of Freud studies is the sheer amount of cross-checking and cross-referencing one has to do, not merely with the letters in the Freud–Fliess correspondence against each other, but also against other correspondence and with various published pieces. The amount of sheer misinformation (sometimes perhaps forgetful, sometimes willful, sometimes strategically rhetorical) contained in Freud's "autobiographical" sketches of his beginnings and the beginnings of psychoanalysis has not yet been assessed to the full, and may never be.

16. This is merely the first of these nearly fatal hemorrhages. As late as Wednesday, March 20, 1895, that is, more or less a month after the original operation, Freud is writing to Fliess:

> Ten days after the second operation, after a normal course, she suddenly had pain and swelling again, of unknown origin. The following day, a hemorrhage; she was quickly packed. At noon, when they lifted the packing to examine her, renewed hemorrhage, so that she almost died. . . . Gussenbauer and Gersuny believe that she is bleeding from a large vessel—but which one?—and on Friday [*i.e., March 22*] they want to make an incision on the outside while compressing the carotid artery to see whether they can find the source. (Masson 1985, 121)

On the question of the *amount* of gauze left behind by Fliess, there appears to be no disagreement among Freudians or anti-Freudians. Was the "half-meter" mentioned in the letter to Fliess another example of Sigmundian hyperbole? Or had Fliess *really* left eighteen inches of gauze in Emma Eckstein's nose? Ear, nose and throat surgeons I have consulted find this an exaggerated claim. And one should recall that these eighteen inches were merely what was "torn off" from the postsurgical packing of Fliess.

17. Once seen as a new bright star in the American psychoanalytic firmament, Masson, with his openly critical stance to received analytic wisdom and especially with his decision to publish the complete Freud–Fliess letters (against the counsel of Kurt Eissler and other guardians of the Freud Archives), rapidly became *persona non grata* to the American analytic community. They closed ranks against him.

As Anthony Clare, professor of psychiatry at Trinity College, Dublin, noted in his review of Masson's later book *Against Therapy*:

> The force of this indictment of psychoanalysis has been superseded by the vitriolic responses of the psychoanalytical establishment. For all the supposed insights that their lengthy training has given them, the critics have manifested the classic pathological defences of repression, denial and projection. Resolutely denying the challenging ideas propounded by Masson, they have gone for the man, speculating on alleged deficiencies in his personality, in his psychoanalytic training, in his relationship with his parents, and in his relationship with Anna Freud. (*The Sunday Times* [London] June 18, 1989, G10)

18. The hushed-up Eckstein fiasco provides, on either alternative reading, the sufficient coup de grâce to psychoanalysis. Either Freud did *not* know how mistaken both he and Fliess were in their diagnostic procedures, and so his ability to comprehend human physiological/psychological difficulties becomes even more phantasmagorical; or, Freud *did* know about their mistakes and invented a post hoc series of confabulations and patient suggestions which were knowingly deceitful. In either case, the medical ignorance at the heart of the 1924 note on the Frau Emmy von N. case is here repeated with a vengeance.

19. See Masson 1985, 132: "I need a lot of cocaine. Also, I have started smoking again, moderately, in the last two to three weeks, *since the nasal conviction has become evident to me.*" Masson explains the italicized phrase in a footnote: "Freud means that he has become convinced of the nasal origin of his cardiac symptoms."

Masson's interpretation is correct, I think, and it fits with other comments on Freud's arrhythmia scattered throughout the correspondence to this effect. For instance, in the letter of April 20, 1895, Freud writes:

> With regard to my own ailment, I would like you to continue to be right—that the nose may have a large share in it and the heart a small one. Only a very strict judge will take it amiss that in view of the pulse and the insufficiency I frequently believe the opposite. (Masson 1985, 125)

Freud's reasons for believing the opposite were non-medical. In a way, of course, Fliess was *right*! The nose was certainly the site of the causes of Freud's heart irregularities (and also the pulse irregularities); but not because of any "nasal reflex neurosis" but because of a decade of massive daily ingestion of cocaine via the painting of the membranes of the nostrils. See the pharmacologist Louis Lewin's chapter on cocaine and its physiological sequelae, especially on the heart, in the chapter from his *Phantastica* reprinted in Byck (1975).

20. Masson gives the original German "*sie war gar nicht abnorm gewesen*" in *The Assault on Truth*, 66. I would tend to keep Freud's pluperfect in English: "[S]he had not been at all abnormal" [with the implied "*until* the operation"].

21. Freud's credulity as far as this operation and Fliess's back-to-front rationalizations of the relationship between the nose and female sexual organs (and hence continuing their joint ignorance of the parasympathetic nervous system) was still being expressed in terms of strong advocacy, accompanied by the usual contempt for those doctors who would not agree, as late as the letter of January 30, 1901.

The significance of this is that over a year after the first publication of *Die Traumdeutung* (*The Interpretation of Dreams*) (1899) and after the first draft of what was to become the Dora case history had been completed, together with most of *The Psychopathology of Everyday Life* (the first part was published in *Monatsschrift für Psychiatrie und Neurologie* in July 1901), Freud was still attached to Fliess's noxious nasal notions. These works have to be reread with the constant remembrance of Freud's psychophysiological beliefs imbibed from Wilhelm Fliess.

This is what Freud writes after a Viennese medical conference (on January 25, 1901) had generally responded unfavorably to a paper by Arthur Schiff, "Über die Beziehungen zwischen Nase une weiblichen Sexualorganen," which supported Fliess's ideas:

> The second discussion in Vienna, I hear, was even more disgraceful than the first. These people are incorrigible. In the same breath with which they should be ashamed to have to admit that they so wrongly dismissed what could be easily proved and yet was quite extraordinary in your book, they now scoff at its more difficult part; and no self-criticism tells them that if they were proved to be wrong and the author right, there might even be something to the other part that they should first reflect on. Incorrigible and therefore enough of it! (Masson 1985, 435)

22. Masson refers to two works by Eckstein on the subject of the upbringing of children. In 1899 *Die neue Zeit* published an article by her entitled "*Eine wichtige Erziehungsfrage*" ["An Important Question in Education"]. In 1904, the Leipzig publisher, Curt Wigand, brought out a thirty-eight-page pamphlet or book by Eckstein, *Die Sexualfrage in der Erziehung des Kindes* [*The Sexual Question in the Upbringing of the Child*], which Masson calls "the most

illiberal piece that Emma Eckstein wrote" (see Masson, *The Assault on Truth*, 244-45).

23. C. G. Jung (1924), "Lecture III. Analytical Psychology and Education," in *Psychology and Education* reprinted in *The Collected Works of C. G. Jung*, vol. 17, Bollingen Series 20 (tr. R. F. C. Hull), Princeton: Princeton University Press, 1969, 102-103.

24. Masson's interpolation "that is, remembers" is not helpful in this instance. Freud's use of the word "Szene" has been variously interpreted by readers of psychoanalytic literature. It seems to me that the essence of the problem is quite simple and has been grossly exaggerated: Freud means "remembers," or he means "agrees" (i.e., with my [Freud's] construction), or he means "enacts." In the suggestive atmosphere of an anamnesis, and given the strangely unreliable reportorial techniques of Freud, I would suggest that it is not of the slightest interest to attempt to discern which of the three possibilities is indicated.

25. Freud had written on April 20, 1895, in response to a request from Fliess:

> The writer of this is still very miserable, but also offended that you deem it necessary to have a testimonial certificate from Gersuny for your rehabilitation. For me you remain the physician, the type of man into whose hands one confidently puts one's life and that of one's family—even if Gersuny should have the same opinion of your skills as *Weil*. (Masson 1985, 125)

Masson mentions that *Weil* is a reference to the surgeon, Moriz Weil, who concludes one article: "We have achieved the insight that *it is less important to discover new operations and new methods of operating than to search for ways and methods to avoid operations.*" (Masson 1985, p. 126; Masson notes that the emphasis is in the original). It would seem, therefore, that Freud's familial trust in Fliess was tempered by an awareness that reputed Viennese surgeons did not think highly of his skills or his methods.

26. At the time of the Harvard University Press publication of the complete correspondence between Freud and Fliess, Masson had already argued that Freud's 1896 paper "The Aetiology of Hysteria" was "Freud's most brilliant" (*The Assault on Truth*, xxvi), and still later in *Against Therapy* (New York: Atheneum, 1988: 48, note 3) he would write of this paper: "I consider that essay to be the greatest that Freud ever wrote." I do not think that Masson is using sardonic praise, alas.

27. That is, an attack of *childhood* convulsions. Freud is continuing the line of inquiry begun two weeks before (letter of January 12, 1897), where he has asked Fliess "to search for a case of childhood convulsions that you can trace back (in the future or in your memory) to sexual abuse, specifically to *lictus*

[licking] (or finger) in the anus." I confess to not understanding the sense of the bracketed phrase "(in the future or in your memory)."

28. Appignanesi and Forrester are mistaken in this assumption. The wish theory of psychosis and dreams was not only *not new* to Freud; it was *not new*! Freud himself, in the extensive survey that prefaces *The Interpretation of Dreams*, was to refer in detail to a book by W. Griesinger (*Pathologie und Therapie der psychischen Krankheiten*) that first appeared in 1845. Freud quotes from the summary of the 1861 second edition in P. Radestock's 1879 *Schlaf und Traum* and adds: "Griesinger . . . shows quite clearly that ideas in dreams and in psychoses have in common the characteristic of being *fulfilments of wishes*" (*P.F.L.*, 4, 163; Freud's emphasis). Far from uncovering new theories in the treatment of Emma Eckstein, Freud was relying on material that had been published half a century earlier.

29. Mark Pendergrast (1996). *Victims of Memory: Incest Accusations and Shattered Lives*. New York: HarperCollins (paperback edition). This book was originally published in 1995 at Hinesburg, Vermont, by Upper Access, Inc.

30. Janet D. Feigenbaum (1997) "Haply I May Remember and Haply May Forget," *The Times Literary Supplement* (August 22): 8-9. This quotation is from page 8. Dr. Feigenbaum is a lecturer in clinical psychology at the Institute of Psychiatry (London). Her review is a comprehensive discussion of three books: Matthew H. Erdelyi, *The Recovery of Unconscious Memories*; Jennifer J. Freyd, *Betrayal Trauma*; and Pendergrast's.

4

Interlude: Voi che sapete che cosa è amor

In this early period there was an obvious split between the *dynamic* understanding of the illness, which emphasized conflict and defense, and the *economic* "explanation," by which symptom formation was explained. The dynamic approach made the case histories read like detective novels; the economic view was modeled on the formulations Freud had used for the actual neuroses. Dynamic and economic views were both contained in the theory that a traumatic experience was the etiological factor in the formation of a hysterical symptom. This idea was taken over from Charcot. WALTER A. STEWART[1]

If the case of Emma Eckstein was not a determining one for psychoanalysis (and I don't believe that it was; the closing down of Freud's mind to serious clinical investigation, unprejudiced by his a priori imaginings about the place and significance of sexuality, or even— surprising as this may sound—what it entailed, was already perfectly apparent in his contributions to *Studies on Hysteria*), it was, nevertheless, the most seriously documented one we have of the early Freud clinical excursions. The space it occupies, week after week, month after month, year after year, in that extensive correspondence with Wilhelm Fliess makes manifest the unusual evidential value of the Emma Eckstein business. In the preceding chapter I have indicated some, but only some, of the travesties that it involved (and I have spared the reader the greater part of the details of Freud's nasal pus problems as well as some of the more unpleasant close-ups of the prone Eckstein, morphine-hazed and nasally butchered).

Careful study of the Fliess letters dealing with the Eckstein affair would produce more than enough arguments to demolish the pretensions of psychoanalysis to serious scientific and/or medical (or even philosophical) foundation. One could, in fact, had one world enough and time, devote a whole volume to this forgotten episode from the heroic years of psychoanalysis. It would make an excellent topic for a Ph.D. dissertation for someone (from medical history or comparative literature) interested in this particular aspect of the intellectual history of late-nineteenth-century Vienna, or for someone—a young Ellenberger?—curious about the origins of certain schools of psychotherapy.

One aspect of Freud's obsession with sexuality, together with his corollary dependence on Fliess, concerns the sustained treatment by suggestion of Eckstein that her many hemorrhages were self-induced neurotic symptoms of her need for him to be by her bedside. I have argued in my earlier book that this is an inescapable instance of Freud's deceit, that he knew the true cause of her hemorrhages, that he knowingly suggested to Eckstein a pattern of physiological consequence that he knew to be wrong, and that he rhetorically embroidered upon these inventions in the following months. In other words, he was knowingly lying to his patient in order to disculpate his friend from Berlin, Fliess, and indeed himself, from any responsibility for Eckstein's present grave state. My fellow Freud critic from London, Allen Esterson, is not sure that the heavy charge of "lying to the patient" can be laid at Freud's door in the case of Emma Eckstein, however horrendous the circumstances.

Esterson's argument, simply stated, runs: given the extraordinarily strange notions that Freud was prey to in these years, it is quite possible that he genuinely credited the suggestions he was giving to Emma. He cannot, therefore, be found guilty of fraud or deception in this specific case. Guilty of credulity, certainly; of incompetence, possibly; but for outright knowing deception, the Scottish verdict: not proven, must prevail. Unfortunately for Esterson, who is a generous thinker and an (almost) intransigent opponent of Freud and of the damage incurred by him and his followers (even the "revisionist" ones), his argument does not hold in the light of the circumstances as reported by Freud himself.

In the weeks after the Fliess operation, Freud wrote regularly to Fliess to inform him of the state of his Viennese patient. The delay in the expected recovery and the worsening condition of her damaged nose caused Freud intense anguish. He did not, at this time, assume that either this delay or this increased pain and suppuration were the consequences of neurotic ideational adventures of Emma herself. He assumed—and the assumption was correct—that there was a physiological problem that needed to be resolved by the intervention of a surgeon. So he called one in. In fact, at least three surgeons—Rosanes, Gersuny, and Gussenbauer—were called in at one time or another. This does not argue for a belief that the patient's physiological impairment was the result of neurotic need expressing itself through bleeding. The now-famous letter of March 8, 1895, recounting Rosanes's discovery of the gauze inadvertently left behind by Fliess discounts Emma's responsibility for her state—"so we had done her an injustice; she was not at all abnormal." When his patient was in danger of dying in her apartment, Freud's immediate response was *not* to call in another psychologist or to attempt his own emerging brand of psychotherapy.

Why not?

I would argue that it was precisely because he knew that the cause of the distress was physical and that it was, in some way, a physiological consequence of the operation. Events proved him right and the patient recovered. For Freud then to spend considerable time attempting to convince his patient that *she* was responsible for her bleeding—"As for Eckstein—I am taking notes on her history so that I can send it to you—so far I know only that she bled out of *longing*. She has always been a bleeder, when cutting herself and in similar circumstances" (letter of May 4, 1896; Masson 1985, 186)[2]—can only be considered as a sign that Freud was either a highly disturbed individual who could separate aspects of his own cognitive medical experiences into such virtually watertight compartments, or that he was capable of massive deception, amounting to fraudulent professional treatment, of a patient in his care. Now Freud *was* a highly disturbed individual; but I find it hard to believe that a doctor who knowingly (and correctly) opted for surgical correction could within a short time genuinely convince himself that the patient, because of her (assumed) hysterical personality, was the one who engendered the continuing moments of hemorrhage.[3] We have to do here with what I call an "excuse of convenience." Esterson gives, I think, far more credit to Freud's credulity than is warranted.

Either way, credulity or hypocrisy, Freud emerges as an incompetent clinician intent on shaping his patient's "symptoms" to his prevailing theories. His investigations of Emma's childhood and adolescent crises involving bleeding are a fairly transparent elaboration of a theme which would enable the patient herself—as well as Freud and Fliess—to consider the disaster of February 1895 as part of a pattern of her own previous responses to the world. Whether Freud's findings about reputed childhood imaginings or remembered realities were in any way accurate (and this we can never know) or worthwhile, is totally irrelevant to the situation of Emma Eckstein in his consulting room, or in her bed at the Sanatorium Loew. The one thing that tends to be forgotten, incidentally, in discussions of her postoperative treatment by Freud is the vexed question of origins, that is, *What* was she ever doing in Freud's office in the autumn of 1894? What were her presenting symptoms? And this takes us back in a "riverrun" way to where we came in with the misdiagnosis of the nasal reflex neurosis.

At the time of the Eckstein business, Freud was still using the hypnotic "pressure technique" (of the hand on the patient's forehead while the patient's eyes are closed) learned from Hippolyte Bernheim. The childhood and adolescent material drawn from Eckstein may have been induced in this manner. In the correspondence with Fliess, however, there is no indication that Freud used this method on her. But in another case history reported to Fliess (that Masson and his team date as probably belonging to the end of 1895), Freud explicitly refers to his continuing use of this Bernheim hand pressure to induce comunication from the patient under what Borch-Jacobsen considers to be a form of hypnosis.

This case is entitled "Draft J. Mrs. P. J. (Age 27)" (Masson 1985, 155-58). It is not a letter, but, like other "Drafts" included in the correspondence, a complete self-contained document. We have in this instance a detailed narrative of an interrupted analysis of just two sessions, apparently set down by Freud on the evening of the second session (his use of "Today she arrived weeping" tends to confirm this conjecture). It concludes with a one-line paragraph: "Interrupted by the patient's flight" (Masson 1985, 158).

The value of this document lies in its combination of freshness of recall by Freud, in the verbatim examples of the questions he asked Mrs. P. J. (we have no instances of Freud's direct questions to Eckstein), in its presentational division into parts "1" and "2," in its movement in contramotion chronologically, and, finally, in the illustration it provides in miniature (even for the restricted audience of one—Fliess) of the remark that Freud had disingenuously placed at the beginning of the "Discussion" section in the case of Fräulein Elisabeth von R. in *Studies on Hysteria*:

> Like other neuropathologists, I was trained to employ local diagnoses and electro-prognosis, and it still strikes me myself as strange that the case

histories I write should read like short stories and that, as one might say, they lack the serious stamp of science. (*Studies on Hysteria*, 160)

The story of Mrs. P. J. (and what Freud sent Fliess certainly reads like an unfinished two-part short story) is, in many ways, a more complete and interesting case history than the letters relating to Emma Eckstein. The Eckstein affair, because of Fliess's surgical error and its sequelae, is more substantially discussed and over a length of years and through many, many letters, than this four-page tale recounted to Fliess about Mrs. P. J. (which, curiously, is never referred to again). Eckstein is, therefore, as I have said, "the most seriously documented" example we have of a treatment procedure by Freud at that period. Yet none of the Eckstein episodes is ever narrated to Fliess as a "tale" with the aesthetic shape and texture of the adventures elaborated in *Studies on Hysteria*. Even the incidents relating to the Gothic discoveries of association between needles, drops of blood, the diabolus, and the Inquisition are presented to Fliess as fragmented moments devoid of narrative drive or situational context. The Freud informing Fliess of the progress of the Eckstein case is not the Freud, master-of-the-séance, who had already drafted the stories of hysteria and who was, in the early years of this century, to draft the four tales ("Dora," "Little Hans," "The Rat Man," "The Wolf Man") which were to ravish the hearts and minds of so many intellectuals in the West. Perhaps the brutal intervention of reality, via the surgery, inhibited the narrative genius in Freud. So the moments of record from Freud's treatment of Emma may be, by virtue of their unaesthetic and existential need, the most authentic we have of that period in Freud's career.

Having said that, however, what do we know about any individual session of Emma with Freud? Nothing whatever. There is nothing, either in the letters to Fliess or elsewhere, that gives an account of her sessional treatment. It may be that the horrifying immediacy of the surgical disaster (real, rather than phantasmagorical)—and Freud's recognition that the intervention had been misplaced—removed the veneer of Olympian serenity that is a feature of *Studies on Hysteria*. And it is precisely this Olympian posture that is present throughout the narration of the case of Mrs. P. J. It never became a "case history" because of the patient's rapid (and wise) departure from Berggasse 19; it afforded, nonetheless, a chance for Freud to hone his skills of narration.

The tale begins *in medias res*, as all good stories should. We can no more date the "real" time of the first three sentences than we can those relating to 'Peachy' Carnahan returning, apparently insane with grief and deprivation, to the office of the unnamed narrator of *The Man Who Would Be King*. Freud's opening sentences place him with Kipling, or at least with Somerset Maugham, as a master narrator who incites the reader to ask for more: "She had been married for three months. Her husband, a traveling salesman, had had to leave her a few weeks after their marriage and had been away for weeks on end. She missed him very much and longed for him" (Masson 1985, 155). "Yes! Yes! And then?" is the anticipated reader response. This is more than an interesting way, it is an *innovative* way to begin a medical case history. The medical reader or the psychiatric reader will ask, "But how did the session begin?" Did the author know this material before accepting the case? Was it revealed in the opening dialogue of the female patient? And, if so, what questions from the doctor prompted this information from the patient? And had the patient been referred to Freud by another doctor? And if so, on what grounds? What was the possible preliminary diagnosis that had guided Mrs. P. J. to Freud's consulting rooms? That such an opening prompts so many questions a hundred years later is a measure of the fascination exerted by Freud's narrative genius. There is a clue in these first sentences that suggests a theme for the tale: a recent marriage happily consummated, the absence of the loved partner, the longing for his return. None of these events indicates the need for Freudian intervention, or indeed for any "medical" intervention—even in late-nineteenth-century Vienna.

Something else, something *more*, must be implied by these sentences. And Freud intends to discover it. Here one has to recall the fact that the author of these lines, written up on the evening of the patient's flight, knew the path of inquiry and significance that he would follow. Why then, one might ask, does he, in this opening paragraph, indulge in what Stanley Fish was to call "withholding the missing portion"?[4] Precisely because such "withholding" produces the dramatic effect of the narrative and imbues it with a quality that requires a double reading (or a triple reading) for the history to be understood. And when it is understood, it is precisely to the credit of the narrator—that is, it is understood *on Freud's terms*, as the Wolf Man case would be. That this has little to do with medical art or science is neither here nor there. Mrs. P. J. is not a patient in any medical sense of the term; she is a prelude to a parable.

The oracular narrator then offers a sentence which at the same time reveals an aspect of her background and suggests why he has met her. Once again we have to imagine the likely conversation that produced the extreme concision of the reported speech in which the patient's situation is given to the reader:

> She had been a singer, or at any rate had been trained as one. To pass the time she was sitting at the piano singing, when suddenly she felt sick in her abdomen and stomach, her head swam, she had feelings of oppression and anxiety and cardiac paresthesias [a tingling sensation in the heart]; she thought she was going mad. (Masson 1985, 155-56)

The remainder of this introductory paragraph offers two interpretative possibilities for Mrs. P. J.'s distress as (presumably) reported by her:

> A moment later it occurred to her that she had eaten eggs and mushrooms that morning, so she thought she had been poisoned. However, the condition quickly passed. Next day the maidservant told her that a woman living in the same house had gone mad. From that time on she was never free of the obsession, accompanied by anxiety, that she too was going to go mad. (Masson 1985, 156)

This opening paragraph is set in an indeterminate time in the past. Freud's use of the pluperfect ("she *had* been married for three months," etc.) does *not* refer to the temporal distance separating these events from the analytic encounter (this becomes clear by extrapolation from the time sequences in part 2). It refers specifically to the antecedents to the crisis at the piano. This one moment of (apparently) recounted difficulty—"suddenly she felt sick in her abdomen and stomach, her head swam, she had feelings of oppression and anxiety and cardiac paresthesias; she thought she was going mad"—is followed by two patient-originated hypotheses as to the causes for the sensation: food-poisoning or "atmospheric" suggestion via the maidservant's remarks. The first possibility is soon eliminated—"However, the condition quickly passed"—but by whom? By Freud? Or by the patient herself in her presenting interview? The second hypothesis, of a kind of contagious atmospheric insanity, is retained by the patient, which explains the last sentence of Freud's opening paragraph—"From that time on she was never free of the obsession"—and the woman's presence in Freud's chambers: she was an obsessional neurotic in need of treatment.

The next paragraph, largely in the present tense, offers to Fliess (or the putative reader) the outline of Freud's argument and of his approach: "The argument runs as follows: I begin with the assumption that her condition at that time had been an anxiety attack—a release of sexual feeling that was transformed into anxiety" (Masson 1985, 156). This 'mechanism' whereby "a release of sexual feeling" is transformed into anxiety is to become a standard article of Freudian faith;[5] it will be used later on to explain the hidden significance of migraine (in females) and in the Dora case history to explain Dora's feeling of disgust ("displacement upwards") at the sudden embrace of Herr K., the neighborhood predator. Freud will naturally ignore the "atmospheric pollutions" of the maidservant's tale. Why, he will ask—and perfectly correctly—did the distressing event occur *before* Frau P. J. had heard the rumors about the female who went mad in the house? He continues:

> An attack of that kind, I am afraid, might take place without any accompanying psychic process. Nevertheless, I do not want to reject the more encouraging possibility that such a process might be found; on the contrary, I take it as the starting point of my work. What I expected was this: she had a longing for her husband—that is, for sexual relations with him; she thus came upon an idea that excited sexual affect followed later by defense; she took fright and made a false connection or substitution. (Masson 1985, 156)

Freud's idea, one must remember, is contemporaneous with (or shortly subsequent to) the writing up of the case of "Frau Emmy von N." where, we recall, he saw her difficulties with life as proceeding from a self-enforced celibacy of more than nineteen years. So long an absence from sexual felicity must create havoc on the human psyche. He was, delightfully, mistaken in those assumptions. Was he similarly mistaken with the young married Frau P. J.? The "starting point" of his work, he asserts, is an anxiety attack (which he defines as "a release of sexual feeling that [is] transformed into anxiety"), and this, he assumes, has happened in the case of young Frau P. J. Thus far, Freud has not suggested why, *if* his hunch is correct, she has continued to have such states of anxiety arousal. She must be an "obsessional neurotic" and therefore a "suitable case for treatment."

One question which arises at this stage concerns the redescription of the scene of feeling sick in the abdomen at the piano (and after the husband's absence of several weeks). Have we been given the full version of that peculiar occasion? Is there, perhaps, a "missing portion" left out by the patient in her narrative of the moment? And, if there is, what does it signify? Freud asks what was the music being played and sung at the moment of the crisis. He continues in a passage that shows firm belief in the powers of Bernheim's "hands-on" approach:

> She had been singing Carmen's aria "Près des remparts de Séville." I asked her to repeat it for me; she did not even know the words exactly.—At what point do you think the attack came on?—She did not know.—When I applied pressure [to her forehead], she said [it had been] *after* she had finished the aria. That seemed quite possible: it had been a train of thought prompted by the text of the aria.—I then asserted that before the attack there had been thoughts present in her which she might not remember. She [said] she really remembered nothing, but pressure [on her forehead] produced *husband* and *longing*. The latter was further specified, on my insistence, as longing for sexual caresses. (Masson 1985, 156)

After Freud's repeated insistence that the recollections of the absent husband were above all recollections of sexual pleasure, Freud momentarily assumes the role of Cherubino (but of a Cherubino who has discussed life with Dr. Fliess) and in one extended direct quotation gallops from Mozart to micturition—the quotation marks in this passage are Freud's own:

> "I'm quite ready to believe that. After all, your attack was only a state of outpouring of love. Do you know the page's song?—
>
> > Voi che sapete che cosa è amor,
> > Donne vedete s'io l'ho nel cor.
>
> There was certainly something besides this: a feeling in the lower part of the body, a cramp and an urgent need to urinate."—She now confirmed this. The insincerity of women starts from their omitting the characteristic sexual symptoms in describing their states. So it had really been an *orgasm*. (Masson 1985, 156)

Freud's redescription of the scene we have just read is a piece of narrative legerdemain which obliges us to reread the scene at the piano of some years previous. It fails to persuade. Its intention is (on the narrative level of Agatha Christie suspense) very impressive; the jocose masculine *bonhomie* about the insincerity of women, however, undoes its value as credible narration or credible case history. On the marginal assumption that the singer–pianist felt some erotic sensation between her legs as she sang and played Carmen's Act I *seguidilla* while remembering her husband's caresses (and that *is* a very *marginal* assumption!), the further assumption of a full orgasm—and, furthermore, of one obviously unrecognized as such by a married woman who probably knew what orgasms felt like—seems quite untenable.[6] The shared clubmen-amongst-clubmen approach of that last sentence—"So it had really been an *orgasm*"—reveals more of Freud's ignorance of human female physiological responses than it does of any psychoanalytic acumen.

"No," one feels like saying, "No, Sigmund, *female* orgasms are really not like male orgasms." Women do not feel "an urgent need to urinate" after an orgasm; men do, often, feel such a need (though one might question the urgency); but it is not part of the biological response of the human female. This simple fact puts into doubt the value—even on the narratological level—of the expressed irritation about "the insincerity of women" not revealing biological sensations which they do not have. In a way, this whole tale is an amusing example of "why can't a woman be more like a man?" from *My Fair Lady*.

Intelligent feminist critics of psychoanalysis, such as the psychologist Hannah Lerman, have inveighed against the ignorance of the later Freud's understanding of female psychosexual development: "when he developed the full-blown theory of female sexuality, the material reads as abstraction built upon abstraction and premise erected upon shaky premise without even the appearance of factual data."[7] The "Frau P. J." early foray into female physical sexual response demonstrates that his understanding of the *bodily* responses of women was just as shaky. Freud's report of the patient's agreement under the continued hand pressure—"She now confirmed this"—is, if accurate (however unlikely), to lead to the piece of self-deception that concludes the paragraph: "So it had really been an *orgasm*" (a phrase where the use of the adverb "really" allows for two possible, but contrasting, implications: "So I was *right!*" or "How bizarre!").

Freud ends this part 1 of his tale with a record of a sexually explicit, "mature?" conversation between himself and Frau P. J., which closes the session. Freud's words are given verbatim, those of Frau P. J. in reported speech:

> "Well, you can surely recognize that a state of longing like that in a young woman who has been left by her husband cannot be anything to be ashamed of."—On the contrary, she said that is the way it is supposed to be—"Correct; but in that case I can see no reason for fright. You were certainly not frightened about *husband* and *longing*; so we still are missing some other thoughts, which are more appropriate to the fright."—But she

added only that she had all along been afraid of the pain that intercourse caused her, but that her longing had been much stronger than her fear of the pain.—At this point we broke off. (Masson 1985, 156-57; the quotation marks and the emphasis are Freud's)

In one session we have come a long way from feeling sick in the abdomen with one's head swimming; a long way from the passing thought of eggs and mushrooms (and possible food poisoning); a long way from the housemaid's legend of contagious insanity. We have entered the world of Freud's favorite fantasies (just as contagious in their own way), where physical sexual desire dominates all forms of human conduct and particularly those moments where it seems neither likely nor necessary in the way that Freud imagines it. If the solution to the patient's problem— the apparent admixture of pleasure and terror—has not yet been found, the next session will surely reveal material that was *unconsciously* present in the patient's original moment of crisis.

In order to read and follow the next section—Freud's part 2—two Freudian hunches have to be accepted (a kind of willing suspension of disbelief on the reader's part): (1) that the patient's original crisis at the piano was *doubly* psychophysically sexual—positively, as far as recollections of the husband are concerned; negatively, as far as "repressed" moments of sexuality are concerned; (2) that the human mind has an "unconscious" which is totally inaccessible to personal introspection (except to Freud himself, of course) and which is chock-full of naughty sexual memories that only a third-party expert can unravel.[8] An archaeologist of Freud's proven ability can, nevertheless, unearth the fragments interred in the unconscious and reassemble them into significant artifacts indicating at each stage what was authentic discovery and what was necessary conjecture, or, as he terms it, "construction." As he was to write some five years later, prefacing the 'Dora' case history, he had no choice but

> to follow the example of those discoverers whose good fortune it is to bring to the light of day after their long burial the priceless though mutilated relics of antiquity. I have restored what is missing, taking the best models known to me from other analyses; but, like a conscientious archeologist, I have not omitted to mention in each case where the authentic parts end and my constructions begin.[9]

The mental muddle inherent in the phrase "I have restored what is missing" is an instance of the inventive but slovenly thinking of Freud in writing this and of the laxity of serious thought among his many admirers in accepting at face value a statement that is asinine. It is not helped by his qualifying phrase "taking the best models known to me from other analyses." The "best models" known to him from "other analyses" are those of his own patients, since no one else (apart from Emma Eckstein) was practicing psychoanalysis when this was written. And how such "other analyses" could conceivably help "restore what is missing" from a particular human experience is quite beyond conjecture (though, doubtless, Appignanesi and Forrester could conjure up some colorful curiosities). The claim in the last sentence of this quotation—"I have not omitted to mention in each case where the authentic parts end and my constructions begin"—is simply a lie. This was not true of the Dora case history (which this passage prefaces); nor is it true of any other Freudian case history. The metaphorical model chosen by Freud—archaeology—was an astute one which gave to his bogus science an aura of profundity, however inaccurate the analogy. Freud was genuinely fascinated by the late-nineteenth-century discoveries in archaeology and was well-read in the subject; but he was not an archaeologist.

Before discussing Freud's part 2, I would like to quote a very sensible observation made by Richard Webster in his chapter 12, "Dreams and Symptoms," of *Why Freud Was Wrong*. Having understood that one of Freud's personal and perverse self-satisfaction strategies was to talk dirty and look smart,[10] Webster maliciously (and correctly) notices the disparity between Freudian theory and Freudian practice:

> Instead of facing up to the fact that his interest in his patients was at least partly erotic, personal and spontaneously human, Freud anxiously and repeatedly denied that his therapeutic relationships afforded him any gratification. While he made it clear that he did not hesitate to discuss sexual matters openly and frankly with young women such as Dora, he insisted that this was for the purest of scientific motives, adding, with that self-deceiving naivety which frequently characterises his attempts at self-analysis, that 'it would be the mark of a singular and perverse prurience to suppose that conversations of this kind are a good means of exciting or gratifying sexual desires.' The assumption which is made here—that the dreams of his patients which do not refer to sexual behaviour are sexually gratifying, whereas the explicitly sexual conversations he has with them are not—is one that recurs throughout his work.[11]

Freud's Act II of his *Voi che sapete* drama is much more turbulent than the initial encounter. It begins in anguish and tears and ends with "the patient's flight." In between, Freud constructs the missing links of negative sexuality that, he believes, had produced the effect of anxiety in the original crisis—what he refers to as "scene 1"—and attempts to piece together the scenario of the woman's life (her *adult* life—there is no mention in this narrative, at least, of explorations into childhood fantasies) in a way that would fit with the scenario implied by his theoretical hunches outlined in the second paragraph of part 1. A sense of unremitting frenzy pervades part 2. This is no doubt in part a combination of three things: the patient's serious emotional upset; Freud's confused and urgent desire to get to the heart of the mystery of scene 1; and his increasing, and increasingly blatant, verbal disrobing of the patient—almost a nineteenth-century equivalent of what Erica Jong was to call, with true American bravura, "the zipless fuck."

Freud opens his account to Fliess with a dry résumé of the problems left by the first encounter:

> It was certainly to be expected that in scene 1 (at the piano), alongside her longing thoughts for her husband (which she remembered), she had entered on another, deep train of thought, which she did *not* remember and which led to a scene 2. But I did not yet know its starting point. (Masson 1985, 157)

Freud begins this second session with a set of assumptions based on his ad hoc interpretation of the material gathered in the first meeting. The interpretation, as we have seen, involves an unrecognized moment of orgasm. The assumptions pertinent to this are: that the recollection of a loved one can by itself produce a sexual climax (there is no suggestion by Freud or by the patient that either masturbation or "thigh-squeezing" excitation of the clitoris is involved); that this situation can create a psychical state in which an unremembered "deep train of thought" manifests itself and causes anxiety; that this "deep train of thought" is also sexual in content; that this deep train of thought only appears when sexual climax is near or present; that this deep train of thought does not provide conscious thoughts of previous experiences, but rather unpleasant bodily sensations ("sick in her abdomen and stomach") without cognitive content for the patient. When Freud writes, "But I did not yet know its starting point," he has shifted his diagnostic position from speculation to certainty. Where the "deep train of thought" began is still, of course, a speculative subject for his investigation. That there *was* such a "train of thought" has become a certainty. The question for Freud is no longer: "Was there one, and did it have the effect that my interpretation of orgasm supposes?" It is now: "There was one, and it did have the effect that my interpretation has hypothesized. But *where* did it begin?"

Although the sentences which follow reveal the patient's upset and Freud's irritation about the appearance of what he calls "resistance," there is no acknowledgment by him (or, perhaps, even realization?) that his very method of treatment may be at fault. We—and this includes Fliess, the recipient of this draft—are never told, by the way, for *what* this woman was being treated. I have suggested some kind of obsessional neurosis that produces anxiety states; but this is merely my hunch from Freud's hunches.[12] This is yet another conundrum of this "medical case history" from which even a basic clinical diagnosis is absent. Nor is there any hint that the previous session's path of inquiry may have been responsible for the young woman's evident distress on entering Freud's rooms on the second occasion.

This case is also peculiar in the sense that at no time is the question of a physical and/or neurological malfunction investigated. Had the woman seen a physician with her problems previously? We do not know, and Freud does not tell us—or Fliess. I am not in a position to invent a post hoc cause for the young woman's reported malaise at the piano; nor can I suggest the possible reasons for her subsequent moments of the fear of becoming mad (was this simply the power of suggestion of the housemaid's remark on a susceptible personality?). I do recall the frequent use of the metaphorical phrase "highly strung" being used of persons of a labile disposition when I was a child in England, and I suspect that Frau P. J. would probably fit into that category; but I have no recollection that the solution was to be found in psychoanalysis. My parents must have moved in the wrong circles.

Freud's reaction to the woman's distress is to ignore the effects of the previous session on her fragile equilibrium and to conceive of an instance of resistance on her part. The consequences of his "impudence"—to use Medawar's term—and the enforced intimacy of the first meeting are brushed aside as human irrelevancies; if the woman is in even more desperate straits now, it is only a sign of the accuracy of the hunches of the first meeting and of her refusal to countenance their truth. He writes: "Today she arrived weeping and in despair, evidently without any hope of the treatment's succeeding. So her resistance was already stirred up and progress was far more difficult" (Masson 1985, 157). This chilling refusal of responsibility for any part in the woman's sense of despair, which may well have issued from the invasive and ignorant strategies of the first session, was to become a continuing feature of Freud's dealings with his patients—male or female—(such sensitive persons as Victor Tausk, Sándor Ferenczi, and even Emma Eckstein when the time came, were coolly given the brush-off, with appropriate psychoanalytic explanation, when they no longer fitted into Freud's schemes or contemporary needs).

"What I wanted to know, then," Freud continues, "was what thoughts that might lead to her being frightened were still present." This is followed by an interesting passage which seems to demonstrate more Freud's tenacity in his blindness than his ability as a concerned and investigative doctor.

> She brought up all kinds of things that could not be relevant: that for a long time she had not been deflowered (which Professor Chrobak had confirmed to her); that she attributed her nervous states to that and for that reason wished it might be done.—This was, of course, a thought from a later time: until scene 1 she had been in good health. (Masson 1985, 157)

The chronology of Freud's report becomes very strange from now until the end. It is difficult to work out *when* the various incidents in the woman's life occurred and their chronological relationship to her marriage and her "crisis" at the piano (when she had been married for three months).[13] In the passage just cited Freud makes the curious statement that "until scene 1 she had been in good health"—and one must assume that he means psychically as well as physically. The observation that her wish to be deflowered to relieve her nervous tension "was, of course, a thought from a later time"—that is, subsequent to the piano crisis—makes no sense. And the reputed "good health" until the "scene 1" attack is difficult to square with Freud's continuing insistence of an important and intrusive (what Freud would elsewhere refer to as "pathogenic") repressed memory of sexual significance which had unleashed her anxiety states. If she was in "good health" how can she nonetheless be harboring noxious repressed memories which will undo her sense of equilibrium when she plays some Bizet on the piano? To pose here the frivolous, skeptical question "Is Bizet that powerful?" is to fall into the trap of accepting Freud's own personal invention, abstracted from his occasional reading of the nineteenth-century German philosophers, of the "repressed unconscious" constructed along the lines of his various broodings about the supposed psychogenic power of sexual experiences.[14]

Freud here has anticipated the French satirist Jules Romains, who, in 1923, invented the former tie salesman, later peanut wholesaler, turned charlatan Doctor Knock. In Act I of *Knock, ou le triomphe de la médecine*, the eponymous hero declares the title of his doctoral thesis *Sur les prétendus états de santé* (On So-called States of Health) and adds his chosen (and totally invented) epigraph attributed to the great nineteenth-century French medical scientist, Claude Bernard: *"Les gens bien portants sont des malades qui s'ignorent"* ("Healthy people are sick people who are unaware of their illness"). Knock, with an organizational flair that Freud would have appreciated, has almost the whole *commune* in bed and under his medical orders within three months—he has ensured the medical "good health" of those essential persons needed to create this triumph of medicine: the local schoolteacher who provides public lectures on hygiene (with terrifying images of the powers of microbes); the local pharmacist (for obvious reasons); the local inn-keeper (whose hotel has been converted into an impromptu sanatorium).[15]

Working on the assumption from the previous session that the feeling of sickness in the stomach had been part of an unrecognized orgasm, and still, apparently, crediting the notion that women who have had orgasms can then have orgasms and not realize what has occurred (one wonders where on earth Freud discovered this gem), Freud pursues his line of inquiry:

> At last I obtained the information that she had already had a similar but much weaker and more transitory attack with the same sensations. (From this I realize that it is from the mnemic picture of the orgasm itself that the path leading down to the deeper layers starts.) We investigated the other scene. At that time—four years back—she had had an engagement at Ratisbon. In the morning she had sung at a rehearsal and it had been a success; in the afternoon, at home, she had had a "vision"—as if she were "planning" something (a row) with the tenor of the company and another man, and afterward she had had the attack, with the fear that she was going mad. (Masson 1985, 157)

Freud's self-congratulatory parenthesis—"From this I realize that it is from the mnemic picture of the orgasm itself that the path leading down to the deeper layers starts"—is probably best left where it so deservedly belongs, in the pages of these wild letters to Fliess. But those still tempted by Freud's reputation for "wisdom" (and who have forgotten his treatment of Dr. Horace Frink) might do worse than to ponder it carefully for an hour or so for what it reveals about the state of mentation of a man who was claiming not merely to heal the sick, but to understand the origins of their sickness and, then, to theorize upon the necessary causations of these origins. The madcap certainty of the phrase "From this I realize" is, we know, par for the course as far as Freud's impromptu revelations to Fliess are concerned; but it is sobering to find such a phrase in the what-should-be reflective aftermath of a treatment session.

If ever one wanted an "inside"—or fly-on-the-wall—picture of Freud-in-action-as-psychotherapist, the *Voi che sapete* scenario offers an unintended, and hence totally authentic, glimpse of just what went on (in Freud's mind and in the consulting room) in Berggasse 19. These four pages offer the alert and unprejudiced reader a view of psychoanalysis that speaks volumes. The *Standard Edition* and all the commentaries upon it can be discarded. The later elucubrations about male or female sexual developmental patterns can be ignored. The deceptive sophistications of *The Psychopathology of Everyday Life* and the autobiographical contrivances that appear to underwrite *The Interpretation of Dreams* can now be read as the fantastical tales they always were. It is at once horrifying, amusing, fascinating, pathetic, and, medically, outrageous.

What Freud has done, we realize, is to take the initial "crisis" at the piano and to split the experience into two sequences of response which he labels "scene 1" and "scene 2." His interpretation of the longing for the absent husband, enhanced by the playing and singing of the Bizet aria, is that this combination of remembrances and the erotically charged *seguidilla* led to an orgasm—this is micro-scene 1. The Freudianly constructed orgasm, however, induces thoughts of an unpleasant nature in the past that will not be denied physiological expression in the present (of the constructed orgasm)—this is micro-scene 2. The phrase "it is from the mnemic picture of the orgasm itself that the path leading down to the deeper layers starts" allows Freud to claim to have found the origin of the "anxiety" from the Ratisbon experience of some four years previous.

> Here then was scene 2, *which had been touched on by association in scene 1.* But we must admit that here, too, her memory had gaps in it. There must have been other ideas present in order to account for the release of sexual feeling and the fright. I asked for these intermediate links, but instead I was told her motives. She had disliked the whole of life on the stage.—"Why?"—The brusqueness of the manager and the actors'

relations to one another.—I asked for details of this.—There had been an old comic actress whom the young men used to make fun of by asking her if they might come and spend the night with her. (Masson 1985, 157-58; my emphasis)

One has to accept the misuse of language which has become a given in psychoanalytic discourse. The phrase "instead I was told her motives" is *not* what is reported (by Freud himself) of her spontaneous reactions to the circumstances of theatrical life. Freud never departs from his initial supposition that the young singer's malaise at the piano had been an unperceived climax followed by a momentary sensation of fear or anxiety which must have been produced by an "unconscious" association with some distressing sexual encounter of an earlier time. He relentlessly pursues his chosen theme of sexual mayhem that has become "repressed"—an interesting example of adult experience being subject to repression and only allowed rememorative expression in another adult action that involves (so he claims) sexual ecstasy. Freud, incidentally, never, either here or in later theoretical essays, describes or demonstrates how adult sexual encounters can become at once "repressed"—that is, not accessible to consciousness—and powerful inhibitors of genuine sexual release. That he may have been in error in his original and gratuitously lascivious redescription of the moment of malaise at the piano is not once considered by Freud in this document, "Draft J." He continues:

"Something further, about the tenor."—He had pestered her, too, at the rehearsal he had put his hand on her breast.—"Through your clothes or on the bare skin?"—At first she said the latter, but then took it back: she had been in outdoor clothes.—"Well, what more?"—Everything about this relationship, all the hugging and kissing among the players had been abhorrent to her.—"Anything else?"—Once again the manager's brusqueness, and she had only stayed there a few days.—"Was the tenor's assault made on the same day as your attack?"—No; she did not know if it had been earlier or later.—My inquiries with the help of pressure [*of Freud's hand on her forehead while her eyes are closed*] showed that the assault had been on the fourth day of her stay and her attack on the sixth.

Interrupted by the patient's flight. (Masson 1985, 158; the quotation marks are Freud's)

This passage is one instance that reminds me of Erica Jong's phrase. The whole paragraph is devoid of any medical or even psychotherapeutic information. It is, on the other hand, replete with the kind of masturbatory prurience that Webster rightly criticizes in his chapter on dreams. "Nudge-nudge wink-wink" seems to have become, at this stage, a standard method of Freudian inquiry into the human distresses presented to him. A whole armory of intellectual theorizing is ready to hide this fact from Freud and to allow his disciples to credit him with extravagant discoveries that some three thousand years of recorded human history had not noticed.[16] The "patient's flight"—the one intelligent action committed by Frau P. J. in this scenario—does not give Freud any second thoughts about his handling of the case, or about his assessment of the origins and nature of the woman's reputed moments of anxiety.

Why not?

We should remember that this "case" was written up for Fliess in the hours following the hasty departure of "Frau P. J." Leaving aside the possible intervention of moments of masculine disappointment and the need for some kind of epistolary revenge for the failure of the treatment—to be taken out via the presentation of the patient, a position later adopted in the case of Dora, who was also to leave in her own good time (much to Freud's annoyance)—one should, nonetheless, ask why Freud, in composing this testament, had nowhere felt obliged to question either the approach he took or its implications: why, in other words, did he neither question his intuited interpretation of the "piano crisis" or his way of discussing his patient's moments of anxiety? It is therefore even more of an unwitting self-indictment than had it been, for instance, a record on an ongoing analysis with its awkward moments and occasional pauses caused by the dilemma of the patient's grasping just how his or her revelations would be understood by the analyst. What this document clearly demonstrates, however, is Freud's fundamental incapacity, or cognitive unwillingness, to investigate "neurotic" ailments (or neurophysiological problems) outside the strange and obsessive parameters of his own prejudices. There clearly were no "second thoughts" that Freud was prepared to contemplate even in the privacy of his letters to Fliess. We must believe that when Freud drafted this example of his current practice to Fliess he was convinced of the correct procedure of his approach to . . . to what? To mental illness? To problems of a neurological origin? To problems of emotional stress? To problems of sexual repression? Or, on a more modest level, to problems of life itself with its inevitable ups and downs? This last suggestion, precisely because of its modest disavowal of "scientific" research possibilities and its lack of operatic drama, seems far too removed from the Wagnerian sensibilities of the *magister ludi*.

Freud, in these years of correspondence with Fliess, appears to have been in thrall to the peculiar genius of the Berlin *Zauberer*. And yet it was that magician who, in one of his most perceptive moments (his nasal and numerological notions may have been grotesque to the point of insanity, but he still retained a critical awareness of friend Freud's weaknesses) was to reveal to Freud how he, in his solipsistic universe, was no more than a kind of self-confirming projector focused on the screen of other psyches. This well-known critique of Freud's methods was quoted, in massive anger, by Freud himself in his letter to Fliess of August 7, 1901.

In one powerful and strange passage—written, one must remind oneself, after the publication of *The Interpretation of Dreams* and the completion of *The Psychopathology of Everyday Life*—Freud suddenly brings up: (1) Josef Breuer's no doubt worldly-wise observations to Ida Fliess that she was lucky to live in Berlin where Freud could not interfere in her marriage and create problems for the couple that probably did not exist; and (2) that, according to Fliess, he (Freud) merely projected his own thoughts onto others. Freud writes in this tempestuous reply toward the end of the friendship:

> What is your wife doing other than working out in a dark compulsion the notion that Breuer once planted in her mind when he told her how lucky she was that I did not live in Berlin and could not interfere with her marriage? In this you too have come to the limit of your perspicacity; you take sides against me and tell me that "the reader of thoughts merely reads his own thoughts into other people," which renders all my efforts valueless. (Masson 1985, 447)

If the Mozartian interlude of the case of Frau P. J. is anything to go by, then Freud's ironic comment to Fliess—"which renders all my efforts valueless"—loses its irony. The value of this brief moment in the history of psychoanalysis lies partly in its illustration of Freud's approach in the intimacy of the consulting room; what it also demonstrates, however, is Freud's self-satisfaction with the paths of inquiry chosen and with the methods adopted to exert emotional and intellectual compliance from the patient. Apart from the devastating effect such clinical behavior may have on a patient, Freud's continuing use of this approach (with or without the assistance of the Bernheim hand pressure) virtually guaranteed that no new medical or psychological knowledge could ever emerge from such encounters. The limpet-like hold of the *a priori* positions was too strong.

Even, as we shall see, with the self rather than some patient as the center of inquiry, the limpet hold was to remain firm. No tides of experience could, it seemed, shake the *a priori* from its piece of rock.

There is, in spite of known instances of obtuse clinical abuse, like the case of Frau P. J., or later Dora, a peculiar passage in Ian Hacking's recent *Rewriting the Soul* which implies, without moral approval it is true, that Freud was a systematic searcher for the Truth (the capital letter is Hacking's).[17] Jim Schnabel in his generally favorable review in *The Guardian* (U.K.) noted that Hacking's book "is a deliberately cool, non-polemical exploration of the origins of multiple personality as a medical entity."[18] And so it is; Schnabel's assessment is generally justified, in my opinion. However, the two moments of intellectual weakness that stand out—to my surprise, given Hacking's track record for careful research—both concern Freud. In the first case, his generous acceptance of Jeffrey Masson's *The Assault on Truth* as a "brilliant attack on Freud for abandoning the so-called seduction theory" (Hacking 1995, 137)—a comment repeated on page 194 ("Masson's well-known and well-aimed assault on Freud")—reveals a fatal misreading of the published histories of Freud and of the correspondence. Masson, as Allen Esterson has shown in a recent article,[19] had been seduced by the deceptive rhetoric of Freud's records of his case histories. By his approval of Masson's inquiries (or rather, of his conclusions), Hacking has also been seduced by the reported findings of the Berggasse 19 consultation sessions. In short, *what* did Freud's female patients tell him? And *what* did *he* tell them to tell him? And how was it all reported?

In the second case, Hacking's "peculiar passage" concerns his vision of the personality differences between Freud and Pierre Janet. The whole paragraph deserves to be quoted for what it reveals about the persuasive (and pervasive) influence of Freud upon a distinguished philosopher and historian of science who is not a member of the psychoanalytic sect:

> I see Freud as driven by a terrible Will to Truth, illustrated by a second contrast with Janet. Ellenberger writes that the values of Freud were those of the romantic era; Janet was an Enlightenment rationalist. That insight is partial at best. Janet was flexible and pragmatic, while it was Freud who was the dedicated and rather rigid theoretician in the spirit of the Enlightenment. His early theory on the specific etiologies of the neuroses would have delighted seventeenth-century intellects; Leibniz would have loved it. Freud aspired after such theories all his life and, like many a dedicated theoretician, probably fudged the evidence in favor of theory.

Freud had a passionate commitment to Truth, deep underlying Truth, as a value. That ideological commitment is fully compatible with—may even demand—lying through one's teeth. The emotionally felt aim is to get at the Truth by whatever means. (Hacking 1995, 195)

I can certainly see Freud using his intaglio ring to formally impress an *imprimatur* on that paragraph. What is terribly wrong with it is the extraordinary confusion in Hacking's mind between "truth" (or, as he writes, as if this confers some different meaning to the word, "*Truth*") and the urgent need of "being *right*." The Freud legend has for years praised its founder's self-proclaimed and unswerving search for "Truth." What is now known about the early (and, indeed, the later) years of the psychoanalytic movement is that Freud was intent on having the last word, intent on being *right*. But the desire, the psychopathological desire, to be *right*,—that is, to consider oneself, and to be considered, *right*—whatever the cost, is not the same as the "Will to Truth" (in Hacking's deliberately Nietzschean phrase).

I do not know why the generally careful thinker that Hacking is decided to go "Nietzschean" in his comments on Freud; nor can I understand how a careful philosopher of science can accept Masson's arguments in *The Assault on Truth*. It cannot be through lack of access to the complete Freud–Fliess correspondence. It must therefore be through a reading of that correspondence which was no more than cursory. If the little aborted case of Frau P. J. shows anything, it is just this foolish, juvenile, one may say, insistence on Freud's part that *he* knows and that the other *doesn't*, and, almost by Freudian definition, *cannot* know. Frau P. J. may well not have understood her panic attack, if such it was; but *Voi che sapete* does not include the "all-knowing" Freud.

Notes

1. Walter A. Stewart, M.D. (1967). *Psychoanalysis: The First Ten Years*. London: Allen and Unwin, 74. This passage is from the introduction to chapter 4 and prefaces Stewart's consideration of the case of Frau P. J. (75-76). Sulloway frequently cites Stewart's pioneering work, but does not mention this case.

2. This letter retails several incidents of juvenile bleeding, including an interpretation by Freud of one of Eckstein's adolescent dreams. He concludes:

Then, in the sanatorium, she became restless during the night because of an unconscious wish [*unbewusste Sehnsuchtsabsicht*] to entice me to go there; since I did not come during the night, she renewed the bleedings, as an unfailing means of rearousing my affection. She bled spontaneously three times and each bleeding lasted for four days, which must have some significance. She still owes me details and specific dates. (Masson 1985, 186)

The last two sentences are a reference to Fliess's numerological games and illustrate Freud's continuing credence in them.

3. In fact the situation is worse (for Esterson's thesis) than I have mentioned here. There were weeks in the spring of 1895 when the beginning of Emma's indoctrination coincided with the continuing recourse to surgical intervention. Freud's treatment of her night "hysterias" at the Sanatorium Loew were contemporaneous with the ongoing postoperative procedures by her surgeons. He *must* have been aware, therefore, of the real reasons for the surgeons' concern.

To argue that he genuinely believed that her *psychological* responses were the *cause* of her present physiological condition is to make of Freud not so much a charlatan as a complete idiot, incapable of recognizing such an elementary category mistake! I refuse to believe that Freud was "a complete idiot," irrespective of the credence he gave to Fliess's versions of mathematics.

4. See Stanley Fish, "Withholding the Missing Portion: Power, Meaning and Persuasion in Freud's 'The Wolf-Man.'" *The Times Literary Supplement* (August 29, 1986): 935-38.

5. Freud seems to have remained for many years genuinely perplexed as to how to fit "anxiety" into a causative sequence within his libido-based schemata of human psychology. All the analytic work up to and including the end of World War I was conceived on the notion that anxiety was caused by sexual repression. In a footnote added as late as 1920 to the fourth edition of *Three Essays on Sexuality* he observes: "One of the most important results of psychoanalytic research is this discovery that neurotic anxiety arises out of libido, that it is the product of a transformation of it, and that it is thus related to it in the same kind of way as vinegar is to wine" (*P.F.L.*, 7, 147).

With the publication of *Inhibitions, Symptoms and Anxiety*, however, in 1926 (the book had been drafted in the previous July), Freud appears (and yet with no new case material to support the change) to do a 180-degree turn, and thereafter anxiety was no longer to be considered as a repression of libido.

6. I am reminded, quite irreverently, of the Scottish comedian Billy Connolly's version of St. Paul's blinding moment of illumination on the road to Damascus, duly sporraned into broad Glaswegian: *"Wha' the fuck was tha'?"* ("Swearing and the Use of Bad Language," now available on "Classic Connolly," including *Wreck on Tour* and *Atlantic Bridge*, Polygram Records, 1994.)

7. See chapter 3, "The Personal Becomes Theoretical," of Hannah Lerman (1986), *A Mote in Freud's Eye: From Psychoanalysis to the Psychology of Women*, New York: Springer. This quotation comes from page 88. Lerman's book is the first, to my knowledge, to take full cognizance of Masson's edition of the complete correspondence between Freud and Fliess.

8. This central conceit of Freudianism, woven with considerable rhetorical skill into the fabric of the vision, has foxed, and continues to fox—as Esterson once reminded me—even scholars not known for being of the psychoanalytic persuasion. As a consequence, the mythological history of the movement has frequently been strengthened to the disadvantage of the truth.

For example, in his introduction to *The Mind's I: Fantasies and Reflections on Self and Soul*, the philosopher Daniel C. Dennett can write:

> [W]hen Freud initially hypothesized the existence of *un*conscious mental processes, his proposal met widely with stark denial and incomprehension. It was not just an outrage to common-sense, it was even self-contradictory to assert that there could be unconscious beliefs and desires, unconscious feelings of hatred, unconscious schemes of self-defense and retaliation. (Hofstadter and Dennett 1982, 12)

None of Dennett's extravagant statements about the reception of Freud (which must be based on hearsay) is true. Freud's shade would be delighted by such unconscious support from the groves of academe.

The opening two sentences of a later paragraph show clearly that Dennett has been duly (and unhelpfully) mesmerized by the one transcultural mythology of our time: "Freud's expansion of the bounds of the unthinkable revolutionized clinical psychology. It also paved the way for the more recent development of "cognitive" experimental psychology" (Hofstadter and Dennett 1982, 12).

9. Sigmund Freud, *Case Histories I: 'Dora' and 'Little Hans,'* P.F.L., 8, 41.

10. This Freudian lesson has been well learned by academics in the humanities. To go to an American academic humanities conference on any aspect of any literature and *not* find some clown (male or female) intent upon talking dirty while claiming to "theorize" or "problematize" a literary text is nowadays well-nigh impossible.

11. Richard Webster, *Why Freud Was Wrong*, 272. The passage quoted from Freud is from his "Prefatory Remarks" to the Dora case history: *S.E.*, 7, 9; *P.F.L.*, 8, 37.

12. I wish to make it clear that when I offer the suggestion "obsessional neurosis" I am following what I can credit as factual from Freud's narrative of the woman's mental state. Having said that, I would be reluctant to make such an ill-informed assessment of a client without other medical history being examined properly. And having said that, if we can credit the "broad lines"—

without the psychoanalytic interpretations—of Freud's presentation, then I suspect that two or three hours with a cognitive reinforcing presence—like that of Anthony Clare or Peter Lomas—would have done Frau P. J. a world of good.

If, in fact, her medical predicament was graver than that, then we are looking at some early incursion of a depressive illness for which a reasonable modern-day response would be some kind of cognitively exploratory and reinforcing psychotherapy accompanied by a chemical antidepressant regime. Freud did not have at his fingertips the psychopharmaceutical possibilities of nowadays. That, of course, is *not* the point. The point about this tale of an interrupted analysis is that from the very beginning the diagnosis was skewered into a nonsense representation of Freud's obsessive interests.

13. It is never revealed by Freud how much time has passed between her "piano crisis" and her presence in his office. By working through the document sent to Fliess one can hazard that she had been married less than four years at the time of their encounter. She had therefore been a young woman of twenty-three when she married. But this is mere conjecture from the material offered by Freud.

14. None of the German philosophers studied by Freud ever referred to an "unconscious" as conceived by Freud with the necessary inaccessibility to consciousness as a consequence of the sexual material therein contained. A contemporary American professor of comparative literature who has investigated Freud's borrowings from the nineteenth-century German speculative tradition which incorporated a concept of the "Unconscious"—*das Unbewusste*—is Peter L. Rudnytsky. See his 1987 volume *Freud and Oedipus* (New York: Columbia University Press). The book is worth consulting for its scholarly examination of the German nineteenth-century literary and philosophical masters from Hegel to Nietzsche. Its intellectual and existential weakness lies in the author's total acceptance of Freudian psychoanalysis as the Truth and, from a scholarly point of view, in its partial and specious reading of the Freud–Fliess letters. Although the Harvard unexpurgated edition of Masson is mentioned and (occasionally) quoted, where psychoanalytic myths have to be preserved, only the censored edition of 1954, *The Origins of Psychoanalysis*, is cited (and with no indication offered to the reader about the missing material).

15. Jules Romains's satire, *Knock, ou le triomphe de la médecine* (currently available in Gallimard's paperback "Folio" edition), is probably even more relevant now as an incisive satire of hypocrisy and medical flummery than when it was first performed in Paris in 1923 with the great Louis Jouvet in the lead role. (Jouvet also directed the play and later appeared in the film version; Romains dedicated the published text to Jouvet.)

The second act is a priceless illustration of several contemporary pieces of nonsense mostly related to psychoanalysis. Examples of "suggestion," of "recovered memory syndrome," of persuasion through the authority status automatically granted a doctor are brilliantly evoked in Act II where Knock offers free consultations to the members of the *commune* (French administrative district) of St. Maurice. From the free consultations he acquires lifelong dependents who swear by his medical insights.

16. An interesting example of Freud's posthumous seduction of the intelligentsia is the French literary historian Marthe Robert. Her French equivalent of Ernest Jones's biography of Freud, *La Révolution psychanalytique* (Paris: Payot, 1964) was translated as *The Psychoanalytic Revolution: Sigmund Freud's Life and Achievement* (tr. Kenneth Morgan, London/New York: Allen and Unwin/Harcourt, Brace, and World, 1966). On her first page she notes: "This man, who perfected an infallible method of understanding the enigma of every individual life—including his own—always took great pains to protect his personal life from the legitimate curiosity of his successors and the malice of his innumerable opponents" (11-12). Her book continues in this vein of unbridled belief in Freud's originality as a discoverer of what makes one tick.

17. Ian Hacking (1995). *Rewriting the Soul: Multiple Personality and the Sciences of Memory*. Princeton, N.J.: Princeton University Press.

18. Jim Schnabel. "Splits in the Search for Self." *The Guardian* (London), June 9, 1995, Books 5.

19. Allen Esterson (1998). "Jeffrey Masson and Freud's Seduction Theory: A New Fable Based on Old Myths," *History of the Human Sciences* 11, no. 1 (February 1998): 1-21.

5

From the Sanatorium to the Theater of the Self

Had Freud better understood Darwin, for example, the world might have been spared such dead-end fantasies as death instincts and Oedipal desires. MARTIN DALY AND MARGO WILSON[1]

[P]erhaps nowhere was the impact of Darwin, direct and indirect, more exemplary or fruitful outside of biology proper than within Freudian psychoanalysis. FRANK J. SULLOWAY[2]

In sum: the Oedipus complex, infantile sexuality, the wish-fantasies, all of Freud's self-proclaimed "discoveries" are arbitrary constructions designed to explain away his patients' stories of incest and perversion while simultaneously excusing the method that provoked them. MIKKEL BORCH-JACOBSEN[3]

The science writer Timothy Ferris, interviewed on CBC radio about his latest vade mecum for debutant cosmologists, *The Whole Shebang*,[4] gave a little illustration of the importance of empiricism in science. He had been asked about the "Heaven's Gate" multiple suicides of those who were convinced that an alien spaceship was following the Hale-Bopp comet. Some of the sect had visited a specialist store and purchased a high-powered telescope to examine the presence of the spacecraft behind Hale-Bopp. When nothing was observed behind the comet, the sectarians returned the telescope to the store and demanded their money back. Ferris observed dryly that this empirical disconfirmation of a belief was so overridden by the power of the sect's a priori assumptions that the *un*empirical (and erroneous) conclusion was reached that the telescope was defective.

One of the metaphorical psychoanalytic equivalents of Hale-Bopp's phantom spaceship is the Oedipus complex, together with its little cluster of satellite notions. Modern neuropsychiatry or cognitive psychology is the equivalent of the telescope in Ferris's cautionary tale. It is not known how many hundreds of thousands of these instruments have been returned by Freudians as "not wanted on voyage" or as malfunctioning. Some Freudians even refuse to purchase them in the first place. And some make sure to doctor their documentation to such effect that the telescopes are considered an unnecessary intrusion into the plutonian nether-regions of life as she is lived. This includes Peter L. Rudnytsky, whose *Freud and Oedipus* quotes the very letter to Fliess where the idea of the universal significance of Oedipal desires is first, and autobiographically, broached by Freud. Rudnytsky, perhaps with the help of the Western New England Institute for Psychoanalysis (dutifully thanked in his acknowledgments), decided that the *full* text of the passage in the letter to Fliess was not necessary for the serious (read "psychoanalytic") understanding of the text. A little parenthesis indicating Freud's debt to Fliess's "observations" on his infant son is missing from Rudnytsky's quotation. Sulloway had already referred, in 1979, to the Fliessian origins of Freud's notions about infantile sexuality (see pages 190-91 of the 1979 or 1992 editions of *Freud, Biologist of the Mind*). Rudnytsky's later circumspection is suspect. Who needs telescopes?

Even the contemporary psychoanalytic anti-Christ, Richard Webster, hedges his discussion about Freud's supposed discovery of his own Oedipal longings with a learned section on Ernst Haeckel's 'biogenetic law'[5] and the theories of the now-forgotten Wilhelm Bölsche as Frank J. Sulloway has recovered them. Webster's extensive discussion of the German antecedents of Freud's "biogenetic" thinking has much to do, I believe, with his uncritical faith in Sulloway's *Freud, Biologist of the Mind*, which on pages 199-202 reprints Haeckel's faked diagrams accompanied by a commentary which implies they are valid. Webster should have attended more carefully to the important reservations of Frank Cioffi in his original review of Sulloway's book. Cioffi wrote:

> Sulloway detects a conspiracy to deny the biological inspiration of Freud's thought. But the myth of Freud as a "crypto-biologist" seems to have been invented by Sulloway. Sulloway confuses the question of whether Freud approached his patients with unshakeable convictions as to the nature of

their difficulties with the question of whether these convictions were, in some sense, biological in character. It was only the first of these that the psychoanalytic establishment had an interest in misrepresenting, for it was on the pretension to diagnostic powers denied those who were untrained in psychoanalytic method that it had a pecuniary as well as an emotional investment. (1979, 503)

Webster also ignores the telling—or tell-tale—Freudian parenthesis that Rudnytsky had chosen to conceal from his readers.

It is totally irrelevant to any investigation of Freud's emerging thoughts (or pseudo-hypotheses) that Darwin was a powerful influence on his thinking and that the German biogeneticists were somehow crucial for its development.[6] It is quite true that in later writings, when he needed to shore up parts of his extravagant versions of human development, Freud had recourse to some of the more mystical nineteenth-century German scientific thinkers (though one may say that his published disagreements with his scientific predecessors or contemporaries was more the hallmark of his originality). But I have come to the conclusion that Sulloway is as mistaken about their real influence on Freud (during the heroic years of the last decade of the nineteenth century) as Webster is in his reliance—in this respect—on Sulloway. This is not to say that Sulloway was wrong to examine the contemporary intellectual *Zeitgeist* to which Freud was no doubt, in some way, responsive. On the contrary, there is a wealth of fascinating and relevant documentation in *Freud, Biologist of the Mind*. The reason that much of this material is irrelevant to the developing theories of Freud is that they—the theories and Freud himself—were in thrall to the *Zauberer* from Berlin, Wilhelm Fliess (whether Fliess himself was hooked on Haeckel or some private version of phylogenetic recapitulation is another issue). There is no evidence, in Freud's correspondence with Fliess or with anyone else, that these theories were in any serious way the consequence of Freud's reading of Darwin or his looking at the fraudulent facsimile fetus drawings of hoaxer Haeckel.[7]

Although he has now moved away to a more critical position about Freud, it should be remembered that in his 1979 book Sulloway was cautious about dismantling the edifice of the then predominant Freudians. His frequent, nonironic, use of the noun "insight" for some of Freud's versions of human experience in the 1890s should be a clear warning signal to new readers. The early Sulloway was a sucker for many of the things that passed for science in some quarters during the nineteenth century. His appreciation of Wilhelm Fliess, for instance, is something that would have amazed—and disconcerted—the nineteenth-century doctor Benjamin "Ry"—or Rischawy—(see my Chapter 3). In *Freud, Biologist of the Mind*, Sulloway writes: "As for the success of Fliess's methods, he himself, at the Medical Society for Sexual Science in 1914 [reference omitted], was able to speak of a 75 percent confirmation of his clinical procedures in over three hundred separate medical publications!" (Sulloway 1979 [1992], 152). (That exclamation point is Sulloway's, by the way.) He concludes this paragraph with the following strange observation: "Only Fliess's more ambitious theory of the "nasal reflex neurosis," together with his method of therapeutic treatment, eventually proved ephemeral" (Sulloway 1979 [1992], 152).

Sulloway's "only" implies that he believes (or "believed" in 1979, anyway) in gastric spots in the nostrils that are responsible for tummy pains, or that a touch of the cocaine brush to the right spot can not only relieve but also cure migraines. Who knows? The Sulloway upon whom Webster relies apparently believed many things that he now no longer credits. It is an advance for science that Sulloway has outgrown his earlier beliefs in the nasal notions of Fliess (if, in fact, he has). It would be a further advance for science if Sulloway, Webster, and company could now accept that the origin of the Oedipus complex was not to be found in philosophical tergiversations about "biogenetics" (nineteenth-century German version thereof), but in the convoluted grappling with what Freud thought were his infantile experiences at a moment in his career when he was least reliable and most intellectually and emotionally dependent on Fliess. Frank Cioffi had a pertinent comment on this deficiency in Sulloway's considerations on Freud:

> Sulloway's conviction that evolutionary biology was the secret inspiration of Freud's thought blinds him to other motives for Freud's adopting the views he did. Sulloway can think of no other reason why phylogenetic inheritance tends to loom larger in Freud's later than in his earlier career than that a long-standing Lamarckianism asserted itself more boldly. Freud's Lamarckianism was mostly opportunism. In 1915 he was denying that a child could come by the idea of *coitus a tergo* except through his own experience. What had become of his Lamarckianism? It surfaced in 1918 when he decided that he didn't want his account of the sources of the Wolf Man's symptoms to be completely dependent on the historicity of Freud's conjecture that he had, as an infant, seen a sexual act in the *a tergo* position. Similarly with Freud's other list of infantile traumas— inadequate nursing, premature weaning, seduction by adults, castration threats—it eventually transpired that all could work their mischief without

having characterised the infancy of a patient, since they were undoubtedly to be found in the lives of his ancestors.[8]

Freud may have been at his least reliable—or at his least stable—when he concocted the "Oedipus" scenario; he nevertheless provoked, by that piece of literary prestidigitation, a whole century of learned journal reports on the "evidence" for or against his fantastical version of infancy. I am aware that my last phrase rings polemically, as if there were no debating the status of the Freudian notions; as if there were no point in even considering the material involved as anything except a literary and/or personal extravaganza. And this may be unfair to the many sociologists, anthropologists, and psychiatrists who have written extensively on the subject. (Not that many of them bothered to put in the spadework needed to discover the weird origins of the concept.)[9]

Even Hans J. Eysenck and Glenn D. Wilson in their, by now, classical overview anthology—*The Experimental Study of Freudian Theories*[10]—devote a whole section (part 2) to "Oedipus and Castration Complexes" (113-69). That they were unimpressed by the studies they reprinted is not really the point. The point is that they, rightly, felt it necessary to include this subject in their survey of clinical writings on Freud, so pervasive and intrusive had this Freudian invention become in the fields of psychology and psychotherapy. (This may be more a reflection of the signs of the times when this book was published—1973[11]—than of any need to refute any claimed empirical or epidemiological studies of the time.)

Stuart Sutherland in a recent double review of Elaine Showalter's *Hystories: Hysterical Epidemics and Modern Culture* and Harrison G. Pope, Jr.'s, *Psychology Astray: Fallacies in Studies of "Repressed Memory" and Childhood Trauma* makes the sensible point that:

> A comparison of the two texts [Showalter's and Pope's] shows that, as is usually the case, the prose style and clarity of the scientist are far superior to those of the professor of English. In this postmodernist world, literary criticism might well fare better if it were taken over by scientists. But God help science if literary critics reciprocated this gesture.[12]

Eysenck and Wilson were writing before what Sutherland calls "this postmodernist world" had come into existence as a force to be reckoned with. But they were writing in a world that had been saturated for nearly half a century with sociological, psychological, anthropological, and—

naturally—psychoanalytical reports which took for granted the existence of the "Oedipus complex" and which sought instances of its universality. It may be that the present infatuation of the world of literary studies with Oedipus and his Freudian avatar has less to do with sloppy writing than with sloppy thinking (the former is often no more than the written demonstration of the latter).

In three succinct paragraphs dealing with "repressed memory," Sutherland notes that the psychiatrist Harrison G. Pope "meticulously destroys the findings of a study by L. M. Williams which is the one most cited by believers in repressed memory"[13] and, furthermore, that "[t]here is no need to invoke repression as the cause of forgetting: indeed there is no evidence for the existence of repression."[14] He ends this part of his review with the sentence: "Pope also demonstrates that the belief that sexual abuse propagates from one generation to the next is equally groundless." Without mentioning Freud, Sutherland suggests that Pope has demolished the grounds for psychoanalysis either as a tool of investigation or as a treatment method. Repression, for Freud, was "the corner-stone on which the whole structure of psycho-analysis rests."[15] Sexual abuse (or precocious sexual experience) was seen in 1896 by the Freud of "The Aetiology of Hysteria" paper[16] as an inevitable instigator of later sexual predation (and although he later revised—or claimed to revise—his opinions substantially, he did not relinquish his belief in this part of his paper).

Repressed memories were understood by Freud to be responsible for psychic (and physiological) distress in later years. Repressed memories were not considered as merely inaccessible memories of momentous upset from the early and even, eventually, the first infantile years (or months); they were considered specifically as "concealed" memories of early *sexual* experiences. Memories of other early experiences—of cruelty, of desertion, of social disaster, or of earthquake, fire, and flood (as they say in insurance policies)—were *only* considered for their hidden sexual content which they were assumed to possess and which was seen as the powerful inhibitor of recall, or of conscious access to (unconscious/repressed) memory. If a memory of some early disaster occurs, then that for Freud (and he followed this schema meticulously throughout *The Interpretation of Dreams*) is merely a manifest congeries of symbols disguising the latent and powerfully sexual memory which has been repressed and which will only become accessible to consciousness and interpretable for its sexual—and, hence, general psychological—

significance with the assistance of Freud himself, or one trained in his procedures.

The tempestuous rupture of the intimate friendship with Wilhelm Fliess in 1904 did not cause Freud to reconsider critically the personal phantasmagoria woven obsessively in the last few years of the nineteenth century. He was to insist on this ability of reputed infantile *sexual* activity to cause repression of memory with consequent adult neurosis and/or hysteria. In *Three Essays on Sexuality* (1905), for example, in the section headed, "Second Phase of Infantile Masturbation" (meaning after the truly "new-born" months, but prior to the fourth year), he writes:

> But all its details [those of pre-four-year-old masturbatory activities] leave behind the deepest (unconscious) impressions in the subject's memory, determine the development of his character, if he is to remain healthy, and the symptomatology of his neurosis, if he is to fall ill after puberty. In the latter case we find that this sexual period has been forgotten and that the conscious memories that bear witness to it have been displaced. (I have already mentioned that I am also inclined to relate normal infantile amnesia to this infantile sexual activity.) Psychoanalytic investigation enables us to make what has been forgotten conscious and thus do away with a compulsion that arises from the unconscious psychical material. (*P.F.L.*, 7, 107)

Every single statement in this passage is false and/or deliberately misleading. It provides one of the most succinct demonstrations of (a) what Freud implies by "unconscious," and (b)—knowing what we now know about the neurological reasons for infantile amnesia—the psychoanalytic need for indoctrinating suggestion, implanted by the "therapist," to be at work in such instances of alleged recall. How right Frederick Crews, Elizabeth Loftus, Richard Ofshe and Ethan Watters, and others have been to see Freud's erroneous—and quite impossible— "lifting of the veil of infantile amnesia" as a precursor of the recovered memory movement.[17] (My previous chapter—"Interlude"—gives an early instance of this mistaken approach to human psychological distress, although it deals with the alleged power of supposedly repressed *adult* sexual memories and not with what Freud was to call "primary repression.")

It was with this terrifying unknown element—the powerful repressed sexual memory—that Freud himself was to contend when he made the personal heroic descent into the regions of darkness of his early life. This is perhaps the real "Wagner" side to Sigmund Freud. One needs the orchestral weight of the lower strings and brass, the rhythmic descent of the gods to the underworld where the tuned anvils of the cavernous smithy hammer out *Das Rheingold* and where, for a few bars, they overwhelm and replace the other instruments.

The Oedipus scenario rivals the gods' subterranean voyage. It is theatrical, overpowering, and has been probably the most aesthetically successful tour de force that Freud ever invented. But is it true? But *was* it true? (i.e., did the alleged findings of Freud about his own early years in any reliable way report *fact* rather than self-dramatized misrememberings?).

I know some professors of literature who have been so terrorized by the thoughts of this unknown darkness reputedly lurking within them that they have actually refused to undergo a psychoanalysis, not out of disbelief but, on the contrary, out of fear of what *might* be uncovered by the process. (Hence their refusal of analysis was, paradoxically, the consequence of their overwhelming credence in its power and in its accuracy.)[18] Richard Wagner aimed at the *Gesamtkunstwerk*, where all the arts would be united in one operatic miracle of persuasion. Freud was more economical; the mere suggestion that his personal journey had been horrifying and revealing, and that it had, once undergone, produced an awareness of the human predicament never before grasped was sufficient to provide him with followers and a whole movement of international dimensions.

To return to the surface for a moment, Stuart Sutherland (1997) in his *Nature* review, "Tales of Memory and Imagination," concludes his comments on Elaine Showalter with this thoughtful remark: "She displays an uncritical acceptance of Freudian beliefs and ways of thought, an act of faith now virtually confined to novelists and literary critics, both professions more interested in a good 'narrative' than the truth."

Sigmund's voyage to the hidden, repressed regions of the inaccessible unconscious is indeed a good 'narrative' and may well have produced the "uncritical acceptance" of Showalter and her accomplice novelists and literary critics, as Sutherland meanly suggests. So intrusive have the ramifications of this underground journey become—"penis envy," "castration anxiety," and the other Hale-Bopp satellite phenomena—that social scientists concerned with psychology who emerged after Freudianism may be divided into three categories: those who, like Stuart Sutherland, find it not worth wasting time over;[19] those who, like Seymour

Fisher and Roger Greenberg, seek to support "the validity of various Freudian theories";[20] and those who seek to refute their validity.

The Canadian researchers Martin Daly and Margo Wilson may be firmly placed in this last category. Their 1990 paper "Is Parent-Offspring Conflict Sex-Linked? Freudian and Darwinian Models"—running-head short title "Oedipus"—demonstrates very clearly, in an article which is sober in style and massively documented (including material selected for Fisher and Greenberg's 1977 attempt to provide "scientific evidence" for Freud's underground adventures), that the Freudian notion of "Oedipal rivalry" is a nonstarter on any level, animal or human. They even spare space to refute, tellingly, Melford E. Spiro's book-length attempt to challenge the anthropologist Bronislaw Malinowski's "famous claim that the Oedipus complex was absent among the matrilineal Trobriand islanders."[21] Just like everywhere else, one is sorely tempted to add.

But their most trenchant rebuttal is that of C. Hall and R. L. van de Castle's efforts to study dream reports "in support of Oedipal theory" from an "empirical" point of view.[22] Daly and Wilson's paragraph on this is worth quoting to show the infelicities that can result from the acceptance by social scientists of theories whose unreliable cocaine- and Fliess-inspired origins they were clearly unaware of. Here it is, as published by the *Journal of Personality*—an example, perhaps, of the free play of ideas in the United States, given that the same journal had been host to the original articles of Hall and van de Castle:

> Hall and van de Castle's (1965) results in support of Oedipal theory are in any case trivially necessitated by their methodology: Exactly symmetrical dreams (e.g., "a male dreams that he is a woman" versus "a female dreams that she is a man") were scored as manifestations of "castration anxiety" or "penis envy" according to the sex of the dreamer, and then the sex difference in these scores was treated as a meaningful empirical result. Although Eysenck and Wilson (1973) pointed out this fatal flaw, the study has continued to be cited as strong evidence for Freud's theories (Fisher & Greenberg, 1977; Liebert & Spiegler, 1982). Note too that positive or negative affect was not relevant to Hall and van de Castle's scoring; the central constructs might just as fairly have been labeled "vagina envy" and "penis anxiety." (Daly and Wilson 1990, 176)

What is the Freudian origin for all this mass of professional publications and refutations? Some lifelong, or at any rate, career-long, reputations have been built on Freud's "explorations" or "discoveries" of the Oedipus complex and its supposed diverse adjuncts. And in the popular domain of general discourse, Freud's inventions have found fertile ground for nearly three-quarters of a century. In France, *"résoudre son oedipe"* means to "resolve one's conflictual relations with one's parents" (or, and by extension, with parental or authority figures). The "oedipus" has become as much a metaphor of common parlance as that other well-known Freudian formula "anally retentive" (from which, presumably, the Americanism "uptight" descends).[23] In fact, by these two terms alone Freud has achieved the lexicographical anonymity normally reserved for propositions which are either objectively verifiable or else sanctified by hundreds of years of traditional belief. A glance at the *Webster's Third New International Dictionary* will show that "anal character" and its cognates and "Oedipus complex" and its cognates are all defined as aspects of human psychological maturation processes without a single reference either to "psychoanalysis" or to "Sigmund Freud." Neither this little book, nor the many forceful forays of the effervescent Frederick Crews, nor even the latest salvo of the British neurologist, Raymond Tallis,[24] will be sufficient to change a dictionary definition. One may hope, however, that in the fullness of time the compounded results of serious investigation into the origins of psychoanalysis will oblige lexicographers to substitute fact for mythology. Samuel Johnson's honest, "up-front" excuse to the lady who queried his idiosyncratic definition in his Dictionary of "pastern" as the "knee" of a horse—"ignorance, Madam, pure ignorance"—is now required of those responsible for the current edition of *Webster's*.

Freud's personal "Oedipal" mythology is first explicitly announced in his letter to Fliess of October 15, 1897. He writes, "[T]he Greek legend seizes upon a compulsion which everyone recognizes because he senses its existence within himself. Everyone in the audience was once a budding Oedipus in fantasy and each recoils in horror from the dream fulfillment here transplanted into reality, with the full quantity of repression which separates his infantile state from his present one" (Masson 1985, 272).[25] Freud's phrase "the full quantity of repression which separates his infantile state from his present one" is a neurological nonstarter. The inability of adults to recollect (even in tranquillity) "memories" of infantile moments is *not* the consequence of an ideational process (which is itself necessary for Freud's "repression" to have any psychological meaning at all—repression without ideation is devoid of significance). It is, at least, the consequence of the immature state of the neuronal formation of the brain in early years.[26] Freud's phrase is, however, also a nonstarter to the extent that it completely ignores 50 percent of humankind—women. It is also, of course, entirely—and specifically—Eurocentric.

But to understand and properly situate this theatrical invention of Freud's we have to step back from the late autumn of 1897, to before the summer months when the Freud family was on holiday in Italy. The year 1897 was in many respects one of Freud's busiest. In February, he tells Fliess that he is working "11½ to 12½ hours daily" and that "I now have ten patients in treatment, including one from Budapest; another one from Breslau is due to arrive. It is probably one hour too much" (letter of February 8, 1897, Masson 1985, 230). He was compiling the material for what would become *The Interpretation of Dreams* and was making notes for an outline of the sources of hysteria (a kind of "theoretical" continuation of the "Aetiology of Hysteria" paper of the previous spring).

Sometime in the second half of March 1897, his eldest child Mathilde nearly died from an attack of septic diphtheria (letters to Fliess of March 17, March 29, and April 6). Two of these letters were omitted from the original edition of the correspondence edited by Anna Freud, Ernst Kris and Marie Bonaparte, and one was seriously censored.[27] The significance of this in relation to the authenticity of the date and the analysis of "The Dream of Irma's Injection"—which in chapter 2 of *The Interpretation of Dreams* stands as the paradigm of dream interpretation—is discussed in Wilcocks (1994).[28]

Freud continued his investigations into ("researches into" would be a misleading description)[29] the origins of hysteria, which he now believed were to be found in infantile sexual material overheard by babies. This was the year which had opened with the infamous "phonographic" recall by an adult female patient of a conversation allegedly overheard when she had been eleven months old (letter of January 24). Much to the irritation and evident embarrassment of the man who was to treat Mathilde during her diphtheria crisis, Dr. Oscar Rie, Freud persisted in expanding the psychological consequences of such infantile material coaxed from, or suggested to, his patients. As he confided to Fliess in his letter of April 6, 1897:

> The point that escaped me in the solution of hysteria lies in the discovery of a different source, from which a new element of the product of the unconscious arises. What I have in mind are hysterical fantasies which regularly, as I see it, go back to things that children overhear at an early age and understand only subsequently. The age at which they take in

information of this kind is, strangely enough, from six to seven months on! Brother-in-law Rie implored me to drop this one point (probably he has been charged with this mission) and repeatedly asked me what you have to say about this novelty. (Masson 1985, 234–35)

Freud did not "drop this one point"—on the contrary, he seems to have relished its development. In the letter of April 28, 1897, he recounts listening to a "hysterical" woman patient (suffering from insomnia) who had come to him, fully aware of his reputation as a sexologist. She confesses that, between the ages of eight to twelve years, her father had regularly taken her to bed and "misused" her, but without penetration. Freud concludes his report to Fliess thus: "Of course, when I told her that similar and worse things must have happened in her earliest childhood, she could not find it incredible. In other respects it is a quite ordinary case of hysteria with the usual symptoms. Q.E.D." (Masson 1985, 238)

There is no indication, beyond Freud's report to Fliess, that this patient's father "*regularly* took her to bed." Whether this is a Freudian embroidery for the sake of prurient effect or an honest report of an honest "confession" we shall never know. The importance of this letter of April 28, 1897, is in the concluding passage noted above. Whatever misdemeanors the father reputedly committed on his prenubile daughter, they are insufficient for Freud's inventive obsessions. There had to be infantile moments of sexual abuse which had been "forgotten"—"primary repression"—for the patient's case to fit into the "ordinary case of hysteria with the usual symptoms," or, one is tempted to add, "the ordinary case of nasal reflex neurosis." For Freud is here following, with a lack of clinical discrimination, the ideas about early sexual abuse elaborated by Fliess in his 1893 lecture (see note 15). The "similar and worse things" which must have occurred in this woman's infancy are clearly a continuing thematic pattern of the notions vented in the "phonograph" letter of January. Freud required some kind of corroboration of infantile molestation for his "seduction theory," and the prepubescent incestuous encounters were insufficient. In the privacy of his correspondence with Fliess, Freud does not bother to claim any mastery over putative "resistances" or "amnesias" of infantile sex; he squarely *tells* his female patient that "similar and worse things must have happened in her earliest childhood"[30] and adds, "she could not find it incredible."

That last phrase is strange and deserves a sentence or two. Why does Freud write "she *could* not" rather than she "*did*" not? A childhood incestuous sexual intimacy has been given to Freud (if we credit his report) and nonetheless he implies that the patient may be prepared to find the occasion of infantile harassment a credible possibility, although she has apparently had no recollection of such activity. This may be an instance of Freud's powers of persuasion (and self-persuasion) rather than an instance that would serve to confirm his theorizing. "She *could* not" may, of course, simply indicate an early stage of the treatment when Freud has yet to give her the details of what he imagines has occurred to her in her diaper stage. And what is implied by the loaded phrase "worse things" that Freud claims to have suggested to his patient? Even in the (relatively) unbuttoned correspondence with Fliess, there are Freudian secrets.

What is really significant about this letter is the revelation, not merely of what Grünbaum was to call "contamination by suggestion" (i.e., of the data of the psychoanalytic encounter), but of the typical procedures of a Freudian "therapeutic" session. "Memories," which may have been neither real, nor available, nor aroused (nor even causative of, or relevant to, the patient's present state), are offered to the patient by Freud as the first steps on the path to recovery. Freud, at this stage, firmly believed that the roots of hysteria were to be discovered in the early months of infantile amnesia. He also believed (apparently) that the patient's health would not return without such discovery. It is in this respect that Freud (given the future organizational strength of his enterprise) has to be considered as the most dangerous and damaging of modern psychologists.

The month of May was particularly fertile for Freud. From the letter of May 2 to the last of the month (May 31, 1897), he sent Fliess enclosures with his letters that are now called "Drafts L., M., and N."[31] These concern, as the title of the first two drafts indicates, "The Architecture of Hysteria." They also provide, in a Cole's or Monarch Notes fashion, an outline of Freud's burgeoning "science" of psycho-analysis. Most of the later key concepts (e.g., fixation, symbolic action, repression, fantasies, repression in the Unconscious, impulses, motives for symptom formation) are already formulated—albeit telegraphically—in these few pages drafted for Fliess. Judging from the mostly anonymous patient examples that occur in between the paragraphs of theorizing, these drafts seem to be an instance of Freud's ability to link his ongoing analyses of patients, some of whose adult and adolescent "memories" are noted (but always, and only, for their genital significance), with his fundamental reliance on the infantile sexual component as the originator of all later distress. It is difficult to know whether Freud in these drafts is demonstrating to Fliess that his own "psychological" advances have been as fruitful as the magician's "organic" advances, or whether he is still so absorbed by the latter's assumed medical and intellectual brilliance that he is trying to signal his own progress in order to retain a measure of companionate respect from him.

Freud begins "Draft L." with a thesis that certainly corresponds with his earlier observations to Fliess about the strange resilience of infantile memories and the fact that what was perceived without intelligence in infancy will become a formative item of the personality upon the later remembrance of the occasion, this later remembrance according the original event a full quotient of sexual meaning:

> The aim seems to be to reach the earliest [sexual] scenes [*Urszenen*].[32] In a few cases this is achieved directly, but in others only by a detour via fantasies. For fantasies are psychic facades produced in order to bar access to these memories. Fantasies simultaneously serve the tendency toward refining the memories, toward sublimating them. They are manufactured by means of things that are *heard*, and utilized *subsequently*, and thus combine things experienced and heard, past events (from the history of parents and ancestors), and things that have been seen by oneself. (Masson 1985, 240)

Such as they are, these sketches show that strange admixture of ingenuity and obsession which were to mark Freud's career henceforth. Whether one says that the "key concepts" of psychoanalysis were already present, or the "key errors" of psychoanalysis were already being honed into convoluted shape, is a matter of critical judgment. One quotation from the second paragraph of Draft M., "Repression," will suffice to give the flavor (and the level of sophistication of the arguments used):

> It is to be supposed that the element essentially responsible for repression[33] is always what is feminine. This is confirmed by the fact that women as well as men admit more readily to experiences with women than with men. What men essentially repress is the pederastic element. (Masson 1985, 246)

If by "pederastic element," Freud means male adolescent homoerotic activities, then his use of the word "repression" is already dangerously misleading. What is *concealed* from a therapist is not *necessarily* the consequence of repression. As Harrison G. Pope writes of the Donna Della Femina study: "As Femina and her colleagues so clearly demonstrated in their 'clarification interviews,' cases of seeming repression on initial interview regularly turn out to represent deliberate non-disclosure" (Pope 1997, 61). "Withholding" does *not* equal "repressing." For Freud to have admitted this elementary point of principle would have meant the end of his "metapsychological" constructions and the necessary hara-kiri of psychoanalysis.

In fact, in less than six months (letter of November 14, 1897), Freud had already rejected one aspect of this hunch. He writes to Fliess:

> This is where I have got to so far—with all the inherent obscurities. I have resolved, then, henceforth to regard as separate factors what causes libido and what causes anxiety. I have also given up the idea of explaining libido as the masculine factor and repression as the feminine one. (Masson 1985, 281)

The summer months were spent hoping for a "congress" with Wilhelm Fliess, in August, at the resort in Aussee. One recalls the phrases of the letter of June 22, 1897: "In Aussee I know a wonderful wood full of ferns and mushrooms where you must reveal to me the secrets of the world of lower animals and the world of children." September was out because the Freuds were going to central Italy; the summer idyll with Fliess was doomed by floods that cut off the railway line to Aussee for a time. This was all explained in Freud's letter of August 5, 1897, to "Excellenza," as he addressed Frau Ida Fliess. Less than ten days later, Freud was writing to Fliess himself about the nuisance of the summer floods and adding in the same letter (of August 14, 1897) hints that he was revising his theories about the neuroses—"tormented by grave doubts about my theory of the neuroses"—and mentioning his difficulties with his beginning self-analysis.

As soon as Freud had returned to Vienna from Italy, he wrote to Fliess the famous letter recanting his *neurotica* (Tuesday, September 21, 1897). It is a very cheerful, high-spirited letter, and Freud himself comments on the strange discrepancy between his feelings and what he *should* be feeling announcing such a defeat. He begins with a private admission of therapeutic and theoretical failure to Fliess—an admission that runs quite counter to the claims made before the psychiatrists and physicians who had heard his "Aetiology of Hysteria" paper the year before.

> The continual disappointment in my efforts to bring a single analysis to a real conclusion; the running away of people who for a period of time had

been most gripped [by analysis]; the absence of the complete successes on which I had counted; the possibility of explaining to myself the partial successes in other ways, in the usual fashion—this was the first group. (Masson 1985, 264)

If these statements by Freud are true (and they have the "ring of truth"), then what he had claimed before the assembled physicians the previous year had been completely untrue. His presentation to them had been a series of extravagant universalist claims (the theories) and untruths (the therapeutic successes)—and one should remember that Freud told his medical audience, which included psychiatrists, that he had invented case histories for their edification and had explained to them that the recounting of a "real" case history would take too much time. Freud seems, indeed, to have relied on that occasion on his own theatrical presence and his emerging brilliance with rhetorical flam. In the whole lecture, "The Aetiology of Hysteria," not one single case history is presented and analyzed for its findings. But, Freud's letter of recantation to Fliess is so full of its own contradictory statements and/or of statements which run counter to his previous assertions that one is at a loss to know where the truth of his predicament begins.

Had he, perhaps, taken to heart the force of the comment of the pioneering sexologist, Richard Krafft-Ebing, who had chaired the meeting? We know from the angry letter of Freud to Fliess of April 26, 1896 (see Masson 1985, 184), how much he was infuriated by the "icy reception" given his paper and by Krafft-Ebing's assessment, *"Es klingt wie ein wissenschaftisches Märchen!"*—"It sounds like a scientific fairy tale." Or had he decided to "brass it out" (as Kipling would say) and continue his explorations of ever-earlier psychological potential sources of adult hysteria? The letters in the year and a half that follow the "Aetiology of Hysteria" paper (April 21, 1896) show, if anything, an increasing reliance on Fliess's notions of male and female periodicity and on infantile sexuality.

In fact three years before this lecture, Freud already appears to have accepted, without any reservation, the etiological arguments of Fliess. From the crucial letter of May 30, 1893, where Freud revealed that he was "making this diagnosis"—that is, of Fliess's nasal reflex neurosis—"very often," it would seem that his grasp of human psychology was to be subject to the approval of Fliess and would henceforth be confined to versions of human reality that issued from Fliess's communications.

Freud's second reason for abandoning his *neurotica* was that "in all cases, the *father*, not excluding my own, had to be accused of being perverse." This was in no way a consequence of the "Aetiology of Hysteria" paper. Those accused in that paper were nurses, servants, females of various sorts, and peer-group members. Freud's other reasons, as given in this letter of September 21, 1897, are all bound up with his own private definitions of the "Unconscious"—a word which from his pen had long since departed from any recognizable origin in German philosophy and had simply come to mean "anything to do with *early sexuality*." And by "early sexuality," Freud seems to include anything from the toilet-training difficulties of infancy that he himself later appeared—or claimed—to remember, to moments of purely physiological healthiness in an infant male that Fliess had recorded (and mentioned) concerning his own young son.

Freud paid a visit to Fliess in Berlin toward the end of September 1897, and claimed, on his return to Vienna, to have been "refreshed" by the encounter. In his letter of October 3, 1897, he writes, in an opening paragraph which in itself is sufficient to dampen any enthusiasm for Sulloway's ingenious invention of a "Freud, biologist of the mind" under the influence of a "Darwinian" Fliess:

> My visit has had the advantage of acquainting me with the framework of your current work in its entirety, so that you can relate further details to me . . . each time I am grateful to you for every little item that you unselfishly let come my way. For example, your comments on the relationship between infection and conception in mother and daughter seemed to me highly significant because these can after all be explained only by a condition in the eternal life of the protoplasm and not by one in the life of the individual—that is, because they must be dependent on absolute time and not on life-time. (Masson 1985, 268)

It is in this same letter that he writes of his struggles to discover the infantile sexual origins of his own self-acknowledged hysteria (a struggle every bit as desperate as the one with the cocaine-brush): "For the last four days my self-analysis, which I consider indispensable for the clarification of the whole problem, has continued in dreams and has presented me with the most valuable elucidations and clues" (Masson 1985, 268).

A little later in the same paragraph, we find the famous passage where Freud uncovers, or invents, or misremembers, an occasion for having seen his mother nude. Peter L. Rudnytsky in *Freud and Oedipus* had access to, and quotes from, the complete Freud–Fliess correspondence edited by Jeffrey Masson; but in this instance he chooses to use the 1954 censored, bowdlerized edition. This is what he quotes (the ellipsis is his):

> Later (between the ages of two and two-and-a-half) libido towards *matrem* was aroused; the occasion must have been the journey with her from Leipzig to Vienna, during which we spent a night together and I must have had the opportunity of seeing her *nudam*. . . . My anxiety over travel you have yourself seen in full bloom.[34]

Rudnytsky tries to relate this to Freud's "Hollthurn" dream in *The Interpretation of Dreams*—"the 'Hollthurn' dream thus provides a textbook example of the psychoanalytic theory of dream formation" (Rudnytsky 1987, 73)—and then quotes Ernest Jones on the episode:

> On the journey from Leipzig to Vienna, a year later, Freud had occasion to see his mother naked: an awesome fact which forty years later he related in a letter to Fliess—but in Latin! Curiously enough he gives his age then as between two and two and a half whereas he was in fact four years old on that journey. One must surmise that the memories of two such experiences had got telescoped.[35]

Why the vision of Amalie Nathanson Freud in the altogether should have been considered "an awesome fact" for the four- (rather than two-and-a-half-) year-old Sigmund, is not revealed by Jones. Jones, of course, and as a matter of course, had read Freud's 1927 paper on fetishism and had, no doubt, remembered the dire consequences proclaimed by Freud for those males (of supposed Oedipal or post-Oedipal age) who saw a nude female full-frontal: "Probably no male human being is spared the fright of castration at the sight of a female genital."[36] The publishers of *Penthouse* have earned great sums of money by wisely (and commercially) ignoring this suggestion. And the young "goldener Sigi" in the night train puffing toward Vienna—if the adult-contrived memory is to be credited—had not yet read this 1927 essay. But, then, neither had the even younger Robert Fliess.

Here now is what Freud wrote to Fliess in the unexpurgated translation of the Harvard Univerity Press edition:

> I can only indicate that the old man [Jacob Freud, father] plays no active part in my case . . . that in my case the "prime originator" was an ugly, elderly, but clever woman, who told me a great deal about God Almighty

and hell and who instilled in me a high opinion of my own capacities;[37] that later (between two and two and a half years) my libido toward *matrem* was awakened, namely, on the occasion of a journey with her from Leipzig to Vienna, during which we must have spent the night together and there must have been an opportunity of seeing her *nudam* (*you inferred the consequences of this for your son long ago, as a remark revealed to me*). (Masson 1985, 268; my emphasis)

Rudnytsky's ferreting away of that final little parenthesis is clever and revealing and very Appignanesi- and Forrester-like in its treatment of texts by Freud. And—as with Appignanesi and Forrester, or, earlier, Anna Freud and company—the only reason (or motive?) for the censorship is that the full revelation of the truth would create problems for the established doctrinal status of the founder's utterances. This letter was written on October 3, 1897; Robert Fliess (Wilhelm Fliess's first child) was born on December 29, 1895. Therefore, at the time of Freud's letter, "your son" was just over one year and nine months old. In that letter—and in the censored parenthesis—Freud notes that Fliess had confided "long ago" the "consequences" of infantile libido.

One must assume—though we have no texts to prove it—that what Fliess revealed to Freud was that the infant son had erections and that the infantile erections were caused by the sight of the naked Ida Fliess in the bedroom. The spontaneous erections of infant males are something that is neither more nor less than the physiological activity of a healthy infant; all parents (I write as a parent and recent grandparent) will have observed this, and all, not terrified by psychoanalysis or some other religion, will have accepted it as an aspect of the infant's physiological normality. Sulloway, in his dealing with this question, writes:

> Prior to Freud's self-analysis, Fliess had even informed Freud that his son Robert, now in the second year of life, *had become sexually aroused by the sight of his mother's naked body*—the same and supposedly quite revolutionary, self-analytic revelation that *later* occurred to Freud in October 1897 when he attempted to penetrate the shroud of his infantile amnesia. (Sulloway 1979 [1992], 191; my emphasis)

Sulloway's presentation of this whole episode is naïve, to put it mildly. At no time does he raise the obvious (one would have thought) point that *spontaneous* infantile erections are just that—*spontaneous*. He incorporates Fliess's apparent interpretation into the body of his text, as if it were in any conceivable way valid. Sulloway's naïveté is shown up in the first sentence of his very next paragraph: "Wilhelm Fliess's *discoveries* on the subject of infantile sexuality bring me to the second question" (Sulloway 1979 [1992], 191; my emphasis). The point is that Fliess made *no* discoveries about infantile sexuality. What he did do was to observe two things and make an erroneous connection: (1) Robert Fliess—aged less than two years—had an erection; (2) Ida Fliess was present and naked: *therefore* the presence of the latter caused the former. It is understandable (just) that the freaked-out Freud of the 1890s should have credited his seductive friend's incestuous interpretation of a physiological contingency that had nothing to do with the presence of a nude mother, and that he should have tried to invent a memory of a similar incestuous infantile arousal from his own infantile existence; what is far less understandable is that a young American graduate in the late 1970s should have complied with such a nonsensical (and antibiological) version of the events.

Fliess's "remark revealed to me" was to operate on Freud's imagination for the rest of his life (for, unlike the "seduction theory," the "Oedipal theory" was never renounced) and to incite him—by its Fliessian inferences, and by the inferences Freud was to draw from those inferences—to elaborate an inventive series of constructs about infantile and childhood sexuality whereby the role of the fantasy-forming consciousness is provoked into action by the chemistry of the body's desires from the earliest months of life. (This is giving an adult consciousness—with all that that implies—to the scarcely formed consciousness of the infant.) In Freud's original parenthetical reference to Fliess's observations on his infant son, the phrase "you inferred the *consequences* of this for your son [my emphasis]" can only refer to the supposed immediate "consequences" of an infant seeing a mother nude. Fliess's sexy and intriguing mistake—unrecognized as such by Freud—allowed the latter to assume (and then to richly embroider upon) two false notions: (1) that male infantile erections are the result of ideational excitement; (2) that the loss of the memory of such moments is an act of repression.

But beyond these two errors, Freud elaborated the "Oedipal" interpretation of infancy and childhood whereby the word "consequences" takes on a significance not evident in Fliess's remarks. Fliess, strangely, one may think, was more modest in his inferences than Freud. For Fliess, the equation was limited to: $A + B = C$ (where A = nude mother; B = infant son; C = erection). For Freud, virtually the whole alphabet was to be employed in the various consequences of the original tripartite equation. These Freud-invented "consequences" cannot have been intended in Fliess's observation to his close friend (or, if they were, then psychoanalysis really was the invention/discovery of Wilhelm Fliess and not of Sigmund Freud).

If the infant male desires the mother, then the infant's father must be the successful rival, and therefore hated (one may ask, in parenthesis, what is revealed of the psychology of someone who assumes rivals should be "therefore hated"?). Some twelve years later (1909), Freud was to note in a circular argument in the "Discussion" section of *Analysis of a Phobia in a Five-year-old Boy: 'Little Hans,'* "But his father, whom he could not help hating as a rival." As he clearly states, elsewhere, in the same case discussion: "Hans really was a little Oedipus who wanted to have his father 'out of the way,' to get rid of him, so that he might be alone with his beautiful mother and sleep with her."[38] This, it is true, is a description of a five-year-old, not of an infant in the first months of life. And a five-year-old may perhaps have ambiguous feelings about his relationship with his parents. Whether these ambiguous feelings are "Oedipal" is another question. In the case of "Little Hans" (son of a psychoanalytically devoted father),[39] Freud has brought his own particular sentiments (or the constructed memories of what he supposed his infantile feelings to have been) to bear on the interpretation of the child's situation.

Young "Hans" is as much a displacement of Sigmund's strange inner world as was the report vouchsafed about young Robert Fliess.[40] Mothers, one might add, in Freud's compendium of Oedipal fantasies, have to be "beautiful." (One wonders why. Aren't maternal devotion and affection sufficient? The answer is "No." They may be sufficient for an infantile sense of security; they are insufficient for the "fantasy"-inspired arousal of infantile libido which apparently requires the adult-recognized aesthetic of sexual beauty.) In his letters to Fliess where he recounts his contrived memories of his childish moments of fear and panic at the supposed loss of a mother (e.g., the letter of October 15, 1897 [Masson 1985, 271]), the mother is represented as "beautiful": "I cried even more until, slender and beautiful, she came in through the door." When this incident is redrafted in *The Psychopathology of Everyday Life*, the same adjective "beautiful" occurs. In the case of Little Hans, the same thing happens—"so that he might be alone with his beautiful mother and sleep with her." We have no idea from the text of "Little Hans" whether his mother was beautiful, ugly, or simply passable; nor do we know what the young hero's aesthetic—or, indeed, sexual—responses to her may have been.

This raises the interesting question that Freud himself may have had, or have given himself (by cocaine-enhanced introspection), a homemade "Oedipal complex"—or the imagined first stages of it—and then, as per usual, grafted a universal and universally inevitable status onto his own (pathological) dilemma. One recalls his strange universalization reported in the letter to Fliess of October 15, 1897: "Everyone in the audience was once a budding Oedipus *in fantasy.*" And, if such is the case, then one is obliged to admit that such a thing as "the Oedipus complex" exists (at least in fantasy). After all, Freud had (or, rather, gave himself) one. The Hale-Bopp evidence is there; the only mistake was to universalize a supposed formative psychological idiosyncrasy of the self. One must remember that Freud's reference to a "budding Oedipus in fantasy" is a theatrical continuation of his brooding announced in the letter of just twelve days earlier about the infant Robert Fliess's swaddling erections. (One sees in these letters the dramatically mythologizing mind at work.) A collateral of this was Freud's insistence that, if there is no recall of such a predicament, then that is a prima facie case of repression—primal repression of the various Freudian sexological versions of the neurologically impossible *Urszene* (or "primal scene"). Once again the fact, and it *is* a fact, that infantile amnesia is not of ideational origin is totally ignored. There is no evidence—in any of Freud's correspondence or in any of the published papers, including the *Three Essays on Sexuality*—that Freud ever considered the ubiquity of infantile amnesia as anything other than an instance of the powerful taboo of sexual experience, exerting, in this case, its force upon the mind of the infant. Freud was still writing about it *as a fact* when he was in his seventies (1932) in the first of the *New Introductory Lectures on Psychoanalysis*, "Revision of the Theory of Dreams." Whatever complexities his inquisitive mind had pursued, they apparently excluded any serious and empirically critical regard toward the notions embraced during those heady days of the 1890s with Wilhelm Fliess as his sole intellectual partner.

In the profoundly unreliable and persuasively written *Autobiographical Study* of 1925, Freud recalls his abandonment of the "seduction theory" and his discovery of the "Oedipus complex" in a way which ingeniously disculpates him from ever having *suggested* to his patients that they had been sexually abused as infants and in a way which, quite wrongly, remembers the Oedipal scenario as having been encountered accidentally, as it were, and not as the enthusiastically crafted fantasy it was. Freud writes:

> I do not believe even now that I forced the seduction-phantasies on my patients, that I 'suggested' them. I had in fact stumbled for the first time upon the *Oedipus Complex*, which was later to assume such an overwhelming importance, but which I did not recognize as yet in its disguise of phantasy. (*S.E.* 20, 34)

As the letter of October 15, 1897—"everyone in the audience was once a budding Oedipus in fantasy"—reveals, Freud had certainly grasped the imaginary power of his invention from its very inception in his writings. And this letter, we recall, was drafted less than two weeks after the hokum memory of the famous *matrem nudam* letter to Fliess.

Freud never drafted—so far as we know—any version of his parents' infantilely perceived coupling; the only remnant of autobio-graphical— and evidently invented—Oedipal memory is of the two-and-a-half-year-old having an erection at the sight of the naked mother. This fictitious and erroneously conceived elaboration of an infantile moment is insufficient to warrant the rhetorical splendor that Freud was to lavish upon it in subsequent years. The later inventions, theoretical and rhetorical—though in Freud's writings, the theoretical and the rhetorical are coterminous— were to create the notions of sexual rivalry with the father; sexual fear of paternal retribution; abject fear of castration (Freud's word for ablation of the penis, not the testes); and a full-blown, uniquely sexualized account of the journey from diaper to jockstrap.

There is more than one mistake here. What Freud *thought* he had (or suffered from), and extrapolated that everyone else had (or suffered from), was a consequence of his own deluded adult responses to what he wrongly assumed had been his own infantile responses. In the case of the infantile erections, and what he assumed had been the reasons for them, the adult Freud's claim to be able to recall specific moments, quite irrespective of the adult mythologizing of their significance, is a virtual guarantee that we are dealing with fiction and not reality. This is where the *Rheingold* Wagnerian scenario begins, with the descent into the alleged resistant depths of his own infantile experiences and memories thereof. Freud is no more credible in the full light of day than Wagner. In the flickering torchlight of his own subterranean smithy, he becomes horribly persuasive. As Justin Wintle notes in an important aside to his review of Crews's *The Memory Wars*, recalling his own anxious nightmares about his gentle, hemophiliac father:

> But then comes Freud, straight out of the sewer, with his occult claptrap
> about repression and the Oedipus Complex. Didn't you know, his books
> tell me, that all along you wanted your father out of the way? That that's
> why the nightmares continue, as covert wish fulfilment? His [Wintle's
> father's] illness must have especially deflected his wife's attention away
> from her son. But your Unconscious has remained busy. Your Unconscious
> has never stopped devising stratagems for your father's demise.[41]

In a sense, for all the vitriol passed between his daughter Anna Freud
and his disciple Melanie Klein, it was in truth Melanie Klein who came
closer to what Freud assumed infantile mentation, and its later disguises,
to have been. This cannot be comforting to that diminishing group of still-
credulous Freudians; but it remains the case that, by precisely situating
infantile experiences as equivalents of adult neurotic and psychopathic
responses, Melanie Klein was continuing the good work of the founder
and benefactor of psychoanalysis.

Here are two brief instances. Neither is "Oedipal"; but both share
with the Oedipus scenario (with which they are contemporaneous) the
argument that the origins of adult nonsexual anxiety will be discovered in
"repressed" infantile memories of "sexual" difficulties.

In the letter to Fliess of October 4, 1897, Freud recounts his struggles
to recall his own infantile moments of unpleasure, and then elaborates
from his recollections an alleged psychopathogenic network of causation
for his later neurosis. Thus he establishes a causal link between infantile
"sexual" experiences—here, toilet training—and later school difficulties,
and, most recently, incompetence as a therapist. He has analyzed a dream
in which the subject matter, he imagines, was related to his infantile
awkwardness. He writes:

> Today's dream has, under the strangest disguises, produced the following:
> she [his nurse, Monika Zajíc] was my teacher in sexual matters and
> complained because I was clumsy and unable to do anything.
>
> (Neurotic impotence always comes about in this way. *The fear of not
> being able to do anything at all in school thus obtains its sexual
> substratum*.) At the same time I saw the skull of a small animal and in the
> dream I thought "pig," but in the analysis I associated it with your wish
> two years ago that I might find, as Goethe once did, a skull on the Lido to
> enlighten me. But I did not find it. So [I was] a "little blockhead" [literally,
> a sheep's head]. The whole dream was full of the most mortifying allusions

to my present impotence as a therapist. Perhaps this is where the inclination to believe in the incurability of hysteria begins. (Masson 1985, 269; my emphasis.)

Towards the end of the year (letter of December 22, 1897), Freud gives an example taken from a female patient. In regard to obsessional neurosis, he reports, "I have found confirmation that the locality at which the repressed breaks through is the *word presentation* and not the concept attached to it. (More precisely, the word memory.)" This novel idea is demonstrated by Freud's illustration of the reluctance of a female patient to accept the termination of a sewing class:

> A girl attending a sewing class that soon will come to an end is plagued by the obsessional idea: "No, you mustn't leave; you have not yet *finished*; you must still *make* more; you must still learn all sorts of things." Behind this lay the memory of childhood scenes in which she was put on the pot, did not want to remain there, and experienced the same compulsion: "You mustn't leave; you have not yet *finished*; you must still *make* more." The word "make" permits the later situation to be brought together with the infantile one. Obsessional ideas frequently are clothed in a characteristic *verbal vagueness* in order to permit such multiple deployment. If one takes a closer (conscious) look at it, one finds alongside it the expression "You must still learn more," which perhaps later becomes the fixed obsessional idea and arises through a mistaken interpretation of this kind on the part of the conscious. (Masson 1985, 287-88)

This is, incidentally, an interesting early instance of Freud's brilliant use of narrative dexterity. Time condensation (a kind of chronological foreshortening), thematic focusing, disappearance of the narrator and his questions to be replaced by the responses elicited (themselves offered with their appropriate interpretation as part and parcel of a psychic *truth*), are such as he was to employ, for example, much later in "Two Lies Told by Children" (1913).[42] Statements which are here presented as narrative *fact*—"Behind this lay the memory of childhood scenes in which she was put on the pot"—are, in reality, authorial intrusions based upon theoretical suppositions. We do not know, and cannot tell, whether the female patient made these connections; nor, indeed, whether, *if she made them*, they were the responses suggested by the thematic line of questioning by the "hidden" narrator. Nor can we tell if the chronology of the tale is twofold or threefold. It begins with a present participle, goes into the future "will soon come to an end," returns to the present "is plagued," before settling into a narrative past "[b]ehind this lay." And the last half is set in the present tense of the narrator explaining the actuality and accuracy of the deductions made. These hypothetic deductions, which, as I have said, are presented as *fact* in the narrative proper, are granted a status of self-evidence in the concluding present-tense statements.

As for the chronology, are we dealing with an adolescent patient and a supposed infantile memory? This is twofold; and the sewing class must be contemporaneous with the visits to Berggasse 19. Or are we dealing with an adult female patient, an adolescent memory and, behind that, an infantile memory? This is threefold; and those opening present and future tenses are highly misleading. In this case, they do not refer to a contemporaneity of events and must be a highly condensed way of producing a vivid account of what may have been obtained by the patient's guided recollections and associations (similar to the use of the dramatic present-tense narratives of dreams in *Die Traumdeutung*).[43] In both chronological possibilities, by the way, we are still dealing with a Freudian investigation which has taken for granted the existence of infantile amnesia based on ideational repression. We may have forgotten that the tale is prefaced by Freud's "I have found confirmation that the locality at which the repressed breaks through is the *word presentation.*" As this basis has no foundation in empirical fact, the story illustrates *Freud's* rather than the patient's "obsessional neurosis" and, at the same time, provides a fascinating sketch of his mastery of narrative technique. It also shows how *not* to conduct a psychological inquiry.

In the next paragraph, as if worried that Fliess may not have been entirely convinced, Freud adds:

> All this is not entirely arbitrary. The word "make" has itself undergone an analogous transformation in meaning. An old fantasy of mine, which I would like to recommend to your linguistic sagacity, deals with the derivation of our verbs from such originally coproerotic terms. (Masson 1985, 288)

His first phrase, "not *entirely* arbitrary," implies by its very presence that the intended reader (Fliess) might well hesitate before accepting the validity of the case presentation. The substance of the case relies in effect upon three features: Freud's narrative contrivance (which is impeccable), the notion of repression behind infantile amnesia (which is wrong), and the linguistic flair for double and dubious etymological inventions (which is attractive and mistaken). In the following paragraph, Fliess is granted a merry assortment of Freud's well-known punster abilities with references to "all the things that resolve themselves into—excrement for me (a new Midas!)." So linguistic connections are established between *Abort* (toilet) and *Abortus* (abortion). These language games were not new, of course, nor were they any more founded on a clinical understanding of psychopathology than Shakespeare's amusing, and bilingual, veiled obscenities in the English lessons of Katharine in *Henry V* (rarely, one might say, have "fuck" and "cunt" been so suavely offered to titillate a knowing public).[44]

This letter of December 22, 1897, has attracted the close attention of Jeffrey M. Masson. His *The Assault on Truth*, aided by extensive quotation, deals with the second half of Freud's letter (*The Assault*, 115-19). There is in Masson's discussion no reference to the high jinks of the first half, nor to the genial self-congratulatory tenor of the whole letter—would this have spoiled his po-faced presentation of the second half of the letter? With deep seriousness, Masson examines the "clinical evidence" (115), later to be called the "critical clinical evidence" (116), later still, the "additional clinical evidence" (117), of Freud's second case concerning an adult female patient which is introduced by Freud with the understated "The intrinsic authenticity of infantile trauma is borne out by the following little incident which the patient claims to have observed as a three-year-old child" (Masson 1985, 288). Note, one should add, Freud's own apparent reservations: "which the patient *claims to have observed* as a three-year-old child." This is a terrifying (or hilarious, depending on one's suspension of disbelief) account of either a strange hysterical psychosis enacted in Freud's consulting room (his narrative makes it hard to decipher what was said, what was psychotically reenacted, what was suggested, what was interpreted) or of the "memories" of degradation of the self and the mother in the patient's infant years.

Freud's account offers paternal rape at age two (and a rape which resulted in the contraction of gonorrhea—it is not revealed when the two-year-old became aware of the gonorrhea infection);[45] buggery of the mother witnessed at age three; and, earlier, a vision of the mother lying bleeding on the bed from the father's assaults. What was the patient's age? Six to seven months! Masson, more intent upon his newfound cause of finding vicious males rampant everywhere than on investigating seriously the material discovered, reports this half of the letter under the varieties of "clinical evidence" mentioned above. For all his splendid archival sleuthing, Masson is no more reliable than Freud himself when it comes to assessing what is meant by "clinical evidence."

Freud spent the fall and winter of 1897 continuing his reports to Fliess on the progress and difficulties of his "self-analysis" and hoping, in vain, for a Fliessian response to his theatrical references to Oedipus and Hamlet in October of that year. Fliess appears to have been silent on this aspect of Freud's self-inventions. As late as November 5, 1897, Freud was complaining:

> You said nothing about my interpretation of *Oedipus Rex* and *Hamlet.* Since I have not told it to anyone else, because I can well imagine in advance the bewildered rejection, I should like to have a short comment on it from you. Last year you rejected many an idea of mine, with good reason. (Masson 1985, 277)

It seems evident from Freud's letters that Fliess never did respond to this request for an outside opinion on the current Freudian fantasia. There is not one reference to a reaction that Fliess may have offered to his Viennese friend. To judge by Freud's replies to the occasional letter from Fliess (and, at this stage of the correspondence, Freud seems to be the one more intent on communicating), the Berlin magician was wrapped up in his numerological combinations involving 23 and 28, and had neither the time nor the inclination to pursue Freud's Oedipus and Hamlet scenarios.

By far the most significant letter of this period is the one written on Wednesday, October 27, 1897, where Freud quotes from Goethe's dedication in *Faust*.

> Und manche liebe Schatten steigen auf;
> Gleich einer alten, halbverklungenen Sage,
> Kommt erste Lieb' und Freundschaft mit herauf.[46]

He also writes about the difficulties of his "self-analysis" and what were to become the key features of a classical psychoanalysis. What is interesting about this letter is its unpretentious presentation of Freud's attempts to understand who he was and how he had come to be who he was. The concern to discover the origins of the self is patent. That the search is hidebound by previous (and ongoing) theories about infantile and child psychology that are largely mistaken lessens the value of the document for contemporary investigators of the psyche; but it is one of the few letters of the correspondence where Freud seems genuinely and undramatically in pursuit of character traits that, he felt, had emerged from early experiences.

The early experiences and the character of the early child are alike seen in a kind of unremitting puritanical Manichaean manner, and the present discomfort with the adult self is felt to be the consequence of these infantile disasters. By the same token, any present self-satisfaction is shown to be a mistaken refusal to contemplate the infantile origins of the personality. Freud writes, linking his findings about himself to his patients' difficulties with their confessions:

> And also first fright and discord. Many a sad secret of life is here followed back to its first roots; many a pride and privilege are made aware of their humble origins. All of what I experienced with my patients, as a third [person] I find again here—days when I drag myself about dejected because I have understood nothing of the dream, of the fantasy, of the mood of the day; and then again days when a flash of lightning illuminates the interrelations and lets me understand the past as a preparation for the present. I am beginning to perceive in the determining factors large, general, framing motives, as I should like to call them, and other motives, fill-ins, which vary according to the individual's experiences. At the same time several, though not yet all, doubts about my conception of neurosis are being resolved. An idea about resistance has enabled me to put back on course all those cases of mine that had gone somewhat astray, so that they are now proceeding satisfactorily. (Masson 1985, 274)

The phrase "All of what I experienced with my patients . . . I find again here" should not surprise us. We know from the correspondence with Fliess to just what extent sessions with Freud were at once a continuation—for him—of his own hunches about the long-term significance of infantile sexuality (as he and Fliess appeared to conceive it), and an accusatory interrogation of the patient (or victim), whereby early sexual mayhem, fantasized, desired, or (perhaps?) actually experienced, was broached by Freud as the principal source of the patient's current "medical" problems. What Freud means by "an idea about resistance" in the last phrase of the above quotation is alarmingly detailed in his immediately subsequent sentences. This is an extraordinary passage which needs to be quoted *in extenso*, and even though masturbation is not mentioned, it is implicitly present throughout, as we shall see by the paragraph which follows it. Freud continues thus:

> Resistance, which finally brings the [analytic] work to a halt, is nothing other than the child's former character, the degenerative character, which

developed or would have developed as a result of those experiences that one finds as a conscious memory in the so-called degenerative cases, but which here is overlaid by the development of repression. I dig it out by my work; it struggles; and the person who initially was such a good, noble human being becomes mean, untruthful, or obstinate, a malingerer—until I tell him so and thus make it possible for him to overcome this character. In this way resistance has become something actual and tangible to me, and I wish that instead of the concept of repression I already had what lies concealed behind it as well. (Masson 1985, 274)

The reader will have noticed that we have departed long since from the realms of medicine. This is not *quite* "quackery," however; the real quackery was to come, from 1902 onward, with the Pickwick-like atmosphere of the Wednesday Evening Meetings (later to become the meetings of the Vienna Psychoanalytic Society) and with the establishment of an international organization to promote the views and methods of the founder (Freud-as-Pickwick?).[47] What Freud is confiding to Fliess is more in the nature of a sincere, but totally misguided (and biologically ill-informed), version of moral and spiritual salvation which requires the client's "dark night of the soul" to be confessed to the guru, who will then "make it possible for him to overcome this character."

In the next paragraph, Freud reveals what he is certain "lies concealed behind" repression. The tone of the letter is still that of one anxious divine to another, albeit transgressed now with direct reference to the imagined physiological and psychic responses of the infantile body. This concluding paragraph appears to allow Freud to rejoin the ranks of medical doctors; the path chosen for his recognition that "medicine" is his field and not ethics or some kind of theological practice, is one that returns (inevitably?) to the dreadful dangers, and consequences, of moments of childish self-pleasure:

This infantile character develops during the period of "longing," after the child has been removed from sexual experiences. Longing is the main character trait of hysteria, just as actual anesthesia (even though only potential) is its main symptom. During this same period of longing fantasies are formed and masturbation is (regularly?) practiced, which then yields to repression. If it does not yield, then no hysteria develops either; the discharge of sexual excitation for the most part removes the possibility of hysteria. It has become clear to me that various compulsive movements represent a substitute for the discontinued movements of masturbation. (Masson 1985, 274-75)[48]

The vocabulary has changed from that of the previous paragraph, but not the argument, nor the destructive, underlying certainty that lives are wrecked by the vile practice of childhood masturbation. The ranks of the medical profession which Freud has rejoined in this paragraph are those of the benighted nineteenth-century specialists in nervous disorders who piously (and literally) poured out the bromide to assuage the itches of desire that inhabited the youthful bodies of children to the hypocritical (but, doubtless, real) embarrassment of their parents. As Sulloway most pertinently argues:

> What is also not appreciated about Freud is how integral his medical views on masturbation were to his overall theory of the neuroses. After the abandonment of the seduction theory in 1897, his theory of the neuroses became, in significant part, a theory about infantile masturbation. It was childhood masturbation that he later blamed for the neurotic phantasies that had misled him in the first place. Such phantasies, Freud wrote, "were intended to cover up the auto-erotic activities of the first years of childhood, to embellish it and to raise it to a higher plane" [reference omitted]. (Sulloway 1979 [1992], 185)

Sulloway's last two sentences, however (including the apposite quote from Freud), should be read with caution. For the truth is not that Freud was misled by his patients' "neurotic phantasies," but that these were induced by his obsessive and suggestive approach to them. Nonetheless, Sulloway was absolutely right in seeing infantile and childhood masturbation as being at the heart of the "medical views" that produced psychoanalysis. The great renegade psychoanalyst Wilhelm Stekel (who broke with Freud over the Unconscious and over the latter's inflexible sexual symbolism for the interpretation of dreams)[49] had this commonsensical observation to make about late-nineteenth-century approaches to childhood masturbation:

> All the terrors of earth and hell are set in motion to keep the child from masturbating. Its hands are tied at night, a girdle of virginity is put on, bromide is ordered by the physician. The child is told that it will be imbecile and crippled if it continues this frightful "vice." *These are the most serious traumas for the children.* For the traumas through servants are not so dangerous.[50]

In the letter to Fliess, Freud began with a quotation from his favorite German poet, Goethe. But Goethe —at least, the Goethe of *Faust*—is too magisterial for the intimate failings that seem to pick at Freud's equilibrium. There is perhaps another poet who better fits the sense of spiritual hypocrisy and existential despair implied by Freud's remarks, and that is Charles Baudelaire. The first two stanzas of the introductory "Au lecteur" that prefaces *Les Fleurs du Mal* were written in 1855 (the year of Sigmund's conception). They provide with cruel concision—and with no clinical sessions to back them up—the essence of Freud's complaints to Wilhelm Fliess (though they are concerned with adult and not infantile lapses):

La sottise, l'erreur, le péché, la lésine,
Occupent nos esprits et travaillent nos corps,
Et nous alimentons nos aimables remords,
Comme les mendiants nourrissent leur vermine.

Nos péchés sont têtus, nos repentirs sont lâches;
Nous nous faisons payer grassement nos aveux,
Et nous rentrons gaiement dans le chemin bourbeux,
Croyant par de vils pleurs laver toutes nos taches.[51]

This chapter began with a skeptical observation by a writer on science who had wryly noted the "Heaven's Gate" disciples' preference for unfounded belief over the empirical evidence offered by the telescope. It has ended—having passed through realms inhabited by Fisher and Greenberg, Eysenck and Sutherland, Daly and Wilson, and the inevitable Sulloway—on a poetic note where stubborn sin and the self-centred complacency of remorse and the slackness of repentance, rather than medical illness, are the dominant themes. This is appropriate to the extent that much of the remainder of this book will be concerned with Freud's enthusiasms for, fascination with, and seduction by, a writer of fantasy and of human frailty and endurance who provided him with one model for his literary artifacts. The other, of course, was Conan Doyle, whose imaginary genius was the subject of a brilliant little monograph by the late Michael Shepherd, *Sherlock Holmes and the Case of Dr. Freud.*[52]

There is, however, one last psychiatric comment which is pertinent and it is from *General Psychopathology* by Karl Jaspers. Jaspers, known nowadays more for his philosophical writings than for his earlier psychiatric career (his first university post was as a psychiatrist, not as a philosopher), wrote about psychoanalysis and Freud's influence on the world of medicine with sympathetic but highly critical acumen at a time when such insights were rare. He had sympathy for Freud's attempts to "interpret" the reactions (physical and verbal) of his patients; but he also was aware of the dangers. Having compared Freudian endeavors unfavorably with the writings of Kierkegaard and Nietzsche—"What Kierkegaard and Nietzsche had achieved at the highest cultural level was again achieved at a lower level and crudely reversed to correspond with the lowest level of the common man and metropolitan civilisation"— Jaspers wrote (with no knowledge of the Freud–Fliess correspondence):

> Interpretation brings with it a basic feeling of 'getting behind the scenes'. One uncovers, exposes and displays, as it were, the art of cross-examination, a police-technique. Almost the whole of psychoanalytic understanding is dominated by this fundamental, negative attitude of unmasking.[53]

For Jaspers this approach was misguided, both ethically and medically. As far as the interpretations invented about supposed remembered infantile life are concerned, Jaspers wrote unambiguously: "We are thus led into a world of hypotheses which are not only unproven but unprovable. They remain pure speculation and leave any meaningful phenomena far behind" (Jaspers 1968, 361).

Notes

1. Martin Daly and Margo Wilson (1996). "Homicidal Tendencies," *Demos* 10, 40. Material in this interesting article on the varieties of death-dealing in society is more fully covered in the authors' *Homicide*. New York: Aldine de Gruyter, Hawthorne, 1988.

An earlier study by Daly and Wilson is also worth consulting: "Is Parent-Offspring Conflict Sex-Linked? Freudian and Darwinian Models," *Journal of Personality* 58, no.1 (March 1990): 163-89.

2. Frank J. Sulloway (1979 [1992]), 275.

3. Mikkel Borch-Jacobsen (1996). "Neurotica: Freud and the Seduction Theory," *October 76* (Spring) 43.

4. Timothy Ferris (1997). *The Whole Shebang: A State-of-the-Universe(s) Report*. New York: Simon and Schuster.

5. A recent article by the English anatomist Michael Richardson of St. George's Hospital Medical School (London) appears to have blown the gaff once and for all about Haeckel's alleged embryonic similarities among the species. See Michael Richardson (1997), "There Is No Highly Conserved

Embryonic Stage in the Vertebrates," *Anatomy and Embryology* 196, no. 2, (August): 91-106.

As far as the outright fraud of Haeckel's work is concerned, it was commented on in 1982 by Francis Hitching, who wrote in his *The Neck of the Giraffe* (London: Pan Books), "Time and again, Haeckel doctored his illustrations outrageously to support his biogenetic law." Hitching's source was a book by J. Assmuth, published in London as long ago as 1918, *Haeckel's Frauds and Forgeries*. The science correspondent for the London *Times*, Nigel Hawkes, has pointed out to Allen Esterson that *the extent of Haeckel's forgeries was common knowledge to his own contemporaries*. I gratefully acknowledge Mr. Esterson's sharing of this additional information.

6. I would argue, accepting the risk of a quirky *ad hominem* rebuttal, that two decades of virtual daily cocaine abuse had a far more, and more long-lasting, effect on Freud's mentation than his reading of Charles Darwin. Freud began taking cocaine (painting of the nostrils with a liquid solution) as early as April 1884, when he was twenty-eight. In the letters to his fiancée from Paris (winter 1885-1886) he reports taking cocaine prior to any social engagement at the Charcot household. These doses ("to untie my tongue," letter to Martha of January 18, 1886) may indeed have been temporarily beneficial to the public persona that Freud wished to present. But the long-term sustained use, as evidenced time and again in the correspondence with Fliess, was to impair seriously the critical abilities of his wide-ranging intellect, and to damage, quite needlessly (by the personality modifications which induced a kind of hypersensitive paranoia), many established relationships.

7. Sulloway (1991), benefiting, as he says in a footnote, from the investigations of Adolf Grünbaum (in *The Foundations of Psychoanalysis*) and Frederick Crews (in *Skeptical Engagements*) as well as from the Harvard University Press edition of the unexpurgated Freud—Fliess correspondence, recognizes this in his paper "Reassessing Freud's Case Histories: The Social Construction of Psychoanalysis," which appeared in *Isis* 82, (1991): 245-75. Sulloway's reassessment of Freud is entirely negative for Freud-as-scientist.

This has not prevented him from repeating the blunder of assuming that "cauterization" is carried out on the *bone*, as opposed to the silver nitrate, or other agent, being applied to tissue or a prominent vein in the nose. *Bones* never are, or were, "cauterized"—even by Wilhelm Fliess. Nor has Sulloway avoided the mistake of assuming that Sigmund Freud and Emma Eckstein underwent the same treatment by Fliess. They did not. Freud was several times cauterized; Eckstein was surgically invaded. As Fliess himself carefully adumbrates in *Die Beziehungen zwischen Nase und weiblichen Geschlechts-organen*, special bone forceps are required for the *removal* of a turbinate bone (or nasal concha). The following statement, completely without foundation, remains in the uncorrected 1992 edition of *Freud, Biologist of the Mind*:

"Freud even permitted Fliess to operate repeatedly upon his own nose and sinuses—Fliess surgically removed and cauterized part of Freud's turbinate bone—in the hope of dispelling certain neurotic symptoms!" (Sulloway 1979 [1992], 143). That exclamation point should be reserved for Sulloway's total ignorance of the skeletal structure of the nose. There is not one "turbinate bone" (as Sulloway's sentence implies); there are *six* nasal conchae (three on each side)—ten minutes spent with *Gray's Anatomy* would have enlightened him. Freud was *never* subject to Fliess's surgery.

8. Frank Cioffi (1979) "Freud—New Myths to Replace the Old," *New Society* (November 29): 503-504. Review of Frank J. Sulloway, *Freud, Biologist of the Mind*, and Sherry Turkle, *Psychoanalytic Politics: Freud's French Revolution*.

9. To be even fairer to these social scientists, let me quote from Frank J. Sulloway's 1991 article in *Isis* on the many difficulties put in the way of serious investigative scholarship by the various incarnations of Cerberus in the psychoanalytic establishment:

> During the last forty years, the Freud Archives has collected numerous letters, reminiscences, and other documents pertaining to Freud only to seal many of them away until the twenty-second century. The whimsical nature of many of the dates chosen to release specific holdings is a marvel to contemplate. Thus one letter from Freud's deceased eldest son is sealed away until 2013, while another must wait an additional nineteen years, until 2032, to be seen. A letter from Josef Breuer (one wonders what could be so special about it) must await the year 2102 to be examined, which will be 177 years after Breuer's death. This kind of seemingly paranoid secrecy reminds one of an experience Paul Roazen once had when he was trying to interview an elderly Viennese analyst. When Roazen asked the analyst, who had agreed to be interviewed, just *when* he had joined the Vienna Psychoanalytic Society, the man replied that it was none of Roazen's business. Later the man blurted out defiantly, "You are not going to get our secrets!" (*Isis* 82 no. 312 (June 1991): 250)

10. H. J. Eysenck and G. D. Wilson (1973). *The Experimental Study of Freudian Theories*. London: Methuen.

11. The year 1973 is the date given at the end of the introduction by Juliet Mitchell to her *Psychoanalysis and Feminism: Freud, Reich, Laing and Women* (New York: Vintage Books, 1975). The straight-faced presentation of the "Oedipal" scenario and all of its supposed consequences would make this book the "Monty Python" version of Freudian psychoanalytic doctrine, were the author's tongue anywhere near her cheek.

12. Stuart Sutherland (1997). "Tales of Memory and Imagination," *Nature* 388 (July 17): 239. Professor Sutherland, a distinguished British experimental psychologist, is currently an emeritus professor at the Laboratory of

Experimental Psychology, University of Sussex (England).

13. For his careful evaluation of the epidemiological errors in the study by Linda Meyer Williams, see Harrison G. Pope, Jr. (1997), *Psychology Astray: Fallacies in Studies of "Repressed Memory" and Childhood Trauma*. Boca Raton, Florida: Upton Books, Social Issues Resources Series, Inc., 65-73.

14. This seems to be a reference to Pope's awkward (for believers in the anamnestic results of psychoanalysis) but empirically unassailable conclusion to his chapter 7. Retrospective studies are often insufficient to test a hypothesis; prospective studies are more useful. Pope concludes:

> The same logic applies in testing the theory that it is possible to repress the memory of a traumatic event. Further retrospective reports, based on cases like those described above, do almost nothing to advance our knowledge on this topic. . . . It is time to test the repression hypothesis in properly designed prospective studies. (1997, 46)

15. Sigmund Freud, *S.E.* (1914) 14: 16.

16. See my discussion of this paper in Wilcocks (1994), chapter 4, 113-57. But note also that three years earlier at the twelfth Congress for Internal Medicine held at Wiesbaden, April 12-15, 1893, Fliess had already suggested *abusus sexualis* as a precondition for his "nasal reflex neurosis"—see my chapter 3 above (page 73). By *abusus sexualis* Fliess means literally abuse or misuse of the sexual function, that is masturbation. Hence, precocious sexual experience need not involve any other person.

17. See, for example, Elizabeth Loftus and Katherine Ketcham (1994), *The Myth of Repressed Memory: False Memories and Allegations of Sexual Abuse*. New York: St. Martin's; R. J. Ofshe and E. Watters (1994), *Making Monsters: False Memories, Psychotherapy amd Sexual Hysteria*. New York: Scribners.

18. Cf. Malise Ruthven's final sentence in a *Times Literary Supplement* review of a book by Russell Miller some years ago:

> It is a pity, however, that he is so reticent in offering explanations, either of Hubbard's unusual powers or the reasons why so many bright and able young people allowed themselves to be ensnared by the cult he created, with its totalitarian power structure, spiritual junk-food and nonsensical quasi-theology.

Ruthven was reviewing Russell Miller's *Bare-Faced Messiah: The True Story of L. Ron Hubbard* in the *Times Literary Supplement*, (January 8, 1988): 32. It is only proper to add that the "bright and able young people" that I have encountered who suffer from this fear of psychoanalysis are middle-aged, or older. This really seems to be a generational issue. My own young students, whatever existential problems they may have, do not seem perturbed by, or interested in, Freudian versions of human psychology. But, then, there are those—principally in literature departments—who are cajoled, seduced, or bullied into "decoding" human experience from Jacques Lacan's revised Oedipal encoding of it. But, then—again—*who* are their teachers?

A recent review of the English translation of Elisabeth Roudinesco's biography *Jacques Lacan* (1997, Oxford: Polity) begins:

> Future historians trying to account for the institutionalised fraud that goes under the name of "Theory" will surely accord a central place to the influence of the French psychoanalyst Jacques Lacan. He is one of the fattest spiders at the heart of the web of muddled not-quite-thinkable-thoughts and evidence-free assertions of limitless scope, which practitioners of theorrhoea have woven into their version of the humanities.

This sane and savage critique was drafted by the professor of geriatric medicine at the University of Manchester (U.K.), Raymond Tallis. See "The Shrink from Hell," *Times Higher Education Supplement* (October 31, 1997): 20.

19. Stuart Sutherland is perhaps a special case in that he speaks and writes as one who had, some twenty-five years ago, been to hell and back and who survived to write an account of the experience in his 1976 book *Breakdown: A Personal Crisis and a Medical Dilemma*. As the late Hans Eysenck noted in his *Decline and Fall of the Freudian Empire*, this account

> is by an outstanding experimental psychologist . . . who recounts the history of his nervous breakdown and his disastrous adventures with several psychoanalysts. . . . [H]is detailed exposition of what happened to him in these encounters will give the reader who has not been psychoanalysed an idea of the terrible effects that the typical psychoanalytic attitude to patients can have on someone who is driven to extremes of anxiety and depression by his neurotic worries, which are not at all alleviated by the cold, interpretative attitude of the therapist. (Eysenck 1985, 61)

20. See the penultimate paragraph of the preface to: Seymour Fisher and Roger P. Greenberg (1978), *The Scientific Evaluation of Freud's Theories and Therapy: A Book of Readings* (New York: Basic Books). As their preface points out, this collection of papers is intended as a companion volume to their earlier (1977) *The Scientific Credibility of Freud's Theories and Therapies* (New York: Basic Books). As a matter of topical interest, I should mention the careful assessment of Edward Erwin, which is unsparing in its critique of the pro-Freudian hopes of Fisher and Greenberg. See E. Erwin (1995), *A Final Accounting: Philosophical and Empirical Issues in Freudian Psychology* (Cambridge, Mass.: MIT Press). Fisher and Greenberg seem (and have seemed for years) innocent of, or totally vacuous about, the hideous implications of their enterprise.

A moral, as well as scientific, critique was published in 1984 in Max Scharnberg's *The Myth of the Paradigm-shift, or How to Lie with Methodology.* Having described the methodological slip from "real problem" (P_r) to "substitute problem" (P_s), Scharnberg writes:

> *Every* psychoanalytic experiment with a positive outcome that I have come across during 24 years uses P_s's that are invalid signs. And we must question the honesty of Fisher & Greenberg: *The Scientific Credibility of Freud's Theories and Therapy*; they give lots of extremely false accounts of cited experiments. The worst instances of the faults that I shall describe below could easily have been avoided without any new knowledge. Better morals are much more important. (Scharnberg 1984, 151)

That "honesty" had been questioned—or, rather, denied—some fifty pages earlier in the introductory pages of his chapter 4, "The Doctrine of the Substitute Problem," where Scharnberg writes: "The only thing that is academic in F[isher] & G[reenberg]'s book is the jargon. Everything else is swindle" (107).

21. Daly and Wilson, 174. Melford E. Spiro's book is *Oedipus in the Trobriands*, Chicago: Chicago University Press, 1982.

22. The title of Hall and van de Castle's article is worth treasuring for its deep innocence: "An Empirical Investigation of the Castration Complex in Dreams." It was published in *Journal of Personality* 33, (1965): 20-29. C. Hall had previously published "Strangers in Dreams: An Empirical Confirmation of the Oedipus Complex," *Journal of Personality* 31, (1963): 336-45. Hall's fondness for the word "empirical" seems unrelated to its normal meaning.

23. A recent instance of the currency of Freud's notions about infantile toilet training is provided by the contemporary guru of British cognitive psychiatry, Raj Persaud. In an article in the (London) *Independent* on February 25, 1994, he claims (without any documentary support) that "there is good evidence that a few of his [Freud's] theories about personality were right, and he correctly predicted that people who are obstinate will also be parsimonious and orderly—the anal character." This kind of circular, unsubstantiated, argument by a (partial) believer is presented as "state-of-the-art" psychiatry; but it is merely one more sign of the limits of human honesty and intelligence. See Raj Persaud, "Freud's Window on the Mind," *The Independent* (London), February 25, 1994.

24. Raymond Tallis (1997). *Enemies of Hope: A Critique of Contemporary Pessimism.* London: Macmillan.

25. This is merely one instance of Freud's generalizations from his own personal hunches. It *does*, however, raise the question of when and where (if ever) Freud actually watched a performance of *Oedipus Rex.* To date the only error of fact in my earlier volume on Freud that I have discovered is that Freud

did not see the French tragedian Mounet-Sully in the role of Oedipus when he was in Paris (1885-1886). Borch-Jacobsen in *Remembering Anna O.* (102) quotes from a restricted letter from Marie Bonaparte to Ernest Jones, dated June 18, 1954, informing him that, contrary to what was believed at the time (including by Jones), Freud did *not* see Mounet-Sully in this role. In Wilcocks (1994), I follow Jones in assuming Freud's presence at a performance of *Oedipe roi* in Paris. I am grateful to Borch-Jacobsen for this correction. It makes the letter to Fliess even more problematic, or "theatrical," in that "Coney Island of the Mind" sense that Freud's dispatches so often have.

26. See the French surgeon Gérard Zwang's (1985) caustic volume *La Statue de Freud*, 578, where he deals with the irremediable nature of infantile amnesia on purely *neurological* grounds. The fact that Freud appeared to apply the same neurological mistakes to his own supposed recollections of his own infantile life may be a sign of some kind of confused and totally mistaken "sincerity," but it is not helpful for the development of a study of any human psychology.

For current American studies on infantile amnesia, see the useful bibliography to Pope (1997). A further argument, relying on the issue of the "encoding specificity principle" rather than on the state of the infant myelination process, is found in Stephen J. Ceci, "False Beliefs: Some Developmental and Clinical Considerations," in Daniel L. Schacter, ed., *Memory Distortion: How Minds, Brains, and Societies Reconstruct the Past*, Cambridge, Mass.: Harvard University Press, 1995, 95-97.

27. The letter of March 7, 1897, with the enclosure dated March 17 (where Mathilde's diphtheria attack is first mentioned) and the letter of March 29 were both omitted from the *Anfänge* edition. The letter of April 6 was seriously censored. See Masson (1985), 476.

28. See Wilcocks (1994), chapter 7, particularly 250-57, and the extensive endnote 68, 277-79. For those in haste to know: "The Dream of Irma's Injection" and its analysis, with its references to Mathilde's near death from diphtheria in 1897, could *not* have taken place during the night and morning of July 23/24, 1895 as claimed by Freud; it was a much later invention and Freud lied to Fliess about it. (And Fliess, incidentally, seems not to have credited the lie.)

29. What would be misleading, even by late-nineteenth-century standards, would be the ascription "research" for the *a priori* hunches which were being confabulated, via patient acquiescence (and sometimes even in the absence of this), into what were to become "foundation theses" of psychoanalysis. It may sound strange, or even incredible to those who have been seduced by Freudian rhetoric, but it needs to be said—if only in an endnote—that no clinical or extra-clinical research was ever carried out to test the emerging hypotheses of Freud; and Freud himself frowned upon the idea that outside empirical studies

could contribute usefully to his program. What Raymond Tallis writes of Jacques Lacan could have been said as truthfully of the originator of psychoanalysis: "[He] did not abandon medicine altogether, only its scientific basis. He chose to be a psychoanalyst where, instead of elucidating diagnoses, he could impose them" (Tallis 1997, 20).

30. One of the many points raised in Allen Esterson's (1998) "Jeffrey Masson and Freud's Seduction Theory: A New Fable Based on Old Myths," as indeed in his earlier book *Seductive Mirage* (1993), is that it was *Freud* who told his patients (male and female) about their precocious seductions and *not* they who had misrepresented their past to him. This issue was raised over nearly a quarter of a century ago in the shrewd assessment by Frank Cioffi (1974), "Was Freud a Liar?"

31. See Masson 1985, 240-42, 246-48, and 250-52 for the three drafts.

32. Masson notes of this early use of *Urszenen* (primal scenes): "Freud means, I believe, the scenes of real seduction—the earliest scenes. 'Primal scene,' in the later sense of intercourse between parents, is first used in the wolf-man discussion [citation omitted]." I agree with his second point; I am not sure whether, at this early stage, Freud means seduction by an adult or whether he is simply referring to infantile sexual arousal.

For instance, the "phonograph" letter of January 24, 1897, does not indicate what Masson calls "scenes of real seduction;" yet it does recall—so Freud claims—a sexually lively conversation overheard by the female baby and which was responsible for her adult hysteria. Freud wrote: "Thus I was able to trace back, with certainty, a hysteria that developed in the context of a periodic mild depression to a seduction, which occurred for the first time at 11 months and [I could] hear again the words that were exchanged between two adults at that time! It is as though it comes from a phonograph" (Masson 1985, 226).

If one unravels the events narrated in this letter of Freud's, one comes to this situation: Freud's adult female patient suffered from a mild depression during her periods, this developed into a "hysteria," and *then* Freud investigated the possible origins of this adult menses crisis. By suggestive therapy, he achieved the artificial report from the patient which allowed him to boast to his friend "with certainty" of his accomplishment. I suppose he could be implying a threesome involving the baby; but this seems as tendentious as the reputed oral accuracy of the report.

33. Masson notes that the word used by Freud is *verdrängende* and not *verdrängt* as given in the *Anfänge* edition. I would translate it by "the repressing" in this context.

34. Sigmund Freud, *The Origins of Psycho-Analysis: Letters to Wilhelm Fliess, Drafts and Notes: 1887-1902,* tr. Eric Mosbacher and James Strachey, 1954. New York: Basic Books, 1954 [1971], 219; quoted by Peter L. Rudnytsky (1987), *Freud and Oedipus,* New York: Columbia University Press, 73.

35. Ernest Jones (1953-1957). *The Life and Work of Sigmund Freud.* 3 vols. New York: Basic Books, vol. 1, 13; quoted by Rudnytsky (1987), 73-74.

36. Sigmund Freud (1927). "Fetishism," in *On Sexuality, P.F.L.* 7, 354.

37. This seems to be a reference to Freud's nurse, Monika Zajíc (see Masson 1985, 270, note 1). Anna Freud thought that the nurse was "in her forties" according to Masson's interview report.

38. Sigmund Freud, *Case Histories I: 'Dora' and 'Little Hans.'* Harmondsworth (U.K.): *P.F.L.*, 8, 269.

39. This phrase is intentionally ambiguous. Was Hans's father devoted to his son? (Yes, as far as we can gather); was he devoted to—and/or seduced by—the tenets of Freudian psychoanalysis? (Yes, as evidenced by his ultra-careful recording of his young son's responses to life for Freud to develop into what has wrongly been called "a case history.") The musicologist Max Graf (the father of "Little Hans") was also an occasional participant in the meetings of the Vienna Psychoanalytic Society.

40. "Displacement" is not a Freudian invention. The concept of the displacement of feelings from the self or the "target-other" onto another human being, or even onto an animal or inanimate object is a long-standing tradition of human psychology. Freud, we know, would not have denied this; he would merely have claimed to have given "scientific" status to this notion—and he would have been mistaken.

41. Justin Wintle, "The Eat a Bull Contest," *The Independent* (London), June 14, 1997. Review of Frederick Crews, *The Memory Wars,* and John Forrester, *Dispatches from the Freud Wars.* Wintle is generous about the excellence of the "scholarly" Forrester's collection of essays; but he has failed to recognize that the latter is a devotee of "the cause," hence his erroneous concluding sentence: "Forrester is on to the old crazy, but doesn't have the horns to finish him off."

42. Sigmund Freud (1913). "Two Lies Told By Children," in *On Sexuality, P.F.L.*, 7, 285-91. One—extended (and rhetorically enhanced)—lie told by Sigmund Freud would be more accurate. The sublime confidence of the concluding paragraph to the first tale, in which the patient, first introduced as "[a] girl of seven," had once purloined fifty pfennig (one nickel) from her father to buy colors for painting Easter eggs, has all the surprise and inevitability—once one has learned the doctrine—of those *Just So Stories* that Freud appreciated: "For psychoanalysts I need hardly emphasize the fact that in this little experience of the child's we have before us one of those extremely common cases in which early anal erotism persists into later erotic life. Even her desire to paint the eggs with colours derived from the same source" (*P.F.L.*, 7, 289).

43. I have given the original title because in the current English translation by Strachey (*The Interpretation of Dreams*), Freud's use of the present-tense

narrative is lost. The 1913 English translation by A. A. Brill does respect Freud's use of the present and is in this respect closer to the effects intended by Freud. See Wilcocks (1994), chapter 7, note 40, 270-71.

44. Katharine: *Comment appelez-vous le pied et la robe?*
Alice: De foot, *madame; et* de coun.
Katharine: De foot *et* de coun! *O Seigneur Dieu! ce sont mots de son mauvais, corruptible, gros, et impudique, et non pour les dames d'honneur d'user je ne voudrais prononcer ces mots devant les seigneurs de France pour tout le monde. Il faut* de foot *et* de coun *néanmoins.*
(*King Henry V*, Act III, Scene iii)

45. Freud writes: "When she was two years old, he [her father] brutally deflowered her and infected her with his gonorrhea, as a consequence of which she became ill and her life was endangered by the loss of blood and vaginitis" (Masson 1985, 288). The uncritical acceptance of statements like these from Freud's writings (whether to Fliess or in published accounts) leads to all kinds of problems. However this material may have been obtained from the patient— that is, whether volunteered by herself at a moment of intense emotion, or "constructed" by Freud from remarks (and/or symptoms, see the G. de B. case in Masson 1985, 220) which, he thought, would allow this interpretation—it raises far more questions than it resolves.

46. Translated in Masson 1985 (275) as:

And the shades of loved ones appear;
With them, like an old, half-forgotten myth,
First love and friendship.

47. As an example, taken almost at random from the minutes of the Vienna Psychoanalytic Society recorded by the secretary Otto Rank, see the "Scientific Meeting of March 6, 1907" (this was the first session ever attended by Jung and Binswanger). Adler gives a paper—simply entitled "A Psychoanalysis"—concerning a wealthy Jewish Russian young man who was being treated for "nervousness." Rank's po-faced minutes are worthy of Dickens:

Adler then presents the analysis of this patient's compulsion, which is connected with bathing.
The compulsion: When he took a bath he *had* to submerge and *had* to remain submerged under water until he had counted either to 3 or to 7 or to 49 (or all three numbers together). . . .
Associations: 3 is the sacred number; one counts 1, 2, 3, when taking a run for jumping; 7 is the Jewish holy number; 7 x 7 = 49; this is the Jewish Jubilee year.
Bath associations: when submerged in the water, he may have his usual palpitations of the heart; he also had them when he was riding a bicycle in Berlin

in front of others. Explanation: because one's pants can easily fall down when one is riding a bicycle. The patient has an inclination to keep his pants on. Even during "intercourse" with girls he frequently keeps his pants on. . . .

DISCUSSION

FEDERN . . . The obsessional need to remain dressed could be connected with a fear of soiling the pants. (He knows of such a case.) . . .

RANK thinks that the numbers 7 and 49—the small and the big Jubilee year—represent the small and the big penis. . . .

FREUD, commenting on these remarks, says that 3 may perhaps represent the Christian penis; 7 the small, and 49 the large Jewish penis. The smaller Jewish penis is represented in the compulsion by the larger number.

(Nunberg and Federn 1962, vol. 1, 138-45)

48. The 1897 notion that "various compulsive movements represent a substitute for the discontinued movements of masturbation" [i.e., presumably, *infantile* masturbation] was a continuing feature of Freud's diagnostic methods. His observations, or, better, his interpretations of what may have been his observations (cf. the case of Dora fumbling with her reticule) are discussed and refuted in Frank Cioffi's introductory essay "Why Are We Still Arguing about Freud?" See Cioffi (1998), *Freud and the Question of Pseudoscience*, 44 ff.

49. See Wilhelm Stekel (1962). *The Interpretation of Dreams: New Developments and Techniques.* Tr. Eden Paul and Cedar Paul. New York: Grosset and Dunlap, 314-99. Pages 395-99 are a maliciously brilliant refutation of Freudian sexual symbolic intransigence.

50. Wilhelm Stekel (1950). *Conditions of Nervous Anxiety and Their Treatment.* Tr. Rosalie Gabler. New York: Liveright, 428 (the emphasis is Stekel's). This is a translation of the last edition of Stekel's *Nervöse Angstzustände und ihre Behandlung*, which first appeared from Urban and Schwarzenberg in Berlin and Vienna in 1908. Freud wrote a preface for the first edition; this was later dropped from all subsequent editions following Stekel's noisy break with Freud.

51. Charles Baudelaire (1968). *Oeuvres complètes.* Ed. Y.-G. Le Dantec and Claude Pichois. Paris: Gallimard, Editions de la Pléiade, 5. Baudelaire's next two verses seem to anticipate Freud's medieval notions on the powers of the Devil:

Sur l'oreiller du mal c'est Satan Trismégiste
Qui berce longuement notre esprit enchanté,
Et le riche métal de notre volonté
Est tout vaporisé par ce savant chimiste.

C'est le Diable qui tient les fils qui nous remuent!
Aux objets répugnants nous trouvons des appas;

Chaque jour vers l'Enfer nous descendons d'un pas,
Sans horreur, à travers des ténèbres qui puent.

52. Michael Shepherd (1985). *Sherlock Holmes and the Case of Dr. Freud.* London: Tavistock.
53. Karl Jaspers (1968). *General Psychopathology.* Tr. J. Hoenig and Marian W. Hamilton. Chicago: University of Chicago Press, 361; the previous quotation is from 360.

6

A Present for the Bride and Groom

Can you imagine what "endopsychic myths" are? The latest product of my mental labor. The dim inner perception of one's own psychic apparatus stimulates thought illusions, which of course are projected onto the outside and, characteristically, into the future and the beyond. Immortality, retribution, the entire beyond are all reflections of our psychic internal [world]. *Meschugge?* Psychomythology. FREUD TO FLIESS[1]

My reply was ever so wise and penetrating; I made it appear as though the most tenuous of clues had enabled me Sherlock Holmes-like to guess the situation (which of course was none too difficult after your communications) and suggested a more appropriate procedure, something endopsychic, as it were. FREUD TO JUNG[2]

When little boys have learned a new bad word they are never happy till they have chalked it up on a door. And this also is Literature. RUDYARD KIPLING, *The Phantom Rickshaw*

"[S]omething endopsychic, as it were," Freud writes to Jung in the summer of 1909 over the latter's extra-clinical attentions to, or involvement with, the young and attractive Sabina Spielrein. Taking up the useful phrase first used to Fliess some twelve years before, Freud hints that he may be able to help Jung off the horn of the dilemma of the erotic relationship with Sabina Spielrein by suggesting that it is all in her head. Not that Jung had observed professional chastity; rather, Freud felt he could "arrange" things by invoking his 1897 discovery that "one's own psychic apparatus stimulates thought illusions, which of course are projected onto the outside and, characteristically, into the future and beyond." In this way, Fräulein Spielrein would be made aware of her own psychic investment in the relationship with Jung and of its solely autogenic source (whatever she and Carl may have got up to physically).

The acknowledgment of his duplicitous use of a "Sherlock Holmes-like" omniscience to help a younger colleague out of an awkward spot with a female patient seems like a moment of jovial paternal disinterestedness on Freud's part. Here, perhaps, after all, is that lovely, wise old gentleman (he was all of fifty-three) "whose children loved him for his 'merry heart'" in the words of Dr. Stephen Wilson, the resident Freudian therapist for the *Times Literary Supplement.*[3] On the other hand, it is very reminiscent of a treatment procedure adopted some fourteen years earlier when another female patient, also victim of a younger colleague's invasions (surgical rather than amatory), was persuaded that it was "all in her head," "that she bled out of *longing*." In the interim, it would seem, Freud had discovered the appropriate scientific-sounding word—"endopsychic"—for an aspect of the human mind which, as he wrote to Fliess, was "the latest product of my mental labor." In fact, the notion mentioned to Fliess was not an invention of Freud's, though he may well have credited himself with its paternity, for the paragraph to Fliess conveys a sense of hard-won triumph from the personal excavations carried out in the private Valley of the Kings.

Roy Porter astutely chose the phrase from William Blake's *London*— "mind-forg'd manacles"—for his documentary survey of the treatment of the insane from the Restoration to the Regency in England.[4] Of his choice of title, he notes:

> I have chosen the quotation from Blake for my title—'Mind-Forg'd Manacles'—to convey the sense in which that society first created instruments of cultural torture, such as a theology of eternal damnation, which drove some out of their minds, and then additionally frequently stigmatized the mad as evil and dangerous. (Porter 1987, xi)

This is a Blakean-friendly observation by Porter which shows him in an unusually Michel Foucauldian mood.[5] The second quatrain of *London* reads:

> In every cry of every Man,
> In every Infant's cry of fear,
> In every voice, in every ban,
> The mind-forg'd manacles I hear.

Blake's powerful lines, however, are more a part of that solipsistic experience where mankind's unease is seen unremittingly as a product of wrongly apprehending the external world. In this sense, the anti-Lockean vision of Blake—what would Blake have made of John Locke's pertinent understanding of children's fear of hobgoblins?—has the flavor and, I suspect, the deep meaning of Hamlet's response to Rosencrantz, "[T]here is nothing either good or bad, but thinking makes it so." And in his next reply (*Hamlet*, II, ii), Hamlet gives an early instance of Blakean bliss: "O God, I could be bounded in a nutshell, and count myself a king of infinite space." But the "mind-forg'd manacles" are still present, obliging him to add the rider: "were it not that I have bad dreams." And this, we recall, allows Guildenstern to refer to Rosencrantz's suggestion of ambition in the Prince: "Which dreams, indeed, are ambition; for the very substance of the ambitious is merely the shadow of a dream."

Three hundred years later, Freud (a one-man Rosencrantz and Guildenstern team) can reveal to Fliess what "endopsychic myths" are and how our very thoughts can, apart from our daily experiences, conjure up "immortality, retribution, [and] the entire beyond," which are "all reflections of our psychic internal [world]." In the next paragraph of his letter to Fliess, Freud recommends a work by Rudolf Kleinpaul, *Die Lebendigen und die Toten* ("The Living and the Dead").[6] The letter ends, nonetheless, on a relatively cheerful note as he recalls a recent performance of Wagner's *Die Meistersinger von Nürnberg*. The presence in the audience of Josef Breuer and Freud's emotional response to Hans Sachs's *Morgentraum-Deutweise* (morning-dream interpretation-melody) "forced upon me," he writes, a parallel between Breuer and Hans Sachs. "Moreover," he concludes, "as in no other opera, real ideas are set to music, with the tones of feeling attached to it lingering on as one reflects upon them" (Masson 1985, 286). Was Sigmund brooding upon a possible self-identification with the young knight, Walther von Stolzing, the successful pupil of Sachs-Breuer about to win the laurels (and the lady) for his prize-winning abilities with words and music? *Meschugge*, as Freud would say.

The fascination with the eclectic possibilities of music, literature, and psychology—especially where it concerned numinous ruminations about "immortality, retribution, the entire beyond"—had been an abiding weakness of Freud; his letters to Fliess over the years are sprinkled with references to the arcana of knowledge, or, more properly, of occult belief. This may be one reason, apart from intellectual snobbery, for his frequent quotations from Goethe's *Faust*, and one reason why he remained entranced by Fliess's numerology long after their break—it was not so much the mathematics, which Freud freely confessed he could not follow, but the *implications* behind the Fliessian system which appeared to place man's fate within an "understandable" scientistic orbit.[7]

Fliess had an ability to amaze and overwhelm Freud with his inventions of an "organic" hermeneutics, whereby not merely the nose, but significant dates of even distant blood relatives could be conjured into seeming life-determining significance. I am firmly convinced that the beginnings of psychoanalysis proper coincide with Freud's acceptance, from 1893 on, of Fliess's propositions about the "nasal reflex neurosis."[8] Toward the end of an introductory section to his recent anthology *Unauthorized Freud*, Frederick Crews seems to have come to the same conclusion. Without specifically mentioning the "nasal reflex neurosis," Crews writes:

> Freud's doctrine became more "Fliessian," not less so, as he was resigning himself to the collapse of the seduction theory. Lacking even one single patient who could supply good evidence for his views, Freud turned at once inward toward his own case and outward toward Fliess's parascientific systematizing. Though he would later grant himself full credit for "clinically" deducing such ideas as infantile sexuality, polymorphous perversity, innate bisexuality, latency, and the psychosexual developmental stages, each with its favored zone and mode and "fixation point," all of those notions owed much to Fliess . . . Freud had become a virtually complete Fliessian, but with no intention of admitting that fact. And that is why Fliess, having come to regard Freud less as a friend than as an outright plagiarist, refused to have anything further to do with him.[9]

If Freud was fatally attracted to Fliess's notions, it had to do with a literary and a "scientific" seduction of the arch-seducer himself by a brilliant and totally misguided younger colleague.

Years before, Freud had discovered the seductive delights of the fiction of the precocious Rudyard Kipling. In particular, he had appreciated the "ghost" stories of Kipling, which he had suggested to Ida and Wilhelm Fliess shortly after their marriage in 1892. He had asked on a couple of occasions what would make a suitable wedding present for the pair who had been married on September 6, 1892. He ends the letter of October 21, 1892, with a strange and yet obviously heartfelt recommendation that may well have been accompanied by the volumes themselves: "Read, my dear couple, Kipling's *Phantom Rickshaw* and *The*

Light That Failed. Highly recommended!" (Masson 1985, 34).

Although Freud made only one visit to England (in 1875), his awareness of the English literary scene was a part of his continuing Anglophilia. There were, of course, those members of the Freud family established there (in Manchester) in industry and business; but Freud's personal interest in England seems to have been genuinely informed from a personal cultural perspective, quite irrespective of the family connections. His early—and enduring—fascination with the works of Rudyard Kipling is a case in point. The young literary lion of the London of 1890-1891—newly returned from a teenage stint as editor in Lahore (India)—had created a sensation with the English printings of his poems on military and administrative life in the India of the Raj. The publication, in England, of *The Phantom Rickshaw and Other Tales* in 1890 was a turning point in young Kipling's career. His London publishers ordered the printers to prepare ten thousand copies. The first English edition of *The Light That Failed* appeared in 1891 with the dedication poem "O Mother o' Mine!" and was published by Macmillan and Co.[10]

We do not know whether Freud ever discovered the true precocity of Rudyard Kipling. The tale, which had transfixed him and which he had so strongly recommended to the newlyweds, was, in fact, the work of a teenager. *The Phantom Rickshaw* had first appeared in a family magazine, *Quartette*, which the four Kiplings—father, Lockwood; mother, Alice; daughter, Trix; and son, Rudyard—had persuaded their friends of the *Civil and Military Gazette* to issue as a Christmas Annual at the end of 1885.[11] This issue was duly typeset, by candlelight, and printed in the early hours of December 18, 1885, according to a detailed and hilarious letter from the nineteen-year-old "Wop of Asia" to his English confidante, "The Wop of Albion," Miss Margaret Burne-Jones.[12] Included in this Christmas Annual was the ingenious, grotesque tale entitled "The Strange Ride of Morrowbie Jukes," set in the land of the living dead. For Angus Wilson, this tale is "for whoever could appreciate it, a work of genius."[13]

In a postscript to a letter sent at the beginning of 1886 from Lahore to his schooldays chum Lionel ('Stalky') Dunsterville, now in India and serving in the regiment of the 20th Punjabis, Kipling notes waggishly: "Ain't *Quartette* thrilling—There's a 'Jenny say qwai' about that Phantom Rickshaw that positively haunts me. I have built up a reputation in the Punjab as a chartered libertine on the strength of it."[14] Whatever reputation in the Punjab he boasted of having achieved, Kipling certainly conquered the thirty-six-year-old Sigmund Freud with his literary legerdemain. There is a reason for this. In later years, Kipling was to assess *"The Phantom Rickshaw"* critically: "Some of it was weak, much was bad and out of key; but it was my first serious attempt to think in another man's skin."[15] In fact Kipling, from the very early literary tales, had an uncanny ability to "think in another man's skin" and one suspects that he was well aware of this gift. In a letter of May 2, 1888, to the American-born wife of an Anglo-Indian meteorologist, Mrs. Edmonia Hill, Kipling describes an evening listening to "anecdote after anecdote—each more grisly than the last" concerned with the details of the criminal law as recounted by his friend, H. Straight. His conclusion shows just how more receptive and perceptive he assessed his own mind compared with those of the judiciary:

> I am not much in love with my own mind—it's a scrubby grubby sort o' thing but my faith! 'tis cream laid, wire wove, triple glazed, ivory bank post note paper compared to the mental condition of one who has sat in judgement professionally upon his fellow men.[16]

There is no sitting in judgment upon a fellow man in *The Phantom Rickshaw*. There is, however, an extraordinary ability to develop a framed narrative where the victim/hero of the tale is allowed to write down his account of his fall from grace. Just as Henry James's celebrated novella, *The Turn of the Screw*,[17] turns on the double ambiguity of the governess's sanity and the seizure (medical or spiritual?) that causes young Miles's death, so *The Phantom Rickshaw* may be read as a ghost story, or—and this possibility is strongly indicated in the framing narrative—as a case history of an unnamed tropical fever which exacerbates a morbid, depressive, hallucinatory state of intermittent psychosis leading to death. Angus Wilson seems to opt for the Gothic version when he writes of the dangers of the closed world of the British hill resort of Simla: "Revellers from evening parties at the Viceregal Lodge can never be sure what figure may meet them on the winding, precipitous road. . . . [I]t may be Mrs Wessington's ghost in her "Phantom Rickshaw" haunting her faithless lover Jack Pansay" (Wilson 1977, 89). This is a fine piece of atmospheric novelistic writing by Angus Wilson; and his novelist's imagination has triumphed over the more measured evocation of Simla in the literary tourist part of his biography of Kipling (he and his photographer friend Tony Garrett visited India in preparation of the volume). It may send an anticipatory shiver of fearful pleasure down the spine of the unknowing reader who has not yet read *The Phantom Rickshaw*. But it is a quite illegitimate reading of Kipling's tale. On more than one occasion the victim/narrator, Jack Pansay, makes it crystal clear that when others are present—whether named characters (like the young fiancée, Kitty Mannering, or the medic, Dr. Heatherlegh), or the anonymous strolling throngs of Anglo-Indians—no one else has access to the spectral presence of the late Mrs. Agnes Keith-Wessington and her four *jhampanies* (or coolies), themselves already dead from the cholera. And when Pansay recounts his rides in the company of the late Mrs. Wessington and his conversations with her along the road, the rumor in Simla is that he is stark raving mad and talking to the empty air. It is not Simla that is haunted; it is Pansay alone. Or is he suffering from psychotic hallucinations? In either case, Wilson's invention is misleading.

A chance conversation overheard on the road to Elysium Hill (on the outskirts of Simla) reveals to Pansay that he has indeed been visited by five ghosts and that the very rickshaw itself hired by Mrs. Wessington no longer exists. Pansay's report of this conversation (between Dr. Heatherlegh and another man) implies that he had at first doubted the supernatural visitation *as being supernatural.*

> "It's a curious thing," said one, "how completely all trace of it disappeared. You know my wife was insanely fond of the woman ('never could see anything in her myself), and wanted me to pick up her old rickshaw and coolies if they were to be got for love or money. Morbid sort of fancy I call it; but I've got to do what the *Memsahib* tells me. Would you believe that the man she hired it from tells me that all four of the men—they were brothers—died of cholera on the way to Hardwar, poor devils; and the rickshaw has been broken up by the man himself. 'Told me he never used a dead *Memsahib's* rickshaw. 'Spoiled his luck. Queer notion, wasn't it? Fancy poor little Mrs. Wessington spoiling any one's luck except her own!" I laughed aloud at this point; and my laugh jarred on me as I uttered it. So there *were* ghosts of rickshaws after all, and ghostly employments in the other world![18]

Whether this "realization" is another twist in the hallucinatory anguishes of Pansay is neither denied nor revealed in the autobiographical account of his sickness, which was itself suggested to him by the authorial "I" of the introductory frame:

> When he recovered I suggested that he should write out the whole affair from beginning to end, knowing that ink might assist him to ease his mind. When little boys have learned a new bad word they are never happy till

they have chalked it up on a door. And this also is Literature. (Kipling n.d., 106)

Kipling's cunning excuse for the possible overwriting of the body of the tale itself—"He was in a high fever while he was writing, and the blood-and-thunder Magazine diction he adopted did not calm him" (Kipling n.d., 106).—at once lends a *verismo* to the confession of Pansay and abnegates any authorial responsibility for accrediting the existence of ghosts.

Three possible explanations are offered for Pansay's experiences, or symptoms. Within Pansay's own narrative, Heatherlegh, as a firm no-nonsense physician of the old school, prescribes a combination of rest, physical exercise (walking), and liver pills:

> "Eyes, Pansay—all Eyes, Brain, and Stomach. And the greatest of these three is Stomach. You've too much conceited Brain, too little Stomach, and thoroughly unhealthy Eyes. Get your Stomach straight and the rest follows. And all that's French for a liver pill. I'll take sole medical charge of you from this hour! for you're too interesting a phenomenon to be passed over." (Kipling n.d., 114)

This sounds perilously like a parody of Flaubert's Voltairean philistine, Homais, refusing to grasp the psychological complexities of Emma Bovary (this, however, is Pansay's report of Heatherlegh's diagnosis, and hence may be suspect). But in the introductory framing section—that is, *after* Pansay's death—Heatherlegh "the dearest doctor that ever was" (a reference to his altruistic concern, not to his fees) has suggested a combination of fever and overwork as the cause of the illness and subsequent death:

> "Pansay went off the handle . . . after the stimulus of long leave at Home. He may or he may not have behaved like a blackguard to Mrs. Keith-Wessington. My notion is that the work of the Katabundi Settlement ran him off his legs, and that he took to brooding and making much of an ordinary P. & O. flirtation. He certainly was engaged to Miss Mannering, and she certainly broke off the engagement. Then he took a feverish chill and all that nonsense about ghosts developed. Overwork started his illness, kept it alight, and killed him, poor devil. Write him off to the System—one man to take the work of two and a half men." (Kipling n.d., 105-106)

This second possible explanation, which includes the psychological aspects of guilt, remorse, and the power of the mind over a weakened body, is the first offered in the tale. It is not original, of course, but a long-accepted part of the theatrical demonstration of guilt—"never shake thy gory locks at me," as Macbeth roars to the ghost of Banquo (that none but he can see) seated in *his* place, allowing Lady Macbeth the socially acceptable lie: "my lord is often thus,// and hath been from his youth: pray you, keep seat;// The fit is momentary." This explanation is refuted by the authorial "I" who immediately states, "I do not believe this. I used to sit up with Pansay sometimes when Heatherlegh was called out to patients, and I happened to be within claim. The man would make me most unhappy by describing in a low, even voice, the procession that was always passing at the bottom of his bed. He had a sick man's command of language" (Kipling n.d., 106). This is a clear example of the authorial "I" as clinical observer noting the presence of, and the effect of, the psychotic hallucinations of the "phantom rickshaw" that Pansay experienced. What this apparently empirical observation does not decide is whether the procession "that was always passing at the foot of his bed" was an instance of psychosis or of spiritual possession.

Just before Heatherlegh's diagnosis of overwork and guilty thoughts acting on an enfeebled body, the authorial "I" has written (almost a mini-framing of Heatherlegh's diagnosis within the frame of the introduction itself): "He [Heatherlegh] has, of course, the right to speak authoritatively, and he laughs at my theory that there was a crack in Pansay's head and a little bit of the Dark World came through and pressed him to death" (Kipling n.d., 105). This third explanation—the second in sequence in the tale—is evidently that of the authorial "I" (*not* necessarily to be confused with Kipling the writer). It suggests at once a psychiatric condition in Pansay such as any empirically based medical alienist would recognize and the possible presence and power of forces—"the Dark World"—beyond the realm of ordinary medical investigation because they lie completely beyond the realm of empirical investigation. *The Phantom Rickshaw* as a tale, is, of course, the complete and only textual record we have of its invented universe; and it is genuinely and deliberately *ambiguous*. It cannot be read solely as a psychiatric case study (though, in a sense, it is that); nor can it be read *solely* as a ghost story (despite the brilliant rhetorical presence of the ghosts). It is, in effect, and perversely, *both* at the same time. And we cannot choose between these interpretations without doing violence to the text, or to the artistic intuitions which created it.

Hence, perhaps, Kipling's jaunty comment to 'Stalky' Dunsterville?

His note to Dunsterville, with its amusing "Jenny say qwai," has all the alertness of Edgar Allan Poe's letter to his correspondent, the druggist Ramsay, denying the reality of the mesmeric suspension of death in his tale "The Facts in the Case of M. Valdemar." Was Poe's tale a "hoax"? Ramsay courteously inquires (and this at a time when some members of the medical profession on both sides of the Atlantic were giving credence to the mesmeric postponement of death recounted in Poe's extravaganza), and Edgar Allan responds with disarming candor:

> Dr Sir,
>
> "Hoax" *is* precisely the word suited to M. Valdemar's case. The story appeared originally in "The American Review," a Monthly Magazine, published in this city [New York]. The London papers, commencing with the "Morning Post" and the "Popular Record of Science," took up the theme. The article was generally copied in England and is now circulating in France. Some few persons believe it—but *I* do not—and don't you. (Poe 1966, vol. 2, 337; Poe's emphasis)

Kipling, one suspects, was not taken in by his fictions (and certainly not by this one).[19] With Freud, on the other hand, the question of the "seducer seduced" is always present, even when (as Borch-Jacobsen, Stanley Fish, and others have shown) there is reason to believe that the Freud of the case histories—from *Studies on Hysteria* onward—was knowingly involved in narrative deception.[20] The "invented universe" of the case histories and the theoretical essays is a continuing difficulty with Freud's works, which—unlike those of Kipling—are *not* (one must assume) intended to be read as fictions of human experience. Many arguments have been made about the need to grasp the complex world of late-nineteenth-century Jewish Vienna before any serious understanding of Freud's medical accomplishments can be attained. These arguments leave aside, naturally, the more medically relevant ones relating to the empirical value and reportorial truthfulness of Freud's writings. They also leave aside that vast interior universe of obsessive confabulation that was both Freud's brilliant achievement and his ultimate downfall.

Jean-Michel Rey, in "Freud's Writing on Writing," refers to Freud's prefatory comments on Wilhelm Jensen's *Gradiva*—now, ironically, famous and read largely thanks to Freud's essay—and underlines the importance of "the very passage in which Freud understands his 'knowledge' as being outflanked by that of fiction, and in which he 'learns' that fiction encroaches upon his own discoveries, anticipates them in its own way, thereby twisting the act of interpretation unforeseeably and forcing it to shift to a new location and indeed to find new resources." This is the passage that Rey quotes:

> But creative writers are valuable allies and their evidence is to be prized highly, for they are apt to know a whole host of things between heaven and earth of which our philosophy [*Schulweisheit*] has not yet let us dream. In their knowledge of the mind they are far in advance of us everyday people, for they draw upon sources which we have not yet opened up for science. (G.W., 7, 33; S.E., 9, 8)

And, Rey concludes, "[f]rom such a confrontation, Freud hopes for nothing less than an insight into the 'nature of poetic production' [*Natur der dichterischen Produktion*]."[21] Jean-Michel Rey, then teaching "psychoanalytic theory at the University of Paris-Vincennes" (Felman 1982, 508), was writing as a "believer," as one of Freud's disciples who accepted without question the "discoveries" of the magus, while questioning the theoretical status of the relationship of psychoanalysis to literature and of language to experience. One consequence of his over-intellectualization of Freud's metapsychological essays is that Rey is frequently snared by Freud's use of humorously ironical (and/or publicly deceptive) self-description.

In the above quote, for instance, the phrase "us everyday people" gets no parsing from Rey, when it should, of course, be highlighted for its devious jocularity and all the intellectual mayhem that has resulted therefrom. The more important, but related, issue that Rey seems to have missed is that the distinction he implicitly accepts between discursive, theoretical prose (the Freud essays) and imaginative literature (Jensen, Hoffmann, Schiller, etc.) is a nonstarter. It is *because* Rey has been long seduced by the rhetorical conjuring genius of Freud that he can ascribe to imaginative constructs—"knowledge," "discoveries," "science" and so forth—the significance that they might have in an essay of scientific inquiry. And if Freud appears to be aware of a potential destabilization of their meaning (i.e., of a potential loss of authority status for his writings), then he ups the ante by inventing more imaginative constructs about the human mind and writes more fictions—in the guise of essays—in order to defend and promote the one biographical fiction that rivals, to this day, the rhetorical success of his writings, and that is the rhetorical success of his public persona—the deeply modest but all-knowing explorer of the human mind to whom the members of the Vienna Psychoanalytic Society paid exaggerated deference.

In the Freud passage just cited by Rey, the very first words should alert us—and should have alerted Rey—to the rhetorical game at work: "But creative writers are valuable allies." The implication readily apparent (though not to Rey) is that "we" (i.e., Freud and other analysts) are not "creative writers." "We" are *scientists* doggedly pursuing, and in a scientific manner, the difficult inquiries that our subject matter demands.[22] Frederick Crews, in his introduction to an excerpt from Sebastiano Timpanaro's *The Freudian Slip*, comments dryly on this aspect of the reception of *The Interpretation of Dreams* and the popular *The Psychopathology of Everyday Life*:

> These are indeed works of detective fiction, featuring a hero who is every inch Holmes's equal as a tracer of the faintest clues and an infallible solver of puzzles that would daunt any ordinary mortal. *And our awe is redoubled by our impression that we are not reading fiction but rather science in agreeably narrative form.* (Crews 1998, 94; my emphasis)

One can understand Freud's enthusiasm for *The Phantom Rickshaw*. It had the literary (and medical) ambiguity that his own future case histories would have—especially those early ones (the drafting of which was contemporaneous with his discovery of Kipling) retailed in *Studies on Hysteria*[23]—and it brought into focus the *unheimlich* or "spooky" side of his interests that he would try (or pretend to try) to remove from his own tales (or "case histories").[24] It had as its essential themes: adulterous sexual passion, betrayal, death, sexual revenge (apparently from beyond the grave). The three medical diagnostic possibilities offered to his patient (Jack Pansay) by Dr. Heatherlegh to explain to the ex-fiancée's family the bizarre hallucinations of the hero/victim/narrator are given thus:

> "This engagement has to be broken off; and the Mannerings don't want to be too hard on you. Was it broken through *D.T.* or epileptic fits? Sorry I can't offer you a better exchange unless you'd prefer hereditary insanity. Say the word and I'll tell 'em it's fits. All Simla knows about that scene on the Ladies' Mile. Come! I'll give you five minutes to think over it." (Kipling n.d., 117)

It is tempting—but mistaken—to see *The Phantom Rickshaw* as a kind of masculine and pessimistic version of *Anna O.* with the Breuer part played by Dr. Heatherlegh and the Freud part (not that Freud was ever clinically involved with this case) played by the authorial "I"—more knowing, more imaginative, more "literary" than the senior physician. Heatherlegh, however, does not play the part of Josef Breuer: he neither connives at Pansay's narrative hallucinations nor does he demand from him some hypnoid continuation of them.

Apart from the "medical" situation of the plot, there is in *The Phantom Rickshaw* a narrative structural device that was to become a hallmark of the Kipling short story (inspired by his study of Poe) and that appears to have been seized upon by Freud for his own writings. This is the brilliant employment of a fictionalized persona—"I"—to whom a tale of personal disaster is told, or confessed, who occasionally probes, prompts, and resumes, and who—as controlling narrator—reveals to the public in the rhetorical shape of a history the situation, events, and circumstances of the episode. What is particularly ingenious in the hands of a skilled writer—such as Kipling or Freud—is the way the controlling "I" is scarcely perceived by the reader as being itself an integral part of the fiction. We tend, for the sake of the tale, to grant to this unnamed narrator an illusion of actual reality (stronger than mere verisimilitude) and to forget, in consequence, three crucial, yet simple, things: (1) the shaping of the story— what is revealed, what is not revealed, when and how the events unfold—is in the hands of this invented "I" (whom we first encounter, inevitably, through the written evidence of its "style"); (2) the psychological acumen, the maturity of judgment, the characteristic traits of this "I" are, of course, *also* an essential and quite deliberately constructed fiction; (3) and, lastly, what we learn in English 101, the first-person narrator is not to be confused with the *author*—the one who really pulls the strings, as it were.

It is less immediately obvious why Freud should have shown equal urgent enthusiasm for *The Light That Failed*, or indeed paired it in his letter to Fliess with *The Phantom Rickshaw*. From a purely technical point of view, this novel lacks all of the precocious mastery of narrative cunning evident in the adolescent work. It was Kipling's first published full-length novel in England and, although it received some critical acclaim, it met with quite justified criticism. Freud must have read this work quite differently, from a totally different perspective, and with a kind of frenzied naïveté. If his delight in *The Phantom Rickshaw* stemmed from a professional, writerly, concern over *how* to conceive and draft the narrative of an ambiguous medical case history, with perhaps a marginal, unrecognized sense of identification with the anonymous "I" of the tale, it seems that Freud's reading of the truly juvenile third-person narrative novel was itself one of unsophisticated self-identification with the artist–hero, Dick Heldar, and his war-correspondent companion, faithful to the end (unlike any of the women in the story), Torpenhow.

If this is so, then it may well be that Kipling's lapse as writer was reciprocated by Freud's lapse as reader: Kipling wrote angrily and resentfully to "get off his chest" the supposed hurts and failures of the recent past; Freud read avidly for the vicarious thrill of seeing Dick Heldar's messy tragedy as potentially his own (both were involved professionally in portraying people, in print or in paint, in difficult situations). As we shall see, Freudian criticism of Kipling has given the trophy for interpretation (of people and texts) to the reader—Freud. In my view this is mistaken; but it does allow for two interesting questions: the power of Freud's rhetoric and the desire of the disciples to imitate it (what Borch-Jacobsen calls "the re-citation of the myth"),[25] and the unusual concordance of personality traits in public presentation of self between Kipling and Freud. (This latter point, I confess, had not occurred to me when I first read Freud's praise of Kipling, and even now I am not sure how valuable such parallels are.)

Many critics have seen Dick Heldar as a far too closely related analogue or projection of Kipling himself and his early difficulties with women and society. In addition to the autobiographical parallels (which, in themselves, need not demonstrate any lack of aesthetic control), the absence of a framing device and a judicious first-person narrator (the whole tale recounted in Torpenhow's voice, for example, would have been an immediate improvement) make of this novel an aesthetic failure—that is, a tub-thumping, self-lacerating disaster. Even Angus Wilson, one of the most generously understanding of Kipling critics, is led to argue that Rudyard's failure to reawaken a reciprocal passion in his newfound boyhood love Flo Garrard (encountered by chance in London in February 1890, she became the model for "Maisie" in *The Light That Failed*) and his painful sense of isolation in London (cf. Freud's sense of isolation in Vienna)[26] were responsible for a recklessly conceived novel. Confusing the Pre-Raphaelite notions of courtly love (memories of Uncle Ned Burne-Jones) and the apparent coldness of Florence Garrard, Kipling stumbled, so Wilson writes, from fantasized wrong to aesthetic mess. Angus Wilson chooses not to discuss critically *The Light That Failed*, out of kindness, one suspects, but this is what he describes in one paragraph:

> In his overcharged imagination the two [the Pre-Raphaelite *belle dame sans merci* and his own sources of inspiration] became mixed. And the

result is a farrago of misogyny and false heroics and self-pity. *The Light That Failed* is a *fin-de-siècle* decadent tale with death as its outcome but this would hardly matter (or at any rate it would have made nothing worse than a modish, mediocre work) but that the mode was not Kipling's. For him, if death there was to be, then that death must be exalted, not melancholy, and, to point the misogynist moral, a manly, heroic death in battle that would wash the mouth clean of woman's petty concerns and selfish ways with a good draught of healthy soldiers' blood. The whole makes a novel that would be very distasteful if it were not absurd. (Wilson 1977, 155-56)

And yet Freud was bowled over by it. Why?

He cannot have been intrigued by the novel's narrative skills, nor by the third-person narrator. What the novel may have offered him was the cozy presence and easy jocularity of the mutually supportive male camaraderie of war correspondents—the plump black Hindu known simply as The Nilghai,[27] Torpenhow, Cassavetti and the rest—this would have offered Freud an "innocent" (because inexplicit) illustration of homoeroticism in action. Thanks largely to Freud's obsession, and to his lasting influence on untrained minds (or minds trained by his precepts), the very notion of men working together in a single-sex enterprise has come to be understood (and almost taken for granted) at the end of this century as an indicator for overt, repressed, or sublimated homosexuality. Would this be an instance of the Churchillian Freud?—"rum, sodomy, and the lash" were mockingly declared to be among the premier "traditions of the Royal Navy." A recent history of the British merchant marine argues convincingly against this hoary canard. As Geoffrey Scammell writes in his *Times Literary Supplement* review of Peter Earle's *Sailors: English Merchant Seamen, 1650-1775*:

> He [Peter Earle] dutifully investigates sex, finding that homosexuality was virtually unknown among crews, notwithstanding that men and young boys were crowded together in the closest proximity, and he cryptically observes that the absence of women on board caused few problems other than frustration. He entertainingly recounts the doings of sailors ashore as the notoriously insatiable clients of whores and brothels.[28]

Was Kipling's love of uniforms and of "men of action" an unavowed aspect of a lurking homosexual nature that, given the ethos of late Victorian England, had to use camouflage wherever possible and outright denial when the camouflage was unavailing? And was it to this hidden side of Kipling that Freud responded?

Or, and this is the other part of the possible answer to Freud's enthusiasm, was it the presence on the page throughout the novel, from childhood through to maturity, of the unspoken presentation of lesbian nature? Maisie's coldness was nothing other than her inability to respond to masculine desire. The unnamed "red-haired girl," Maisie's sole and constant companion (in England and in France) is Dick Heldar's nemesis. A passage from chapter 5 suggests this and reveals, at the same time, the horrible, gauche quality of the writing—whether dealing with Maisie or with the masculine sense of closeness between men that is so clumsily described:

> Half-way to the studio, Dick was smitten with a terrible thought. The figure of a solitary woman in the fog suggested it.
>
> "She's all alone in London, with a red-haired impressionist girl, who probably has the digestion of an ostrich. Most red-haired people have. Maisie's a bilious little body. They'll eat like lone women,—meals at all hours, and tea with all meals. I remember how the students in Paris used to pig along. She may fall ill at any minute, and I shan't be able to help. Whew! this is ten times worse than owning a wife."
>
> Torpenhow came into the studio at dusk, and looked at Dick with his eyes full of the austere love that springs up between men who have tugged at the same oar together and are yoked by custom and use and the intimacies of toil. This is a good love, and, since it allows, and even encourages, strife, recrimination, and the most brutal sincerity, does not die, but increases, and is proof against any absence and evil conduct. (Kipling n.d., 450)

The stylist in Freud could not but have been repulsed by this explanation of human activities; it is almost as if an excuse were needed by the narrator for his daring use of the word "love" in this passage. But the nascent "metapsychologist" in him must have rejoiced at finding his evolving theories so "sincerely" depicted by a foreign novelist.

As far as we know, Florence Garrard's sexual inclinations were indeed uniquely lesbian (unbeknownst to young Rudyard). In his elegantly insightful and unprurient manner, Angus Wilson describes Kipling's late-adolescent dilemma in this way:

> Whatever the girl-boy attachment, there is no evidence to suppose that Flo was still alive to it when she met him again by chance in February 1890. Years later, it seems, she spoke of it as *his* infatuation. A visit that Rudyard

paid to her in May 1890 in Paris, where she was sharing a studio with a friend, Mabel Price, certainly gave him no encouragement. The fact that she was apparently still with her friend over thirty years later may lead one to wonder whether he had not, by chance, embarked upon a romantic quest that was stillborn from the start. But enough conjecture has pursued the unfortunate Miss Garrard, simply because a young man of literary genius fell deeply in love with her in his early youth. (Wilson 1977, 154)

This, it seems to me, is as much as one can responsibly deduce from the personal pain of "disprized love" apparent in *The Light That Failed*. Physicians are warned not to offer diagnosis of an unexamined patient (for obvious practical reasons), and psychiatrists usually accept the restraint of not pronouncing on unseen patients (for the same reasons). One famous exception to this elementary medical deontology was Jacques Lacan, who, in 1933, published his diagnosis of the murderesses Christine and Léa Papin in the surrealist journal *Minotaure*,[29] without having ever met them or examined their medical records. Aware of this unprofessional intrusion, Lacan wrote of a senior psychiatrist, Dr. Benjamin Logre, who had argued for diminished culpability on grounds of insanity, and, as if this excused his conduct,

> He [Dr. Logre] had not one but several hypotheses about the suspected mental anomaly of the sisters: persecutory ideas, sexual perversion, epilepsy or hysterical epilepsy. If I believe that I can formulate a clearer solution to the problem, *I should first of all pay my respects to his authority, not only because it defends me against the criticism of making a diagnosis without actually having examined the patient*, but because it allows the appropriate use of certain obscure facts, which are, as we shall see, essential for the demonstration of my thesis. (Crichton and Cordess 1995, 568; my emphasis)[30]

Lacan's phrase which I have italicized is an early example of the Lacanian non sequitur. He is in no way "defended against" the (accurate) charge of forming a diagnosis without ever having met the patients. Lacan, however, is not alone in his misdemeanor. Freud himself was the first of the psychoanalysts to belabor unseen patients with diagnoses of his own imagined invention—the most famous being, perhaps, the essay on the psychotic German judge, Daniel Paul Schreber.

But Freud also instituted the practice of treating famous literary and artistic figures to his own homegrown postmortem analyses. This practice rapidly caught on. What began as essays in "metapsychology" (though in fact they were, quite literally, no more than rhetorically persuasive attempts to fit Freud's unsubstantiated doctrines to the famous dead), was largely responsible for the creation of a new and increasingly popular academic version of literary criticism. It was for most of its practitioners neither literary nor criticism, but rather a fastidious attempt to "read" phallic images and remnants of supposed infantile memories of "primal scenes" (for which the "Wolf Man" case history provided the scatological foundations) in works of literature. Nowadays, it is rare to find a discussion of a literary figure that does not include some acknowledged debt to Freud's dubious methods of understanding human behavior. As Peter Brooks noted at the beginning of *Reading for the Plot*, there are three basic ways of proceeding: analyzing the text; analyzing the author; analyzing the reader's response. In each case, however, the interpretation will depend on the application of Freudian theses, and especially on those concerning Freud's mis-understanding of infantile sexuality (its nature and its imagined long-term effects). But, as I. A. Richards pointed out well over sixty years ago,

> The difficulty is that nearly all speculations as to what went on in the artist's mind are unverifiable, even more unverifiable than the similar speculations as to the dreamer's mind. The most plausible explanations are apt to depend upon features whose actual causation is otherwise. (Richards 1934, 30)

Kipling, who once fascinated Freud, has been for some years now the object of psychoanalytic scrutiny. This is the triumph of Freud's rhetoric over Kipling's. It is not the triumph of truth over fiction, or of medicine over art. The two most evident excursions of psychoanalytic interpretation into the supposed interior world of Rudyard Kipling are by the psychoanalyst Leonard Shengold, M.D., and the biographer, Martin Seymour-Smith.

Shengold, who certainly appreciates Kipling's prowess as a writer, was taken by the phrase "soul murder" (used by Daniel Paul Schreber and earlier, in the mid–nineteenth century, by Anselm von Feuerbach in his study of the enigmatic Kaspar Hauser)[31] and used this phrase as a center-piece in his explanations for Kipling's tone and choice of subject. Shengold rightly emphasizes the pain and difficulties of the years of involuntary exile at Southsea from the age of six that young Rudyard passed with "Aunty Rosa." What he does with these years, however, is to refuse Kipling's own assessment of them and to impose on them—like laying down a predrawn Freudian cellophane grid over the life—a doctrinaire "psychoanalytic" interpretation of young Rudyard's experiences.

Shengold begins his "Summary and Conclusions" with these (apparently) disarming phrases: "The psychoanalyst who is only a reader has no special source of insight. His view of the author's childhood is of necessity superficial."[32] If taken literally, this disclaimer by a psychoanalyst would put all of Freud's writings out of bounds (as far as enabling their reader to have a "special source of insight" is concerned). It is, however, only by *reading* Freud that one can come to the doctrines expounded in his texts (one certainly doesn't come to them by experience with living infants, adolescents, or adults). It may be unfair to accuse Shengold of a "come-on" here; but once one starts reading *his* weird interpretation of Kipling's childhood, one realizes that the Freudian kaleidoscope has been applied. We learn from Shengold that, at the age of six, Rudyard was "at the height of his oedipal development" (Orel 1989, 107), which includes, so we are informed, "castration anxiety" and other Freudian obsessions. The paragraph before this shows Shengold at his Freudian best:

> Fears about his anger and sexual feelings must have been evoked in Rudyard by the births of his sister and the stillborn sibling. These births were probably linked to fantasies about parental intercourse and the first trip to the "dark land": England. The lifelong, obsessive metaphors of light and darkness, vision and blindness show the importance of primal scene fantasies for Kipling, fantasies that had exciting and terrifying con- notations. Another evidence for his fixation is his lifelong, intense curiosity and need to be "in the know"—mysteriously transmuted into his creative gifts as an observer, describer, and evoker of realistic detail. (Orel 1989, 107)

One should ignore the phrase "another evidence for his fixation," which implies (a) that the "fixation" has been established as a fact and (b) that what conjectures have been already offered are, indeed, "evidence" and not conjectures at all. Shengold is here following the rhetorical pattern established by Freud in "From the History of an Infantile Neurosis (The 'Wolf Man')" with a fidelity that does credit to his expensive training. The "lifelong, obsessive metaphors of light and darkness" had far less to do with the facile and erroneous Freudian invention of "primal scene fantasies" and much more to do with the real threatening onset of blindness (unrecognized by his foster parent or his schoolteachers), which was to lead to a diagnosis of severe myopia and to the immediate application of glasses. The only reference that Shengold makes to this *real* childhood difficulty is in the following passage:

> There was, after his near-blindness and breakdown, a flowering of Kipling's creative writing in the predominantly male atmosphere of school. He emerged as a writer and poet, specifically as a master of rhyme. The ambition to become a writer crystallized in adolescence at a time when there must have been a renewal of conflict over masturbation. (Orel 1989, 108)

The unsubstantiated amalgamation of "near-blindness" (biographically and empirically affirmed) with "breakdown" (for which psychiatric disorder there is no evidence whatever—however miserable Rudyard may have been before his mother's return) is, unfortunately, typical of the dishonesty that is so frequent in the self-serving reports of psychoanalysts. Shengold's repeated use of the hopeful "must have been" is an indication, if ever there was, of the "fingers-crossed" guessing that is at the heart of this wretched essay. The truth is that Shengold has not the slightest idea of Rudyard Kipling's youthful experiences. Shengold is intrigued by sex and sexual perversion and by supposed sexual infantile and adolescent imaginings and their subsequent formative importance (thanks, one assumes, to his own Freudian indoctrination—or, one may wonder, did Shengold actually think this way as a medical student, and prior to any close encounter with Freudian texts?). Meanwhile, the *reality* of the near-blind child falsely accused of deliberate destructiveness for his unrecognized myopic clumsiness and unfairly blamed for lying about his school progress is ignored as an important element of the hurt foisted on the young Rudyard.

Kipling's powerful autobiographical tale, "Baa, Baa, Black Sheep," is far more lucid and honest in its description of what happened to a young boy and his sister (Trix, the three-year-old sister, is ignored by most psychoanalysts in their inventions; but Shengold manages the indiscretion of writing "I have speculated that there may have been sexual play between Trix and Rudyard which had some saving effect on his masculinity") than anything that any Freudian has invented. And even the recognition that a returning mother's love could not *totally* remove the psychological damage that had occurred was recognized by the young author himself, then aged twenty-three, in the concluding paragraph of his tale, which gently rebukes the optimistic childish delight of young "Punch" (Aunty Rosa's 'Black Sheep') on his mother's return ("It's all different now, and we are just as much Mother's as if she had never gone") with the narrative persona's assessment:

> Not altogether, O Punch, for when young lips have drunk deep of the bitter waters of Hate, Suspicion, and Despair, all the Love in the world will not wholly take away that knowledge; though it may turn darkened eyes for a while to the light, and teach Faith where no Faith was. (Kipling n.d., 975)

The recurring metaphor of the loss of sight and its description in actuality is an instance of Kipling's artistic triumph over personal experience (two of the better sections of *The Light That Failed* are the visit to the oculist in chapter 10 and chapter 11 where Dick Heldar's failing eyesight is finally and irremediably extinguished). A physiological impairment (Kipling's myopia) is changed into damage to the optic nerve (Dick Heldar's earlier head wounds), and the whole is subsumed into the event-as-metaphor, now become a wide-ranging symbol, that is hinted at in the very title, *The Light That Failed*, with all its manifold implications. In this respect, at least, Kipling continued his brilliant ability to invent the portmanteau title (a gift he shared with Edgar Allan Poe, where the meaning of the title of a tale changes its hues as one's reading progresses, like a laser holograph held up at different angles to the light).

At the time of his first reading of *The Light That Failed*, Freud could not have had knowledge of the autobiographical transpositions that dominated this complex but, ultimately, unsuccessful novel. Later readers and critics, and, of course, biographers, have had the advantage of a life (Freud's or Kipling's) lived through to the end, the perspective of time, and the availability of new documentary material. Martin Seymour-Smith has rolled up his sleeves and gone to work like a Trojan to produce a volume naughtily entitled, in its latest Papermac edition, *Rudyard Kipling: The Controversial New Biography* (1990). All that is "controversial" in Seymour-Smith's book (apart from its relentless pubescent vulgarity) is the proposition that Kipling's "nature" was homosexual. Now, as Seymour-Smith is not a psychoanalyst but a professional biographer, it may be worthwhile to examine briefly how he has approached his assignment. His comments on the opening chapter of *The Light That Failed*, of which more later, give the jejune interpretative information that a goat = lust (symbolically) and a revolver = phallus (symbolically). More interesting, for their evidence of carefully learned

Freudian rhetoric, are the observations in the introduction and in the foreword to the second edition.

In the introduction to the original edition, Seymour-Smith dutifully pays respect to, and declares his gratitude to, literary critics such as the late Joyce Tompkins (for her *The Art of Rudyard Kipling*, 1959) and to earlier biographers, including Philip Mason, Angus Wilson, and Charles Carrington. Of Wilson he notes, "I will say now only that I believe his remark 'Freudianism is too easy' begs the question." In the next few sentences, Seymour-Smith distances himself from the kind of approach taken by Shengold and in a way which implies that we will be treated to a more mature, more sophisticated, psychological exploration of Rudyard Kipling:

> Certainly any old-fashioned attempt to see Kipling in terms of some over-rigid application of 'classical' Freudian tenets, such as one used to see in some biographies of fifty and even fewer years ago, would be absurd. I suspect him [Angus Wilson], here, of uncharacteristically fudging the issue: he is not using 'Freudianism' in its proper sense. All too often it is used to mean, simply, 'intimate psychological exploration,' even if that exploration be along Adlerian, Jungian or even Reichian lines! There are now two distinct senses of the word, anyway: one is 'along the lines of official psychoanalytical dogma,' and the other is the rich sort of speculation practised by Freud himself in some of his own investigations. Yes, the latter is sometimes infected by the former, and the same man was responsible for both; but surely everyone now knows that they are two different things? (Seymour-Smith 1990, xxix)

That rhetorical question is mischievous. Not only does "everyone" not now know that between Freud's "rich sort of speculation" and psychoanalytical dogma there is an enormous gulf, but the significance of Freud's adventures in metapsychology are all dependent upon the tenets invented for his discipline. Without those tenets being taken for granted, the Freudian essays are without scientific significance, and are mere prose poems based on persuasively expressed hunches. Seymour-Smith seems to have fallen into the same misprision of genre that caught Jean-Michel Rey.

One may reasonably ask whether, when he came to the final draft of his *Rudyard Kipling* in 1989, Seymour-Smith had read with attention (as he should have) the 1985 publication by Harvard University Press of the complete Freud–Fliess correspondence. Some of the "rich sort of speculation" perpetrated in those letters would surely have given him pause for thought. In his next paragraph, Seymour-Smith, in an inelegant and unconvincing about-face, claims that—whatever he may have written—he is not what Grünbaum would call a "believer":

> I need carefully to add, at this stage, that I am not in any way a dogmatic Freudian—or, indeed, a Freudian at all, or anything else like that—and that I do not think psychoanalysis itself is of much use to anyone except as self-fulfilling fantasy or as a means of passing time or spending money, or both. (Seymour-Smith 1990, xxix)

Well, "Lah-di-dah!" as Woody Allen's Annie Hall might say.

In this later foreword to the second edition (dated 1990), Seymour-Smith noisily engages with the outraged Kiplingites who had attacked his first edition as a "sex-slur" on their favorite author. "The 'sex-slur'? There is no 'sex-slur.' There is in this book no more than confident psychological speculation that Kipling experienced powerful homosexual desires, and was for a time conscious of them" (Seymour-Smith, xvi). Freud's famous use of a mere hypothesis, or hunch, later to be renamed as an "indisputable fact" or "irrefragable" evidence uncovered by psychoanalysis, is becoming, at long last, a recognized aspect of his rhetoric of deceit (and often of self-deception); it is in this way that his essays and *all* his case histories were constructed. Seymour-Smith has learned this useful technique of Freudian presentation. In the above quotation from his foreword to the second edition," Seymour-Smith claims that his book is "no more than confident psychological speculation." We are not told the grounds for the confidence; and we may wonder, having read his book, whether the "confidence" was not as horribly misplaced as that which Freud had placed in the scientific phantasmagorias of Wilhelm Fliess.

Nonetheless, we should note the modesty of Seymour-Smith's claim—"confident psychological speculation"—not fact, not evidence, not witnessed testimony, just "speculation" (like Shengold on Rudyard's relations with Trix). Now, the reader should turn to the last paragraph of this foreword where he or she will find the book's achievement described in somewhat different terms. I quote: "I deal, therefore, in psychological realities as uncomfortable to me as to my reader" (Seymour-Smith 1990, xviii). All of a sudden, and with no intervening justification, "speculation" has become "realities"—in the plural, note. This attempt at a rhetoric of massive deception is a clear indication that, whatever his disclaimers, Seymour-Smith has learned the tricks of the trade and is writing as a

Freudian would. When we look at his handling of the first chapter of *The Light That Failed*, we discover that he is employing what he would call an "old-fashioned" form of psychoanalytic criticism—and with an obsessive sexual prurience that is at once hilarious and deeply disturbing (for the limitations to the understanding of human experience that Freud's influence has wrought).

Kipling's novel begins on a late afternoon on a seashore at low tide with two children in early adolescence (but Kipling uses the noun "children"), Dick Heldar and his fellow pensioner at his guardian's house, the orphan Maisie, accompanied by her pet goat Amomma whom she had brought with her four years before when she was first assigned to Mrs. Jennett's care by her lawyers. "The children," Kipling writes whimsically, "had discovered that their lives would be unendurable without pistol-practice." They have saved up their pennies and bought a hundred cartridges and a cheap, ill-made Belgian revolver. Three things happen on this eventful afternoon: the two children, for the first time, engage in target practice at a breakwater; Maisie tells Dick that she is going away (to a finishing school in Switzerland); Dick tells Maisie that he loves her and the pair kiss as young lovers rather than as children:

> Amomma looked on from afar. He had seen his property [Maisie] quarrel frequently, but he had never seen kisses exchanged before. The yellow sea-poppy was wiser, and nodded its head approvingly. Considered as a kiss, that was a failure, but since it was the first, other than those demanded by duty, in all the world that either had given or taken, it opened to them new worlds, and every one of them glorious, so that they were lifted above the consideration of any worlds at all, especially those in which tea is necessary, and sat still, holding each other's hands and saying not a word. (Kipling n.d., 421)

This is one of Kipling's more successful passages in *The Light That Failed*. The magical first moment when children experience themselves and others as adults, with the sudden shift in perspective of the glance and the significance that that implies, is captured by Kipling with a wry, almost facetious, but tender, anthropomorphism. Amomma has long been the animal confidant of Maisie, receiving her hidden tears of anguish on his neck ("Amomma is mine, mine, mine!" Maisie has shouted defiantly at the puritanical Mrs. Jennett); here the terms are reversed as the pet is allowed thoughts of possession. In the same way, sea-poppies are given degrees of wisdom.

Irrespective of the charming drollery Kipling employs to offset the gravity of the moment, this is conceived of as a powerful memory for Dick Heldar. And at the end of chapter 2, set years later during the unsuccessful Sudanese campaign to rescue General Gordon at Khartoum from the troops of the Mahdi, when Dick collapses and succumbs to a state of delirium after an Arab sword has gashed his skull, he confuses the present with contorted memories of that long-ago and magical afternoon. Kipling intended the memory of Maisie to be pervasive, if not obsessive, in Dick Heldar's life.

Seymour-Smith, who patently lacks Kipling's psychological depth of perception and stylistic qualities (even in the severely strained and uneven quality of this novel), has decided—à la Freud—that if there is a sexual possibility to be squeezed out of an event, a description, or an image, he will squeeze it out. Before quoting some of the more egregious nonsense of Seymour-Smith, I should point out that, for him, Maisie is a young American publisher's agent: Wolcott Balestier (whose photograph is included in Seymour-Smith's volume under the "confident" rubric: "Wolcott Balestier, the man Kipling loved").

Seymour-Smith starts his shenanigans with the end of chapter 2 and Dick's failed shot just before the Arab blade felled him. He relates this to the scene by the sea of the two children with Amomma in attendance:

> An interesting detail is that Dick's 'aim' is once again spoiled. In the first chapter it was spoiled by—as the girl's hair is blown by the rising wind and she calls the goat Amomma 'a little beast'—a sudden darkness 'that stung'; here it is spoiled by the memory of that incident, a voice saying, 'Ah, get away you brute!', the voice of someone scaring something away, a crack in the head, a darkness 'that stung.' . . . Here is a vivid sense of the blindingness of sexual encounter, not experienced by Kipling with women. He does not know what he will find. (Seymour-Smith 1990, 175)

This is followed by the comment that Freud has made us all self-conscious and by the implication that Victorian literature (and, presumably, *all* literature prior to the advent of psychoanalysis?—otherwise Seymour-Smith's phrase is sheer uninformed gibberish) needs the special decoding powers of an expert in human experience, someone like Seymour-Smith, for instance—someone who *knows*:

> Victorian symbolism, as in some of the very early Henry James, was obvious, 'innocent' and in a sense pure. Freud had not yet come to make everyone self-conscious, and the symbolism worked much better and less

consciously. Blindness here is impotence, lack of creative virility, fear that homosexuality may cripple creativity— and the goat and the 'brute' are lust. They may also represent, although more remotely, the cultural obligation that a man feels to desire women. . . . The 'spoiling of the aim' in this novel is an adumbration of the blindness theme; desire (goat, brute) destroys the will to work. At the same time, the firing of a revolver has an unmistakably phallic significance. It is silly and immature (just as men usually are), over-obvious, and irritatingly and glibly over-used—but one that is responsible for much death and destruction. In *The Light That Failed* the case of the bullets whining away off target is poignant, a hint of something else the author wants. In the first chapter, the 'thoroughly fouled revolver' kicks 'wildly' in Dick's hands—a reminiscence of onanism (although Onan actually seems to have been guilty of *coitus interruptus* rather than masturbation—but we will give the word Kipling would have used if he had dared) when he was not too tired at USC [United Services College]? The bullet of the spoiled aim goes 'singing out to the empty sea.' In the second chapter the bullet goes out over the desert. There is a sense of hopelessness in 'firing' at all. (Seymour-Smith 1990, 175-76)

The last two disasters of biography produced by Seymour-Smith concern Kipling's chance meeting with Flo Garrard in London and Kipling's thought processes on his wedding night. I leave the reader to choose whether these little scenes exhibit Seymour-Smith's "confident psychological speculation" or Seymour-Smith's alternative "psychological realities," or, perhaps, neither. And I leave the reader to ponder whether he or she would buy a second hand car from this man. Of the chance encounter, Seymour-Smith (with no evidence whatever for his version) writes:

Kipling was prompted to write the book [*The Light That Failed*] in the way he did by two events: his accidental meeting with Flo in the street, and his meeting with Wolcott. He could express his passions outwardly by use, so to say, of running into the *femme fatale*. Probably he lurked in alleyways until she emerged, so as to 'run into her.' He knew very well where she was to be found. (Seymour-Smith 1990, 176)

Of Kipling's marriage to Caroline Balestier, sister of Wolcott Balestier who had died of typhoid in Dresden, Seymour-Smith offers a well-known general truth, followed by a gross impertinence in "confident psychological speculation" that perhaps even Freud himself may have resisted:

Many marriages break down when erotic and romantic love break down. Kipling knew from the beginning that there was no romance. Romantically, Carrie was simply the ghost of Wolcott. He would have intended to change that. But can anyone make that sort of change? Doing his marital duty, was he not sodomising (O shameful thought!) Wolcott? No wonder he was confused, and no wonder he became fanatical about his privacy. (Seymour-Smith 1990, 204)

Freud may not be directly responsible for the comical combination of prurience and vulgarity that is at the heart of Seymour-Smith's biography of Kipling; but his influence, or that of his international organization, is ever-present and ever-disastrous.

Whether the Freud, who was so taken by Kipling's fictions, would have appreciated the psychoanalytical tergiversations on his favorite living author is another question. The Freud who recommended *The Phantom Rickshaw* and *The Light That Failed* to Fliess and his bride would, perhaps, have been dismayed at the way things have turned out. To the extent that contemporary discussion of Kipling requires awareness of the Freudian viewpoint, Freud might have felt some sense of justification in his probings of his patients' stories about themselves and in his own incursions into the lives of people (long since dead) that he knew only through their artistic achievements. And, as for his motives in recommending these two particularly lugubrious texts of Kipling to a newlywed pair (Wilhelm and Ida), one can only wonder at the lack of self-knowledge, or the sadistic delight, that such a choice implied.

Notes

1. Freud, letter to Fliess of December 12, 1897 (Masson 1985, 286).

2. Freud to Jung, letter of June 18, 1909. See William McGuire (1974), ed. *The Freud/Jung Letters*. Princeton: Princeton University Press, 234-35.

3. Stephen Wilson (1997), "Fragments of the Truth," *Times Literary Supplement* (December 12): 6. This is a brief review of Paul Ferris, *Dr. Freud: A Life*. For a more accurate and clinically detailed review of Paul Ferris's book, see Anthony Clare (1997), "That Shrinking Feeling," *Sunday Times* (London), November 16, 8.10 Books.

4. Roy Porter (1987). *Mind-Forg'd Manacles: A History of Madness in England from the Restoration to the Regency*. London: Athlone Press.

5. Porter is properly critical in the body of his text for the *anti*historical

tenor of Foucault's massive generalizations about the treatment of the insane during the Age of Reason (at least as far as England is concerned). See Porter 1987, 279-80, for example.

6. Rudolph Kleinpaul, (1898). *Die Lebendigen und die Toten in Volks-glauben, Religion und Sage*. Leipzig: G. J. Gröschen. See Masson 1985, 286-87, note 2.

7. Whether Freud's celebrated superstitious behavior about the supposed hidden and divinatory significance of hotel room numbers, telephone numbers, the more than once numerologically calculated age at which he would die, and so on, was a leftover from his infatuation with Fliess, or whether his cabalistic gullibility (and ingenuity) preceded the encounter with the Berlin *Zauberer* will probably remain an area for amused speculation. There is certainly no trace of this later obsession in the early playful, and precocaine, correspondence (1871-1881) conducted largely in self-taught Spanish with his student friend, Eduard Silberstein. It may be that Fliess found in the older man an apt example of Goethe's *Zauberlehrling* ("Sorcerer's Apprentice") and, Disney-like, offered pails and brooms with reckless abandon.

8. In fact, Freud's interest in Fliess's nasal hypotheses goes back at least to 1892. The first letter which Freud signs with the intimate *Dein* (October 4, 1892) is the one which Freud begins: "Herewith the first proofs of your reflex neuroses" (Masson 1985, 33). This was a reference to Fliess's book *Neue Beiträge zur Klinik und Therapie der nasalen Reflexneurosen* (*New Contributions to the Clinical Treatment and Therapy of the Nasal Reflex Neuroses*). If my hunch is right, psychoanalysis should be renamed "nasalreflexanalysis" and its practitioners should declare themselves "nasalreflexanalysts." Is this idea—at first bizarre—any less weird than "psychoanalysis"? Or any less marketable? Once the concept has become acceptable, the natural professional use of the abbreviation would follow: "I'm an N. R. A. specialist myself; what branch of medicine are you in?" or "There's an N. R. A. meeting in New York next month."

9. Frederick Crews (1998). "Overview, 1," in *Unauthorized Freud: Doubters Confront a Legend*. New York: Viking/Penguin, 8.

10. For details of the fraught publication of *The Light That Failed* (versions with the "happy ending" versus versions with the "sad ending") and detailed information on the appearance in print of Kipling's works, see Flora V. Livingston (1927 [1968]) *Bibliography of the Works of Rudyard Kipling*. New York: Burt Franklin.

11. See Charles Carrington (1986). *Rudyard Kipling, His Life and Work*. Harmondsworth: Penguin, 105.

12. See Carrington (1986), 106-108. Margaret Burne-Jones, daughter of the Pre-Raphaelite painter, Sir Edward Burne-Jones (Kipling's beloved 'Uncle Ned'), was the maternal cousin (and trusted confidante) of Rudyard Kipling. As

Carrington explains, "It was a nursery joke between them that each addressed the other by the name of 'Wop'" (Carrington 1986, 106). Margaret was to be the model for Burne-Jones's Sleeping Beauty in his "Briar Rose" series of paintings (see Lindsay Duguid, "In Faery Lands Forlorn," *Times Literary Supplement*, [November 6, 1998]: 10-11).

13. Angus Wilson (1977). *The Strange Ride of Rudyard Kipling: His Life and Works*. London: Secker and Warburg, 102. Earlier, Wilson had assessed the tale thus:

> Only the inartistic and improbable escape of Jukes at the end of the story prevents it from being among the first dozen of all Kipling's stories. As it is, it remains one of the most powerful nightmares of the precariousness of a ruling group, in this case of a group haunted by memories of the Mutiny not yet twenty years old. And, so incredibly, written by an author not yet twenty years old himself. (72)

Wilson's judgment strikes me as being spot-on. Psychologically, the interest of the tale lies as much in the brilliant interplay set up by Kipling in the precarious position of the young English officer with his Indian "neighbors" and in the exchange of authority status and what that implies in the various verbal subterfuges evoked. This is indeed a "nightmare" of power structures subverted and, indeed, overthrown.

14. Letter of January 30, 1886. Quoted in Carrington (1986), 110-11.

15. Quoted in Carrington (1986), 105. Kipling's most recent biographer, Andrew Lycett, would no doubt see this phrase as an instance of Rudyard's latter-day self-removal from the torments narrated in some of his texts. Lycett notes perceptively:

> He [Kipling] later described both 'The Phantom Rickshaw' and 'The Strange Ride of Morrowbie Jukes,' slightly cagily, as ghost stories. But they were considerably more than that . . . they were briliant meditations on the dilemma of someone such as himself, who is struggling to balance being both a colonist and an artist eager for the truth of India. (Lycett 1999, 114.)

16. Letter from Kipling at Allahabad to Mrs. Hill at Mussoorie. In The Kipling Papers, quoted by Carrington (1986), 136.

17. Henry James, who had assisted Caroline Balestier over her brother Wolcott's sudden typhoid death in Germany and was best man at the wedding of Rudyard and Caroline on January 18, 1892, shared Kipling's fascination with, and mastery of, the ambiguous tale where the reasons for the events narrated owe their very ambiguity to the cunning and the craft of the narrative itself.

18. Rudyard Kipling (n.d.). *The Works of Rudyard Kipling*. One volume edition. New York: P. F. Collier and Son, 112.

19. I can think of two later tales that Kipling may well have wished to have been taken in by: "They" (1904), which invents the exquisitely imagined kiss on the narrator's hands clasped behind his chair by the spirit child (surely a fictional transposition of his grief and yearning for the dead little daughter, Josephine); and "The Gardener" (1926), written after his work on the war graves commission and the death of his son, John, in the trenches of the First World War, which is, at once (as far as the plot is concerned), the least autobiographically inspired of his works and the most movingly Christian statement that he—the ambiguous unbeliever—ever drafted.

Although many (most, in fact) of Kipling's tales hover between the gritty world of the everyday and the troubling appearance of, in Freud's words, "immortality, retribution, the entire beyond" which Freud claimed to Fliess were "all reflections of our inner psychic world," there is in Kipling an unresolved hankering, without credence, for a spiritual dimension to human experience. J. I. M. Stewart puts it well in his sensitive essay on Kipling's late fiction: "What Kipling himself saw as overarching this earth was not Heaven, but a void—and into that void he is here [in "On the Gate"] injecting something for which his heart hungers, but which is unsanctioned by his belief" ("The Mature Craftsman," in Orel 1989, 137).

20. Against this position is the other—equally, if not more, damaging—*medical* position which argues that Freud really did *not* realize the extent of his errors in diagnosis, even many years later in revised editions of his works. This certainly appears to be the case for his footnote material in the revised edition of *Studies on Hysteria* (see my discussion of this in chapter 2).

21. Jean-Michel Rey, "Freud's Writing on Writing," in Shoshana Felman (1982), ed. *Literature and Psychoanalysis: The Question of Reading: Otherwise*. Baltimore: Johns Hopkins University Press, 328.

22. This may be the place to mention that Jean-Michel Rey, and others seduced by the brilliant Freudian rhetoric of exposition, would do well to read carefully Kenneth Burke's "Antony in Behalf of the Play" [on Shakespeare's ingenuity in his writing of Mark Antony's speeches in *Julius Caesar*] in his (1967) *The Philosophy of Literary Form: Studies in Symbolic Action,* 2d ed., Baton Rouge: Louisiana State University Press; and the classic work on irony: Wayne C. Booth (1975), *A Rhetoric of Irony*, Chicago: Chicago University Press.

23. One may wonder whether the famous passage opening the "Discussion" section of the case of "Fräulein Elisabeth von R." was not some kind of self-imposed challenge with Kipling in mind. And the last sentence is pure Kipling in its masterly denial of the rhetoric of fiction:

> I have not always been a psychotherapist. Like other neuropathologists, I was trained to employ local diagnoses and electro-prognosis, and it still strikes me

myself as strange that the case histories I write should read like short stories and that, as one might say, they lack the serious stamp of science. I must console myself with the reflection that the nature of the subject is evidently responsible for this, rather than any preference of my own. (*Studies*, 160)

24. Having said this, many of the metapsychological essays have the "uncanny" aspects of life and literature as an area of interest or investigation, and not merely the essay (*Das Unheimliche*) on E. T. A. Hoffmann. Freud, who alarmed Ernest Jones by his private pursuit of possible psychic or spiritist phenomena and a belief in the potential of telepathy, was very, very careful in his public presentation of self—which remains an important subtext of his writings—to give the public the appearance of an open-minded and yet sternly empirical scientist. One instance is the following passage from the last chapter, "Determinism and Superstition," of *The Psychopathology of Everyday Life* where Freud allows for the possibility of "spiritualist events" and adds that he, himself, has never experienced them:

> If the existence of still other phenomena—those, for example, claimed by spiritualists—were to be established, we should merely set about modifying our 'laws' in the way demanded by the new discovery, without being shaken in our belief in the coherence of things in the world.
>
> In the compass of these discussions the only answer I can give to the questions raised here is a subjective one—that is, one in accordance with my personal experience. To my regret I must confess that I am one of those unworthy people in whose presence spirits suspend their activity and the supernatural vanishes away, so that I have never been in a position to experience anything myself which might arouse a belief in the miraculous. (Freud, *P.F.L.*, vol. 5, 324)

The mischievous humor of that last sentence (which does not deny the supernatural) is on a par, rhetorically, with the opening sentence of young Kipling's *The Strange Ride of Morrowbie Jukes*: "There is, as the conjurors say, no deception about this tale." Freud's frequent numerological excesses with hotel room numbers, telephone numbers, and birth dates are whisked away from public view and replaced with the presence on the page of the eminently sane, safe, and pragmatically empirical, Herr Professor Freud. Almost a Heatherlegh in short.

25. Mikkel Borch-Jacobsen (1996), 13. Borch-Jacobsen's argument at this stage is primarily about the *content* of the myth, rather than the rhetoric of its presentation, but this is, as he recognizes (and as Freud's disciples have recognized), consubstantial with the content.

26. Freud's sense of isolation in Vienna (whether justified or not) is contemporary with his first reading of Kipling and precedes by some years the Fliess-recommended withdrawal from professional involvement following the

Eckstein disaster of 1895. In the holiday letter of August 1, 1890 from Reichenau, Freud writes:

> I still feel quite isolated, scientifically dulled, lazy, and resigned. When I talked with you and saw that you thought well of me, I even used to think something of myself, and the picture of absolutely convincing energy that you offered was not without its effect on me. Moreover, medically I undoubtedly would have profited from your presence and perhaps from the atmosphere in Berlin as well, since for many years now I have been without a teacher; I am more or less exclusively involved with the treatment of neuroses. (Masson 1985, 27)

27. This seems to be a reference to his bulk and color. The word comes from the Hindi *nilgaw* blue bull (fem. *nilgai*) and refers to a large bluish gray antelope of India.

28. Geoffrey Scammell (1998), review of Peter Earle, *Sailors: English Merchant Seamen 1650-1775* (London: Methuen), *Times Literary Supplement*, (August 7), 24.

29. See the "abridged and free" English translation of this article, followed by a brief discussion, in Paul Crichton and Christopher Cordess (1995), "Motives of Paranoid Crime: The Crime of the Papin Sisters," *The Journal of Forensic Psychiatry* 6, no. 6, (December): 564-75.

The reference to the original ("*Minotaure*, 2: 25-8") given by Crichton and Cordess is wrong. The second number of this celebrated surrealist review contains nothing by Jacques Lacan. The correct reference is to Jacques Lacan, "Motifs du crime paranoï aque: Le crime des soeurs Papin," *Minotaure* 1, no. 3-4 (numéro double) (1933): 25-28. Those who read French may be interested to know that Lacan had a piece in the very first number of the review: "Le problème du style et la conception psychiatrique des formes paranoï aques de l'expérience," *Minotaure* 1, no. 1 (1933): 68-69. The same issue contains an essay by Salvador Dali, "Interprétation paranoï aque-critique de l'image obsédante 'L'Angélus' de Millet," 65-67, which tries to do with several Millet paintings (reproduced here) what Freud tried to do with (or to?) Leonardo da Vinci and the vulture wing.

30. Lacan's French reads here: "Si nous croyons pouvoir formuler une solution plus univoque du problème, nous voulons d'abord en rendre hommage à son autorité, non seulement parce qu'elle nous couvre du reproche de porter un diagnostic sans avoir examiné nous-même les malades, mais parce qu'elle a sanctionné de formules particulièrement heureuses certains faits très délicats à isoler et pourtant, nous allons le voir, essentiels à la démonstration de notre thèse" (*Minotaure* 1, nos. 2-3 (1933): 26). Note that in his original article, Lacan correctly uses the plural "malades" (sick persons), that is, *both* the Papin sisters.

31. See the editorial notes by Harold Orel (1989) in *Critical Essays on Rudyard Kipling*, 105-106.

32. Leonard Shengold, "An Attempt at Soul Murder: Rudyard Kipling's Early Life and Work," in Harold Orel (1989), ed., *Critical Essays on Rudyard Kipling*, 106.

7

The Finest Story in the World

Long before the Viennese scientists formulated the new psychology of
the unconscious, the writers of the nineties focused attention on these
problems, thus creating the mental climate in which the new
psychology was born. CHARLES CARRINGTON *Rudyard Kipling, His
Life and Work.*[1]

When Carrington wrote his life of Kipling in the early 1950s, it was still
rare, even in England, to come across substantial evidentially based
criticism of the foundations of psychoanalysis. Carrington was not alone
in writing of the "Viennese scientists" and their formulations of the "new
psychology of the unconscious." There had been those (like Virginia
Woolf before the Second World War) who had found Freudian tenets
risible. And there were those who didn't "believe"; but the archival
material necessary for the demonstration of, not merely the inadequacies,
but the pseudo-scientific mumbo jumbo, and the hair-raising notions of
Wilhelm Fliess, was simply not available.

In fact, when Carrington began his extensive work on the Kipling
biography, the first volume of the famous English Strachey-based
translations of Freud's works—now known as *The Standard Edition of
the Complete Psychological Works of Sigmund Freud*—had not yet
appeared. Neither had the highly censored version of the *Freud–Fliess*
correspondence. The English translation of these letters, edited by Anna
Freud, Ernst Kris, and Marie Bonaparte, did not appear until 1954. The
researches and publications of the last forty years have begun to remedy
this. With the admirable exception of the careful textual analyses of
inference and evidence contained in the early essays of Frank Cioffi and

the medical and/or scientific demonstrations of the late Sir Peter Medawar, serious arguments against Freud's invention had to wait until the mid-1980s (nearly a century after their elaboration) to make their appearance.

Only now (toward the end of the 1990s) has the extent of this monumental hoax—a real-life instance of "The Finest Story in the World"—come to the attention of the literati and the cognoscenti. Predictably, shrieks of outrage have greeted those resourceful searchers after evidence, such as Frederick Crews or Malcolm Macmillan; and, even now, the uncovering of the reality is fraught with emotional, intellectual, academic, and (in the university publishing world) commercial resentment[2] which renders widespread access to the discoveries of the last twenty years difficult in the extreme. The academic cognoscenti (mainly in the humanities) have, in the interim, found in the writings of Jacques Lacan (themselves largely a Hegelian and surrealist version of Freud's writings) an excuse to continue the charade. The recent (winter 1998-1999) exhibition of the sculptures of the venerable eighty-seven-year-old "Spiderwoman," Louise Bourgeois, allowed the *Guardian Weekly* art critic Adrian Searle to note: "Her work might be described as an act of revenge against the past. But she hasn't much time for the psychoanalysts or the analytically inclined theorists who would claim her. She knew Jacques Lacan and described him as a word-gargler."[3] The force of the devastating assessment of Lacan by Raymond Tallis, in his review in the *Times Higher Education Supplement*, "The Shrink from Hell," has not yet made itself felt in the syllabuses of American and English humanities faculties. It should, and in time, one trusts, it will. As Tallis writes of Lacan toward the end of his review:

> His lunatic legacy also lives on in places remote from those in which he damaged his patients, colleagues, mistresses, wives, children, publishers, editors, and opponents—in departments of literature whose inmates are even now trying to, or pretending to, make sense of his utterly unfounded, gnomic teachings and inflicting them on baffled students. Aleister Crowley, the 20th-century thinker whom Lacan most resembles, has not been so fortunate in his afterlife.[4]

We are now in the strange position where known evidence (concerning Freud and the early years of psychoanalysis) is readily available and has been carefully assessed by scholars from all over the world and where they have all found, quite independently, a concatenation of deception, duplicity, and totally unscientific (if not *anti*scientific) practice to be at the origin of the enterprise. The "strange"—Freud would no doubt write "uncanny"—quality of this position is that, irrespective of the genuine discoveries of unbiased research, most humanities faculties in the West continue their Freudian indoctrination of their students, as if the present state of knowledge were merely some passing fashion, unimportant for their disciplines. It is not "some passing fashion," and it is of crucial importance to their disciplines. And here one comes across that inevitable difficulty—how to separate "knowledge" from "belief."[5]

What is now *known* about psychoanalysis and its origins makes it supremely unhelpful for departments of anthropology, sociology, or psychology. It still has a fascination for departments of literature where, it is often argued, even if Freud was not a conscientious and honest scientist, he was, at least, a writer of great fluency and a brilliant literary critic. The apt reply to this is that, as to the first, yes; as to the second, no. He was, without doubt, a most gifted and persuasive writer of tales of all kinds; tales of memory retrieval, almost superhuman in their ingenious grasp of supposed past experiences lost to the conscious awareness of the patient (the very subject of this chapter, in fact). But he was not, in any serious way, a considerable literary critic. His literary essays constitute in every respect attempts to impose his psychoanalytic doctrine (the supposed mechanisms of supposed infantile sexual need and their supposed inevitable sequelae in adulthood) upon the characters and the authors that he discusses. This peculiarly blinkered approach to human behavior, recorded and imagined, in literature was, of course, itself a novelty. And a novelty that was forcefully advanced by his brilliant rhetorical flair.

If he is of interest to departments of literature, it is uniquely because of the immense skill of his own rhetoric of confabulation—whether in the few case histories (*all* of which were unqualified medical disasters—something which tends to be forgotten by the Freudian literati), or in the so-called "theoretical" essays of various aspects of what he was pleased to call "metapsychology" (which may now be seen, thanks to the work of thinkers like Cioffi and Timpanaro, to be also unqualified disasters of careful consecutive thought—never Freud's forte). Freud, in other words, has had a most perverse effect upon the thinking and feeling of the West in this century. To such an extent, in fact, that one feels, vicariously, the pangs of withdrawal as one sizes up the true predicament of teachers who slowly begin to realize that they are teaching their students ideas about human behavior that are completely without foundation.

The more one examines carefully Freud's excursions into "literary criticism"—whether the essay on the Three Caskets riddle in *The Merchant of Venice*, the "Uncanny" in Hoffmann's *Der Sandmann*, or the supposed elucidation of Jensen's *Gradiva*—the more it becomes apparent that what we are reading are mere applications of the sexual theories which were being worked out, or brooded over, in the correspondence with Wilhelm Fliess. Once the heady spice of these hypotheses is removed from the essays, little remains, in terms of literary perception and original aesthetic, or even psychological, acuity, beyond some platitudes worthy of Goldsmith's village school master. (To those who find this judgment harsh, or hard to credit, let me recommend that they reread Freud's literary commentaries with their own psychoanalytic beliefs momentarily suspended.)[6]

Carrington, in the epigraph to this chapter, may have been naïve—or too trusting?—in his ascription of "*scientists*" to the Viennese psychoanalysts. But the significant words in the sentence quoted are, "Long before"; and his argument is, in effect, a salutary rebuttal to the famous phrase of W. H. Auden. Rather than being, or initiating, "a whole climate of opinion," Freud and his epigones were following, and responding to, a widely established European tradition which had made itself felt in literature as much as in psychology. Carrington's "the writers of the nineties focused attention on these problems, thus creating the mental climate in which this new psychology was born," although accurate as far as it goes, leaves unspoken the climate from which *those* writers emerged. And that mental climate has a long and convoluted history in recent modern European literature, antedating psychoanalysis by a good half-century at least.

In France, Zola, Maupassant, Flaubert, Balzac, and Stendhal (to name the 'greats') had explored and illustrated aspects of the real psychopathology in everyday life with far more sureness of touch than Freud in the unreal inventions which, as Timpanaro noticed, are splattered, accompanied by ingenious Poe-like reasoning, across the pages of *The Psychopathology of Everyday Life* as if they were instances of human psychology closely observed and thoroughly understood. As Richard Webster rightly points out, using a pertinent confession by Sainte-Beuve culled by those devious diarists, the brothers Goncourt, "the idea that human behaviour is influenced by impulses or feelings of which we sometimes remain unaware has long been a commonplace both of vernacular and of poetic psychology" (Webster 1996, preface to the paperback edition, xii-xiii). In England, one can return to the happy adventures of that amateur natural scientist, Pickwick, and his band of accomplices, of over half a century before. As early as 1836-1837, *The Pickwick Papers* had offered to the public several illustrated case histories of psychological disturbance. In a serious, even Gothic, vein, there is, for instance, the terminal psychosis of a former wife-beater (chapter 3, "The Stroller's Tale"). In the humorous vein, Dickens provides the comic presentation of a case of female hysteria (chapter 18, "Briefly illustrative of two points,—first, the Power of Hysterics, and, secondly, the Force of Circumstances"). The tale of the Stroller is almost an early picture of the young Kipling at work:

> 'There is nothing of the marvellous in what I am going to relate,' said the dismal man; 'there is nothing even uncommon in it. Want and sickness are too common in many stations in life, to deserve more notice than is usually bestowed on the most ordinary vicissitudes of human nature. I have thrown these few notes together, because the subject of them was well known to me for many years. I traced his progress downwards, step by step, until at last he reached that excess of destitution from which he never rose again.'[7]

Perhaps the most gruesome of Dickens's inventions in the *Pickwick Papers* is chapter 21 ("In which the Old Man launches forth into his favourite Theme, and relates a Story about a queer Client"). This tale— "THE OLD MAN'S TALE ABOUT THE QUEER CLIENT"—begins as a Freudian case history or a Kipling short story should begin (i.e., *not* at the beginning):

> 'It matters little,' said the old man, 'where, or how, I picked up this brief history. If I were to relate it in the order in which it reached me, I should commence in the middle, and when I had arrived at the conclusion, go back for a beginning. It is enough for me to say that some of it passed before my own eyes. For the remainder I know them to have happened, and there are some persons yet living, who will remember them but too well.' (Dickens 1972, 365)

This may sound like a recipe for film narrative as proffered by Jean-Luc Godard in an expansive mood, or the narrative sequence of Freud's "Zwei Kinderlügen" ("Two Lies told by Children") of 1913, which show the master at his narrative best and at his pyschological worst.[8] Dickens's success as a novelist is one of the surest indications that the "mental climate" mentioned by Carrington had been a widely recognized part of middle-class European culture for fifty years prior to Sigmund Freud's attempt to "disturb the sleep of the world." In point of fact, the Danish scholar Max Scharnberg, in his painstaking *The Non-Authentic Nature of Freud's Observations*, argues persuasively that Dickens provided a crucial element to the Dora case history. Freud's report of Dora having gone "as white as a sheet" on encountering Herr K. while walking with her cousin was, suggests Scharnberg, a useful and deliberate "borrowing" of a scene from Dickens's *Nicholas Nickleby* where Kate Nickleby turns pale upon seeing her would-be seducer, Sir Mulberry Hawk, at the theatre. Kate's mother's "quickness of perception" (as Dickens ironically puts it) assumes that the loss of color is the sure sign of love—Freud, perhaps unaware of Dickens's irony—reads Dora's "white as a sheet" with all the acumen of Mrs Nickleby.[9]

If the "mental climate" is taken to refer to the predominant interest in, and supposed pervasive and enduring formative force of "infantile sexuality fantasies" in adult behavioral patterns, then Freud certainly may be said to have started a trend which is with us still. However, Freud was neither the first to write explicitly about sex, nor were the Viennese scientists (among whom one could legitimately include Richard von Krafft-Ebing) the only medical authorities writing on sexual matters. What *was*, perhaps, original—and wrong—in Freud's sexual beliefs was an error in diagnosis and causality in every way as misguided as Wilhelm Fliess's back-to-front version of the relation between the nose and female sexual organs.

When Kipling was newly arrived in London in 1890, he had few intimates and was grateful for the presence of relatives such as the Burne-Joneses and cousins such as Ambrose Poynter. Carrington's remarks about 'Ambo' Poynter and his importance for the evolution of what was to become "The Finest Story in the World" are worth quoting:

'Ambo' Poynter was the nearest thing Kipling possessed to a confidant; he would come into Embankment Chambers [where Kipling had his first rented London flat in Villiers Street] and lay bare his soul, hour after hour, until he was turned out at one or two in the morning. His trouble, apart from mere green-sickness, was the common misfortune of a successful man's son; he had inherited his father's nervous temperament without his father's talent. What he had to exhibit was a five-act tragedy in verse, full of allusions which Kipling, with his meagre classical knowledge, found formidable. 'Ambo,' of course, was grateful for advice and eager to help, but unwilling to be told the truth about his work. It was to Mrs Hill that

Rudyard wrote a candid opinion.

He estimates his poems not by the thing actually put down in black and white but by all the glorious inchoate fancies that flashed through his brain while his pen was in his hand.[10]

Though 'Ambo' Poynter had his own career, as an architect, his poetical aspirations had their consequence in providing 'copy' for Kipling, who throughout his life was haunted by the notion that buried and even inherited memories reveal themselves in dreams.[11] . . . The conflict between 'Ambo' Poynter's unrealized visions and inadequate expression suggested to Rudyard the plot of a story which, again, showed an advance in human sympathy and understanding. 'The Finest Story in the World', his tale of a London clerk who almost, but not quite, recalls memories inherited from a remote past, owes much to 'Ambo' Poynter. (Carrington 1986, 188)

But Ambrose Poynter was not, as Carrington later reveals, the only autobiographical source for "The Finest Story in the World"; there was also—as part of Kipling's assiduous exploration of the common horde of the London lower class—"the clerk who came up to Rudyard's rooms to tell the life-history which, combined with 'Ambo' Poynter's, became the framework for "The Finest Story in the World" (Carrington 1986, 190).

In the last third of his biography, Charles Carrington discusses later works which show the predictive side of Kipling. Carrington mentions, for example, "As Easy as A.B.C." (which stands for "Aerial Board of Control"). Carrington (writing in the early 1950s) is evidently impressed by this "H. G. Wells" aspect of Kipling-the-futurologist and sees in this tale and in "With the Night Mail" and "Wireless" a Rudyard Kipling not readily appreciated by the world at large. (Angus Wilson, to his credit, called "As Easy as A.B.C.," "surely one of the best science-fiction stories of all time" [Wilson 1977, 248].) In fact, this side of Kipling—in a way rarely present in his earlier tales—is one that needs careful attention. George Orwell (a Bengali by birth, whereas Kipling was born on the other side of the subcontinent, in Bombay), so much the opposite of anything recognized about the imperialist Kipling legend, was nonetheless appreciative, and when it was not "politically correct" to be so, of the forthright power of Kipling as a writer. It is a measure of Orwell's intransigence and of his honesty that he could write so perceptively of Kipling.

His own dystopia, *1984*, was much less a projection into the future of what the world may become than a severe warning about what—in the totalitarian Soviet system under Stalin—it had already become. In "As Easy as A.B.C." (1912), Kipling had produced a sequel to his earlier "With the Night Mail: A Story of 2000 A.D." (1909) in which he envisages a future world ensnared in the supranational power of the technocrats. Carrington's 1950s commentary, in its innocence and its misunderstanding of Orwell's achievement, is nevertheless an interesting insight into Kipling's prescient vision. For us, in the 1990s, it would appear—as it could not to Carrington in the 1950s—that Kipling had, got it more or less right (with the notable exception of the abolition of war in 1967):

> It is not Utopia: there is no suggestion that this is what Rudyard would have wished to come about; nor is it, like George Orwell's *1984*, a forecast of horror; it is a mere statement of what might occur when the technocrats should have made the progress which, to a seeing eye in 1907, they seemed likely to make. Broadcasting techniques were foreseen with uncanny accuracy and the transmission of energy by radio is carried to much greater length in his fantasy than has yet been achieved in real life, with the consequence that an international Utility Company of radio technicians, the 'Aerial Board of Control,' has imperceptibly taken over the administration of the planet. The sovereign states have withered away, and political ideologies exist only as picturesque survivals or atavistic patches of superstition. The solution is 'easy as A.B.C.'; power must pass to the organization that directs traffic through the world-wide radio network. Of its structure he has nothing to say except that it is cosmopolitan. (Carrington 1955, 1986, 439)

One has to shake oneself to realize that Kipling was inventing these fantasies before the First World War, before the general broadcasting use of radio, before the discovery of radar, before the advent of television, before the existence of huge multinational corporations owing allegiance to no state, and before the most recent realization of his dream (or nightmare?), the Internet and the World Wide Web. The sinister arachnid sense of that last invention is implicit in Kipling's vision of the future. (Perhaps the only comparable fictional attempt at technological prophecy is Jules Verne's posthumously published *Paris au XXième siècle*, which foresees, quite brilliantly, the use of fax messages.)

It is well known that gadgets (mechanical and electrical) were a source of constant, almost boyish, pleasure for Kipling. He was fascinated by the Royal Navy's Channel Squadron experiments with radio communications in 1898. He was intrigued by military and civilian engineering accomplishments. He had a lifelong love affair with the automobile (his adventures at the wheel, whether driving around Sussex or on holidays through rural France, have an element of a carefree Mr. Toad about them).

There is, however, a quite different dimension to Kipling's prophetic side, something which has nothing to do with technology and everything to do with unusual, even "poetic," manifestations of human behavior. This concerns his intuitive grasp of psychology and of "religious" organizational structures. In this respect, "The Finest Story in the World"—itself one that will never be completely told, although 'authentic' fragments may arise—is one of Kipling's greatest suggestive successes in narrative. Its predictive qualities, in particular concerning the rise and crisis of psychoanalysis, were more an instance of serendipity than of anything else. The only explicit reference to Freud in his fiction that I have come across is in the very late tale of 1928, "Dayspring Mishandled" (collected in the 1932 *Limits and Renewals*), where the narrator writes of the unpleasant Chaucer scholar, Castorley: "He also, 'for old sake's sake,' as he wrote to a friend, went out of his way to review one of Manallace's books with an intimacy of unclean deduction (this was before the days of Freud) which long stood as a record."

I make no claim in this book that Kipling had access to censored 'inside' information about the movement founded by Freud—and, indeed, when "The Finest Story in the World" was written, there *was* no "Movement" yet. Freud had been corresponding with Fliess for less than three years and had not even moved into Berggasse 19 (that *déménagement* took place in the second week of September 1891). This makes Kipling's Cassandra-like qualities the more impressive. The only overt reference in the tale itself to some form of psychological "therapy," or rather to some kind of memory retrieval through hypnosis and suggestion, is to what the narrator calls "a professional mesmerist." Kipling had known, if only through his father's detached and devastating ironic observations, of Madame Blavatsky and her international organization of believers;[12] the rich spiritual background, furnished by his Indian boyhood and the later adolescent return to his origins, had provided him with insights into the Hindu religious imaginings of, not life after death, but of lives after deaths.

The benign agnosticism of his father and mother no doubt tempered a mind that seemed, if not torn between religiosity and outright Voltairean disdain for organized religion, at least frequently hesitant about which side to take. The spiritist atmosphere in some quarters of London was not unknown to him, and Andrew Lang, one of his early patrons, was sufficiently interested in a psychological investigation of medium-trance states to write "Three Seeresses," on Joan of Arc, the nineteenth-century American medium Mrs. Piper, and the Swiss medium known as Hélène Smith.

The latter—in real life Élise-Catherine Müller (1861-1929)—was the subject of the Swiss philosopher and psychologist Théodore Flournoy's best-seller of 1899, *Des Indes à la Planète Mars: Étude sur un cas de somnambulisme avec glossolalie*. The 1901 English translation by Daniel B. Vermilye was reissued in 1994 in an edition by Sonu Shamdasani under the title, *From India to the Planet Mars: A Case of Multiple Personality with Imaginary Languages*.[13]

Shamdasani explains his modification of the original title in his informative introduction (xi-li), "Encountering Hélène: *Théodore Flournoy and the Genesis of Subliminal Psychology*." He takes the reader through a detailed (and impeccably footnoted) history of "subliminal psychology" from the mid–nineteenth century to the early years of the twentieth century. "*From India to the Planet Mars*," he writes, "was the first psychological study of multiple personality that became a best-seller, which played a key-role in its dissemination" (Flournoy 1994, xxxi). (The strange grammar of this sentence is doubtless unpremeditated. Shamdasani is silent about whether this "dissemination" should be a cause for celebration or dismay.) He discusses the interest that the surrealists took in Flournoy's work and its importance for the promotion of "creative states" producing automatic writing and suchlike. The subject of Flournoy's volume, 'Hélène Smith,' "experiences" lives lived before, as Marie-Antoinette, and as a Hindu Indian princess, as well as extra-terrestrial visits to Mars (the cover of the current Princeton edition offers a reproduction of one of her paintings of a Martian cityscape). Shamdasani gives a clear and fascinating account of this neglected aspect of late-nineteenth-century psychology. He quotes from the many favorable reviews that Flournoy's book received (including the highly laudatory letters to Flournoy of the inimitable William James); but he also notes the criticisms in the otherwise favorable review of F. C. S. Schiller who, in *Mind*, was critical of Flournoy's attempts to explain his subject's behavior:

> They neither account for the persistence with which such cases assume a spiritistic form, nor do they supply a principle to account for the selection

of recondite and pseudo-evidential memories in lieu of those which ordinary paths of association would normally reproduce. (*Mind* 1900, 539; cited in Flournoy 1994, xxx)

"For some commentators," adds Shamdasani, "the powers that Flournoy was claiming for the subliminal creative imagination seemed to require no less a leap of faith than the spiritualist hypothesis" (Flournoy 1994, xxx).

It all ended badly, of course—as these things tend to—that is, in the banal empirical realm of reality. In that realm (as Freud had so wisely, and so publicly, proclaimed in the 1901 *Psychopathology of Everyday Life*) the spirits no longer operate; and subliminal imagination was amazingly replaced, in this instance, by an intelligent shop-girl's appropriate awareness of her socioeconomic situation, or predicament. Élise Müller broke with Flournoy; she accused him of persecuting her; she claimed she had been made the laughingstock of her peers, and of the public at large in the Genevan press reports of Flournoy's work; and she demanded (and received) 50 percent of the royalties of *From India to the Planet Mars*. Furthermore, as Shamdasani adds, without, I am sure, a hint of malice, "Hélène Smith attracted the attention of a wealthy American benefactress whose patronage enabled her to leave her job and devote herself to her calling" (Flournoy 1994, xxxii).

Keeping that precarious balance between reality and "the subliminal creative imagination" was a perpetual problem, not always successfully attacked, by the anonymous narrator—himself a professional writer—in Kipling's extraordinary (and pre-Flournoy) tale, "The Finest Story in the World." It was first published in *The Contemporary Review* for July 1891. Two years later it was collected with three other tales and published in book form by Macmillan under the title *Many Inventions*. Within a short time it had appeared in French and German translations. There was, as Shamdasani's "introduction" to Flournoy's scientific romance indicates, a ready market for stories of this kind.

The subject of "cryptomnesia"—etymologically, *memory which is hidden* (and, implicitly, hidden from the conscious awareness of the one remembering)—provides the subject matter of Kipling's tale. The topic was of great interest in Rudyard Kipling's time and has, in a vicious way, returned to popular fascination with the explosion in the West (and not just in the United States, Max Scharnberg instances many examples from the Swedish law courts[14]) of tales told in therapy of memories of incestuous molestation in early childhood, and, more whimsically and perhaps less harmfully for existing family structures, tales of abduction by aliens in spacecraft. Shamdasani has a short section in his introduction entitled "Cryptomnesia," and it is worth quoting here.

> Since the time of the magnetists, attention has been paid to the hypermnesic properties of the trance.[15] These capacities seem to suggest that there was a great deal of information that, although once perceived, now lay outside the reach of conscious attention. The unconscious was designated as the location of these hidden memories. It was principally Flournoy who attempted to map the extent of this phenomena [sic] and trace the transformations that such memories were subject to while in a latent state.
>
> Cryptomnesia plays a crucial role in Flournoy's analysis as the main alternative paradigm to the spiritualistic hypothesis.[16] The significance of the phenomenon had been noted by [Pierre] Janet, who refers to a piece in the *Revue Spirite* by M. Goupil on automatic writing that presents an example of cryptomnesia.[17] Janet notes that he has seen and described similar facts and can supply an explanation:
>
> > When a certain sensation finds itself bound to subconscious acts, there is, at that moment, a particular and corresponding anesthesia for the ordinary personality. When automatic writing manifests a certain memory with persistence, there is a corresponding amnesia for the normal consciousness. (Janet, "Le Spiritisme contemporain," 428, trans. mine [i.e., Sonu Shamdasani])
>
> Janet finds such descriptions valuable and regrets that there are not more like it. It was precisely this lacuna that was filled by *From India to the Planet Mars*.
>
> Flournoy's account of cryptomnesia presented a model of memory that attempted to account for the interrelation of memory and fantasy. For Flournoy what was presented as a memory—in the case of Hélène, of an anterior existence—in actuality represented a hidden and forgotten memory that had been through a process of subconscious elaboration [note omitted]. Significantly enough, this was presented in the interregnum between Freud's confessional retraction of his seduction theory in private to Fliess and his public retraction several years later. (Flournoy 1994, xxv-xxvi)

This little excursion into Shamdasani's preferred territory of how it may have been, should—at the very least—have offered the reader an indication of how *not* to read psychological texts of the last century. Pierre Janet's quoted statements (or even his whole paper) do not in any way correspond with Shamdasani's "can supply an explanation." Janet does not explain; he describes—as, incidentally, does Flournoy—and his description is not intended as an explanation: that is Shamdasani's no doubt "subliminal creative imagination."

The whole issue of "memory" in its "depersonalized" presentation may be quite easily categorized as follows:

(1) it is the consequence of the vivid experience of previous lives intruding into the consciousnesss of the present person; or

(2) it is the consequence of possession of the medium by spirits of the dead or some otherworldly origin; or

(3) it is the consequence of "repression" of memories of early childhood which reappear with all their force and "possess" the consciousness of the present person; or

(4) it is the combined consequence of the interplay between suggestion and compliance in a hypnotic setting.

I know of no other possibilities, except for deliberate play-acting, confabulation, and/or outright fraud—none of which, by definition, has anything to do with cryptomnesia.[18] All of Freud's reported cases fall into categories 3 and/or 4, according to his own writings. Current research into the historical reality of what transpired between Freud and his clients would put all his reported material clearly into category 4 alone (irrespective of the current standing of "repression").

The cryptomnesia at the heart of "The Finest Story in the World" is very strictly limited to category 1: "the consequence of the vivid experience of previous lives intruding into the consciousnesss of the present person." Kipling himself (or rather the authorial narrative "I") is aware of the dangers of categories 3 and 4, compounded by the addition of possible outright lying. As he writes just over halfway through the tale:

I wondered whether it would be wise or prudent to lure Charlie into the hands of the professional mesmerist there [at the London Aquarium], and whether, if he were under his power, he would speak of his past lives. If he did, and if people believed him . . . but Charlie would be frightened and flustered, or made conceited by the interviews. In either case he would begin to lie through fear or vanity. He was safest in my own hands. (Kipling 1992, 30)[19]

This temptation of the narrator to seek outside "professional" help has occurred because of the frustrations provoked in him by the intermittent nature of the appearance in Charlie Mears of cryptomnesia and by young Charlie's lack of recall or serious concern when he is not in a "hypnoid" state of altered consciousness. This state, however, is never provoked by the listener who for the most part responds quietly and warily when the mood of remembrance has taken hold of Charlie.

The gulf between the state of intense urgent pouring forth of the details of past lives and the "everyday" awareness of his personality of the young bank clerk is insisted on by "I" throughout the story. The narrator takes great care not to overstep the delicate limits of his inquiries, and at times fumbles disastrously and spoils the chemistry of the moment (or, in Kipling's more accurate metaphor, "The current was broken for the time being") and unwittingly returns Charlie Mears's mind to its present-day preoccupations—concern for worldly status, ambition for poetic immortality, desire for a girl to love him.

The tale is drafted like an extended case history with an immediate presentation, from the very first line, of the details of the "patient:" name, background, occupation, hobbies, how encountered.

His name was Charlie Mears; he was the only son of his mother who was a widow, and he lived in the north of London, coming into the City every day to work in a bank. He was twenty years old and was full of aspirations. I met him in a public billiard-saloon where the marker called him by his first name, and he called the marker "Bullseye." Charlie explained, a little nervously, that he had only come to the place to look on, and since looking on at games of skill is not a cheap amusement for the young, I suggested that Charlie should go back to his mother.

That was our first step towards better acquaintance. He would call on me sometimes in the evenings instead of running about London with his fellow-clerks; and before long, speaking of himself as a young man must, he told me of his aspirations, which were all literary. He desired to make himself an undying name chiefly through verse, though he was not above sending stories of love and death to the penny-in-the-slot journals. It was my fate to sit still while Charlie read me poems of many hundred lines, and bulky fragments of plays that would surely shake the world. My reward was his unreserved confidence, and the self-revelations and troubles of a young man are almost as holy as those of a maiden. Charlie had never fallen in love, but was anxious to do so on the first opportunity. (Kipling 1992, 14)

This economic introduction provides at once the characteristics of the "patient" and the disequilibrium in the relationship: the narrator is older, wiser, more experienced in the ways of the world, a successful literary man, and has an intuitive ability to recognize literary wheat and to distinguish it from the chaff. He can also recognize the deep veracity of the events babbled thoughtlessly by Charlie and separate them from Charlie's attempts to write them down in poetry form. This is initially revealed on the second page when "I" shows irritation at the written work just accomplished in his study by Charlie Mears.

> "It needs compression," I suggested cautiously.
> "I hate cutting my things down. I don't think you could alter a word here without spoiling the sense. It reads better aloud than when I was writing it."
> "Charlie, you're suffering from an alarming disease afflicting a numerous class. Put the thing by, and tackle it again in a week."
> "I want to do it at once. What do you think of it?"
> "How can I judge from a half-written tale? *Tell me the story as it lies in your head."* [my emphasis]
> Charlie told, and in the telling there was everything that his ignorance had so carefully prevented from escaping into the written word. I looked at him, wondering whether it were possible that he did not know the originality, the power of the notion that had come his way? It was distinctly a Notion among notions. Men had been puffed up with pride by ideas not a tithe as excellent and practicable. But Charlie babbled on serenely, interrupting the current of pure fancy with samples of horrible sentences that he purposed to use. I heard him out to the end. It would be folly to allow his thought to remain in his own inept hands, when I could do so much with it. Not all that could be done indeed; but, ah so much!
> "What do you think?" he said at last. "I fancy I shall call it 'The Story of a Ship.'" (Kipling 1992, 15-16)

This whole tale—"The Finest Story in the World"—is indeed the story of a ship. More than that, it is the story of two ships. And of two lives—a thousand years apart—previously led. It is the story of a Greek slave galley and of an early Viking longboat exploring North America as recorded in the Vinland saga. Kipling has asked the reader to accept (for the sake of the tale) the hypothesis of metempsychosis. Further, Kipling has asked the reader to accept (also for the sake of the tale) that such "leaks" of previous existences as infiltrate the present consciousness of a subject occur precisely at moments of unguarded inattention, and are not recognized for what they are by the subject—who may even be a disbeliever in metempsychosis (as indeed Charlie Mears appears to be).

One might at this stage mention (as a quick public service) two confusing howlers by earlier critics of this text, concerned, as it is, with hidden memory. In the first place, Angus Wilson has forgotten (or not absorbed) what he has read. He writes in his biography of Kipling:

> No doubt the London clerk who has visions half-recaptured of his previous lives as a Roman galley slave and in a Viking ship comes from Poynter's search to express himself to his famous cousin. . . . But the real core of the story lies in the clerk's recalling, both in prose and in verse, of the atmosphere of the Roman galley. It shows Kipling being led by concern for navigational techniques into a period of time that was to be the setting of some of his best later historical work—the Roman Empire. (Wilson 1977, 168)

"It" does no such thing. There is *no* mention of a Roman galley, nor anything whatever to do with the Roman period—Empire or Republic—in Kipling's tale; this is pure Wilsonian invention—no doubt from a false memory of an earlier (and uncorrected) reading. (The dangers of "false-memories" are with us, even without hypnosis or suggestive therapy.) Wilson does not once mention the Greek slave galley. His reading ignores—as, logically, it must—Kipling's prank invention of demotic ancient Greek scratched onto a sheet of notepaper by the ignorant Charlie in one of his reveries (Kipling's discreet version of glossolalia). Asked by the narrator what it may mean, he replies: "'Oh, I don't know. I mean it to mean "I'm beastly tired." It's great nonsense,' he repeated, 'but all those men in the ship seem as real as real people to me.'" (Kipling 1992, 20). When the scratched Greek characters are offered to the elderly "Greek antiquity man" at the British Museum for deciphering, there is a moment of gentle academic comedy:

> "What does this mean? H'mm," said he. "So far as I can ascertain it is an attempt to write extremely corrupt Greek on the part"—here he glared at me with intention—"of an extremely illiterate—ah—person." He read slowly from the paper, *"Pollock, Erckmann, Tauchnitz, Henniker"*—four names familiar to me. [This is Kipling's little joke; having the narrator, who knows almost no Greek, note down the *sounds* heard as if they were the names of German scholars.]
>
> "Can you tell me what the corruption is supposed to mean—the gist of the thing?" I asked.

"I have been—many times—overcome with weariness in this particular employment. That is the meaning." He returned me the paper, and I fled without a word of thanks, explanation, or apology. (Kipling 1992, 21)

Wilson was not alone in misreading this intriguing tale. Martin Seymour-Smith in his "controversial new biography" writes of Charlie Mears that "[h]e can only talk of his pasts when hypnotized by a gas-flame in a fire" (Seymour-Smith 1990, 229). This statement is completely untrue. It has no support in the text of the tale. It is a reference to a passage near the end of the story where Charlie relives a Viking adventure:

He was sitting by the fire staring at the red coals. "*I* can't understand what you find so difficult. It's all as clear as mud to me," he replied. A jet of gas puffed out between the bars, took light, and whistled softly. "Suppose we take the red-haired hero's adventures first, from the time that he came south to my galley and captured it and sailed to the Beaches."

I knew better now than to interrupt Charlie. I was out of reach of pen and paper, and dared not move to get them lest I should break the current. The gas-jet puffed and whinnied, Charlie's voice dropped almost to a whisper, and he told a tale of the sailing of an open galley to Furdurstrandi. (Kipling 1992, 37-38)

Seymour-Smith has taken this one incident and generalized a state of "hypnosis by firelight" for Charlie's memories of previous lives. This incident is, in fact, the only one in the whole tale which appears to require the hypnotic effect of gas flares from a coal fire. One may question Seymour-Smith's judgment; but, more interestingly from a literary point of view, one may question the relevance for the narrator, or for Kipling, of including this morsel. If anything, it is a clear indication that, although this tale may deal with a supposed case of metempsychosis, it does *not* deal with hypnosis. It may well be one of those artless (but so artful) traps for the unwary that Kipling was fond of embedding in his tales. If you think metempsychosis requires hypnosis, or a hypnotic state, for expression, you will be misled by this passage—as Seymour-Smith was.

For the most part, Charlie talks of his early lives with spontaneous enthusiasm and without an awareness of the discrepancy between these feelings expressed and his present life as lived, and then, just as suddenly, forgets what he has said and its significance. For instance, one day the narrator encounters Charlie by chance in Gracechurch Street in the City, and accompanies him over London Bridge. A barge passing under the bridge has a tethered cow on deck which bellows. This is the narrator's observation:

> Charlie's face changed from the face of the bank-clerk to that of an unknown and—though he would not have believed this—a much shrewder man. He flung out his arm across the parapet of the bridge and laughing very loudly, said:
> "When they heard *our* bulls bellow the Skraelings ran away!"
> I waited only for an instant, but the barge and the cow had disappeared under the bows of the steamer before I answered.
> "Charlie, what do you suppose are Skraelings?"
> "Never heard of 'em before. They sound like a new kind of sea-gull. What a chap you are for asking questions!" he replied. (Kipling 1992, 28)[20]

The narrator has, carefully, been "a chap for asking questions" throughout the tale. One way he assures himself of the veracity of the recalled memory is to ask for specific details of ancient maritime technologies and for close-up descriptions of galley conditions and fights. He assures himself (and virtually convinces the reader) that Charlie cannot have gained his knowledge anywhere, except as *first hand experience*. As a kind of double-trick to ensure himself of the authenticity of Charlie's previous lives, the narrator offers him a copy of the then popular novel on soul travel and notes Charlie's irritation and incredulity concerning voyages to the planet Mars:

> I did not press him further, but to satisfy myself that he lay in ignorance of the workings of his own mind, deliberately introduced him to Mortimer Collins's *Transmigration*, and gave him a sketch of the plot before he opened the pages.
> "What rot it all is!" he said frankly, at the end of an hour. "I don't understand his nonsense about the Red Planet Mars and the King, and the rest of it. Chuck me the Longfellow again." (Kipling 1992, 25-26)[21]

A little before this, Kipling has introduced a comic episode where the narrator's indulgence—in offering the use of his library of great authors—has horribly misfired and produced in young Charlie, a voracious reader, a tendency to "poeticize" his memories along the lines of Byron, Shelley, or Keats.

> "I've given you the story," he said shortly, replunging into "Lara."

"But I want the details."

"The things I make up about that damned ship that you call a galley? They're quite easy. You can just make 'em up for yourself. Turn up the gas a little, I want to go on reading."

I could have broken the gas globe over his head for his amazing stupidity. I could indeed make up things for myself did I only know what Charlie did not know that he knew. But since the doors were shut behind me I could only wait his youthful pleasure and strive to keep him in good temper. One minute's want of guard might spoil a priceless revelation: now and again he would toss his books aside—he kept them in my rooms, for his mother would have been shocked at the waste of good money had she seen them—and launched [sic] into his sea-dreams. Again I cursed all the poets of England. The plastic mind of the bank-clerk had been overlaid, colored, and distorted by that which he had read, and the result as delivered was a confused tangle of other voices most like the mutter and hum through a City telephone in the busiest part of the day. (Kipling 1992, 22)

There is thoughout this tale an atmosphere of Hindu reincarnation notions. When the narrator is in a busy London street assailed by gloomy reflections about the chance of success of his enterprise in gleaning, and then writing down, the *whole* truth of Charlie's past lives, his thoughts are interrupted:

"They are very funny fools, your English," said a voice at my elbow, and turning round I recognized a casual acquaintance, a young Bengali law student, called Grish Chunder, whose father had sent him to England to become civilized. (Kipling 1992, 30)

Grish Chunder, a minor character (and yet as important for what he reveals—that Charlie is, unbeknownst to himself, a seer— as the narrator), appears in the last half of the tale and allows the narrator to reveal to the reader the Hindu beliefs that inform the story. It is Grish Chunder who intimates that the full story of the past lives will never be revealed, *can* never be revealed without the ending of the world, and that the love of a woman will erase the memories of previous existences from Charlie's mind. And this is what happens.

In spite of the very evocative passages where Kipling's narrator produces (or reproduces—Freud would say "constructs") some aspects of Charlie's past lives, the whole of what is known to the narrator is only revealed in Hindi to Grish Chunder. We get, in effect, toward the end of the tale, not so much a Gidean *mise en abyme*, as an untold (but briefly reported) retelling of the whole tale in Hindi, the language appropriate to the matter.

> I began to tell the story of Charlie in English, but Grish Chunder put a question in the vernacular, and the history went forward naturally in the tongue best suited for its telling. Grish Chunder heard me, nodding from time to time, and then came up to my rooms, where I finished the tale.
> *"Beshak,"* he said philosophically. *"Lekin darwaza band hai.* (Without doubt the door is shut.) I have heard of this remembering of previous existences among my people. It is of course an old tale with us, but, to happen to an Englishman—a cow-fed *Mlechh*—an outcast. By Jove, that is *most* peculiar!"
> "Outcast yourself, Grish Chunder! You eat cow-beef every day. Let's think the thing over. The boy remembers his incarnations."
> "Does he know that?" said Grish Chunder quietly, swinging his legs as he sat on my table. He was speaking in his English now.
> "He does not know anything. Would I speak to you if he did? Go on!"
> "There is no going on at all. If you tell that to your friends they will say you are mad and put it in the papers. Suppose, now, you prosecute for libel." (Kipling 1992, 31)

This line of attack suggests the young law student in Grish Chunder and is not pursued by the narrator. The more thoughtful side of the Bengali is in his first questioning of the narrator's statement: "The boy remembers his incarnations." Grish Chunder asks, "Does he know that?" And, of course, the discrepancy is immediately apparent to the narrator: Charlie has vivid recollections but *does not know* that they are recollections.

There is a telling passage—in the context of Kipling's extraordinary prophetic psychological acumen perhaps the most significant passage in "The Finest Story in the World"—immediately prior to the narrator's encounter with Grish Chunder, where the anonymous narrator contemplates the quasi-theological authority that will be his once he has induced Charlie Mears to disburden himself of the sagas within him. (When I reread it the other evening, I could not help thinking of the transcendental ambitions of Freud and of some of the more effusive outbursts directed at the *confidant*, Wilhelm Fliess.) But the passage curiously transcends those ambitions, and leaps imaginatively into a world (ours and that of our future) where the international institutionalization of a movement such as psychoanalysis, dependent on the recovery and construction of "lost" memory, has already taken place and the "theological" schisms have long since begun their inevitable destructive work on the doctrinal authority of a founding father, such as Freud.

Kipling's anonymous narrator frames his musings and his visions of a potential future (provided Charlie Mears is able to be induced to relate the complete memory of his past lives) within a Hindu, or hinduistic, struggle with the mythical "Lords of Life and Death." There is a powerful antiphonal effect achieved by Kipling as he has his narrator project a putative *future* from his triumph in having had access to a putative repressed remembered *past* from his young acquaintance. Readers who are familiar with Freud's immense personal ambitions (as revealed in various unguarded moments in his correspondence, long after Fliess had dropped him—in the letters to Jung or Karl Abraham, for example) on the one hand, and with the subsequent history of the many psychoanalytic squabbles of internecine dimension on the other, will, I suspect, find the following passage from Kipling's tale highly surprising, articulately prophetic, and, at the same time, (if one may be oxymoronic) strangely familiar—we have lived with these dissensions for nearly three-quarters of a century now, and serious journals in science. medicine, psychology, and sociology have published attempts to demonstrate the originality and the scientific accuracy of Freud's inventions.

Here, *in ovo*, from the last years of the nineteenth century is a succinct parable of the history of the founder and, in effect, of the whole movement of psychoanalysis. Almost, one might say, one of those favorites of Freud's, a "Just So" story. Musing by himself through the streets of London, Kipling's anonymous narrator ponders young Charlie's impetuous scorn for the "Skraelings" blurted out on London Bridge, and wonders how a Greek galley slave could have intimate knowledge of the Viking expeditions to North America. He confides (for this passage is, in effect, a strict narrative equivalent of 'thinking aloud'):

> One thing only seemed certain, and that certainty took away my breath for the moment. If I came to full knowledge of anything at all, it would not be one life of the soul in Charlie Mears's body, but half a dozen—half a dozen several and separate existences spent on blue water in the morning of the world!
> Then I reviewed the situation.
> Obviously if I used my knowledge I should stand alone and unapproachable until all men were as wise as myself. That would be something, but, manlike, I was ungrateful. It seemed bitterly unfair that Charlie's memory should fail me when I needed it most. Great Powers

Above—I looked up at them through the fog-smoke—did the Lords of Life and Death know what this meant to me? Nothing less than eternal fame of the best kind, that comes from One, and is shared by one alone. I would be content—remembering Clive, I stood astounded at my own moderation,—with the mere right to tell one story, to work out one little contribution to the light literature of the day. If Charlie were permitted full recollection for one hour—for sixty short minutes—of existences that had extended over a thousand years—I would forego all profit and honor from all that I should make of his speech. I would take no share in the commotion that would follow throughout the particular corner of the earth that calls itself "the world." The thing should be put forth anonymously. Nay, I would make other men believe that they had written it. They would hire bull-hided self-advertising Englishmen to bellow it abroad. Preachers would found a fresh conduct of life upon it, swearing that it was new and that they had lifted the fear of death from all mankind. Every Orientalist in Europe would patronize it discursively with Sanskrit and Pali texts. Terrible women would invent unclean variants of the men's belief for the elevation of their sisters. Churches and religions would war over it. Between the hailing and restarting of an omnibus I foresaw the scuffles that would arise among half a dozen denominations all professing "the doctrine of the True Metempsychosis as applied to the world and the New Era;" and saw, too, the respectable English newspapers shying, like frightened kine, over the beautiful simplicity of the tale. The mind leaped forward a hundred—two hundred—a thousand years. I saw with sorrow that men would mutilate and garble the story; that rival creeds would turn it upside down till, at last, the western world which clings to the dread of death more closely than the hope of life, would set it aside as an interesting superstition and stampede after some faith so long forgotten that it seemed altogether new. Upon this I changed the terms of the bargain that I would make with the Lords of Life and Death. Only let me know, let me write, the story with sure knowledge that I wrote the truth, and I would burn the manuscript as a solemn sacrifice. Five minutes after the last line was written I would destroy it all. But I must be allowed to write it with absolute certainty.

There was no answer. (Kipling 1992, 29-30)[22]

Kipling ends his tale, the narrator having been visited by Charlie Mears, ecstatic because a tobacconist's assistant has declared her love for him, with the two-sentence paragraph: "Grish Chunder was right. Charlie had tasted the love of woman that kills remembrance, and the finest story in the world would never be written" (Kipling 1992, 40). It is only with that last sentence of the tale that the full ironic, if not mocking, significance is given to the quotation marks that embrace Kipling's cleverly, deviously, chosen title. Writing of Kipling's tale, I have referred here to "The Finest Story in the World." To be pedantically accurate, and to give the flavor of the sad joke contained within the title, I should have written: ""'The Finest Story in the World.'"" What Kipling did, of course, was to defy this self-imposed challenge and to write the tale "of a tale"—of "The Finest Story in the World."

Most of Kipling's more successful stories are precisely conceived and structured along these lines. "The Man Who Would Be King," for instance, is itself the narrative of a narrative told to an inquiring, inquisitive, yet discreet, listener who will reveal to the reader the genesis and the outcome of the story "told to him." We have to trust the constructions and their presentation, and their sequential ordering, by this authorial "I"—we have no choice. Kipling was a master of this telling of tales about tales that were (perhaps) told to him. He was also, of course, a master of the invention of such situations where "tales" could be imagined as having been told to him. Rudyard Kipling and Sigmund Freud have more in common, as writers of inventive, seductive prose fiction, than either would have appreciated. To his credit Kipling did not create, or argue for, an international organization that would perpetuate his skillful fictions as fact.

This takes me back to Sir Peter Medawar's trenchant definition of psychoanalysis: "the most stupendous intellectual confidence trick of the twentieth century." Perhaps that is simply another way of referring to an impossible enterprise. Kipling may, in fact, have concurred that, between a "finest story" and a "most stupendous intellectual confidence trick," there was, in the end, little difference. The early tale, "The Strange Ride of Morrowbie Jukes," is indeed constructed on this assumption.

Psychoanalysis was an enterprise conceived in the realms of fiction (Charcot's presentation of hysterics at La Salpêtrière) and myth (Fliess's understanding of the nose as a repository of diagnostic certainty), sustained by the founder's abuse of cocaine and his emotional and scientific reliance on Wilhelm Fliess, and propounded by lesser mortals, themselves seduced by the magisterial presence of the Master, who regarded "disconfirmation" as a lack of understanding, based, most probably, on "repression."

The Master, himself, lived in a world inhabited by the products of his own Gothic imagination (far removed from the everyday realities of Jewish Vienna), not so distant from the tribal exuberance sometimes manifested in Rudyard Kipling's tropical writings. In the year of Wilhelm

Fliess's marriage to Ida Bondy, a reminiscence of imperial reading occurs in Freud's letters to his friend. On July 12, 1892, he chortles over the choice of books that he had been offered from the estate of his late professor of psychiatry, Theodor Meynert: "Last week brought me a rare human pleasure: the opportunity to select from Meynert's library what suited me—somehow like a savage drinking mead from his enemy's skull" (Masson 1985, 32).

Indeed.

This anthropological moment is perhaps the time to mention the power of myth over reality in the human experience and to ask, yet again, why and how such insubstantial fabrics seem so immune to empirical correction. In fact, the very essay especially commissioned to introduce Frank Cioffi's most recent collection, *Freud and the Question of Pseudoscience*, is entitled "Why Are We Still Arguing about Freud?"[23] At the end of what Richard Dawkins calls "Derek Freeman's detective story"—*The Fateful Hoaxing of Margaret Mead: A Historical Analysis of Her Samoan Research*—Derek Freeman recalls Plato's question in *The Republic* about the possibility of creating a magnificent myth that would carry conviction with the whole community. Freeman argues that such a creation is possible and that, once credited, brings anathema on those who would—and can—discredit it. He writes:

> It was just such a myth that Margaret Mead created in *Coming of Age in Samoa*, and although it was based on entirely false information derived directly from her hoaxing on the island of Ofu on March 13, 1926, this myth, after *Coming of Age in Samoa* had been vouched for by Franz Boas, Bronislaw Malinowski, Ruth Benedict, and other cognoscenti, came to carry conviction with a whole community of anthropological and other cognitively deluded believers, in America as elsewhere in the world. Such magnificent myths, once a sufficient number of individuals have come fervently to believe in them, achieve an aura of invincible propriety and are defended, when challenged, with the utmost vehemence.[24]

Those of us who have worked on the Freud material and who have discovered the inadequacies of the founder and of his thoughts on life have, without exception, been confronted, at one time or another, "with the utmost vehemence" that Derek Freeman encountered in his long, solo journey to uncover the reality behind the glorious (and ludicrous) fictions of Margaret Mead. As Richard Webster tells the reader in the preface to the paperback edition" of his *Why Freud Was Wrong*, "Precisely because some people do find psychoanalytic ideas comforting, any work which criticises Freud is liable to provoke passionate resentment." (Webster 1996, xi) In the case of Margaret Mead, many people took not merely comfort, but voluptuous, if vicarious, delight in the belief in the unbridled sexual adventures of her Samoan adolescents.

Margaret, and Sigmund, and Rudyard were all magnificent writers. They created worlds in words that seemed more real for the poetry of their prose than that inhabited by mere human beings. They were all extraordinary personalities. Margaret, the Earth Mother to the world tramping to conferences with her stout Devon thumb-stick; Sigmund, the Viennese commander in chief of a worldwide organization unrivaled until Scientology arrived; Rudyard, the mischievous Mr. Toad so agin authority and yet so authoritative.

The worlds created, and perhaps imaginatively inhabited, by these master writers cannot be destroyed; they remain an integral part of our diverse cultural experiences. But where, as with Mead and Freud, they lay claim to a unique methodology for the interpretation of, and a theoretical grasp of, areas requiring thorough empirical investigation, then those claims must be challenged—on grounds of intellectual integrity and (particularly with Freud) on ethical grounds of minimizing future personal disasters. Mead was genuinely hoaxed by her female informants, but her greater intellectual 'sin' was in her later refusal to recognize this; Freud claimed (albeit quite tendentiously) to have been hoaxed by *his* female informants. In his case, however, the perpetrator of the errors (of the so-called seduction theory) was already deeply involved in the duplicities of his Fliess-inspired diagnoses. Whether Franz Boas played for Margaret Mead the determining role that Wilhelm Fliess seems to have played for Sigmund Freud is a moot point.

One observation to end on. Richard Webster notes in his preface to the paperback edition that "any critique of psychoanalysis which uses poetic, vernacular or empirically based insights in an attempt to analyse the behaviour of Freud himself (as I do in this book), is seen by some as self-contradictory or as a covert exercise in the very psychoanalysis it seeks to repudiate" (Webster 1996, xiv). Webster goes on to lambast the ignorance of those intellectuals who have lazily accepted a version of Freudianism which is an expansion of theories that Freud specifically held. He writes:

These still tend to be characterised not by their actual content so much as by the general impression that they deal with aspects of human nature which are dark, hidden or complex. Psychoanalysis comes in consequence to be seen not as the highly specific theory of mental functioning and sexual development which it is, but as an affirmation of human complexity. (Webster 1996, xiv)

Webster is quite right to preempt such criticism. He is mistaken, however, if he believes that such a caveat will prevent the "believers" from using the *tu quoque* argument. Freud himself, incidentally, was the first to make of "the highly specific theory" a grab-all for human psychology. One of the things that appealed to Freud in the personality of Carl Jung was the latter's enthusiasm for expanding the realm of their "expertise" to the fields of literature, art, and culture generally. Witness this comment in a letter to Jung after their trip to America:

I am glad you share my belief that we must conquer the whole field of mythology. Thus far we have only two pioneers: Abraham and Rank. We need men for more far-reaching campaigns. Such men are so rare. We must take hold of biography. I have had an inspiration since my return. The riddle of Leonardo da Vinci's character has suddenly become clear to me. (McGuire 1974, 255)

These do not sound like the words of a man who has evolved, with appropriate care and caution, a "highly specific theory of mental functioning and sexual development." They do sound, on the other hand, like those of the man who would be king, or who would write the Finest Story in the World.

Notes

1. Charles Carrington (1955 [1986]). *Rudyard Kipling, His Life and Work.* London: Macmillan; Harmondsworth: Penguin, 188.

2. It is high time that the general public were informed of the state of affairs governing the offer to American university publishers of refereed manuscripts contesting the truth and the well-found status of Freudian psychoanalysis.

Allen Esterson, the author of *Seductive Mirage: An Exploration of the Work of Sigmund Freud,* had great difficulty in placing his manuscript, and it was some years after completion before Open Court of Chicago was discovered and accepted his manuscript. Even recently, the young scholar who teaches at Claremont McKenna College in California, John Farrell, had an enormous number of university press refusals before New York University Press accepted to publish *Freud's Paranoid Quest: Psychoanalysis and Modern Suspicion* in 1996.

In my own case, *Maelzel's Chess Player: Sigmund Freud and the Rhetoric of Deceit* was refused by more than a dozen leading American university presses (even when accompanied by a three-page letter of serious recommendation by the chair of psychiatry at Trinity College, Dublin, Dr. Anthony Clare). Rowman and Littlefield accepted it after a very positive response from an anonymous American referee. But that was after three and a half years of attempts to find an American university press for my book. Not one of the university presses approached was even prepared to read chapters of the manuscript.

This type of endnote information is usually rejected on the grounds that it smacks too much of "authorial sour grapes." We are dealing here, however, not with a psychology of authorial resentment, but with a "marketplace of ideas" situation where certain investigations into the truth of established myths are refused a public airing because (1) they may upset persons in senior academic posts in psychiatry and (2) the publishers concerned have already hugely invested in the continuation of publishing texts for university courses where Freud is taken as an indisputable authority on matters affecting psychiatry and as one who has added immeasurably to our knowledge of human psychology.

3. Adrian Searle. "Come into the Parlour, My Dear." *Guardian Weekly*, (December 6, 1998): 27.

4. Raymond Tallis (1997). "The Shrink from Hell." *Times Higher Education Supplement* (London) (October 31): 20.

5. A similar situation exists in the aftermath of the 'Sokal Hoax' essay in the American postmodernist journal, *Social Text*. The subsequent publication in France of *Impostures Intellectuelles* by the two physicists (one American, one Belgian), Alan Sokal and Jean Bricmont, was met with a widespread but low-level critical response. The later publication (1998) in England of *Intellectual Impostures* has produced a much more vigorous debate, and yet the overwhelming presence of 'theorists' (who, interestingly enough, are frequently concerned to attach the writings of Jacques Lacan to their cause) demonstrates, in effect, just how much work for "under-labourers," in John Locke's words, remains to be done "in clearing ground a little, and removing some of the rubbish that lies in the way to knowledge" (Locke, n.d., "Epistle to the Reader").

As Patrick McGuinness of Jesus College, Oxford, noted in his letter to *The London Review of Books* responding to John Sturrock's unfavorable review of the English translation:

For every book that challenges or debates 'theory' there are probably a hundred that don't. A look at publishers' catalogues and academic job adverts is enough to establish that theory is the orthodoxy in the humanities, and its foundational texts just as canonical as whatever canons they have displaced, questioned or enriched . . . Book for book, market for market, debate for debate, Sokal and Bricmont are so outnumbered that the sight of Sturrock stamping them down is disturbing. . . . It is just as well for Sokal and Bricmont that they are scientists, because they are now shafted in the humanities job market. (*London Review of Books*, August 20, 1998, 5)

6. This may be a much harder recommendation to follow than I had assumed when I first wrote this.

What appears to have occurred in many humanities programs—in Britain as in the United States—which go under the generic "cultural studies" (in itself a most worthwhile concept, though not as innovative as some would have us believe)—is a wholesale importation and incorporation of Freudian vocabulary (and associated notions) concerned with masturbation, phallic penetrations, and vaginal receptiveness, rhythms leading dangerously to ejaculatory states and so on. Gershwin's "I got rhythm . . . who can ask for anything more?" has no doubt been the subject of more than one Freudian-inspired deconstructive seminar. Few of the "cultural studies" authors seem to have recognized what was going on in the Freudian texts, and none (to my knowledge) has investigated impartially the obsessional grounds for a sick, deluded mind coming to the universal generalizations, and the quite false extravagances, that it did. The splendid exception to this is the American psychologist Hannah Lerman whose 1986 examination of Freud, *A Mote in Freud's Eye: From Psychoanalysis to the Psychology of Women*, should be required reading in every humanities course that deals with Freudian concepts.

I. A. Richards's fear in 1934 of what might happen to a reading of Coleridge's *Kubla Khan* with the unhelpful assistance of psychoanalytic notions was far more justified than even he could have known: "The reader acquainted with current methods of analysis can imagine the results of a thoroughgoing Freudian onslaught" (Richards 1934, 30).

We now have had that "onslaught" for a good half-century. We no longer need to "imagine" its results—we know them. With the widespread expansion of cultural studies, the dangers that Richards perceived have increased exponentially. Why? Simply because one unacknowledged item on the agenda of cultural studies aficionados has been to include Freudian and Lacanian interpretations of human behavior—irrespective of their irrelevance to reality. The answer to this objection is that Freud and Lacan are indeed representative of the "culture" of our time; my response to this is a request for instruction not to be coercive and for students to be encouraged to think *critically* about the course material.

A recent example of this (and by no means the worst) from the New Cultural Studies Series launched by the University of Pennsylvania Press, is Robert A. Erickson's *The Language of the Heart, 1600-1750* (Philadelphia: University of Pennsylvania Press, 1998). As Rob Iliffe writes, with quotation, about Erickson's treatment of the great British medical scientist William Harvey's *De Motu Cordis* in his, not unfavorable, *Times Literary Supplement* review:

> For Erickson, the "minute anatomist as surgical knight with his lance" offers an "unmistakably phallic—even masturbatory" depiction of the heart, and there is "a strong phallic impulse in his love of handling daggers, needles and 'lances' . . . surgical knives, probes and pincers". The systolic heart is ejaculatory, although when it ails in creatures such as doves, Harvey steps in to revive it. (Iliffe 1998, 7)

We are back, once again, to the unwarranted but confident assertion of Freud's 1911 edition of *The Interpretation of Dreams* where we read (as the sole commentary vouchsafed on a male patient's dream of being accused by his piano-teacher of insufficient piano practice): "It is fair to say that there is no group of ideas that is incapable of representing sexual facts and wishes." (*P.F.L.*, vol. 4, 491). (Freud should have added: "Especially when presented to me by a patient.") That extraordinary piece of medical nonsense has become, in recent years, a foundation argument for perpetrators of "cultural studies."

7. Charles Dickens (1972). *The Pickwick Papers*. Harmondsworth, U.K.: Penguin, 105.

8. Sigmund Freud, "Two Lies told by Children," *S.E.*, 12, 305-309; *P.F.L.*, vol. 7, 285-91. Of the narration of these two "lies" perhaps the first is the most misleading, beginning as it does—like the Dickens tale—in the middle, with the account of the dilemma of a seven-year-old girl trying to find the money to buy the paints for the Easter eggs. But this is all "construction in analysis"— there is no seven-year-old girl with these problems—there is, however, a mature woman being interrogated by Freud about her childhood memories. What we read at the opening of this tale is what he has already deduced from his sessions with her. Nowhere in this narrative do we learn why she ever visited Freud in the first place, and no indication is given in the story of what her medical symptoms may have been (assuming she had any). The last paragraph deserves quotation, if only to demonstrate how far removed from medicine Freud had become by 1913:

> For psycho-analysts I need hardly emphasize the fact that in this little experience of the child's we have before us one of those extremely common cases in which early anal erotism persists into later erotic life. Even her desire to paint the eggs with colours derived from the same source. (*S.E.*, vol. 12, 307; *P.F.L.*, vol. 7, 289)

We have no knowledge of what Freud calls "this little experience of the child's;" we merely possess his "construction in analysis" from the remarks of an adult woman as interpreted by him. No information is provided in Freud's tale about this woman's "later erotic life" (about which Freud may have been in as much ignorance as he was about the sexual conduct of Frau Emmy von N.). This tale, cunningly drafted, is completely useless as a piece of medical or psychiatric evidence.

9. See Max Scharnberg (1993). *The Non-Authentic Nature of Freud's Observations: Vol. 1: The Seduction Theory.* Uppsala: Acta Universitatis Upsaliensis (Uppsala Studies in Education 47), 52-54. The Dickens incident occurs in chapter 27 of *The Life and Adventures of Nicholas Nickleby* (London: Michael Joseph, 1982, 177).

10. This is indeed an important aspect of Charlie Mears's difficulties as described in "The Finest Story in the World."

11. Seymour-Smith, chastised in the last chapter for facile Freudianism, requires a rap over the knuckles for his presentation (from Carrington, unacknowledged, unreferenced, and, worse, misunderstood) of this very simple passage. He writes: "Ambo, in the manner of Victorians, 'throughout life was haunted by the notion that buried and even inherited memories reveal themselves in dreams'" (Seymour-Smith, 1990, 227). Seymour-Smith's "in the manner of Victorians" gives the game away. The massive generalization— unsupported by any evidence about the "Victorians"—is sheer hocus-pocus, relying on the ignorance or inattentiveness of his readers (a learned Freudian technique?). As Carrington's passage makes perfectly clear, one would have thought, the reference to the psychological power of dreams and memories is *uniquely* attributed to Rudyard Kipling—it has nothing whatever to do with the worldly architect and failed dramatist, Ambrose Poynter, nor with any hypothesized Victorian predilection for the magic of recovered memory.

12. Carrington quotes from Kipling's autobiographical sketch, *Something of Myself,* how Lockwood Kipling had visited the Simla house of Edward Buck and "attended these seances [of Mme. Blavatsky], and quietly observed that Madame Blavatsky was 'one of the most interesting and unscrupulous imposters he had ever met'" (Carrington 1986, 104).

13. Théodore Flournoy (1994). *From India to the Planet Mars: A Case of Multiple Personality with Imaginary Languages.* Edited with a new introduction by Sonu Shamdasani. Princeton: Princeton University Press. The subject of Flournoy's inquiries was called either Élise Catherine Müller (if one credits Shamdasani's introduction) or Catherine Élise Müller, if one credits the "Appendix One: The Making of Martian: The Creation of an Imaginary Language," by Mireille Cifali which Shamdasani produces at the end of Flournoy's account.

14. See, for example, Max Scharnberg (1993). *The Non-Authentic Nature*

of Freud's Observations: Vol. 1 The Seduction Theory. Uppsala: Acta Universitatis Upsaliensis, Uppsala Studies in Education 47, "The Contemporary Aftermath of The Seduction Theory: Incest Trials in the Courts," 269-334.

15. This is true, and totally misleading; it ignores the many studies of "memory recall in hypnosis" that completely exclude any enhancement of recall because of hypnosis (American police studies dealing with simple, but crucial, testimonial evidence of recall-under-hypnosis of car license plate numbers, for example). I recommend once again the bibliography and arguments of Harrison G. Pope's *Psychology Astray.* "Hypermnesic" is precisely *not* the term to apply to material collected under these conditions. "Hyperinvented," or "hypersuggested" may, perhaps, be more accurate adjectives.

16. Another paradigm, of course—and by far the most likely—is sheer ingenious confabulation; with the natural ingredients of fraud, on the one hand, and "the willing suspension of disbelief" on the other. The theatrical connotation of Coleridge's phrase is here particularly relevant. The fact that Flournoy did not credit the "spiritist" origins of his subject's performances does not imply that his own invented "explanations" were not subject to the kind of seduced deception that Mikkel Borch-Jacobsen has so rightly adduced in the case of Bertha Pappenheim, "Anna O.," and Josef Breuer.

17. Any article written in a "Revue Spirite" and signed by one named "Goupil" requires the most careful attention. *Goupil* is the old French name, and still popular archaism, for "Reynard the Fox," and it seems to me, ignorant as I am in these spiritualist matters, that any article so signed should be regarded with the utmost caution. Was Janet caught out? Or was he teasing? Or was there, *mirabile dictu*, a genuine nineteenth-century explorer of the supposed hidden realms of consciousness who was so-named? After all, the twentieth century has accepted the existence of an American, Dr. A. Foxe, editor of the American *Psychoanalytic Review* in the 1940s, who proclaimed, quite seriously, the medical genius of Edgar Allan Poe in his *Poe as Hypnotist.*

18. This last suggestion is the one unambiguously chosen by the doyen of American science writers, Martin Gardner, in his chapter "Psychic Astronomy" from *The New Age: Notes of a Fringe Watcher* (Buffalo, N. Y.: Prometheus Books, 1988). Of the Smith/Flournoy encounters, Gardner writes:

> Only a hopeless paranormalist could suppose that these miracles were anything but conscious fraud. She [Hélène Smith] is best known, however, for her frequent out-of-body trips to Mars. . . . Théodore Flournoy, a Swiss psychologist, investigated Hélène's claims and, . . . concluded that her Martian language was a form of French glossolalia, and that her visits to Mars revealed nothing except what was inside her head. (Gardner 1988, 256)

19. Rudyard Kipling (1992). *John Brunner Presents Kipling's Fantasy: Stories by Rudyard Kipling*. Ed. John Brunner. New York: Tom Doherty (A Tor Book). All future page references will be to this edition.

20. John Brunner (Kipling 1992) in his notes refers to the Canadian writer, Farley Mowat, who suggests in *Westviking* that "Skraelings" were most likely Cape Dorset Inuit (Eskimos)—hence the Viking expedition was far north of the putative Rhode Island of Kipling's guess. Cape Dorset is on the western side of Baffin Island on the Hudson Strait and lies 64N and 77W.

21. This is a reference to Longfellow's "My Lost Youth" and "Seaweed," both quoted in Kipling's text.

22. Dr. Alan A. Stone in his recanting keynote address to the American Academy of Psychoanalysis (December 9, 1995) also uses the image of a religious creation and its later, disastrous, consequences. He uses the image of John "Jock" Murray of the Boston Psychoanalytical Society comparing "what we were doing to the construction of the great cathedral at Chartres, where workers toiled for more than a century." But rather than dwarfs standing on giants, Stone says:

> Those who stand on Freud's shoulders have not seen further, they have only seen differently and often have seen less. Rather than building a cathedral, psychoanalysts have built their own churches. Consider from this perspective the two great women, Anna Freud and Melanie Klein, who dominated psychoanalysis after Freud's death. Each of them thought she was standing on Freud's shoulders and extending his true vision. And their adherents certainly believed they were building Freud's cathedral and they accommodated both their psychoanalytic practice and thinking accordingly. Today, at least in my opinion, and I am not entirely alone in thinking this, neither Anna Freud's Ego Psychology nor Melanie Klein's Object Relations Theory seem like systematic advances on Freud's ideas. Rather they seem like divergent schools of thought, no closer to Freud than Karen Horney who rebelled against Freudian orthodoxy.
> (Stone 1997; see: <http://www.harvard-magazine.com/jf97/original.html>)

23. Frank Cioffi (1998). *Freud and the Question of Pseudoscience*. Chicago: Open Court, 1-92.

24. Derek Freeman (1999). *The Fateful Hoaxing of Margaret Mead: A Historical Analysis of Her Samoan Research*. Boulder, Colo.: Westview Press, 202. Richard Dawkins's comments are from a prepublication appreciation printed on the back of the dust cover. On the same dust cover both Martin Gardner and Mary Lefkowitz have praise for Freeman's retrieval of truth from the realms of fallacious myth. Mary Lefkowitz writes: "Both anthropologists and everyone who cares about truth should regard Freeman (rather than Mead) as a 'culture hero' for our times and society."

8

Coda:
"You have been in Afghanistan, I perceive."
The Papers on Technique

Naïveté is out of place in psychotherapy. The doctor, like the educator, must always keep his eyes open to the possibility of being consciously or unconsciously deceived, not merely by his patient, but above all by himself. The tendency to live in illusion and to believe in a fiction of oneself—in the good sense or in the bad—is almost insuperably great. . . .

Since there is no nag that cannot be ridden to death, all theories of neurosis and methods of treatment are a dubious affair. . . . A doctrinal system like that of Freud or Adler consists on the one hand of technical rules, and on the other of the pet emotive ideas of its author. C.G. JUNG[1]

Psychiatry has long been troubled by the danger of labelling, and how the act of diagnosis can in certain circumstances do more harm than good. SIMON WESSELY[2]

84 Charing Cross Road was always a renowned place for bibliophiles; the firm no longer exists, of course, and has become a kind of hallowed cultural memory. One aspect of that memory not revealed by Helene Hanff, but recently vouchsafed by the owner's son, Leo Marks, in his memoir *Between Silk and Cyanide: The Story of S.O.E.'s Code War*, was the moment of "anal osmosis" when, sitting in the chair Freud had sat in on one of his visits to the establishment, he recognized the unconscious as "the greatest of all code rooms."[3] The elegant wit and intelligence of Leo Marks allow for a certain humorous response to the 'reality' of "anal osmosis" (perhaps not even a first in the annals of the Freudian tales). It may be placed with his record of Wing Commander Yeo-Thomas's explanation of his choice of *nom de guerre* when working undercover in Occupied France. Why did he choose "the White Rabbit" as a code name? Because, as Leo Marks wryly reveals, Yeo-Thomas thought that the organization he worked for (the Special Operations Executive [S.O.E.]) was "a fucking Mad Hatter's tea party."

Peter Medawar, who may privately have thought the same thing about the whole shambolic structure (theoretical, clinical, and methodological) of psychoanalysis, was always careful in his public refutations of psychoanalysis to give Freud himself the maximum credit and respect. As an instance of this, witness the paragraph in his rejoinder to the (unnamed) psychotherapist Anthony Storr who had criticized Medawar's Oxford Romanes lecture for 1968:

> To go now to the other extreme: the psychoanalytic critic I referred to above thinks it probable that 'neurosis is the result of faulty early conditioning' rather than of brain disease or an inborn error of metabolism. No doubt; but does he not also think that constitutional or organic influences may raise or lower the susceptibility of his patients to these disturbing influences? Of course he does—and so did Freud. It is normally a mistake, I suggest, to trace any psychological disorder to wholly mental or wholly organic causes. Both contribute, though sometimes to very unequal degrees, and the contributions made by one will be a function of the contribution made by the other.[4]

Later in the same paper, Medawar lets loose, if not on Freud then on those followers of the Master who have accepted doctrine as knowledge and have interpreted their patients' complaints in the light of the Freudian doxology. It is here that Medawar reveals the vacuity of the psychoanalytic endeavor, or, rather, the emptiness of its overarching explanatory claims:

> I shall not attempt a systematic treatment, but shall merely draw attention to a few of its more serious methodological, doctrinal and practical defects.
>
> The property that gives psychoanalysis the character of a mythology is its combination of conceptual barrenness with an enormous facility in explanation. To criticise a theory because it explains everything it is called on to explain sounds paradoxical, but anyone who thinks so should consult the discussion by Karl Popper in *Conjectures and Refutations*, particularly the passages that make mention of psychoanalysis itself. (Medawar 1984, 66)

Medawar then decides to quote from the authors' summaries of their own contributions to the Twenty-third International Psychoanalytical Congress held in Stockholm in 1963 to make his point. "I choose," he writes, "the proceedings of a congress rather than the work of a single author so as to get a cross-section of psychoanalytic thought" (Medawar 1984, 66). His examples include the psychoanalytic treatment of a sufferer of ulcerative colitis—"A disease of the kind psychoanalysts would be well advised not to meddle with"—and he concludes caustically:

> I have not chosen these examples to poke fun at them, ridiculous though I believe them to be, but simply to illustrate the Olympian glibness of psychoanalytic thought. The contributors to this congress were concerned with homosexuality, anti-Semitism, depression, and manic and schizoid tendencies; with *difficult* problems, then—problems far less easy to grapple with or make sense of than anything that confronts us in the laboratory. But where shall we find the evidence of hesitancy or bewilderment, the avowals of sheer ignorance, the sense of groping and incompleteness that is commonplace in an international congress of, say, physiologists or biochemists? A lava-flow of *ad hoc* explanation pours over and around all difficulties, leaving only a few smoothly rounded prominences to mark where they might have lain. (67-68)

In other words, Medawar's attack is two-pronged: he argues that both the substance and the *style* of psychoanalytic presentation are dangerously lacking in clear, responsible argument. This fault he traces back, toward the end of the paper, to Freud himself.

> Nevertheless, psychoanalysts are wont to say that Freud's work carried conviction because it was so firmly grounded on basic biological principles. I am therefore sorry to have to express the professional opinion that many of the germinal ideas of psychoanalysis are profoundly unbiological, among them the 'death-wish,' the underlying assumption of an extreme fragility of the mind, the systematic depreciation of the genetic contribution to human diversity, and the interpretation of dreams as 'one member of a class of *abnormal* psychical phenomena.'
>
> I said earlier that the mythological status of psychoanalytic theory revealed itself in its combination of unbridled explanatory facility with conceptual barrenness, a property to which I have not yet referred. Ever since Freud's factually erroneous analysis of Leonardo, psychoanalysts have tried their hand at 'interpreting' the life and work of men of genius, and many of the great figures of history have been disinterred and brought to the post-mortem slab. The fiasco of Darwin's retrospective

psychoanalysis has already been held up to ridicule. But, Darwin apart, how can we not marvel at the way in which the whole exuberant variety of human genius can be explained by the manipulation of a handful of germinal ideas—the Oedipus complex, the puzzlement of discovering that not everyone has a penis, a few unspecified sado-masochistic reveries, and so on: surely we need a more powerful armoury than this? Evidently we do, for these analyses always stop short of explaining why genius took the specific form that interests us. (70-71)

In the Dora case history, written some ten years before the first of the six Papers on Technique, Freud introduced the notion of "symptomatic acts" which were for him clear indices of significant aspects of the patient's personality and possible neurosis. Freud writes:

I give the name of symptomatic acts to those acts which people perform, as we say, automatically, unconsciously, without attending to them, or as if in a moment of distraction. They are actions to which people would like to deny any significance, and which, if questioned about them, they would explain as being indifferent or accidental. Closer observation, however, will show that these actions, about which consciousness knows nothing or wishes to know nothing, in fact give expression to unconscious thoughts and impulses, and are therefore most valuable and instructive as being manifestations of the unconscious which have been able to come to the surface. . . .

On some other occasion I will publish a collection of these symptomatic acts as they are to be observed in the healthy and in neurotics. They are sometimes very easy to interpret. Dora's reticule, which came apart at the top in the usual way, was nothing but a representation of the genitals, and her playing with it, her opening it and putting her finger in it, was an entirely unembarrassed yet unmistakable pantomimic announcement of what she would like to do with them—namely, to masturbate. (*P.F.L.*, vol. 8, 113-14)

Medawar's phrase "Olympian glibness" comes to mind. Some historians of psychoanalysis have taken Freud's ingenious but deadly monotonous obsessions as instance of his insightfulness. Thus Peter Gay in *Freud: A Life for Our Time* writes in a footnote to his chapter on the Dora case:

Laurence Sterne, that psychological novelist before his time, had already said something very much like it a century and a half earlier: "There are a thousand unnoticed openings, continued my father, which let a penetrating eye at once into a man's soul; and I maintain it, added he, that a man of sense does not lay down his hat in coming into a room—or take it up in going out of it, but something escapes, which discovers him." (*Tristram Shandy*, book VI, ch. 5). (Gay 1988, 254, note 3)

Sterne (or his character, Tristram's father) was probably less intent on discovering traces of childhood masturbation or supposed infantile incestuous fantasies in "a man of sense" than in unearthing more significantly revealing character traits. Incidentally, Peter Gay's footnote may also be a Freudian trap for the unwary as it is, in fact, an unacknowledged quote from the 1920 revision of *The Psychopathology of Everyday Life* in which Freud had written: "Wilhelm Stross has drawn my attention to the following passage in Laurence Sterne's celebrated humorous novel, *Tristram Shandy*" (*P.F.L.*, vol. 5, 271).[5]

We will encounter Freud's "symptomatic acts" again in the papers devoted to introducing neophyte analysts to the mysteries of conducting the analytic session. But, to quote once more from the Dora case, the passage which ends with the "revelation" of the mime of masturbation carried out by Dora, is followed by a self-congratulatory paragraph reminiscent (as Gay supposed) of the detective powers of observation of Tristram's father:

> There is a great deal of symbolism of this kind in life, but as a rule we pass it by without heeding it. When I set myself the task of bringing to light what human beings keep hidden within them, not by the compelling power of hypnosis, but by observing what they say and what they show, I thought the task was a harder one than it really is. He that has eyes to see and ears to hear may convince himself that no mortal can keep a secret. If his lips are silent, he chatters with his finger-tips; betrayal oozes out of him at every pore. And thus the task of making conscious the most hidden recesses of the mind is one which it is quite possible to accomplish. (*P.F.L.*, 8, 114)

Freud may well have read Sterne (thanks to Wilhelm Stross)—as well as Poe, Kipling, and Dickens—but a writer whose influence he did acknowledge, Conan Doyle, had published a decade and a half (1887) before "Fragment of an Analysis of a Case of Hysteria," the first of the Holmes–Watson adventures entitled *A Study in Scarlet*. Of the article headed "The Book of Life" that Watson was reading at breakfast one March 4, the doctor–narrator observes:

It struck me as being a remarkable mixture of shrewdness and absurdity. The reasoning was close and intense, but the deductions appeared to me to be farfetched and exaggerated. The writer claimed by a momentary expression, a twitch of a muscle, or a glance of an eye, to fathom a man's inmost thoughts. Deceit, according to him, was an impossibility in the case of one trained to observation and analysis. His conclusions were as infallible as so many propositions of Euclid. So startling would his results appear to the uninitiated that, until they learned the processes by which he had arrived at them, they might well consider him as a necromancer.[6]

Watson, as we know, after much disbelieving "resistance" comes to credit his flatmate's method and his genius at retrodiction. Dupin's associative links established during the fifteen minutes of silent strolling near the Palais Royal that Holmes judged so "showy and superficial" are in every respect a precursor of Holmes' investigative methods (and, of course, of Freud's). In the last chapter of *A Study in Scarlet* the obtuse Watson is still not clear about the secret of Holmes's success and the latter has to explain: "In solving a problem of this sort, the grand thing is to be able to reason backward." The rarity of his triumph is explained: "There are fifty who can reason synthetically for one who can reason *analytically*."

Adolf Grünbaum in his *The Foundations of Psychoanalysis* has made much of Freud's ability to detect the danger of that *pons asinorum* of rudimentary logic—the fallacious use of *post hoc ergo propter hoc*. I have suggested in these chapters that running throughout Freud's *metapsychological*[7] works (i.e., *all* the case histories and the various papers on technique as well as the "applied" psychoanalysis of the essays on Leonardo and Moses) lies a disguised *post hoc ergo propter hoc* formulation.[8] I have also suggested that *sometimes* such an approach may well be warranted by the evidence of the circumstances—for instance, the miraculous disappearance of the "grands hystériques" from the Salpêtrière following the death of Jean-Martin Charcot. This is perhaps merely the most famous instance of a diagnosed complaint disappearing in a puff of smoke with the doctor who made the diagnosis. Fliess's "nasal reflex neurosis" would, I suppose, be another.

Sherlock Holmes's method relies on a very astute employment of the post hoc argument. In a sense, the retrodiction of Holmes (transferred to the sphere of sexuality, where adult experiences have their origins in infantile sexuality and its imagined fantasies) is the real realm of psychoanalysis. It rarely predicts. Holmes is given a short speech in the last chapter of *A Study in Scarlet* which aptly sums up his own and (unbeknownst to Conan Doyle) Freud's method of approach:

> Most people, if you describe a train of events to them, will tell you what the result would be. They can put those events together in their minds, and argue from them that something will come to pass. There are few people, however, who, if you told them a result, would be able to evolve from their own inner consciousness what the steps were which led up to that result. This power is what I mean when I talk of reasoning backward, or analytically. (Conan Doyle n.d., 127)

Freud's cases are full of this type of argumentation *backward* in an attempt to perceive, or invent, what must have led to the "illness" established in the patient's presentation. The most flagrant example is that recorded in the adventures of 'Little Hans' which are pressed into service in several essays (see *P.F.L.*, vol. 7, "On Sexuality"), often mendaciously. Freud writes, for instance, in the essay *"Zur Sexuellen Aufklärung der Kinder"* ("The Sexual Enlightenment of Children"):

> I know a delightful little boy, now four years old, *whose understanding parents abstain from forcibly suppressing one part of the child's development*. Little Hans has certainly not been exposed to anything in the nature of seduction by a nurse, *yet* he has already for some time shown the liveliest interest in the part of the body which he calls his 'widdler.' (*P.F.L.*, vol. 7, 176; my emphasis)

In spite of the statement italicized, Freud reports in the case history itself ("Analysis of a Phobia in a Five-Year-Old Boy") the mother's threat of penile ablation when the child, aged three and a half, was found with his hand on his penis. "If you do that, I shall send for Dr. A. to cut off your widdler" (*P.F.L.*, vol. 7, 171). Freud writes later in the case of the boy, now five years old: "It would be the most completely typical procedure if the threat of castration were to have a *deferred* effect, and if he were now, a year and a quarter later, oppressed by the fear of having to lose this precious piece of his ego" (*P.F.L.*, vol. 7, 198).

Since Freud's access for experimental purposes to five-year-old children was (fortunately) extremely limited—even Martha kept him at arm's length from the nursery—his statement "the most *completely typical procedure*" refers *not* (as the reader is led to believe) to any empirical data that Freud may have (in fact, he had none from direct observation), but back to the unsubstantiated home-brew theories we have read about in the letters to Fliess.

We have here an example of lies to the public ("whose *understanding* parents abstain from forcibly suppressing one part of the child's development") in what one must believe was a misguided attempt to *prove*, by the psychological harassment of a young child (conveniently the son of Freudian disciples), the spurious tenets of his universal "castration anxiety" theory. Freud's seductive rhetoric has indeed been singularly successful if one is to judge by the frequency with which this 'case' is cited as 'evidence' for his theory. One who was not seduced by the rhetoric was the Irish psychiatrist Anthony Clare, who wrote:

> The case of Little Hans is often used to support Freud's theory of castration anxiety, although in truth what it shows is the effort of a Freudian-inclined mother to induce castration anxieties in her perfectly normal son. . . . The conclusion that Hans's phobia disappeared as a result of the resolution of his Oedipal conflict has to be seen in the light of the remarkably fragile evidence in support of the notion that Hans had such an Oedipal complex in the first place.[9]

The 'case' (it is not so much a case history—'Little Hans' was never in analytic therapy with Freud—as an epistolary romance between Freud and Hans's father who supplied, and certainly contributed to, the data) is also indicative of Freud's inadequate grasp of proper inferential conclusions. Despite his manifest (and, no doubt, latent) lies in this narration, it does not save his universal castration-fear theory because— and this is even more significant for his understanding of the rules of correct inference—*had* the mother made *no threat of penile ablation*, and *had* 'Little Hans' *nevertheless* shown fears "of having to lose this precious piece of his ego" this would not in itself in the least warrant a universal "castration anxiety" theory (or, more properly, a universal penile-ablation-anxiety theory). It would not even warrant such a theory for the tiny sub-class of humanity: middle-class Viennese Jews known to practice infantile circumcision. We are back to the problems of "an inference from a relatively small sample to the entire human population" raised by the philosopher Barbara Von Eckardt.[10]

The six "Papers on Technique" are all to be found in volume 12 of the *Standard Edition*. They were translated into English in 1924 by Joan Rivière. I list them here in their order of apppearance in German, the date in parenthesis after each paper indicating the first German publication date.

The Handling of Dream-Interpretation in Psycho-Analysis (1911);
The Dynamics of Transference (1912);
Recommendations to Physicians practising Psycho-Analysis (1912);
On Beginning the Treatment (1913);
Remembering, Repeating and Working-Through (1914);
Observations on Transference-Love (1915).

To these one could perhaps add the very late essay (published in December 1937) which concerns Freud's 'archaeological' digging in the case histories of the Rat Man, the Wolf Man, and the unnamed (even unnicknamed) homosexual girl: "Constructions in Analysis" (*S.E.*, vol. 23, 255-70). In this essay, Freud holds fast to the notions of infantile sexuality (as he understood it) and to its determining effects (and, of course, to its necessarily inaccessible repressed unconscious nature) that were first bruited in the Fliess correspondence almost a half-century earlier. Between those letters of the forty-year-old Freud and this essay, drafted in his early eighties, there is a total absence of evidence of concern for empirical investigation of the hypotheses presented. Freud's notions are expressed in "Constructions in Analysis" with a rhetorical cunning, however, that was powerful enough to seduce the literary critic Peter Brooks (see, as evidence, his *Reading for the Plot*, where "Constructions in Analysis" is presented as an infallible *vade mecum*).

The "Papers on Technique," given their intended audience, are probably among the most damaging and reprehensible that Freud ever wrote. The "monumental certainties" in them—something previously restricted to the weekly evenings of the Vienna Psychoanalytic Society— allowed him to make the kind of "first glance" appraisal of a new victim that would henceforth be a beacon to guide the path the anamnesis should take. Such, Watson believed, was Holmes's approach; but Holmes did not allow circumstances to be interpreted overwhelmingly by preexisting theory. Freud inevitably did. In spite of "modifications" to his theory[11] and qualifications about the unique therapeutic value of psychoanalysis toward the end of his life (qualifications that may be either a published awareness of the practical therapeutic failure of his enterprise, or a last-ditch attempt to save belief in his theories via a newfound rhetoric of modesty), his writings on technique must count as the most subversive of his works for the way they present 'knowledge' of human psychology and 'knowledge' of how to succor those who have come for relief from mental and/or affective distress.

This was not 'knowledge' for Freud himself alone; it was to be shared with those he taught. In the paper for apprentice analysts called "On Beginning the Treatment," Freud says, without any scientific, clinical, or even anecdotal evidence to support the statement: "The first symptoms or chance actions of the patient, like the first resistance, have a special interest and may betray a complex which governs his neurosis" (*S.E.*, vol. 12, 138). In other words, the "chance actions" of the patient are equivalent to the "first symptoms" and will betray the root of his or her problems. When Freud says "first symptoms" he means, though he does not say as much, the *first behavioral patterns* observed by the psychoanalyst upon the presentation of, or the introduction to, the patient. Furthermore, he means the "first symptoms" *from the psychoanalytic point of view*. Freud immediately continues in this lecture—intended, let us not forget, for trainees—with an illustrative instance of what he understands by such "first symptoms" and how these should be properly interpreted:

> A clever young philosopher with exquisite aesthetic sensibilities will hasten to put the creases of his trousers straight before lying down for his first hour; he is revealing himself as a former coprophilic of the highest refinement—which was to be expected from the later aesthete. (*S.E.*, vol. 12, 138)

It is not the *appearance* of the victim that produces the conviction about his illness (we shall not know whether *he* has been in Afghanistan), it is what Freud has already classified in the Dora case as the "symptomatic act." In Freud's presentation to his neophytes the symptomatic act is resumed by the observation of the young philosopher that he "will hasten to put the creases of his trousers straight before lying down for his first hour." This is his "symptomatic act." Freud at once interprets the action and defines the man—"a former coprophilic"—then places him within the sub-group (coprophilics) "of the highest refinement." This is followed by a smug Q.E.D.: "which was to be expected from the later aesthete." If Freud was playing for laughs, the laughter targeted has many unpleasant overtones, none suited to intending therapists for people in distress.[12]

Several things are at work here, and they do not support the idea that Freud thought, acted, or even taught, scientifically (and here I mean "scientifically" in the broadest possible definition of the term). Nor do these particulars indicate a firm grasp of the twin principles of modesty and decency that the finer medical pedagogues try to teach to their interns.

It is an established practice that interns will be asked to judge their patients on first acquaintance and to be alert to signs as well as symptoms. By "signs" I mean those gestures, mannerisms, presentations of the social self that may indicate such disparate things as social class, marital status, occupation, likely pastimes, and so on. By "symptoms" I mean the specifically medical aspect of the patient's presentation. Some ten years ago, I heard a CBC (Canadian Broadcasting Corporation) radio interview with the then ninety-one-year-old father of Canadian cardiology, Dr. Harold Segall, in which he estimated for these patient presentation guesses a "batting average" of no more than 40 percent accuracy as far as the social signs were concerned.

Freud, in this paper "On Beginning the Treatment," has borrowed this medical rhetoric and is here promoting himself as the experienced general practitioner he never was[13] who, by virtue of this borrowed rhetoric, will instruct his novice followers in the arcane secrets of "making conscious the most hidden recesses of the mind." As a consequence of this, he not only offers impromptu discoveries of mental distress (neuroses, in his designation), he also offers impromptu discoveries of social ontology. And both are given with the same magisterial certainty. We are presented with one action, isolated in the beam of Freud's fascination for reminiscences of nursery naughtiness in adults who come for treatment, which is taken as a *"symptomatic act"* that "may betray a complex which governs his neurosis."

So far the patient has not said a word. But he has already been classified as a neurotic and as a former coprophilic. Anything he actually says will be fitted into the grid of this preliminary diagnosis. If the patient does not fit, then *he*, and not the diagnosis, will be shortened or lengthened according to the laws laid down by that ancient who should count as the patron saint of psychoanalysis, Procrustes.[14]

As we can see from the case of the young philosopher, in spite of the (often legitimate) complaints of the feminists, Freud could be as thoughtless toward male patients as toward female ones—and as thoughtless in his suggestions for future practitioners: we should recall that the subtitle of this paper is "Further Recommendations on the Technique of Psycho-Analysis." There is, however, an engaging display of impartiality in this paper. The aesthetic philosopher and the young girl introduced as the very next example of how to begin the therapeutic treatment are instances of it.

Her first actions will also be judged in the same severe (or comic) manner as those of the philosopher; and they will also be seen as *symptomatic acts*. Freud writes:

> A young girl will at the same juncture [i.e., at the beginning of the treatment] hurriedly pull the hem of her skirt over her exposed ankles; in doing this she is giving away the gist of what her analysis will uncover later: her narcissistic pride in her physical beauty and her inclinations to exhibitionism. (*S.E.*, 12, 138)

Neither "narcissistic pride" nor "inclinations to exhibitionism" seem to be medical problems, nor yet socially disabling characteristics, though doubtless they will be made to seem so by the time she is through with her medical Svengali who will assure her that they originate in inaccessible unconscious infantile experiences, or, rather, fantasies. Freud in fact predicts as much when he prefaces his description of her sauciness by what is, in effect, an alternative description: *"the gist of what her analysis will uncover later."* If that is indeed what the "gist" of her "treatment" will uncover, it sounds uncommonly like the tenebrous soothsaying of the "cross-my-palm-with-silver" type more frequently encountered in tents at country fairs, to which have been adroitly added a whiff of medspeak and a strong dose of "most miserable offender" sermonizing.

We do not know, and will not learn, what miseries brought her to Freud's attention in the first place—nor, incidentally, are we vouchsafed what the consequences were of such attention. Freud's first interest, as he here instructs his students, is neither in the medical nor the social distress that occasioned her visit, but in the culpable fantasies of the self that her "symptomatic act" reveals. She, like the philosopher before her, has not yet said a word. The interpretation of the brief reflexive gesture is Freud's alone, unaided by dialogue or dream work or free association. We are not far removed from the doctor who wrote about Dora: "I added that she was now on the way to finding an answer to her own question of why it was that precisely she had fallen ill—by confessing that she had masturbated, probably in childhood" (*P.F.L.*, vol. 8, 112).

Ironically, Freud's extraordinary commentary on the girl's "narcissistic pride" and "inclinations to exhibitionism" precedes, by just over a page, his admonition that "[i]t is certainly possible to forfeit this first success if from the start one takes up any standpoint *other than one of sympathetic understanding, such as a moralizing one*" [my italics]. Whose leg is he pulling?[15] As J. Allan Hobson has written, "By 1936, his thinking was characterized by arbitrariness, authoritarianism, and a failure to specify rules or imagine data that could contradict his theory" (Hobson 1988, 58-59). But, as we can see from this early demonstration of the patriarchal style, the rot had set in very much sooner. This influential paper was first published in German in the *Internationale Zeitschrift für Psychoanalyse* in 1913. It was reprinted at least four times before 1936. In 1924, the first English translation, by Joan Rivière, appeared. The burgeoning psychoanalytic world was well-served with means of ready access to the instructions on technique emanating from Berggasse 19.

The "Papers on Technique" form a cluster of nontheoretical and non-case-history material written between 1911 and 1915 (the last two were contemporaneous in production with the writing-up of the Wolf Man case). They were didactic in intention and presentation but, unlike the *Introductory Lectures* or *The Psychopathology of Everyday Life*, they were not written for a general readership. One readily discernable effect on the rhetoric used in these papers of this decision to limit their audience was that Freud appears blunter in his statements (witness the above remarks about the philosopher and the young girl). It is not that he is more "unbuttoned" but that he feels less need to seduce with wise saws and modern instances, less need to present, as he does to great effect, for instance, in *The Psychopathology of Everyday Life*, his invented discipline in the most disarming of lights. The other most noticeable effect is his double assumption (perfectly reasonable in the circumstances) that his audience would (a) be familiar with psychoanalytic theory and (b) be accepting of it. There is, in consequence, an absence of demonstration of evidence for basic tenets about infantile sexuality and its supposed later manifestations in adult relationships. Since Freud appears as a *magister ludi* he does not bother to question aloud his own basis for what he offers, and, furthermore, what is offered is indeed offered as proven evidence, not as unsubstantiated hypothesis.

The rhetorical trick of the 'epistemic split' whereby Freud can at once present his 'science' as other than himself and himself as an informed teacher of that 'science' is used throughout these lectures. And so, for instance, that clever little phrase "psychoanalysis has shown that" (and its variants) is used to considerable advantage. This backfired in the 1896 lecture on the aetiology of hysteria because he was *in partibus infidelium*; but with the present audience of knowledgeable believers Freud can take theoretical shortcuts which will only enhance the faith. What, in these lectures, he states as fact will most assuredly be accepted as such by the intended public. For example, in the first paper, on "The Handling of Dream-Interpretation," Freud can note, taking his metapsychological constructs and his clinical experience for granted:

> I know that it is asking a great deal, not only of the patient but also of the doctor, to expect them to give up their conscious purposive aims during the treatment, and to abandon themselves to a guidance which, in spite of everything, still seems to us 'accidental.' But I can answer for it that one is rewarded every time one resolves to have faith in one's own theoretical principles, and prevails upon oneself not to dispute the guidance of the unconscious in establishing connecting links. (*S.E.*, vol. 12, 94)

A passage such as this appears to have such an air of common-sense experience behind it that one is likely to forget that the presentation of self as the successful therapist—*"one is rewarded every time one resolves to have faith in one's own theoretical principles"*—is highly misleading when measured against the now-known reality of Freud's recorded case histories. One is also tempted to forget that the "unconscious," whose guidance one should follow, is a very particular beast formed, or originating, from the "primary" sexual repressions between the ages of one and three.

By the same token, in the second lecture on "The Dynamics of Transference" Freud can divide the "positive" transference into two parts, one of "friendly or affectionate feelings which are admissible to consciousness" and another which is constituted by "prolongations of those feelings into the unconscious." These prolongations, we learn in the next sentence, are the consequence of the infantile sexualization of human experience[16] between ages one and three which determines all future relationships:

> As regards the latter, analysis shows that they invariably go back to erotic sources. And we are thus led to the discovery that all the emotional relations of sympathy, friendship, trust, and the like, which can be turned to good account in our lives, are genetically linked with sexuality and have developed from purely sexual desires through a softening of their sexual aim, however pure and unsensual they may appear to our conscious self-perception. Originally we knew only sexual objects; and psychoanalysis
>
> shows us that people who in our real life are merely admired or respected may still be sexual objects for our unconscious. (*S.E.*, vol. 12, 105)

Although not intended for the lay public, this passage is charged throughout with the rhetoric of the 'middle mode' of discourse, including a double example of the 'epistemic-splitting': "analysis shows us that . . ." and "psychoanalysis shows us that."

The last two papers, "Remembering, Repeating and Working-Through" and "Observations on Transference-Love," have acquired a reputation for introspective sophistication that, at first glance, seems not wholly undeserved. But, alas, once one starts reading them carefully with an awareness in mind of what (impossible) theoretical inventions underpin them, the sophistication vanishes and the introspection is seen to be no more than a kind of brooding, in the first instance over the (possibly phylogenetic) 'primal scene' constructions of the Wolf Man case; and, in the second, over the amatory entanglements of certain colleagues like Ferenczi.

If in this coda I have described Freud's "Papers on Technique" as the most damaging and reprehensible that he wrote, it is because they pretend to science and medical method in a context where both are lacking and in a context where both were believed by gullible apprentices who themselves were one day to purvey their content and their style to a later generation of practitioners. In an amusing aside to the introduction to *Pluto's Republic*, Medawar mentions his mother's response to his review of Teilhard de Chardin's *The Phenomenon of Man*:

> My aged mother was very shocked by my review of Teilhard: 'How *could* you be so horrid to that nice old man?' she asked me. The reason, I told her, was that Teilhard had described his book as a work of science— and one executed with 'remorseless logic'—and as a work of science it has been accepted by its more gullible readers. If only he had described it as an imaginative rhapsody 'based on science' in much the same way as some films are said to be based on books to which in the outcome they seem to bear little resemblance, then *The Phenomenon of Man* would have caused no offence. (Medawar 1984, 23)

In my own case—and I am not a Medawar, but merely one of John Locke's "under-labourers" engaged "in clearing ground a little, and removing some of the rubbish that lies in the way to knowledge"—the facts are slightly different. My own ancient mother (now deceased) did not consider Freud "that nice old man" and was delighted in her last year when my first Freud critique had found a publisher.

Since completing this volume, I have discovered the excellent recent account of what Frederick Crews calls "psychiatry's Late Middle Ages" in Edward Dolnick's *Madness on the Couch: Blaming the Victim in the Heyday of Psychoanalysis* (1998). Dolnick deals with the disasters of leucotomy and ice-pick brain surgery as well as with the three big disaster areas of psychoanalytic treatment: schizophrenia, autism, and obsessive-compulsive disorder. It is a brilliant piece of work by a senior science reporter and should be required reading for all medical residents interested in psychiatry and by those in the humanities (whether in departments of literature or the social sciences) who still believe that Margaret Mead, Gregory Bateson, R. D. Laing, and, of course, Freud himself have anything worthwhile to tell us about human mental distress or psychic dysfunction when the medical problems involved are specifically neurological rather than psychological.

Quoting from "Obsessive Actions and Religious Practices" (*S.E.*, vol. 9, 115-27; *P.F.L.*, vol. 13, 27-41), Dolnick writes of the performance:

> Such virtuoso displays were a speciality of Freud's—he happily ventured off into literature and anthropology whenever he could slip his therapeutic leash—but Freud did not rely on literary artistry to win over his peers. The proof of *this* pudding, he noted repeatedly, was easy to find: he cured obsessive patients. (Dolnick 1998, 258)

This is Dolnick being ironic and slightly misleading, since Freud *did* indeed rely on his literary legerdemain. Dolnick, in effect, recognizes Freud's way with words (even including the false literary presentation of cures that never took place) in his comments on the following page on the 1926 paper "The Question of Lay Analysis," where he notes Freud's clever comments about the apparent lack of "magic" in psychoanalysis since the treatment takes so long. Dolnick's concluding paragraph on this paper shows his astuteness as a reader:

> Appropriately, Freud is practicing sleight of hand here. By admitting so openly that psychoanalysis is slow to cure, he draws our attention away from the real question—never mind speed, does it cure at all? While we are left pondering whether a slow miracle is a true miracle, Freud has snatched our wallet and darted off. (Dolnick 1998, 259)

Dolnick, on his last page, is critical of the famous Medawar remark about psychoanalysis being "the most stupendous confidence trick of the twentieth century." His objection to Medawar is that psychoanalysts (and their founder) were not confidence men, *they were believers.* "Brilliant scientist and caustic writer though he was, Medawar was surely wrong here. Con men know exactly what they are up to" (Dolnick 1998, 294). So, in a sense, did Freud. And Dolnick himself on an earlier page has castigated Freud's repeated dishonesty in the reporting of his own cases. He writes:

> It is no rebuke to Freud to say that he did not cure his obsessive patients— even today, they are notoriously difficult to treat. But Freud's behavior here was dishonest, in fact doubly so. He claimed, first of all, to have cured patients *though he knew those claims were false or exaggerated.* Second, he advanced those same fictional cures as proof that his theory of obsessional neurosis was valid. (Dolnick 1998, 261; my italics)

If that is not an instance of a long-term confidence trick, what is? Medawar had already answered criticisms of this sort in the papers collected in *Pluto's Republic.* In the 1968 Romanes Lecture, he had railed against willful obscurity and had argued that the intellectual labor of a reader confronted with a text dealing with a difficult subject was different in essence from the intellectual labor involved in trying to comprehend a text "made hard to follow because of *non sequiturs*, digressions, paradoxes, impressive-sounding references to Gödel, Wittgenstein and topology, 'in' jokes, and a general determination to keep all vulgar sensibilities at bay." In the first case, "the reasoning was the author's" whereas "in the other case our own. We have thus been the victim of a confidence trick" (Medawar 1984, 52).

In "Further Comments on Psychoanalysis" Medwar replies to Anthony Storr's critique about the implication of deliberate malfeasance by modern psychoanalysts.

> *Of course* I don't think a psychoanalyst would knowingly attempt to treat a brain tumour or a victim of Huntington's Chorea by psychoanalytic methods, but he may not realise the degree to which he is being wise after the event. Being a sensible man he naturally repudiates the idea of treating those psychological ailments of which physical causes are, in general terms, already known. But psychoanalysts do treat and speculate upon the origins of schizophrenic conditions and manic-depressive psychoses. *These* are the test cases: what are we to make of *them*? (Medawar 1984, 63)

What indeed? The point is that nothing within the Freudian arsenal provides ammunition to counter these maladies and, worse (and this is Medawar's point), once one has accepted the Freudian theories of human mental operations, one is in effect lost within a labyrinth of notions where no scientific help is possible. With his great journalistic gift for the memorable analogy, Edward Dolnick has captured the inevitable effects of doctrinal Freudianism on the American psychoanalytic community:

> But in the end, a system without outside feedback is doomed. As crashes go, the final crash of the analysts who had taken on madness was not especially spectacular. What marked it as special was that this time the pilots themselves were the ones who had disabled the warning lights in the cockpit and shut off communication with air traffic control on the ground. (Dolnick 1998, 279)

I do not think that Edward Dolnick's splendid book is undermined by the modish criticism of Medawar on his last page. It is sad, but true, that in too many areas of intellectual activity it is fashionable to be critical of Peter Medawar and his caustic commentaries on those whose apparent efforts to decipher humanity to itself have resulted in more confusion than clarity. Medawar, Dolnick, and I share, however, one important thing: we are meliorists. Freud wasn't; and he never claimed to be one. His Romantic pessimism, and the Lacanian versions of his pessimistic writings (the title of Tallis's review article "The Shrink from Hell" says it all), must be contested—and this may be a very long battle—especially in the universities, if the arts and sciences of life are to recover some firm foundation where critical knowledge is allowed to replace irresponsible and quite unfounded belief.

Notes

1. Carl Gustav Jung. "Lecture III. Analytical Psychology and Education," In *Psychology and Education* (from *The Collected Works of C. G. Jung*, Vol. 17, Bollingen Series 20). Tr. R. F. C. Hull. Princeton University Press, 1969, 102-103. This is from the last of three lectures originally drafted by Jung in English and given in London in 1924 at the International Congress of Education.

The commonsense criticism of dogmatic Freudian procedures in the treatment setting should not, however, blind one to the astrological bent evident in Jung's works from the time he was still writing as a friend and disciple of Freud. For example in the letter to Freud of June 12, 1911, Jung waxes extravagantly about the presumed diagnostic powers of astrology:

My evenings are taken up very largely with astrology. I make horoscopic calculations in order to find a clue to the core of psychological truth. Some remarkable things have turned up which will certainly appear incredible to you.[Jung had no access to the Freud–Fliess correspondence.] In the case of one lady, the calculation of the position of the stars at her nativity produced a quite definite character picture, with several biographical details which did not pertain to her but to her mother—and the characteristics fitted the mother to a T. . . . I dare say that we shall one day discover in astrology a good deal of knowledge that has been intuitively projected into the heavens. For instance, it appears that the signs of the zodiac are character pictures, in other words libido symbols which depict the typical qualities of the libido at a given moment. (McGuire 1974, 427)

Incidentally, Max Scharnberg argues convincingly that Freud's "Anal Theory" and the personality traits thereby subsumed are themselves no more than a transformation of "Astrology into Psychiatry" whereby the characteristics of the Virgo personality are those of the orderly "anal" personality. Max Scharnberg (1993), *The Non-Authentic Nature of Freud's Observations. Vol. II: Felix Gattel's Early Freudian Cases, and the Astrological Origin of the Anal Theory.* Uppsala: Acta Universitatis Upsaliensis, Uppsala Studies in Education 48. See 134 ff.

2. Simon Wessely (1989). "It's not *all* ME." *The Observer* (London), May 21, 40. Dr. Wessely, then Research Fellow in Epidemiology at the Institute of Psychiatry (London), was referring to the kind of ill-effect on a patient's sense of self-worth or psychic integrity that a negative (i.e., denigratory) diagnosis may have. He does not mention Freud, but Freud's papers on technique often propose such an approach.

3. Quoted in the review by Ian Ousby, "Mental One-time Pad," *The Times Literary Supplement* (December 25, 1998): 25. Raymond Tallis, and probably most modern neurologists, would posit consciousness itself as the "greatest of all code rooms." Certainly this would be the view of the Harvard neuroscientist and psychiatrist, J. Allan Hobson, whose recent beautiful book on the brain is simply entitled *Consciousness* (New York: Scientific American Library, 1999).

4. Peter Medawar (1984). "Further Comments of Psychoanalysis." In *Pluto's Republic*, 65.

5. It is perhaps a sign of the times, as much as a sign of Freud's personal obsessions, that at the end of the twentieth century Madelon Sprengnether can write (in Bernheimer and Kahane, *In Dora's Case: Freud-Hysteria-Feminism*) of the momentous revealing of Dora's childhood masturbation: *"hardly a remarkable discovery."* Freud and his invention, psychoanalysis, are a time- and culture-bound production of European history. They represent, in short, no more than an obverse *Biedermeirei* of the mind. Perhaps that is why Peter Gay is so fond of them.

Freud's younger contemporary and one-time disciple, Wilhelm Stekel, wrote a succinct paragraph about childhood masturbation that deserves quotation for its sheer hygienic common sense. In *Conditions of Nervous Anxiety and Their Treatment* (first published in 1908 as *Nervöse Angstzustände und ihre Behandlung*) he clearly distinguished his position from that of his erstwhile tutor:

> Masturbation is harmless so long as human unreason does not make it a crime, and load it with the consciousness of religious and hygienic guilt. All children masturbate—some more, some less. Mankind would be a race of pitiable objects of utter imbeciles if masturbation were injurious. But the well-meant warnings of guardians and the false notions of physicians have turned many a masturbator into a neurotic. I recommend all parents, physicians, and educators not to trouble about masturbation in the children and at most to try by distractions and by tiring them out to get them to give up excessive masturbation. (Stekel 1950, 428; his emphasis.)

Against this example of clear, and heretical, thinking by Stekel one should weigh in the balance the strange 1943 essay by the analyst Otto Fenichel, "The Psychopathology of Coughing," which relies heavily on the 'Dora' case for "evidential" information about the phenomenon of *hysterical conversion* of which coughing is one instance. Fenichel does not dispute Freud's initial diagnosis of hysteria and accepts as Gospel all the masturbatory constructions that Freud put upon his patient's presentation. In consequence we get several pages of "facts" which turn out to be no more than a naïve reading of the Master. For example, Fenichel introduces the material thus:

> Freud, in one of his earliest cases, had the opportunity to psychoanalyze a classical example of hysterical cough (combined with aphonia) as a conversion symptom. His patient, Dora, produced coughing spells, the analysis of which showed the following factors involved: (a) Dora imitated the sickness of an acquaintance, Mrs. K., who happened to be the wife of the man with whom Dora was unconsciously in love; (b) the cough expressed the rejection of the fantasy of being raped by Mr. K., which rape (out of certain facts and fantasies in Dora's earlier life) was imagined as a fellatio. (Fenichel 1954, *The Collected Papers of Otto Fenichel*, 2nd Series, 239)

The rest of this paper (one of the two series of Fenichel's writings recommended—still!—for training analysts) continues in the same vein. This leads me to suggest that at least three things should be required of those preparing to become analysts:

(1) a sound knowledge of modern neurology;

(2) a thorough reading of the complete Freud–Fliess correspondence;

(3) a *literary* training in the 'deconstruction' of Freudian rhetoric.

6. Arthur Conan Doyle (n.d.). *The Best of Sherlock Holmes.* New York: Grosset and Dunlap, 15-16. The article that Watson is reading is, of course, by Holmes himself who shortly demonstrates his unique powers. When Watson compares him to Poe's Dupin, Holmes responds with the following commentary on the "association" exercise of *The Murders in the Rue Morgue*:

> Now, in my opinion, Dupin was a very inferior fellow. That trick of his of breaking in on his friend's thoughts with an apropos remark after a quarter of an hour's silence is really very showy and superficial. He had some analytical genius, no doubt; but he was by no means such a phenomenon as Poe appeared to imagine. (Doyle n.d., 18)

The title of the present chapter, *aficionados* will have realized, is from the first sentence that Holmes ever addresses to Watson upon being introduced to him in the chemical laboratory of Bart's Hospital by their mutual acquaintance, the surgical dresser Stamford.

Long after an earlier version of this chapter had been drafted, Professor Anthony Clare kindly brought to my attention the delightful monograph (based on the 1984 Squibb History of Psychiatry lecture) by the late Michael Shepherd entitled *Sherlock Holmes and the Case of Dr. Freud* (London: Tavistock, 1985). This closely argued paper examines the history of "retrospective prophecy" from the sixteenth-century tales of the sons of the king of Serendippo, via Voltaire's *Zadig*, and Poe and Conan Doyle and the Italian physician-cum-art detective Giovanni Morelli (who apparently knew Conan Doyle's uncle, the director of the Dublin Art Gallery), to Sigmund Freud himself. Shepherd's splendid text, which is stuffed with carefully documented historical *minutiae*, begins and ends, quite appropriately, in the doubly fictitious realms of Nicholas Meyer's *The Seven Per Cent Solution*.

Incidentally, a rare secret not revealed by Shepherd, the title of the first Sherlock Holmes tale, *A Study in Scarlet*, is a humorous reference by Conan Doyle to the choice of canvas titles by the American painter Whistler.

7. I am using this word in Freud's sense as expressed in the letter to Fliess of March 10, 1898, that is, for "[his] psychology that leads behind consciousness." There he maintains that "the source of the unconscious" and "the etiology of all the psychoneuroses" as well as "dream life" all derive *biologically* "from the residues of the prehistoric period of life (between the ages of one and three)" (See Masson 1985, 301-02).

This *neurologically untenable theory* was never repudiated by Freud and indeed may be said to form the underlying theoretical basis of *all* his later papers—and not just the five extant of the twelve 1915 papers intended for publication as a book to be called *Zur Vorbereitung einer Metapsychologie*

(*Preliminaries to a Metapsychology*); see editor's introduction, 101-104, to *On Metapsychology*, *P.F.L.*, vol. 11. The only alteration to this theory was the addition of the notion of a phylogenetic programmation that has been called Lamarckian, though in fact this seems to have been inspired less by Lamarck than by a curious combination of theoretical rivalry with Carl Jung and a need to put his analytic constructions of infantile circumstances beyond the range of scientific scrutiny (cf. the 'Wolf Man' case and the 'invention' of the putative 'primal scene' irrespective of any lived experience or recall of such an event).

8. This is, perhaps, made most clear in the arguments elaborated toward the end of Freud's life in *An Outline of Psycho-Analysis*. The *Outline*, dated July 1938, only adds to the disguised post hoc statements of his Fliess period the more recent belief in phylogenetic forces (which, being undemonstrable, is post hoc one-upmanship). Having argued, for instance, of the mother that "[b]y her care of the child's body she becomes its first seducer," Freud writes:

> In all this the phylogenetic foundation has so much the upper hand over personal accidental experience that it makes no difference whether a child has really sucked at the breast or has been brought up on the bottle and never enjoyed the tenderness of a mother's care. In both cases the child's development takes the same path; it may be that in the second case its later longing grows all the greater. (*S.E.*, vol. 23, 188-89)

This comes from the passage in chapter 17 of the *Outline* where the wretch Sophocles is chided for having deviated from Freudian dogma (here called "analytic *facts*"): "The Greek hero [Oedipus] killed his father and took his mother to wife. That he did so unwittingly, since he did not know them as his parents, is a deviation from the analytic facts which we can easily understand" (*S.E.*, vol. 23, 187). For Freud to accuse Sophocles of having deviated, however understandably, from psychoanalytic (i.e., Freudian) doctrine is an excellent example of *Chutzpah*.

9. Anthony Clare (1985). "Freud's Cases: The Clinical Basis of Psychoanalysis." In *The Anatomy of Madness*, Vol. 1 (ed. Bynum, Porter, and Shepherd). London: Tavistock, 1985, 277.

Clare refers the reader to the trenchant critique of the 'case' and the massive contamination by suggestion of any worthwhile clinical data reported in the 1960 paper of Joseph Wolpe and Stanley Rachman, "Psychoanalytic Evidence: A Critique Based on Freud's Case of Little Hans," *Journal of Nervous and Mental Disease* 131, 135-48. Max Scharnberg dedicated the first volume of his *The Non-Authentic Nature of Freud's Observations* to these two scholars, noting in his preface that "[they] were the first to apply textual analysis to Freud's writings. Their re-analysis of the case-study of Little Hans is the most important paper ever written on psychoanalysis" (Scharnberg 1993, vol. 1, 13).

10. Barbara Von Eckardt (1986). "Grünbaum's Challenge to Freud's Logic of Argumentation: A Reconstruction and an Addendum." *Behavioral and Brain Sciences.* 9, no. 2, (June): 262-63. See also Barbara Von Eckardt, "Why Freud's Research Methodology was Unscientific," *Psychoanalysis and Contemporary Thought* 5, (1982): 549-74; and her "Adolf Grünbaum: Psychoanalytic Epistemology," in *Beyond Freud: A Study of Modern Psychoanalytic Theorists*, ed. J. Reppen (Erlbaum Associates, 1985).

11. One has to be very cautious about approaching these "modifications of theory." Whether we consider the id-ego-superego schemata, or those sometimes "economic" sometimes "topographic" constructions that appear to show "new" insight, we are *not* dealing with any new information obtained from *outside* the earlier Freudian system. We are only dealing with Freud's original deck of cards, reshuffled according to the agonized whim of the moment. From the time when he abandoned neurology at the end of the nineteenth century, Freud paid not the slightest attention to any of the developments in that rapidly developing medical science. Most orthodox analysts have, alas, followed his path up this blind alley.

12. It is *just possible* that this example is in the nature of a tasteless in-joke and that the young philosopher is none other than Heinrich Gomperz referred to in the Freud–Fliess correspondence as "my philosopher." Of his experiences with Freud (he was *not* a patient, by the way, but a volunteer guinea pig), Heinrich Gomperz wrote in an autobiographical sketch in *The Personalist* 24, 1943, 254-70:

> When his *Interpretation of Dreams* was first published in 1899 I offered myself as a 'victim' for testing his theory and for several months, during the second half of that year, we tried to interpret my dreams according to the method he had just worked out. The experiment proved a complete failure. All the 'dreadful' things which he suggested I might have concealed from myself and 'suppressed' I could honestly assure him had always been clearly and consciously present in my mind. I offered no 'resistance' and I have learned later that Freud had told a disciple he had met with two persons only whose dreams he had been unable to analyze and that I had been one of them.

Gomperz would have been twenty-six years old at the time of the experiment. Freud's comment to Fliess on the outcome of this, after lamenting that in general (regarding the connection between the infantile sexual theory and the dream theory) he had "too little strict proof," was:

> I did not even succeed in convincing my philosopher, though he was providing me with the most brilliant confirmatory material. Intelligence is always weak

[meaning?], *and it is easy for a philosopher to transform inner resistance into logical refutation.* (Letter of Saturday, December 9, 1899. Masson 1985, 391; my emphasis)

The "Heads I win, tails, you lose" criticism of psychoanalysis that Freud was later to dispute seems to be in full swing here. "Inner resistance" was an hypothesis attached to his theory, *not an evidence*; the "logical refutation" *was*, on the other hand, something of which Freud indeed had evidence (as, presumably, did Gomperz). Nontheless, the evidence is sacrificed for the hypothesis. One has the impression of the encounter of two world views from two fundamentally incompatible temperaments.

I am reminded of the death-bed conversation between the cancer-stricken David Hume who had achieved that conscious equanimity, *ataraxy*, recommended by Epicurus and the terror-stricken James Boswell unable to comprehend or believe that one could confront death without the fear of Hell-fire. Gomperz evidently felt no need to conceal from himself the "dreadful things" that so tormented Freud. And Freud, evidently, felt that his own torments must be universal, and that if people would not agree to this, then that was a sure sign of 'repression' on their part rather than of Boswellian error on his.

However, even if this identification is correct (this is merely a hunch on my part), Freud's presentation in an international journal is highly misleading (the man was *not* a patient, there was *no* neurosis for treatment; the "symptomatic act" becomes even more a hermeneutic figment of Freud's febrile imagination). On the assumption that this passage refers *not* to Gomperz, but, in truth, to a real patient, then Freud's remarks are simply and crassly irresponsible.

13. The brilliant success of Freud's rhetoric has led many to believe that his claim to elementary medical practice was as assured as his claim to a research specialization in neuropathology.

In fact, this was not an accurate reflection of the situation. By leaving neurology and biology, his research "specialization" came to be a series of ingeniously misleading rhetorical extravaganzas on his own (in Jung's words) "pet emotive ideas" carried out with people who were (in his own words to Fliess) "especially irrational and suggestible."

As for his claim to "general practice" experience, the letter to Fliess toward the beginning of their correspondence (August 29, 1888) indicates very clearly, and with unusual modesty, Freud's status in that direction:

To go into general practice instead of specializing, to work with all possible means of investigation, and completely to take charge of the patient—that is certainly the only method which promises personal satisfaction and material success; but for me it is too late for that. I have not learned enough to be a medical practitioner, and in my medical development there is a flaw which later on was laboriously mended. I was able to learn just about enough to become a neuropathologist. And now I lack, not youth, it is true [he was 32], but time and independence to make up for it. (Masson 1985, 23-4)

Thomas Szasz in his *Karl Kraus and the Soul-Doctors* suggests that the editor/publisher of the satirical *Die Fackel* was unique in not being hoodwinked by Freud's medical reputation:

After all, was Freud not a brilliant doctor and a courageous experimenter with new treatments to combat dreadful diseases? He said he was. And even his enemies treated him as if he were a physician and a therapist, albeit a wrongheaded and mistaken one. Evidently, only Kraus saw what others were unwilling to see—that Freud was not a real physician, and that his psychoanalytic method was not a real treatment. "Psychoanalysis," Kraus insisted, "is the disease of which it claims to be the cure." (Szasz 1976, 23-4)

14. *Procrustes* means "the stretcher" (i.e., "the one who stretches") and was the nickname of the famous ancient robber, Polypemon, or, according to some, Damastes. See William Smith, Ll.D., *A Classical Dictionary of Biography, Mythology and Geography*. London: John Murray, 1866, 616.

15. This "first success" refers to the creation of an "attachment and link" to the doctor so that "one of the imagos of the people by whom [the patient] was accustomed to be treated with affection" may be established (*S.E.*, vol. 12, 139-40). In spite of the famous and repeated claims that suggestion had naught to do with psychoanalysis, Freud has just directed in this paragraph that: "It remains the first aim of the treatment to attach him [*the patient*] to it [*the treatment*] and to the person of the doctor (*S.E.*, 12, 139).In the earlier (1912) "The Dynamics of Transference" Freud had already more openly accepted that "suggestion" was indeed part and parcel of psychoanalytic therapy:

If we 'remove' the transference by making it conscious, we are detaching only these two components [this appears to refer to the preceding remarks about the alleged "unconscious" sexual aspects of all positive relationships] of the emotional act from the person of the doctor; the other component, which is admissible to consciousness and unobjectionable, persists and is the vehicle of success in psycho-analysis exactly as it is in other methods of treatment. *To this extent we readily admit that the results of psycho-analysis rest upon suggestion*; by suggestion, however, we must understand, as Ferenczi (1909) does, the influencing of a person by means of the transference phenomena which are possible in his case. (*S.E.*, vol. 12, 105-106; my emphasis)

Freud was to return to this issue in the twenty-eighth of the *Introductory*

Lectures (*S.E.*, vol. 16, 448-77) where he contrasts hypnotic and analytic suggestion: "The first works cosmetically, the second surgically." Again, he argues that the transference is the key to the question and this is 'controlled' *as is the patient by the power of suggestion*: "we are able to control it; the patient alone no longer manages his suggestibility according to his own liking, but in so far as he is amenable to its influence at all, we guide his suggestibility."

16. Otto Fenichel in a 1945 paper, "The Means of Education," credits Freud with the 'discovery' of infantile sexuality in a passage of either remarkable stupidity or remarkable ignorance of the history of medicine (let alone of philosophy, religion, or letters):

> If one remembers that prior to Freud science did not even know of the existence of infantile sexuality, one realizes how intensely mankind must have wished that it actually did not exist. Awareness of this wish should warn us against subscribing to the idea that infantile sexuality is dangerous, since this idea may be the product of the same tendency. (Fenichel 1954, 332)

One paragraph from Henri Ellenberger's *The Discovery of the Unconscious* will suffice to illustrate the poverty of Fenichel's historical knowledge, or the mendacious extravagance with which he embraced and furthered Freud's self-serving lies:

> While physicians generally considered child sexuality as a rare abnormality, *it had been taken for granted for a long time by priests and educators.* Father Debreyne, a moral theologian who was also a physician, insisted in his books upon the great frequence of infantile masturbation, of sexual play between young children, and of the seduction of very young children by wet nurses and servants [footnote omitted]. Bishop Dupanloup of Orleans, an eminent educator, repeatedly emphasized in his work the extreme frequency of sex play among children and stated that most children acquired "bad habits" between the ages of one and two years [footnote omitted]. (Ellenberger 1970, 295-96; my emphasis)

Ellenberger is referring to works written between 1846 and 1866! It is not that these earlier writers were any more accurate than Freud; but rather that Freud was not only *not original* but *profoundly and Catholically nineteenth-century* in his understanding of human growth patterns.

Stekel has a pertinent comment that Fenichel should have considered:

> *In sexual matters people's behavior is incredibly naive. They shut their eyes and will not see.* With what good reason does Frank Wedekind scoff at a world which has secrets from itself [Stekel is thinking of *Frühlings Erwachen* (Spring's Awakening), 1891]. Thus infantile sexuality is a secret which all the initiated know. If only parents kept it in mind! (Stekel 1950, 430; his emphasis)

Selected Bibliography

Abraham, Hilda C., and Ernst L. Freud, eds. 1965. *A Psycho-Analytic Dialogue: The Letters of Sigmund Freud and Karl Abraham, 1907-1926.* Tr. Bernard Marsh and Hilda C. Abraham. London: Hogarth Press and the Institute of Psycho-Analysis.

Andersson, Ola. 1997. *Freud avant Freud: La préhistoire de la psychanalyse (1886-1896).* "Présentée" by Elisabeth Roudinesco and Per Magnus Johansson. Le Plessis-Robinson, France: Synthélabo Groupe, Collection Les Empêcheurs de penser en rond.

Appignanesi, Lisa and John Forrester. 1992. *Freud's Women.* London: Weidenfeld and Nicolson.

Baudelaire, Charles. 1968. *Oeuvres complètes.* Ed. Y.-G. Le Dantec and Claude Pichois. Paris: Gallimard, Pléiade.

Bernfeld, S. 1953. "Freud's Studies on Cocaine." *Journal of the American Psychoanalytical Association* 1: 581-613.

Bernheimer, Charles, and Claire Kahane, eds. 1985. *In Dora's Case: Freud-Hysteria-Feminism.* New York: Columbia University Press.

Binet, A., and Charles Féré. 1885. "L'hypnotisme chez les hystériques: Le transfert." *La Revue philosophique* 19 (janvier-juin): 1-25.

Bonaparte, Marie. 1933. *Edgar Poe: Étude psychanalytique.* Avant-propos de Sigmund Freud. 2 vols. Paris: Denoël et Steele.

Booth, Wayne C. 1975. *A Rhetoric of Irony.* Chicago: University of Chicago Press.

Borch-Jacobsen, Mikkel. 1997. "L'effet Bernheim (fragments d'une théorie de l'artefact généralisé)." *Corpus* (Nanterre), no. 32: 147-73.

———. 1996. "Neurotica: Freud and the Seduction Theory." *October 76.* (Spring): 15-43.

———. 1996. *Remembering Anna O.: A Century of Mystification.* New York: Routledge.

———. 1997. "Sybil — The Making of a Disease: An Interview with Dr. Herbert Spiegel." *New York Review of Books.* (April 24): 60-64.

Bowie, Malcolm. 1987. *Freud, Proust and Lacan: Theory as Fiction.* Cambridge, U.K.: Cambridge University Press.

Breuer, Josef, and Sigmund Freud. 1957. *Studies on Hysteria.* Tr. and ed. James Strachey in collaboration with Anna Freud. New York: Basic Books.

Burke, Kenneth. 1967. *The Philosophy of Literary Form: Studies in Symbolic Action.* 2nd ed. Baton Rouge: Louisiana State University Press.

Byck, Robert, ed. 1975. *Cocaine Papers: Sigmund Freud.* New York: Meridian Books.

Bynum, W. F., Roy Porter, and Michael Shepherd, eds. 1985. *The Anatomy of Madness.* 2 vols. London: Tavistock.

Carrington, Charles. (1955) 1986. *Rudyard Kipling, His Life and Work.* London: Macmillan; Harmondsworth U.K.: Penguin.

Cioffi, Frank. 1986. "Did Freud Rely on the Tally Argument to Meet the Argument from Suggestibility?" *Behavioral and Brain Sciences* 9 no. 2 (June): 231.

———. 1998. *Freud and the Question of Pseudoscience.* Chicago, Illinois: Open Court.

———. 1979. "Freud—New Myths to Replace the Old." *New Society* (November 29): 503-504.

———. 1974. "Was Freud a Liar?" *The Listener* 91: 72-74.

Clare, Anthony. 1989. "Mad, Bad and Dangerous." *Sunday Times* (London), June 18, G.10 (review of Masson, *Against Therapy*, English edition, London: Collins).

———. 1980. *Psychiatry in Dissent: Controversial Issues in Thought and Practice.* 2nd ed. London: Tavistock Publications.

———. 1997. "That Shrinking Feeling." *Sunday Times* (London), November 16, 8.10 Books.

Clark, Roland W. 1980. *Freud: The Man and The Cause.* London: Granada, Paladin Books.

Conan Doyle, Arthur. n.d. *The Best of Sherlock Holmes.* New York: Grosset and Dunlap.

Cooper, Irving S. 1974. *The Victim Is Always the Same.* New York: Harper and Row.

Crews, Frederick. 1998. *Unauthorized Freud: Doubters Confront a Legend.* New York: Viking/Penguin.

———. 1986. *Skeptical Engagements.* New York: Oxford University Press.

Crews, Frederick, et al. 1995. *The Memory Wars: Freud's Legacy in Dispute.* New York: New York Review Books.

Crichton, Paul, and Christopher Cordess. 1995. "Motives of Paranoid Crime: The Crime of the Papin Sisters." *Journal of Forensic Psychiatry* 6, no. 6 (December): 564-75.

Daly, Martin, and Margo Wilson. 1990. "Is Parent-Offspring Conflict Sex-Linked? Freudian and Darwinian Models." *Journal of Personality* 58 (March 1): 163-89.

———. 1988. *Homicide*. New York: Aldine de Gruyter, Hawthorne.

———. 1996. "Homicidal Tendencies." *Demos* 10: 40 passim.

Damasio, Antonio R. 1994. *Descartes' Error: Emotion, Reason, and the Human Brain*. New York: Grosset/Putnam.

Dickens, Charles. 1972. *The Pickwick Papers*. Harmondsworth, U.K.: Penguin.

Dolnick, Edward. 1998. *Madness on the Couch: Blaming the Victim in the Heyday of Psychoanalysis*. New York: Simon and Schuster.

Edmunds, Lavinia. 1988. "His Master's Choice," *Johns Hopkins Magazine* 40, no. 2 (April): 40-49.

Ellenberger, Henri F. 1970. *The Discovery of the Unconscious: The History and Evolution of Dynamic Psychiatry*. New York: Basic Books.

Erwin, Edward. 1995. *A Final Accounting: Philosophical and Empirical Issues in Freudian Psychology*. Cambridge, Mass.: MIT Press.

Esterson, Allen. 1998. "Jeffrey Masson and Freud's Seduction Theory: A New Fable Based on Old Myths." *History of the Human Sciences* 11, no. 1 (February): 1-21.

———. 1993. *Seductive Mirage: An Exploration of the Work of Sigmund Freud*. Chicago, Illinois: Open Court.

———. 1994. "Freud the Fraud." The Sunday Times (London), (May 29): 10.6-9.

Evans, Martha Noel. 1991. *Fits and Starts: A Genealogy of Hysteria in Modern France*. Ithaca: Cornell University Press.

Eysenck, H. J. 1985. *Decline and Fall of the Freudian Empire*. New York: Viking/Penguin.

Eysenck, H. J., and G. D. Wilson. 1973. *The Experimental Study of Freudian Theories*. London: Methuen.

Farrell, John. 1996. *Freud's Paranoid Quest: Psychoanalysis and Modern Suspicion*. New York: New York University Press.

Feigenbaum, Janet D. 1997. "Haply I May Remember and Haply May Forget." *Times Literary Supplement* (August): 8-9.

Felman, Shoshana, ed. 1982. *Literature and Psychoanalysis: The Question of Reading: Otherwise*. Baltimore: Johns Hopkins University Press.

Fenichel, Otto. 1953 and 1945. *The Collected Papers of Otto Fenichel*. First and second series (collected and edited by Dr. Hanna Fenichel and Dr. David Rapaport). New York: W. W. Norton.

Ferris, Timothy. 1997. *The Whole Shebang: A State-of-the-Universe(s) Report*. New York: Simon and Schuster.

Fish, Stanley. 1989. *Doing What Comes Naturally: Change, Rhetoric, and the Practice of Theory in Literary and Legal Studies.* Durham, N.C.: Duke University Press.

———. 1986. "Withholding the Missing Portion: Power, Meaning and Persuasion in Freud's 'The Wolf-Man.'" *Times Literary Supplement* (August 29): 935-38.

Fisher, Seymour, and Roger P. Greenberg, eds. 1978. *The Scientific Evaluation of Freud's Theories and Therapy: A Book of Readings.* New York: Basic Books.

———. 1996. *Freud Scientifically Reappraised: Testing the Theories and Therapy.* New York: John Wiley and Sons.

Flournoy, Théodore. 1994. *From India to the Planet Mars: A Case of Multiple Personality with Imaginary Languages.* Edited with a new introduction by Sonu Shamdasani. Princeton, N.J.: Princeton University Press.

Fogel, B. S., R. B. Schiffer, and S. M. Rao, eds. 1996. *Neuropsychiatry.* Baltimore: Williams and Wilkins.

Forrester, John. 1997. *Dispatches from the Freud Wars.* Cambridge, Mass.: Harvard University Press.

Foxe, Arthur. 1978. *Poe as Hypnotist.* New York: Tunbridge Press.

Freeman, Erika. 1971. *Insights: Conversations with Theodor Reik.* Englewood Cliffs, N.J.: Prentice-Hall.

Freud, Ernst L., ed. 1960. *Letters of Sigmund Freud, 1873-1939.* New York: Basic Books.

Freud, Sigmund. 1950. *Aus den Anfängen der Psychanalyse: Briefe an Wilhelm Fliess.* Abhandlungen und Notizen aus den Jahren, 1887-1902. Ed. Marie Bonaparte, Anna Freud, and Ernst Kris; introduction by Ernst Kris. London: Imago Publishing. See also *Origins.*

———. 1980. *Briefe, 1873-1939.* Herausgegeben von Ernst und Lucie Freud. Frankfurt am Main: S. Fischer Verlag (new edition).

———. 1977. *Case Histories I: 'Dora' and 'Little Hans.'* Tr. Alix Strachey and James Strachey; ed. James Strachey, assisted by Angela Richards and Alan Tyson. Present volume ed. Angela Richards. Harmondsworth, U.K.: Penguin (*The Pelican Freud Library*, vol. 8).

———. 1979. *Case Histories II: 'Rat Man,' Schreber, 'Wolf Man,' Female Homosexuality.* Tr. James Strachey. Present volume ed. Angela Richards. Harmondsworth, U.K.: Penguin (*The Pelican Freud Library*, vol. 9).

———. 1985. *Civilization, Society and Religion: Group Psychology, Civilization and its Discontents and Other Works.* Tr. under the general editorship of James Strachey. Present volume ed. Albert Dickson. Harmondsworth, U.K.: Penguin (*The Pelican Freud Library*, vol.12).

———. 1959. *Collected Papers.* Vol. 5. Tr. and ed. James Strachey. New York: Basic Books.

———. 1985. *The Complete Letters of Sigmund Freud to Wilhelm Fliess, 1887-1904*. Tr. and ed. Jeffrey Moussaieff Masson. Cambridge, Mass.: The Belknap Press of Harvard University Press.

———. 1982. *Die Traumdeutung*. Freud-Studienausgabe, Band II. Frankfurt am Main: S. Fischer Verlag.

———. 1976. *The Interpretation of Dreams*. Tr. James Strachey; ed. James Strachey, assisted by Alan Tyson. The present volume edited by Angela Richards. Harmondsworth, U.K.: Penguin (*The Pelican Freud Library*, vol. 4).

———. 1976. *Jokes and Their Relation to the Unconscious*. Tr. James Strachey; ed. Angela Richards. Harmondsworth, U.K.: Penguin (*The Pelican Freud Library*, vol. 6).

———. 1960. *Letters of Sigmund Freud*. Selected and ed. Ernst L. Freud; trans. by Tania Stern and James Stern. New York: Basic Books.

———. 1984. *On Metapsychology: The Theory of Psychoanalysis*. Tr. James Strachey. Present volume comp. and ed. by Angela Richards. Harmondsworth, U.K.: Penguin (*The Pelican Freud Library*, vol. 11).

———. 1973. *New Introductory Lectures on Psychoanalysis*. Tr. James Strachey; ed. James Strachey, assisted by Angela Richards. Harmondsworth, U.K.: Penguin (*The Pelican Freud Library*, vol. 2).

———. 1954. *The Origins of Psycho-Analysis: Letters to Wilhelm Fliess, Drafts and Notes, 1887-1902*. Ed. Marie Bonaparte, Anna Freud, and Ernst Kris; tr. Eric Mosbacher and James Strachey; intro. Ernst Kris. London and New York: Imago Publishing and Basic Books. For original German, see Freud, *Aus den Anfängen* (1950).

———. 1987. *A Phylogenetic Fantasy: Overview of the Transference Neuroses*. Ed. Ilse Grubrich-Simitis; tr. Axel Hoffer and Peter T. Hoffer. Cambridge, Mass.: The Belknap Press of Harvard University Press.

———. 1979. *On Psychopathology*. Tr. under general editorship of James Strachey. Present volume comp. and ed. by Angela Richards. Harmondsworth, U.K.: Penguin (*The Pelican Freud Library*, vol. 10).

———. 1975. *The Psychopathology of Everyday Life*. Tr. Alan Tyson; ed. James Strachey and Angela Richards. This volume ed. by Angela Richards. Harmondsworth, U.K.: Penguin (*The Pelican Freud Library*, vol. 5).

———. 1977. *On Sexuality: Three Essays on the Theory of Sexuality and Other Works*. Tr. James Strachey; ed. Angela Richards. Harmondsworth. U.K.: Penguin (*The Pelican Freud Library*, vol. 7).

———. 1953-1974. *The Standard Edition of the Complete Psychological Works of Sigmund Freud*. 24 vols. Ed. by James Strachey; translated in collaboration with Anna Freud, assisted by Alix Strachey and Alan Tyson. London: Hogarth Press and the Institute of Psycho-Analysis.

Gardiner, Muriel, ed. 1971. *The Wolf-Man by the Wolf-Man*. New York: Basic Books.

Gardner, Martin. 1966. "Freud's Friend Wilhelm Fliess and His Theory of Male and Female Life Cycles." *Scientific American*. 215, (July): 108-12.

———. 1998. *The New Age: Notes of a Fringe Watcher*. Buffalo, N.Y.: Prometheus Books.

Gasman, Daniel. 1971. *The Scientific Origins of National Socialism: Social Darwinism in Ernst Haeckel and the German Monist League*. New York: Macdonald.

Gay, Peter. 1988. *Freud: A Life For Our Time*. New York: W. W. Norton.

Gellner, Ernest. 1985. *The Psychoanalytic Movement, or The Coming of Unreason.* London: Granada, Paladin Books.

George, François. 1979. *L'Effet 'Yau de Poêle de Lacan et des Lacaniens*. Paris: Hachette.

Grosskurth, Phyllis. 1980. *Havelock Ellis: A Biography*. Toronto: McClelland and Stewart.

Grünbaum, Adolf. 1986. "Response." *Behavioral and Brain Sciences* 9, no. 2 (June): 266-81.

———. 1988. "The Role of the Case Study Method in the Foundations of Psychoanalysis." *Canadian Journal of Philosophy* 18, no. 4 (December): 623-58.

———. 1993. *Validation in the Clinical Theory of Psychoanalysis*. Madison, Conn.: International Universities Press.

———. 1979. "Is Freudian Psychoanalytic Theory Pseudo-scientific by Karl Popper's Criterion of Demarcation?" *American Philosophical Quarterly* 16: 131-40.

———. 1984. *The Foundations of Psychoanalysis: A Philosophical Critique*. Berkeley: University of California Press.

Hacking, Ian. 1995. *Rewriting the Soul: Multiple Personality and the Sciences of Memory*. Princeton, N.J.: Princeton University Press.

Hale, Nathan G., Jr. 1971. *Freud and the Americans: The Beginnings of Psychoanalysis in the United States, 1876-1917*. New York: Oxford University Press.

———. 1995. *The Rise and Crisis of Psychoanalysis in the United States: Freud and the Americans, 1917-1985*. New York: Oxford University Press.

Hall, C., and R. L. van de Castle. 1965. "An Empirical Investigation of the Castration Complex in Dreams." *Journal of Personality* 33: 20-29.

Hall, C. 1963. "Strangers in Dreams: An Empirical Confirmation of the Oedipus Complex." *Journal of Personality* 31: 336-45.

Hinsie, L. E., and R. J. Campbell, eds. 1970. *Psychiatric Dictionary*. 4th ed.. New York: Oxford University Press.

Hobson, J. Allan. 1988. *The Dreaming Brain*. New York: Basic Books.

Hoffman, Frederick J. 1967. *Freudianism and the Literary Mind.* 2nd ed. Bâton Rouge: Louisiana State University Press (first published 1957).

Hofstadter, Douglas R., and Daniel C. Dennett, eds. 1982. *The Mind's I.* New York: Bantam Books.

Iliffe, Rob. 1998. "Cardiac Arrest." *Times Literary Supplement,* (August 21): 7.

Izenberg, Gerald N. 1976. *The Existentialist Critique of Freud.* Princeton, N.J.: Princeton University Press.

James, Henry. 1966. *The Turn of the Screw.* Ed. Robert Kimbrough. New York: W. W. Norton.

Jaspers, Karl. 1968. *General Psychopathology.* Tr. with introduction by J. Hoenig and Marian W. Hamilton. Chicago: University of Chicago Press.

Jones, Ernest. 1953-1957. *The Life and Work of Sigmund Freud.* 3 vols. London: Hogarth Press.

Jones, Steve. 1997. "Crooked Bones." *New York Review of Books.* (February 6): 23.

Jung, Carl G. 1974. *Psychology and Education.* Tr. R. F. C. Hull. Princeton, N.J.: Princeton University Press, Bollingen Series 20.

Kipling, Rudyard. 1992. *John Brunner Presents Kipling's Fantasy: Stories by Rudyard Kipling.* Ed. John Brunner. New York: Tom Doherty (A Tor Book), 1992.

———. n.d. *The Works of Rudyard Kipling.* One volume edition. New York: P. F. Collier and Son.

Koestenbaum, Wayne. 1989. *Double Talk: The Erotics of Male Literary Collaboration.* New York: Routledge.

Kramer, Heinrich, and James Sprenger. 1971. *The Malleus Malificarum of Heinrich Kramer and James Sprenger.* Tr. with introductions, bibliography and notes by Rev. Montague Summers. New York: Dover.

Kushner, Howard I. 1999. "From Gilles de la Tourette's Disease to Tourette Syndrome: A History." *C N S Spectrums (The International Journal of Neuropsychiatric Medicine)* 4, no.2, (February): 24-35.

———. 1999. *A Cursing Brain? The Histories of Tourette Syndrome.* Cambridge, Mass.: Harvard University Press.

Lacan, Jacques. 1966. *Écrits.* Paris: Éds du Seuil.

———. 1980. *De la psychose paranoï aque dans ses rapports avec la personnalité.* Paris: Éds du Seuil (reprint of doctoral thesis originally published in Paris by Le François in 1932).

———. 1978. *The Four Fundamental Concepts of Psycho-Analysis.* Ed. by Jacques-Alain Miller; tr. Alan Sheridan. New York: Norton.

———. 1933. "Motifs du crime paranoï aque: Le crime des soeurs Papin." *Minotaure* 1, nos. 3-4 (numéro double): 25-28.

Laplanche, J. and J.-B. Pontalis. 1973. *The Language of Psycho-Analysis.* Tr. Donald Nicholson-Smith. London: Hogarth Press and the Institute of Psycho-Analysis.

———. 1984. *Vocabulaire de la Psychanalyse.* 8th ed. Paris: Presses Universitaires de France (first published 1967).

Leibin, Valerii. 1986. "Psychoanalysis: Science or Hermeneutics?" *Behavioral and Brain Sciences* 9, no. 2 (June): 247.

Lerman, Hannah. 1986. *A Mote in Freud's Eye: From Psychoanalysis to the Psychology of Women.* New York: Springer.

Lewin, Louis. 1924. *Phantastica: Die Betäubenden und Erregenden Genussmittel für Ärzte und Nichtärzte.* Berlin: Verlag von Georg Stilke. The chapter "Der Kokainismus" translated in Robert Byck (q.v.).

Livingston, Flora V. 1927 [1968]. *Bibliography of the Works of Rudyard Kipling.* New York: Burt Franklin.

Locke, John. n.d. *An Essay Concerning Human Understanding.* London: George Routledge and Sons.

Loewenstein, R. M., Lottie M. Newman, Max Schur, and A. J. Solnit, eds. 1966. *Psychoanalysis: A General Psychology—Essays in Honor of Heinz Hartmann.* New York: International Universities Press.

Loftus, Elizabeth, and Katherine Ketcham. 1994 *The Myth of Repressed Memory: False Memories and Allegations of Sexual Abuse.* New York: St. Martin's Press.

Lycett, Andrew. 1999. *Rudyard Kipling.* London: Weidenfeld & Nicolson.

Macmillan, Malcolm. 1984. "Delboeuf and Janet as Influences in Freud's Treatment of Emmy von N." *Journal of the History of Behavioral Sciences* 20: 340-58.

———. 1997 *Freud Evaluated: The Completed Arc.* Cambridge, Mass.: MIT Press.

Mahony, Patrick. 1982. *Freud as a Writer.* New York: International Universities Press.

Malcolm, Janet. 1985. *In the Freud Archives.* New York: Vintage Books.

———. 1982. *Psychoanalysis: The Impossible Profession.* New York: Vintage Books.

Masson, Jeffrey Moussaieff. 1988. *Against Therapy: Emotional Tyranny and the Myth of Psychological Healing.* New York: Atheneum.

———. 1985. *The Assault on Truth: Freud's Suppression of the Seduction Theory.* New York: Farrar, Straus, Giroux, 1984; paperback with new preface, New York: Viking-Penguin.

———. 1985. *The Complete Letters of Sigmund Freud to Wilhelm Fliess, 1887-1904.* Tr. and ed. Jeffrey Moussaieff Masson. Cambridge, Mass.: The Belknap Press of Harvard University Press.

———. 1990. *Final Analysis: The Making and Unmaking of a Psychoanalyst.* Reading, Mass.: Addison-Wesley.

McGrath, William J. 1986. *Freud's Discovery of Psychoanalysis: The Politics of Hysteria.* Ithaca, N.Y.: Cornell University Press.

McGuire, William, ed. 1974. *The Freud/Jung Letters: The Correspondence between Sigmund Freud and C. G. Jung.* Tr. Ralph Mannheim and R. F. C. Hull. Princeton, N.J.: Princeton University Press, Bollingen Series 94, 1974.

Medawar, P. B., and J. S. Medawar. 1983. *Aristotle to Zoos: A Philosophical Dictionary of Biology.* Cambridge, Mass.: Harvard University Press.

Medawar, Sir Peter. 1984. *Pluto's Republic.* New York: Oxford University Press.

———. 1975. "Victims of Psychiatry," *New York Review of Books* (January 23): 17.

Merskey, Harold. 1992. "Anna O. Had a Severe Depressive Illness." *British Journal of Psychiatry* 161: 185-94.

Mitchell, Juliet. 1975. *Psychoanalysis and Feminism: Freud, Reich, Laing and Women.* New York: Vintage Books.

Neu, Jerome, ed. 1991. *The Cambridge Companion to Freud.* Cambridge: Cambridge University Press.

Nicolson, Nigel, ed. 1977. *A Change of Perspective: The Letters of Virginia Woolf*, vol. 3 (1923-1928). London: Hogarth Press, 1977.

Nunberg, Herman, and Ernst Federn, eds. 1962-1975. *Minutes of the Vienna Psychoanalytic Society*, vols. 1-4. New York: International Universities Press.

Obholzer, Karin. 1980. *Gespräche mit dem Wolfsmann.* Reinbek bei Hamburg: Rowohlt Verlag.

———. 1982. *The Wolf-Man: Conversations with Freud's Patient—Sixty Years Later.* Tr. Michael Shaw. New York: Continuum (translation of previous entry).

Ofshe, R. J., and E. Watters. 1994. *Making Monsters: False Memories, Psychotherapy and Sexual Hysteria.* New York: Scribners

Orel, Harold, ed. 1989. *Critical Essays on Rudyard Kipling.* Boston: G. K. Hall.

Ousby, Ian. 1998. "Mental One-time Pad," *The Times Literary Supplement.* (December 25): 25.

Pappenheim, Else. 1980. "Freud and Gilles de la Tourette: Diagnostic Speculations on 'Frau Emmy von N.'" *International Review of Psychoanalysis* 7: 265-77.

Pendergrast, Mark. *Victims of Memory. Incest Accusations and Shattered Lives.* New York: HarperCollins, 1996.

Poe, Edgar Allan. 1966. *The Letters of Edgar Allan Poe.* 2 vols. Ed. J. Ward Ostrom. New York: Gordian Press.

―――. 1980. *The Portable Poe*. Ed. Philip Van Doren Stern. Harmondsworth, U.K.; New York: Viking/Penguin.

―――. 1967. *Selected Writings*. Ed. David Galloway. New York: Penguin.

Pope, Harrison G. Jr. 1997. *Psychology Astray: Fallacies in Studies of "Repressed Memory" and Childhood Trauma*. Boca Raton, Florida: Upton Books, Social Issues Resources Series, Inc.

Porter, Roy. 1987. *Mind-Forg'd Manacles: A History of Madness in England from the Restoration to the Regency*. London: Athlone Press.

―――. 1987. *A Social History of Madness: Stories of the Insane*. London: Weidenfeld and Nicolson.

Richards, I. A. 1934. *Principles of Literary Criticism*. London: Kegan Paul, Trench, Trübner; New York: Harcourt, Brace, (1st ed. 1924).

Richardson, Michael. 1997. "There Is No Highly Conserved Embryonic Stage in the Vertebrates." *Anatomy and Embryology* 196, no. 2 (August): 91-106.

Robert, Marthe. 1964. *La Révolution psychanalytique*. Paris: Payot, (Republished, Paris: Gallimard, Collection Tel, 1976).

―――. 1966. *The Psychoanalytic Revolution: Sigmund Freud's Life and Achievement*. Tr. Kenneth Morgan. London: Allen and Unwin; New York: Harcourt, Brace, and World (translation of previous entry).

Romains, Jules. 1972. *Knock*. Paris: Gallimard, Folio.

Rothgeb, Carrie Lee, ed. 1973. *Abstracts of the Standard Edition of the Complete Psychological Works of Sigmund Freud*. New York: Jason Aronson.

Rudnytsky, Peter L. 1987. *Freud and Oedipus*. New York: Columbia University Press.

Rycroft, Charles. 1990. "Freud's Best Face," *The Times Literary Supplement* (July 6-12): 725. (review of Peter Gay's *Reading Freud*, 1989).

―――. 1971. "Not So Much a Treatment, More a Way of Life." *New York Review of Books*, October 21. (review of Muriel Gardiner's *The Wolf-Man by the Wolf-Man*; reprinted in Rycroft 1985 92-100).

―――. 1985. *Psychoanalysis and Beyond*. Ed. Peter Fuller. London: Chatto and Windus/Hogarth Press.

Schacter, Daniel L, ed. 1995. *Memory Distortion: How Minds, Brains, and Societies Reconstruct the Past*. Cambridge, Mass.: Harvard University Press.

Scharnberg, Max. 1984. *The Myth of Paradigm-Shift, or How to Lie with Methodology*. Uppsala, Swed.: Acta Universitatis Upsaliensis, Uppsala studies in Education 20.

―――. 1993. *The Non-Authentic Nature of Freud's Observations: Vol. II: Felix Gattel's Early Freudian Cases, and the Astrological Origin of the Anal Theory*. Uppsala, Swed.: Acta Universitatis Upsaliensis, Uppsala Studies in Education 48.

————. 1993. *The Non-Authentic Nature of Freud's Observations: Vol. I: The Seduction Theory.* Uppsala, Swed.: Acta Universitatis Upsaliensis, Uppsala Studies in Education 47.

Schmidl, Fritz. 1955. "The Problem of Scientific Validation in Psycho-Analytic Interpretation." *International Journal of Psychoanalysis* 36. (March-April): 105-113.

Schnabel, Jim. 1995. "Splits in the Search for Self." *The Guardian* (London), (June 9): Books 5.

Seymour-Smith, Martin. 1990. *Rudyard Kipling: The Controversial New Biography.* London: Macmillan (first published by Queen Anne Press, 1989).

Shepherd, Michael. 1985. *Sherlock Holmes and the Case of Dr. Freud.* London: Tavistock.

Shone, Tom. 1991. "Review of *A Derrida Reader.*" *Observer* (London), (May 12): 55.

Sokal, Alan, and Jean Bricmont. 1997. *Impostures intellectuelles.* Paris: Odile Jacob.

Spiegel, Herbert. 1974. "The Grade Five Syndrome: The Highly Hypnotizable Person." *The International Journal of Clinical and Experimental Hypnosis* 22: 303-19.

Spinoza, Benedict de. 1862. *Tractatus Theologico-Politicus.* London: Trübner (translator unacknowledged).

Steiner, George. 1988. "The Great Liberator" *The Sunday Times* (London), May 22, G2 (review of Gay, *Freud: A Life for Our Time*).

Stekel, Wilhelm. 1950. *Conditions of Nervous Anxiety and Their Treatment.* Tr. Rosalie Gabler with an introduction by Samuel Lowy, M.D. (Prague). New York: Liveright (translation of last, much expanded, German edition of the 1908 entry below).

————. 1962. *The Interpretation of Dreams: New Developments and Techniques.* Tr. Eden Paul and Cedar Paul. New York: Grosset and Dunlap (first U.S. publication, New York: Liveright, 1943).

————. 1908. *Nervöse Angstzustände und ihre Behandlung.* Mit einem Vorworte von Professor Dr. Sigmund Freud. Berlin: Urban und Schwarzenberg.

Stewart, Walter A. 1967. *Psychoanalysis: The First Ten Years.* London: Allen and Unwin.

Stone, Alan A. 1997. "Where Will Psychoanalysis Survive? What Remains of Freudianism When Its Scientific Center Crumbles?" *Harvard Magazine* 99, no. 3 (January-February): 34-39.

Storr, Anthony, 1997. "Battle for the No Man's Land of the Mind." *The Times* (London), June 12.

Sulloway, Frank J. 1979, 1992. *Freud, Biologist of the Mind: Beyond the Psychoanalytic Legend*. New York: Basic Books; Cambridge: Harvard University Press.

———. 1991. "Reassessing Freud's Case Histories: The Social Construction of Psychoanalysis," *Isis* 82, no. 312 (June): 245-75.

Sutherland, Stuart. 1976. *Breakdown: A Personal Crisis and a Medical Dilemma*. London: Weidenfeld and Nicolson.

———. 1997. "Tales of Memory and Imagination." *Nature* 388 (July 17): 239.

Szasz, Thomas. 1976. *Karl Kraus and the Soul-Doctors. A Pioneer Critic and His Criticism of Psychiatry and Psychoanalysis*. Baton Rouge: Louisiana State University Press.

Tallis, Raymond. 1996. "Burying Freud," *The Lancet*. 347, no. 9002 (March 9): 669-71.

———. 1999. "Deconstruction in Performance." *Times Literary Supplement* (March 12) 17.

———. 1997. *Enemies of Hope: A Critique of Contemporary Pessimism*. London: Macmillan.

———. 1988. *Not Saussure: A Critique of Post-Saussurean Literary Theory*. London: Macmillan Press.

———. 1997. "The Shrink from Hell." *Times Higher Education Supplement* (October 31): 20.

Taylor, Michael Alan. 1989. "Editorial." *Neuropsychiatry, Neuro-psychology, and Behavioral Neurology* 2, no. 4: 237-38.

Thornton, E. M. 1983. *Freud and Cocaine: The Freudian Fallacy*. London: Blond and Briggs.

Timpanaro, Sebastiano. 1976. *The Freudian Slip. Psychoanalysis and Textual Criticism*. Tr. Kate Soper. London: New Left Books (originally published as *Il Lapsus Freudiano* by La Nuova Italia in 1974).

Torrey, Edwin Fuller. 1992. *Freudian Fraud. The Malignant Effect of Freud's Theory on American Thought and Culture*. New York: HarperCollins.

Turkle, Sherry. 1990. "Dynasty," *London Review of Books* (December 6): 3, 5-9. (Review of Elisabeth Roudinesco, *Jacques Lacan and Co.: A History of Psychoanalysis in France, 1925-1985*. Tr. Jeffrey Mehlman. London: Free Association Press, 1990.)

———. 1978. *Psychoanalytic Politics: Freud's French Revolu-tion*. New York: Basic Books.

Vickers, Brian. 1993. *Appropriating Shakespeare: Contemporary Critical Quarrels*. New Haven: Yale University Press.

Von Eckardt, Barbara, 1986. "Grünbaum's Challenge to Freud's Logic of Argumentation: A Reconstruction and an Addendum," *Behavioral and Brain Sciences* 9, no. 2 (June): 262-63.

———. 1982. "Why Freud's Research Methodology was Unscientific." *Psychoanalysis and Contemporary Thought* 5: 549-74.

Webster, Richard. 1995. *Why Freud Was Wrong. Sin, Science and Psychoanalysis*. New York: Basic Books; reprinted 1996. London: Fontana Press (paperback).

Wessely, Simon. 1989. "It's not *all* ME," *The Observer* (London), May 21, 40.

White, Edmund. 1991. "When the Genders Got Confused: The Odd Woman, the New Woman and the Homosocial." *Times Literary Supplement* (April 12): 5-6 (review of Elaine Showalter, *Sexual Anarchy*).

Wilcocks, Robert. 1996. "Freud and His Defenders," *Times Literary Supplement* 11 (October): 19.

———. 1994. *Maelzel's Chess Player: Sigmund Freud and the Rhetoric of Deceit*. Lanham, Md.: Rowman and Littlefield.

Wilson, Angus. 1977. *The Strange Ride of Rudyard Kipling: His Life and Works*. London: Secker and Warburg.

Wilson, Stephen. 1997. "Fragments of the Truth." *The Times Literary Supplement* (December 12): 6.

Wollheim, Richard, and James Hopkins, eds. 1982. *Philosophical Essays on Freud*. Cambridge: Cambridge University Press.

———. 1979. "The Cabinet of Dr. Lacan." *New York Review of Books* (January 25): 36-45.

Wolpe, J., and S. Rachman. 1960. "Psychoanalytic Evidence: A Critique Based on Freud's Case of Little Hans." *Journal of Nervous and Mental Disease* 131: 135-48.

Zwang, Gérard. 1985. *La Statue de Freud*. Paris: Robert Laffont.

Zweig, Stefan. 1987. *Briefwechsel mit Hermann Bahr, Sigmund Freud, Rainer Maria Rilke und Arthur Schnitzle*. Herausgegeben von Jeffrey B. Berlin, Hans-Ulrich Lindken und Donald A. Prater. Frankfurt am Main: S. Fischer Verlag.

Index

About the Author

Robert Wilcocks is professor of modern French literature at the University of Alberta, Edmonton, Canada. He was educated at Dulwich College (London, U.K.), and at the Universities of Hull and London (King's College). He has taught English literature at the Institut médico-psychologique de Sceaux (University of Paris). He taught French at the University of Khartoum (Sudan) and, later, was head of the department of French and German at the University of Makerere (Uganda), before joining the University of Alberta in 1969. He has published and edited books on Jean-Paul Sartre. His first book on the origins of psychoanalysis was *Maelzel's Chess Player: Sigmund Freud and the Rhetoric of Deceit* (1994).